WAYS TO WRITING

WAYS TO

PURPOSE, TASK,

Macmillan Publishing Company
New York

WRITING
AND PROCESS

Linda C. Stanley
David Shimkin
Allen H. Lanner

QUEENSBOROUGH COMMUNITY COLLEGE
CITY UNIVERSITY OF NEW YORK

Collier Macmillan Publishers
London

For their support and encouragement these five years, we thank our students, our families, and our friends.

ACKNOWLEDGMENTS

The authors would like to thank the following authors and publishers for permission to reprint various selections in this book:

Excerpt from ''50,000 on Beach Strangely Calm as Rocket Streaks Out of Sight'' by Gay Talese reprinted from *The New York Times*, 21 February 1962. Copyright © 1962 by The New York Times Company. Reprinted by permission.

Excerpt from ''The Angry Winter'' in *The Unexpected Universe* by Loren Eiseley, copyright © 1969 by Loren Eiseley. Reprinted by permission of Harcourt Brace Jovanovich, Inc.

Excerpt from ''Encouraging Honest Inquiry in Student Writing'' by David Harrington, reprinted from *College Composition and Communication*, Volume XXX, No. 2 (May 1979). Reprinted with the permission of the National Council of Teachers of English.

(continued on p. xx)

Macmillan Publishing Company
866 Third Avenue, New York 10022

Collier Macmillan Canada, Inc.

Library of Congress Cataloging in Publication Data

Stanley, Linda.   (date)
  Ways to writing.

  Includes index.
  1. English language—Rhetoric.   2. Exposition
(Rhetoric)   I. Shimkin, David.   II. Lanner, Allen H.
III. Title.
PE1408.S684   1985   808'.042   84-11244
ISBN 0-02-415500-4

Printing: 1 2 3 4 5 6 7 8   Year: 5 6 7 8 9 0 1 2 3

ISBN 0-02-415500-4

PREFACE

Ways to Writing has emerged from the authors' belief that students best understand the writing process when it is presented through a series of integrated activities that take the writer through each stage of the process. For example, if they are asked to write on a personal experience or to develop an idea from their reading, students benefit from being shown how their decisions as to purpose, invention, audience, arrangement, revision, and style are crucial to the effectiveness of their writing. Too often, however, students come away from textbook explanations of these rhetorical elements with only a fragmented view of their application to specific writing assignments. Instead, we have created a coherent, unified sequence of methods and activities intended to guide students as they seek ways to solve the problems that arise in the act of writing.

In their effort to write more effectively, our students have taught us the urgency of starting with what the writer already knows. They remind us that even very good writers do not use personal experience or expressiveness merely as a springboard to writing about something outside themselves, namely the world of ideas or abstractions, and that their work is in the fullest sense ''expressive'' of their own voice and vision. Thus, in Chapters 1–3 we emphasize the value of the journal, of free writing, of a first-person perspective on things, ideas, and institutions. Because we want our students to become more conscious of themselves as writers writing, we guide them first to what they can express or explain with the power that comes from having experienced life directly.

With increased ability to write about their perceptions, students can do better with the complex demands of expository writing. In Chapters 4–6 we ask them to examine and explore their environment and values by gathering, analyzing, and interpreting information. In Chapters 7–9 we introduce them to library research, methods of argumentation, and the special problems associated with writing about literature.

The central focus of our book is the task that sets each writing assignment in motion. We lead the student writer through a series of prewriting activities that culminate in the preparation of an essay. To this end, we have placed the task for each chapter after the prewriting sections, which suggest ways of generating ideas for completing a task as well as of analyzing audience considerations. The sections following the presentation of the task guide the writer through the various stages of writing the essay. They encourage students to apply what they have learned in the prewriting sections to the task at hand, and they suggest patterns of arrangement, present a professional essay based on a similar task, and offer the rough draft of a student essay in fulfillment of the task.

Concluding each chapter is a ''Focus'' section stressing matters of style and structure; a ''Rewriting'' section suggesting different approaches to revising the student essay in the chapter and the students' own essays as well; and ''Becoming Aware of Yourself as a Writer,'' a series of questions on the chapter's writing process that encourage students to become more conscious of what they do when they write. An easy-reference handbook of common grammatical and mechanical problems is included at the end of the book.

We have found many advantages for the student in this task-centered approach. First, the student benefits from a ''hands-on'' approach that provides concrete, specific assistance for an actual writing assignment. Second, the task itself enables the student to draw from a broad range of experiences and, through a sequence of self-designed strategies, to arrive at a conclusion that follows naturally from the student's own cognitive processes. Third, and probably most important for the student writer, each task builds on the skill and awareness acquired in completing the previous tasks. Beginning with expressive writing, the writer is encouraged to move beyond narrative writing to tasks requiring more complex analytic and interpretive thought. In fact, it was our desire to help students to make this transition that drew us to this cumulative, task-centered method.

We believe our task-centered approach will also be of practical advantage to the instructor, who can relate the writing strategies to the actual assignment at hand. The many rhetorical exercises and examples of readings should also help the instructor focus on the problems that often arise in discussions of ''good'' and ''bad'' writing. The task format yields even greater benefits, we believe, in assignments on the research essay and the interpretation of a work of literature. Here the student is guided through the difficult stages of writing these essays, from formulating the shaping idea to revising the rough draft.

The authors feel that both student and teacher will benefit from the unity of design and purpose that we have created in each chapter. Of course, no approach to teaching writing can or should presume to be prescriptive or definitive in its methods, and we encourage the users of this text to choose what they think useful and to modify what they think does not respond expressly to the needs of their own students. The ''Generating Ideas'' and ''Audience'' sections are not bound to the process of writing on a particular task and can be used in other chapters or in class activities devised by the instructor. An instructor can quite easily restructure some of the tasks to suit a particular expressive or expository demand. Although the chapters cover most of the customary writing assignments undertaken in college writing classes, an instructor need not use every chapter, for each individual chapter provides the student with parallel purposive activities. One of our intentions has been to encourage instructors to modify or augment our tasks and activities with their own.

The authors wish to express their admiration for, and indebtedness to, James Moffett's *A Student-Centered Language Arts Curriculum: K–13*. We have drawn from Moffett's work the central role of the task in the formulation of a writing consciousness, as well as his important contribution to the study of how and why students write, and of the interplay between "concrete" and "abstract" as the basis for the development of sound thinking and writing. We are also most obviously indebted to James Kinneavy for his analysis of the different underlying purposes in writing; expressive, referential, persuasive, and literary.

Ways to Writing offers instructor and student concrete direction through the process of writing but without the reductive "by-the-numbers" approach of many basic writing texts or the exhaustive minutiae of the all-encompassing rhetoric. By engaging student writers in activities that are both interesting and immediately useful, we hope to give them ways to gauge their own progress in expressing themselves effectively, and to direct their vision beyond the classroom to the world that they have already experienced and observed.

We have also prepared an instructor's manual that introduces the pedagogy of the text, offers suggestions for approaching the tasks, includes a twelve-week and fifteen-week syllabus, and lists sources for the instructor who seeks more information on both traditional and current approaches to the teaching of writing.

The authors wish to thank the many students who over the five-year gestation period of this book have good humoredly submitted themselves to the trials and errors that we have put them through while developing both approach and materials in their classrooms. We wish to thank particularly the students whose work—both in rough and more polished stages—we have used as models for each task: Donna DiMaggio, Christine Domanoski, Michael Donovan, Italo Ferrari, Liliana Gonzalez, Jolene Gottlieb, Kathy Greene, Hennessy Levine, Virginia McLaughlin, Steve Medvedeff, Audrey O'Leary, Marc Pressman, and Patricia Sadhoff.

For their encouragement and contributions, we should like to thank the following colleagues: Marcia Keizs, Joyce Sigurdsson, Sheena Gillespie, Elaine Levy, David Greetham, and Arnold Asrelsky; also, for their help in typing various stages of the manuscript, Evelyn Pomann, Margaret Cavanaugh, and Tina Packer.

We are indebted to those reviewers who gave us valuable suggestions and comments throughout the process of writing this text: George Haich, Georgia State University; Dr. Barbara J. Craig, Del Mar College; Russell Peterson, College of Lake County; Kathleen L. Bell, University of Miami; Michael J. Hogan, University of New Mexico; Ralph Jenkins, Temple University; George Miller, University of Delaware.

At Macmillan we thank Eben Ludlow, Executive Editor for the College Division, for his intelligent guidance and patience; Robert Hunter, our production editor, for seeing the manuscript through production; Christine Cardone, marketing manager, for her thorough approach to marketing; and Holly Reid McLaughlin, designer.

L. C. S.

D. S.

A. H. L.

TO THE STUDENT

By now you must have arrived at some definite view of yourself as a writer. After many years of writing in one school or another, you probably have concluded that you are either a "good" or a "bad" writer. Those words are written with quotation marks around them for a specific reason: they really have no meaning. Or at least no meaning that can be of any usefulness in evaluating yourself as a writer. The words *good* and *bad* imply some kind of absolute standard of judgment—perhaps the grade you received on a high-school essay exam or a report on gerbils you prepared in the third grade. But they just won't do for an evaluation of writing once you become aware of all the complexities involved in any act of written expression. This textbook attempts to take those complexities and arrange them into a coherent pattern so that they can be studied and perhaps even mastered.

But writing, as you know, is not plane geometry or biology or accounting. When you write, you don't necessarily begin at the beginning. You write because you have something to communicate, and often only after you have already begun to write do your thought processes go to work to determine the form that your writing will take. Our textbook is based on the assumption that you will write more effectively if you clarify your purpose in writing and if you are aware of how the ways you develop ideas, as well as what your audience expects, can give direction and weight to your writing. We have arranged the text in a way that we feel will increase your skill in these elements of communication.

The central focus of each chapter in *Ways to Writing* is a specific writing task. In the earlier chapters, the tasks are more personal: you may be asked to evaluate something you have learned about yourself by keeping a journal, or something you have learned about your attitude toward a place by visiting and studying that place. In the latter chapters of the book, the tasks become more analytic, and you will be asked, for example, to explain why an idea that you hold is sensible or to argue why a position that you take is valid. In completing each task, you will be invited to employ a different way of developing ideas, and you will be asked to write for a different kind of audience. To guide you through these tasks, we have arranged our text so that the completion of a writing assignment is supported on one side by general prewriting activities and on the other by prewriting, writing, and rewriting activities directed specifically to the completion of the task at hand.

Beginning each chapter is a "Purpose" section that provides a brief explanation of the writing aim for that chapter. Following this is a section called "Generating Ideas" that offers ways for you to get started writing. Some ways are traditional; others are relatively new. Some require no deliberation; others demand logical concentration. You will find that you can apply these procedures in writing to the tasks in other chapters. They form a kind of cumulative reserve to draw on when you need to develop ideas for an essay.

Another important consideration before you begin writing is, naturally enough, your audience. You don't usually write in a vacuum: you write to and for others. Thus you need to know who your readers are, how to interest them, what kind of stance you need to take toward them. Clarity is important, but more than that is required to move an audience, to make it see what you want it to see. Through discussion and exercises, we hope to make you more conscious of the crucial role that an audience plays in determining the shape of your writing.

After announcing the task in each chapter, we guide you through the writing of an essay, showing you how to use the prewriting techniques, stressing the importance of a shaping idea, suggesting ways to arrange your discussion, directing you to the structural and stylistic characteristics of effective writing. As you will notice in your own writing, revision is an indispensable follow-up to any writing effort. By studying the rough drafts of other students, as well as peer evaluations of their work, you will become more aware of the contribution that these activities can make to your own writing.

Finally, we ask you some questions to encourage you to think about your own writing process, to become aware of the tentative, provisional nature of all writing as the unfolding of a mind. Clearly, this is not the same thing as counting the errors in each of your papers and then trying to find the mathematical formula for determining a grade. If we succeed in conveying to you some of the satisfaction you can derive from expressing yourself effectively to others through the act of writing, we will have accomplished our purpose in preparing this text.

CONTENTS

Preface / v
To the Student / ix

Part I
SELF-EXPRESSION   1

1 Writing About Yourself   3

Purpose / 3
Generating Ideas: The Journal / 4
  Keeping a Journal / 4
  Using Your Journal as a Source of Ideas for Writing an Essay / 9
Addressing Your Audience: Authentic Voice / 11
  Your Authentic Voice / 11
  Discovering Your Own Voice / 13
  How Others Hear You / 14
Task: Writing an Essay Based on Your Journal / 18
  Based on ideas generated by keeping a journal, you write an essay about yourself. Audience for task: A sympathetic reader
Writing the Essay / 19
  Using the Journal as a Source of Ideas / 19

Developing Your Own Voice / 21
Arranging the Essay / 21
Finding a Shaping Idea / 21
Determining What You Want to Say About Your Subject / 22
Writing the Rough Draft / 22
''This Really Isn't Me'' (Rough Draft of Student Essay) / 22
Focus: Shaping the Subject / 25
Rewriting / 28
  Obtaining Feedback on Your Rough Draft / 28
  ''This Really Isn't Me'' (Revised Student Essay) / 29
  The Final Product / 31
  Presentation / 31
  Your Title / 31
  Proofreading / 31
Becoming Aware of Yourself as a Writer / 32

2 Writing About an Incident   33

Purpose / 33
Generating Ideas: The Journalist's Questions / 34

*Using the Journalist's Questions in
    Writing an Essay / 37*
**Addressing Your Audience: Frame
    of Reference / 39**
The Writer's Frame of Reference / 40
The Reader's Frame of Reference / 43
Interview / 44
Inference / 45
Role Playing / 46
**Task: Writing About an Incident /
    47**

You search your memory for an
incident that you observed or were
involved in that in some way affected
the course of your life. Audience for
task: Your peers.

Writing the Essay / 48
Using the Journalist's Questions / 48
*Determining Your Audience Frame of
    Reference / 49*
*Bridging the Gap Between Your
    Audience's Point of View and
    Your Own / 49*
Arranging Your Essay: Narration / 50
Duration / 51
    *Essay Model: ''The Angry Winter'' by
        Loren Eiseley / 51*
Details / 53
    *''Sensuous Sounds'' (Rough Draft of
        Student Essay) / 54*
Arranging the Details of Your Essay / 55
Writing the Rough Draft / 56
Focus: Transitions / 56
Rewriting / 62
*Obtaining Feedback on Your Rough
    Draft / 62*
    *''Sensuous Sounds'' (Revised Student
        Essay) / 63*
Revising / 64
Adding / 65
Editing / 66
Adding / 66

Transitions / 66
Mechanics / 66
**Becoming Aware of Yourself as a
    Writer / 66**

3 Writing About a Phase 68

Purpose / 68
Generating Ideas: Free Writing / 69
*Free Writing as a Source of Ideas for
    Writing an Essay / 71*
*Free Writing and the Writing Process /
    73*
**Addressing Your Audience:
    Selecting a Voice for Your
    Reader / 73**
*Selecting a Voice as a Means of Self-
    Expression / 73*
*Selecting a Voice as a Bridge Between
    the Writer and the Reader / 74*
Task: Writing About a Phase / 76

You present an episode in your life that
represented a break from your earlier
behavior or outlook. Audience for task:
Your English instructor.

Writing the Essay / 77
Free Writing as a Source of Ideas / 77
*Selecting a Voice as a Bridge Between
    You and Your Audience / 79*
*Arranging Your Essay: The Shaping
    Idea, Narration, and Exposition /
    80*
The Shaping Idea / 80
*Narration and Exposition in the Service of
    Narration / 81*
*Using Narration in Writing on a
    Significant Episode / 82*
Exposition in the Service of Narration / 83
    *''My Phase with the Devil'' (Rough
        Draft of Student Essay) / 84*

*Using Exposition in Writing on a
Significant Episode / 85*
**Writing the Rough Draft: Cutting and
Pasting / 86**
*Model Student Essay: ''Daydream
Believer'' / 86*
Focus: Paragraph Structure / 88
Rewriting / 95
**Obtaining Feedback on Your Rough
Draft / 95**
*''My Phase with the Devil'' (Revised
Student Essay) / 96*
Rearranging / 97
Editing / 98
Transitions / 98
Topic Sentences / 98
Mechanics / 98
**Becoming Aware of Yourself as a
Writer / 99**

someone with the same interest or
hobby.
Writing the Essay / 112
Using the Explorer's Questions / 112
Audience Depth of Information / 113
Arranging Your Essay / 115
Narrative Patterns / 115
Patterns of Exposition / 116
Patterns of Description / 117
Dialogue / 118
The Overriding Impression / 119
*Model Essay: ''On a Kibbutz'' by Saul
Bellow / 119*
Writing the Rough Draft / 122
*''The Assembly-Line Method of
Reproductive Health'' (Rough Draft of
Student Essay) / 123*
Focus: Paragraph Development / 125
Rewriting / 130
**Obtaining Feedback on Your Rough
Draft / 130**
*''The Assembly-Line Method of
Reproductive Health'' (Revised
Student Essay) / 131*
Revising: Substituting / 133
Editing / 134
Substitutions / 134
Transitions / 134
Paragraphs / 135
Mechanics / 135
**Becoming Aware of Yourself as a
Writer / 135**

Part II
EXPLORATION   101

4 Writing About a Place   103

Purpose / 103
**Generating Ideas: The Explorer's
Questions / 104**
**Addressing Your Audience: Depth
of Information / 107**
Task: Exploring a Place / 111

Exploring a place about which a myth
may have been created for you by
others, you write to explain your
perceptions as fully and richly as
possible. Audience for task: Someone
interested in your findings about the
place, a class in your curriculum,

5 Writing a Case   137

Purpose / 137
**Generating Ideas: The Classical
Questions / 138**
**Addressing Your Audience: The
Common Reader and Writing
for Publication / 142**

Task: Writing a Case / 145

Choosing an ongoing event or situation which you have prejudged in some way, you write a case study in which you test your prejudgment or prejudice against the information that you have amassed. Audience for task: Your college newspaper, a newsletter at work, a local weekly newspaper, or a hobby magazine.

Writing the Essay / 146

Generating Ideas with the Classical Questions / 146

Addressing the Reader Common to Your Publication / 148

Arranging the Essay / 149

The Shaping Idea / 149

Cause and Effect / 150

Comparison and Contrast / 150

Process Analysis / 151

Model Essay: ''Stalking Muskrats'' by Annie Dillard / 152

Writing the Rough Draft / 154

''Your Right to a Good Education'' (Rough Draft of Student Essay) / 155

Focus: Sentence Combining / 156

The Base Sentence / 157

Subordinate Clauses / 158

Free Modifiers / 158

Noun Cluster / 158

Verb Cluster / 159

Adjective Cluster / 159

Adverb Cluster / 159

Varying Sentence Length and Rhythm / 160

Punctuation / 162

Transitions / 162

Rewriting / 165

Obtaining Feedback on Your Rough Draft / 165

''Your Right to a Good Education'' (Revised Student Essay) / 167

Distributing / 169

Editing / 169

Distributing / 169

Sentence Combining and Transitions / 169

Paragraphs / 170

Mechanics / 170

Becoming Aware of Yourself as a Writer / 170

Part III
EXPLANATION   171

6 Writing About What You Know   173

Purpose / 173

Generating Ideas: The Classical Questions / 174

''What Has Been Said About My Topics by Others?'' / 174

''What General Ideas and Values Does My Topic Exemplify?'' / 176

Addressing Your Audience: A Shared Sense of Form and Value / 180

Task: Writing About What You Know / 182

From your reading or other media experience, you explain an attitude, an action, an idea, or a belief that is reasonable to you but that others might not fully understand. Audience for task: peers who are studying the art of the essay and are familiar with the language and form of educated discourse.

Writing the Essay / 182

Using Your Reading or Other Media Experience as a Way of

Generating a Subject and/or Generating Ideas / 182
Using Generalization as a Way of Generating Ideas / 185
Using a Shared Sense of Form and Value in Addressing Your Audience / 186
Arranging Your Essay: The Shaping Idea, Generalization, and Specification / 187
The Shaping Idea / 187
Generalization and Specification / 187
Model Essay: ''Riposte'' by E. B. White / 188
Writing the Rough Draft / 190
''Horrors'' (Rough Draft of Student Essay) / 190

Focus: Style / 194
The Components of Style / 194
Ways of Adjusting Style / 195
Adjusting for Concreteness / 195
The Verbal Sentence / 196
Adjusting for Abstractness / 196
The Nominal Sentence / 197
How to Write More Eloquently / 197
Balanced Phrasing / 197
Loose and Periodic Sentences / 197
Figurative Language / 198
Irony / 198

Rewriting / 201
Obtaining Feedback on Your Rough Draft / 201
''Horrors'' (Final Draft of Student Essay) / 202
Consolidating / 207
Editing / 208
Consolidating / 208
Style / 208
Mechanics / 208

Becoming Aware of Yourself as a Writer / 209

7 Writing About Research   210

Purpose / 210
Generating Ideas Through Induction / 213
Addressing Your Audience: The Lay Reader / 216
Task: Writing About Research / 219

You write an article for a college magazine that presents the work of students exploring the sciences and social sciences. Audience for task: Students and professors interested in the writings of students on the sciences and social sciences.

Writing the Essay / 220
Using Induction as a Means of Generating Ideas / 220
Finding a Topic / 221
Gathering Sources: Preparing a Preliminary Bibliography / 223
Taking Notes / 225
Outlining / 228
Considering Your Audience / 229
Putting Your Notes Together / 232
Writing the Introduction / 234
Writing the Rough Draft / 235
''Achieving a Tie Score: One Boy to One Girl'' (Rough Draft of Student Essay) / 235

Focus: Methods of Documentation / 241
Using Footnotes / 241
Using Bibliography / 242
Using the New Method / 244

Rewriting / 246
Obtaining Feedback on Your Rough Draft / 246
Eliminating Deadwood / 247

*"Achieving a Tie Score: One Boy to One
    Girl" (Final Draft of Student Essay) /
    249*
**Becoming Aware of Yourself as a
    Writer / 259**

Part IV
PERSUASION   261

8 Writing
    Persuasively   263

Purpose / 263
**Generating Ideas: Induction,
    Deduction, and The Classical
    Questions / 264**
Induction / 264
Deduction / 272
Deductive Fallacies / 275
*The Classical Questions in Support of
    Persuasion / 277*
*How to Apply the Principles of
    Induction and Deduction in
    Generating Ideas for a
    Persuasive Essay / 278*
**Audience: Persuading Your
    Audience / 281**
Establishing Credibility / 281
Adopting the Proper Tone / 282
Analyzing Your Audience / 283
Presenting an Ethical Appeal / 283
**Task: Writing a Persuasive Essay /
    286**
You construct a life situation or "case"
in which you take the role of one of the
participants in the situation and write
an argument to convince one or more
other participants of your point of view
about an issue that has arisen. Audience
for task: One or more other participants
in your case.

Writing the Essay / 288
*Generating Ideas Through Induction,
    Deduction, and the Classical
    Questions / 288*
Persuading Your Audience / 289
Arranging Your Essay / 290
*Essay Model: "The Declaration of
    Independence" / 293*
Writing the Rough Draft / 296
*"Bodybuilding: The Shape of the Future"
    (Rough Draft of Student Essay) / 297*
**Focus: Persuasive Language and
    the Appeal to the Emotions /
    299**
Connotation / 299
Figurative Language / 300
Allusion / 301
Repetition / 301
Humor and Satire / 302
Categorical Statements / 303
Logical Terms / 303
Tone and Audience / 303
Rewriting / 308
*Obtaining Feedback on Your Rough
    Draft / 308*
*"Bodybuilding: The Shape of the Future"
    (Revised Student Essay) / 309*
**Becoming Aware of Yourself as a
    Writer / 311**

Part V
INTERPRETATION   313

9 Writing About
    Poetry   315

Purpose / 315
**Generating Ideas: Figurative
    Language / 317**

Analogy / 317
Metaphor and Simile / 319
Metonymy / 320
Personification / 320
Symbol / 321
Imagery / 321
Irony / 322

Audience: The Informed Reader / 324

Task: Writing About Poetry / 329

You write an interpretative essay on one or more poems, an essay that will explain your own understanding and appreciation of what the poems mean and how they convey that meaning. Audience for task: Your English instructor.

Writing the Essay / 330

Generating Ideas for Writing on a Poem / 330
Writing on Poetry for an Informed Audience / 341
Arranging the Essay / 344
First Responses: Journal Entries / 344
Comparison and Contrast / 345
Writing the Rough Draft / 346

''*Howard Nemerov's 'The Vacuum' and Adrienne Rich's 'Trying to Talk with a Man': A Comparison''* (Rough Draft of Student Essay) / 347

Focus: The Sound of Poetry / 350

Rewriting / 352

Obtaining Feedback on Your Rough Draft / 352
''*Howard Nemerov's 'The Vacuum' and Adrienne Rich's 'Trying to Talk With a Man': A Comparison''* (Final Draft of Student Essay) / 353
Quoting Lines of Poetry / 355

Becoming Aware of Yourself as a Writer / 356

Handbook   359

Grammar / 361
Punctuation / 390
Mechanics / 406

Index   423

RHETORICAL CONTENTS

PURPOSE

Expressive—Chapters 1–3
   From journal to essay—Chapter 1
   Narrative—Chapter 2
   Narrative and expository—Chapter 3
Expository—Chapters 4–7
   Exploration—Chapters 4 and 5
   Explanation—Chapters 6 and 7
Persuasive—Chapter 8
Literary—Chapter 9

GENERATING IDEAS

The Journal—Chapter 1
The Journalist's Questions—Chapter 2
Free Writing—Chapter 3
The Explorer's Questions—Chapter 4
The Classical Questions—Chapters 5–8
Induction—Chapters 7, 8
Deduction—Chapter 8
Figurative Language—Chapter 9

AUDIENCE ANALYSIS

Voice—Chapter 1
Frame of Reference—Chapter 2
Selecting a Voice—Chapter 3

Depth of Information—Chapter 4
The Common Reader—Chapter 5
A Shared Sense of Form and Value—
   Chapter 6
The Lay Reader—Chapter 7
Persuading Your Audience—Chapter 8
The Informed Reader—Chapter 9

ARRANGEMENT

Duration—Chapters 1–4
Shaping Idea—Chapters 1–9
Exposition (Introduction to)—Chapter 3
Description—Chapter 4
Cause and Effect—Chapter 5
Comparison and Contrast—Chapters 4–9
Process Analysis—Chapters 4, 5
Generalization and Specification—
   Chapter 6
The Scientific Research Paper—
   Chapter 7
Argumentation—Chapter 8

FOCUS

Shaping the Subject—Chapter 1
Making Transitions—Chapter 2
Paragraph Structure—Chapter 3

Paragraph Length and Development—
    Chapter 4
Sentence Combining—Chapter 5
Style—Chapter 6
Research Techniques—Chapter 7
Persuasive Language—Chapter 8
The Sound of Poetry—Chapter 9

REVISING STRATEGIES

Self, Peer, or Instructor Feedback—
    Chapter 1

Adding—Chapter 2
Rearranging—Chapter 3
Substituting—Chapter 4
Distributing—Chapter 5
Consolidating—Chapter 6
Eliminating Deadwood—Chapter 7
Incorporating Audience Response in
    Writing a Persuasive Essay—Chapter 8
Quoting Lines of Poetry—Chapter 9

HANDBOOK

ACKNOWLEDGMENTS *(continued from p. iv)*

Excerpt from *Introductory Lectures on Psychoanalysis: A General Introduction to Psychoanalysis* by Sigmund Freud. Published by Liveright, 1977. Reprinted by permission of the publisher.

Excerpt from *To Jerusalem and Back* by Saul Bellow. Copyright © 1976 by Saul Bellow. Reprinted by permission of Viking Penguin Inc.

Specified excerpt from pp. 190–192 in *Pilgrim at Tinker Creek* by Annie Dillard. Copyright © 1974 by Annie Dillard. Reprinted by permission of Harper & Row, Inc.

Excerpt from *Calcutta* by Geoffrey Moorhouse. Published by Weidenfeld & Nicolson Ltd., 1971. Reprinted by permission of the publisher.

Excerpt from ''Sounds That Bring Us Closer Together'' by Tracy Early in *The Christian Science Monitor,* 1 January 1980. Reprinted by permission of the author.

Excerpt from ''Riposte'' by E. B. White, reprinted from *Essays of E. B. White*. Published by Harper & Row, Inc., 1977. Reprinted by permission of The New York Times Company.

Excerpt from ''The Pentagon of Life'' is reprinted from *Ever Since Dawn* by Stephen Jay Gould, by permission of W. W. Norton & Company, Inc. Copyright © 1977 by Stephen Jay Gould. Copyright © 1973, 1974, 1975, 1976, 1977, by The American Museum of Natural History.

Excerpt from ''Emotions Found to Influence Nearly Every Ailment'' by Jane Brody, reprinted from *The New York Times,* 24 May 1983. Copyright © 1983 by The New York Times Company. Reprinted by permission.

Excerpt from *The Dragons of Eden* by Carl Sagan. Copyright © 1977 by Carl Sagan. Reprinted by permission of Random House, Inc.

Excerpt from ''Abraham Lincoln and the Self-Made Myth'' reprinted from *The American Political Tradition and the Men Who Made It* by Richard Hofstadter. Copyright 1948, © 1973 by Alfred A. Knopf, Inc. Reprinted by permission of the publisher.

Excerpt from *The Magic Years* by Selma Fraiberg. Copyright © 1959 by Selma H. Fraiberg. Reprinted with the permission of Charles Scribner's Sons.

Excerpt from ''It's Failure, Not Success'' reprinted from *Close to Home* by Ellen Goodman. Copyright © 1979 by the Washington Post Company. Reprinted by permission of Simon & Schuster, Inc.

Excerpt from *The Lives of a Cell* by Lewis Thomas. Copyright © 1971, 1972, 1973 by the Massachusetts Medical Society. Copyright © 1974 by Lewis Thomas. Originally published in the *New England Journal of Medicine.* Reprinted by permission of Viking Penguin Inc.

Excerpt from ''Sport: If You Want to Build Character, Try Something Else'' by Bruce C. Ogilvie and Thomas A. Tutko, in *Psychology Today,* October 1971. Reprinted by permission of Ziff-Davis Publishing Company.

Excerpt from ''Speech to Graduating Class of '79'' by Woody Allen, reprinted from *The New York Times,* 10 August 1979 (Op-Ed page). Copyright © 1979 by The New York Times Company. Reprinted by permission.

Specified excerpt from ''Letter from a Birmingham Jail, April 16, 1963,'' from *Why We Can't Wait* by Martin Luther King, Jr. Copyright © 1963 by Martin Luther King, Jr. Reprinted by permission of Harper & Row, Inc.

''Danse Russe'' by William Carlos Williams, reprinted from *Collected Earlier Poems of William Carlos Williams*. Copyright 1938 by New Directions Publishing Corporation. Reprinted by permission of New Directions Publishing Corporation.

''Trying to Talk with a Man'' is reprinted from *Poems, Selected and New, 1950–1974* by Adrienne Rich, by permission of W. W. Norton & Company, Inc. Copyright © 1975, 1973, 1971, 1969, 1966 by W. W. Norton & Company, Inc.

''The Oven Bird'' by Robert Frost from *The Poetry of Robert Frost,* edited by Edward Connery Lathem. Copyright 1916, © 1969 by Holt, Rinehart and Winston. Copyright 1944 by Robert Frost. Reprinted by permission of Holt, Rinehart and Winston, Publishers.

''Nothing Gold Can Stay'' by Robert Frost from *The Poetry of Robert Frost,* edited by Edward Connery Lathem. Copyright 1923, © 1969 by Holt, Rinehart and Winston. Copyright 1951 by Robert Frost. Reprinted by permission of Holt, Rinehart and Winston, Publishers.

''The Vacuum'' by Howard Nemerov, reprinted from *The Collected Poems of Howard Nemerov*. Published by The University of Chicago Press, 1977. Reprinted by permission of the author.

PART I

SELF-EXPRESSION

INTRODUCTION

Imagine yourself describing an incident to a close friend, a member of your family, or a schoolmate. Everything about you—your voice, your facial expressions, your body movements, even your dress—establishes a unique physical presence that gives force to your story. Like a musical instrument, your voice rises and falls, emphasizing key words at moments of high drama or anxiety. Every gesture of your hands, every arching of your eyebrows reveals to the other person the unity of your voice and being. A filmed and recorded version of this conversation would represent for you and others authentic evidence of your self, of your presence as a human being in a unique moment of time.

Now imagine yourself wishing to transform this spoken narrative into a written account. Immediately your hand freezes, your brain numbs, and your eyes gaze fixedly at pen and paper. What was so easy and spontaneous an act of language now becomes weighted with the difficulty of premeditation, the self-consciousness of beginnings. To some anthropologists, in fact, the entrance into literacy for preliterate cultures signifies the rupture of a magical fusion of humans and nature, of language and the objective world.

Ironically, our membership in a literate culture further inhibits our powers of self-expression because we so often experience events through the language of others, for example, the press, government, business, and artistic communities. How, we might ask, can we then develop in our writing an authentic voice of our own? If we write on a sports event, must we see it only through the television language of the "thrill of victory and the agony of defeat"? What if we were more impressed by the third baseman's casual grace, the relief pitcher's menacing mustache, or some of the spectators' ferocity? If we already have a cultural overlay of meaning to apply to experience, we do not express the world as *we* have seen and experienced it.

We hope to provide a context for writing in Part I that will encourage you to develop an authentic voice of your own. By reporting on the world as you see and experience it directly, you will engage in what is fundamentally an act of self-expression, even as you begin to learn how to adjust your voice so that it is appropriate to your subject and understandable to your audience.

1 WRITING ABOUT YOURSELF

PURPOSE

If you wish to set down your day-to-day experiences and observations and responses to life as directly, completely, and honestly as possible, you may seek a form of writing that is flexible enough so that you do not have to be overly concerned with the effect on others of what you write or how you write it. For many writers, this form has been the journal.

A journal is a record, often kept daily, of one's life, a kind of personal account book. In the privacy of your journal, you can write about your conflicts and pleasures with family, friends, and associates without worrying about offending or embarrassing anyone. You can try out your responses to events, people, and things without worrying about the critical eye of a teacher or the difficulty of writing without error. You can open up and express yourself without fear of being poorly understood or harshly judged by anyone other than yourself. In short, you can discover your own uniquely personal voice.

To some students, the keeping of a journal or notebook seems a useless indulgence, a waste of time that has little to do with the next required theme or the grade that will be given to it. But this view is as impractical as it is misguided. Most writers are in constant search of new material, or of old material seen from a new perspective. How much easier it is to draw from a full well than to try to reclaim a few drops from the bottom. Thus many writers fill their journals or notebooks with materials as diverse as they can find.

It was customary for writers in the past to keep a personal notebook of their reading and observations by collecting sayings, quotations, philosophical reflections, lines from favorite poems, and formulas for success, anything that struck their interest. Such a collection was called a *commonplace book,* not only for its ordinary, everyday usefulness but also for its ability to supply fresh material for the common places, or topics, of writing. One modern compiler of a commonplace book, W. H. Auden, called it "a map of my planet." Like every map, it marks out boundaries, it locates the topics of deepest interest to a writer, and at the same time, it offers the possibility of new topics to explore.

The journal acts for many writers as a means of testing the self in its confrontations with the world. In your journal entries, you can express your confusion and disillusionment, your whimsicality and curiosity toward all the eccentric shapes of daily experience. Often, writing in your journal about an experience you have had can reveal to you something about yourself or your perceptions that you might not have realized as clearly before.

In this chapter, we ask you to keep a daily journal as a means of learning about yourself and also as a means of looking into the storehouse of your mind to obtain the raw material with which to forge a formal essay.

GENERATING IDEAS: THE JOURNAL

Keeping a Journal

Keeping a journal every day is a kind of contract with yourself. You agree to record your observations and reactions over an extended period of time and expect in return a writer's bounty: some usable glimpses of yourself or others that you can work into a finished essay, or perhaps some developing pattern of feeling or thought that reveals you in the act of resolving some personal conflict or perceiving a subject in a new way. Although you receive no guarantee that your entries will be more interesting, less common, or even less boring than your daily routine or your usual thoughts may seem to you, what is surprising is how often the bright hue of fresh observation emerges from the uniform gray of the workaday world.

Here are selections from a student's journal entries:

Sun., Sept. 19

    8:00 A.M.—I don't know why I agreed to work today 'cause I am beat! It's money anyway so I better take advantage of it. My boyfriend hasn't called me in 16 hrs I worry about him. . . . hmm.—

    2:00 P.M.—Well here I am at break. I really miss my roommate. She's a real doll. We've grown close since we first met at school. She's closer to me so far than most people are to me whom I've known for years!

11:00 PM.—As I was coming home from work, a stranger told me I was the most beautiful girl he's ever seen. I told him he must've been blind and just regained his sight.

Mon., Sept. 20

10:00 A.M.—Ah! here I am back at school! (Now I miss my mother and sister!) I also missed first period 20th Cent. Lit. I hate missing classes. Especially when I tried so hard to get to class on time. I got a big greeting from my friends here!

12:30 P.M.—I'm back at classes now. I enjoy classes very much. I guess I'm just beginning to realize it now. This strange guy called out my name suddenly in the hallway. I felt frightened at first. But it really is quite flattering that guys like you and find out your name through mysterious sources. Mari and I talked during lunch. I really think she's great.

11:00 P.M.—I'm getting ready for bed. I just came out of the shower and my mind's at ease. I just realized that a guy I met at the beginning of the semester is really quite a nice guy. I wonder if he thinks the same of me?

Tues., Sept. 21

9:00 A.M.—I had a lot of trouble getting out of bed to go walking with my "roomie" Mari. She's inspiring me to get in shape. What a sweet lady she is! (She doesn't want me to get fat—so the guys will stay in touch—) I couldn't express how much we've grown to like each other as friends. I treasure her friendship very much. (Of course our next door neighbor Martha is great with equal intensity.)

12:00 noon—Today Martha and Mari and I went to dinner. Dave (the hunk I referred to before) winked at me. He's definitely interested. Just a bit shy.

9:00 P.M.—I want to write a quickie here. I really am head over heels for Dave. God forgive me 'cause I love my boyfriend. But there's definitely an element of attraction from both sides here. I hope no one gets hurt along the way.

Wed., Sept. 22

9:00 A.M.—I'm getting ready to go to class now. My roommate's still asleep. I can't help but wonder why she's so sweet. Our relationship has not changed one bit. We still get along fine.

12:00 noon—Lunchtime! Classes have been great—so far. A really strange thing happened to me. This girl came out across to me in a very rude way at lunch. I snapped back at her and she smiled. Later I found out that I had met her prior to that and that she was only trying to be humorous. I thought it odd and forgot it.

10:00 P.M.—I saw Dave today. He made a very sexual gesture but excused himself after I expressed my disapproval. I'm beginning to realize that he's been coming on to all the women in our dorm. I guess I'll forget about him. Now I have to get ready to go to the PUB to meet my friends for a drink.

Fri., Sept. 24

9:00 A.M.—I'm shocked I got up early today. I have no classes. Yeah! I have to go home this afternoon. I'm looking forward to it.

12:00 noon—I'm having lunch and I miss school already. There's a funny feeling coming over me lately. As I sit here thinking I can't help but realize that I'm suddenly feeling torn between school and home. When I'm at school I feel as if I've lost my family. It's a weird feeling I hope I'll soon overcome. However, I believe my roommate has been a great help in my keeping whole throughout my stay here at college. I believe that she's the source of my pulling through thus far.

9:00 P.M.—Nothing extremely unusual happened. Except that I had a fight with my boyfriend. We're breaking up—I know it!

Sat., Sept. 25

8:00 A.M.—I got up late today. I'm about 20 min late for work. I'm very tired and already miss my roommate.

12:00 noon—I just got out to lunch. The most terrible thing has just happened to me! I just got mugged. The two creeps that mugged me caught me off guard. I mean, who would expect two clean-cut American kids to mug you on 86th St. and 3rd Avenue? I'm really shocked to hell! I think I've never been so afraid of New York City in all the 19 years that I've lived here.

10:00 P.M.—I was excused from work earlier as I was too upset to work. At this point I wish that I was back at school near my friends. They've become more close to me than the people back home.

Sun., Sept. 26

12:00 noon—I overslept. I'm still shocked a bit, and no one seems to understand why. The reason, I believe, is that the two muggers (yesterday) have robbed me of far more than just money; they robbed me of my self-confidence.

9:00 P.M.—I called my roommate today. I told her of the incident. She was very supportive and helped me feel a bit better. Something my own mother found difficulty in doing.

Tues., Sept. 28

8:00 A.M.—Off to class—I'm tired and very sleepy. I must get some sleep!

12:00 noon—Lunchtime! I am beginning to get over my feelings of bitterness about the mugging—my roommate's been quite a lot of help! She's helped me through a great deal.

10:00 P.M.—I called my boyfriend today. We are trying to communicate to get our problems straightened out. We've drifted apart since I came to stay on campus. He loves me a great deal and I know we'll stay together. I'm afraid, however, that for the meantime the relationship will be rocky.

What experiences has the student focused on in her journal? What feelings does she express in her entries? In what ways are her feelings in conflict with one another? What thoughts does the student have about her experiences? Just how random are her entries? What developing patterns of thought or feeling emerge from them?

Begin now to keep a journal. Your instructor may have a preference, but otherwise use a notebook or the blank diaries available in bookstores or stationery departments.

If you can't think of anything to start with, there are various ways to get yourself writing. You might take down a remark of a television personality or copy a quotation from a magazine article. Then write a few sentences in which you apply these comments to an experience you have had recently or to an idea that you have been thinking about. Also keep an eye out for unusual contrasts that might be puzzling or amusing or otherwise interesting. An article in *New York* magazine for July 5, 1982, called "Unappreciated New York" describes a Japanese Zen garden in the middle of Brooklyn. A meditative retreat in the midst of urban clamor is a fascinating kind of incongruity.

Another way of getting started is to do some free writing, which is also an effective way of getting in touch with your most authentic feelings and thoughts. Free writing is based on the belief that writers need to free themselves from the image of the perfectly formed and finished writing product in order to let the free play of language emerge in all its roughness, incoherence, and occasional imaginative sparkle. In free writing, you simply let the pen move as spontaneously and automatically as possible without the intervention of rational thought and order, without pause, and without lifting pen from paper. The result may be something like this:

Blue skies today no clouds to block the sun great tennis if the wind doesn't start up beat Mark last week don't know if I can get him today blue headband makes him look like McEnroe but not as fierce imagine him throwing his racket off the court not mild Mark cant think of anything to write so what what's a psyche anyhow can't think records almost over a guy in accounting didn't know who Springsteen was maybe he's been living in a cave.

How long could this have taken to write? Perhaps no more than a minute. Remember, our language-making power never stops working, not even during sleep. In fact, in a way, free writing resembles the flow of language in dreams. There is no "correct" order of events in dreams, and rules of grammar and sentence structure are irrelevant. Try to tap this flow of verbal energy and put it to work for you. Free writing, for timed intervals, is a practical means of "priming the pump." It helps a writer to overcome that initial fear of beginning, and it is another way of discovering what is going on within your mind. We will work more with free writing in Chapter 3.

Using Your Journal as a Source of Ideas for Writing an Essay

Our reactions to people and events seldom occur in isolation. Usually, we can trace a thought or feeling through a series of journal entries and discover that seemingly random observations actually have a shape, an order, a logic. In other words, your private journal may reveal a pattern of ideas or emotions connected to one subject. This pattern can become the basis for a public piece of writing, a formal essay. As you continue to write in your journal, you may find yourself noting over a period of time sufficient ideas on enough different topics for all the formal writing you must do, whether the subject is personal experience or, more objectively, thoughts about the world you live in.

SOME PRACTICE IN USING YOUR JOURNAL

The following exercises suggest topics and/or ask you to experiment with your journal as a method for discovering ideas that can give content and form to an essay:

1. Suggested Topics

   a. Reserve the same time each day for several days for writing in your journal. Note the difference in your attitude from day to day. What has caused you to have these differing feelings? Can you trace your feelings to a specific incident that occurred that day? Does any pattern of response emerge as you reread your entries for the preceding days?

   b. Write a number of entries, preferably on successive days, that record your activities with, and feelings toward, one person. What do these comments reveal about the nature of your relationship to this person? Can you notice a change in this relationship or recognize a phase that you are going through with this person?

   c. Forever, it seems, humankind has been afflicted by, and sometimes consumed by, boredom. In the Middle Ages, monks feared the onset of midday, the "demon of noontide," when life seemed particularly empty and joyless. Is there any time of day when you feel the regular approach of the demon boredom? Select this time to record your response in your journal, preferably over a period of several days. Explain how you attempted to slay the demon. In addition, become an observer of others' boredom, writing down what you see of boredom in its public forms, namely, in shopping centers, in the student lounge, at airline terminals, or on mass transportation.

   d. Over a period of time, note your reactions to a particular public personality: a television performer, a newspaper columnist, or an author. What do your reactions tell you about yourself? What do they tell you about the subject you have been studying?

e. Has a public issue, local or national or even international, captured your attention? As it develops in the press, record your reactions and interpretations. How does the issue affect you personally? What contributions might you make to general opinion about the subject?

2. Experiments with Your Journal Entries

a. After you have written entries for a week or longer, write a commentary on one of your previous entries in which you related your feelings about an emotional confrontation with another person. Do you see this encounter in the same way you did when you experienced it? If you see it differently, how would you have changed your original response? How do you explain your change of attitude? What implications could your thoughts about this encounter have for the next time you have a similar experience?

b. Rewrite a previous journal entry so that it ends in a way that you find more satisfying or pleasing to your view of yourself. What kinds of changes did you make? Would another reader be able to see through your deception?

c. Are there any previous entries that now appear to you false or inaccurate, either because you failed to observe carefully or because you willfully distorted the "facts"? Rewrite, this time giving a more reliable account and adding an explanation of the inaccuracies, along with a summary of the differences in the two versions.

d. Reread the entries in your journal that relate different encounters that you have had with others during a period of at least a week, in school, at work, or at home. Is there any pattern to these encounters? For example, was there a kind of forced casualness with other students, an unexpected tenseness at home, or a pleasing sense of friendship at work? What do these various encounters say about you and your social relations? Is there anything inconsistent in your different responses to other people?

e. In preparing your entries, seek for some evidence of the serendipitous, that is, an unexpected yet fortunate occurrence. For example, a fellow student you thought to be aloof and unfriendly surprisingly turns out to be quite helpful and concerned in explaining a mathematics problem. Can the writer always recognize these fortunate circumstances when they occur? What might prevent the writer from seeing them?

f. After you write an entry about an experience, write another in which you see yourself as a writer would see you going through the same experience. Change the narrative point of view (the voice telling the story) from the personal "I" to the impersonal "he" or "she." What differences are there in the two versions? What possible advantages are there in this change?

ADDRESSING YOUR AUDIENCE: AUTHENTIC VOICE

Your Authentic Voice

Writing in a journal is like talking to yourself. Because there is no one around, you can say what you want to without worrying about whether anyone is listening to you, judging your sincerity, or evaluating your skill as a writer. You can test out your thoughts and feelings, as well as your ability to express them openly and directly. You can also discover your authentic voice.

This is not necessarily an easy discovery to make. For one thing, you may not wish to hear your authentic voice, your most honest and original expression of yourself; there may be feelings you wish to hide from, to keep out of your own conscious awareness. Keeping a journal can be a way of tapping those feelings, but only if you allow it to.

Even if you are quite uninhibited about revealing your feelings, you may find that the language you use to convey them has a false note to it, is not unique or original enough, does not really sound like you. When we write, we often imitate one or another public voice that seems to us to command wide attention, or we adopt the voice of a close associate or a friend or a parent, or we rely on trite, clichéd expressions because they come readily to mind.

You may feel, for example, that it is a good idea to draw your ideas and language from the world of advertising, television, or popular journalism, for these media provide us with a stock of ready-made expressions and current attitudes. But in a way, allowing your voice to be an echo of someone else's is like wearing someone else's name on your clothes, applying to yourself a kind of designer's label of the mind. And this process may actually make you even more inhibited about expressing your most original ideas and observations.

For example, think of how often you, as a student, are tempted to imitate a teacher in order to make a good impression. In yielding to this temptation, you may feel uncomfortable, even guilty, about pretending to be someone that you're not. Feeling this way, you may reveal even less about yourself and hide your thoughts even more, rather than express them in an inauthentic way.

Consider the student who wrote the following note:

Dear Professor Ames,

Due to circumstances beyond my control, the paper on <u>Hamlet</u> was not submitted. I shall complete said paper and submit it as soon as possible prior to the final date of failure previously determined by the departmental authorities.

The student begins by sounding like a television announcer, then goes on to employ a pretentious, abstract style of phrasing that is perhaps meant to echo the academic language of the classroom. The effect is phony, unnatural, and unconvincing.

Nor would this student make a much better case if he or she tried to convey a false sense of familiarity that actually says little:

Dear Professor Ames,

I'm sorry I can't hand in my paper on Hamlet today. I've been having a rough time lately. But I'm getting myself together now, so I definitely should have the paper done by next week, OK?

Again the writing is unconvincing because it hides more than it tells. Phrases like "getting myself together" are so trite and commonplace that we use them most often as a way of avoiding telling what we really feel.

But what if the student wrote the following:

Dear Professor Ames,

I'm sorry that I don't have my paper on Hamlet for you today. I had a biology test yesterday and now I've got a math test today, and I'd fallen behind in my studying for both. So I didn't get the paper done. Would you still accept it if I write it tonight and get it to you first thing tomorrow?

Might this note have more success? Whether or not it would depends, of course, on the sort of person and teacher Professor Ames is. But at least the student sounds more forthright.

This might not always be the best strategy to take when you write. If you honestly feel that *Hamlet* is a rotten play and Professor Ames is a rotten teacher for making you write a paper on it, you probably would be wise to exercise a certain diplomacy and to edit these feelings out of your note. Sometimes you will have thoughts and feelings that you rightly choose to keep to yourself. Often you will want to adjust your voice to the expectations and values of your audience (a subject we take up in Chapter 2 and examine in most of the audience sections thereafter). But you do want to develop a firm sense of your own most direct and original voice, because even when you edit this voice, it will remain the foundation of all the writing that you do.

Discovering Your Own Voice

Other than simply trying to write about your observations and experiences as freely and honestly as possible, what can you do to discover your most authentic voice, the way of writing that is uniquely an expression of yourself?

Ken Macrorie, in his book *Telling Writing,* speaks of truthfulness in writing as the way to achieve an authentic voice. By *truthfulness* he does not mean simply the avoidance of lies and dishonesty; rather, he means the willingness to figure out what we really do want to say and to find a way of saying it. This approach recognizes, first, that we do not often know what we think unless we write about it and, second, that in order to express exactly what we think we need to find the words and the examples that will best convey it. We do not, in other words, think and then write. A process is involved in which thinking and writing are intertwined. This process is an arduous one; the right words do not always flow easily from the pen of even the greatest writer.

What you write about is less a problem than how you approach the subject. Taking an approach that allows you to learn something new from writing about the subject and to see the subject in a new, perhaps even contradictory, light will help you locate the truth.

Looking for unexpected perceptions that contrast with the perceptions of others or even with perceptions you have previously held yourself is, in fact, an excellent way of discovering something new, fresh, and original to say about a subject. If you feel there really is something rotten about a play that everyone tells you is a great classic, this feeling may be worth exploring in a paper. Perhaps the personality of one of the characters is offensive to you, and by writing about it, you may discover something new and vital about the character and about yourself as well. Macrorie suggests that the writer would be wise always to look for unexpected or opposing perceptions. Consider the positive aspects of a subject that strikes you as negative and vice versa. You thus treat a subject in all of its complexity and give yourself the opportunity to reveal the complexity of your own character.

Finding the words and phrases that reveal rather than mask this complexity is a challenge. By trying to be as concise and, at the same time, as detailed as possible in your choice of words, you can at least avoid sounding overly imitative of others.

On the one hand, you do not want to waste words. A phrase may convey more than a sentence or even a paragraph. Try not to use more words than you need to make your point. Why write, "When a black cat crosses my path, I am a superstitious enough person to believe that it is apt to be prophetic of misfortune," when you can write, "When a black cat crosses my path, I fear it will bring me bad luck"? Why be long-winded when you can be direct and to the point?

But truthfulness in writing is not just bare-bones economy. Although empty phrases should be pared from your writing, details that convey the uniqueness of your observations and experiences should be included. Work to find the specific nouns and the active verbs, adjectives, and adverbs that will bring your thoughts and feelings to life. Why write, "I felt very uptight," when you can write, "My stomach was doing triple somersaults, and every time I swallowed, I felt like a wad of cotton had been stuffed down my throat." Try to make your ideas more specific, more concrete, by offering detailed examples of what you mean. Try to re-create the feel of your experiences by telling the reader how they were like or unlike comparable experiences.

How Others Hear You

The test of how truthful you have been will be the response of the reader. Have you expressed yourself clearly, colorfully, and concisely enough so that your reader believes in your experiences, trusts your feelings, and understands and respects your thoughts? Have you given the reader a good sense of who you are and what you are all about?

Once you are writing for an audience* and not just for yourself, you may feel reticent about expressing yourself openly and honestly. If your subject itself is very private, you may decide not to write about it for a particular audience or not to write about it at all. But when this is not the case, the chances are that your reader will draw you along the path to honesty by his or her interest in your subject, rather than putting up roadblocks that will inhibit you.

For example, review the journal entries written by the student who was mugged. There are many feelings expressed here. Is there one overriding feeling or tone that seems most "authentic," most heart-felt, most "truthful"? Now read through the following rough draft that the student wrote on the mugging incident. To what degree has the student emphasized an authentic tone of voice in the rough draft?

Just two hours ago I got mugged. The two muggers were pushy, and for the first time in my life, I was actually afraid. I was so angry, not just at the muggers but at New York in general.

Before this incident occurred, I was very confident about living in New York. I mean, for nineteen years, I lived in the Bronx and never had any problems whatsoever. I guess one can say that all the years in New York gave me some kind of instinct for distinguishing the good from the bad. It turned out to be wrong, at least in my case. I never

---

*We use *reader* and *audience* interchangeably here to mean either a group of readers or an individual. Each task in the book will specify whether your audience is to be a group or a particular individual.

thought that the two "gentlemen" that approached me would turn out to be two of the "bad" guys. I always pictured the "bad" guy as a shabbily dressed, dirty-looking being. However, my stereotyping cost me 150 bucks!

If I had been a lot wiser about who I allowed to come near me (whether shabbily dressed or not), this would never have happened to me. I should have applied caution to everything and everyone. I should never trust anyone right off. My problem was that I applied caution in only one area (bad neighborhoods and shabby-looking people), instead of all neighborhoods and all people.

I guess it's not fair to blame all of New York; however, for a while there, I was really upset and I still carry a lot of the bitterness around with me. I blame the city because it disappoints me to see and feel that I could be harmed in a place and an area in which I've been brought up and have grown accustomed to. It really hurts to feel afraid suddenly when you've never known that feeling before; and it's really awful to have to think that two people can make you fear a whole city.

How authentic is the voice in this essay? Does the student offer as honest or complete a sense of herself in her rough draft as she does in her journals?

When her classmates read her essay, they felt that her concise style and use of slang conveyed her anger and disappointment well. But they did not feel that her fear came through fully, even though she refers to it throughout the essay.

To be as convincing as possible, she may need to convey her fear more thoroughly. How might she accomplish this?

Her classmates suggested that she describe her attackers and the mugging incident itself in detail. They felt that a more concrete narrative of what actually happened might capture more of her feelings and attitudes and might allow a reader to get to know her more fully. Here, in response, is what the student added between the second and third paragraphs of her original draft:

I was on my way out to lunch from work when the two creeps caught me off guard. I mean, who would expect two clean-cut American types to mug you on 86th St. and 3rd Avenue. Maybe that made it worse. They were nice-looking guys.

One minute they were walking past me; then before I knew what was happening, the big one reached out and grabbed my arm hard. His hand was so big, it fitted all the way around my arm muscle. I must've looked shocked, 'cause all of a sudden he laughed in my face. He didn't have his two front teeth. For some reason, I keep remembering that.

The next thing I knew they'd pushed me against the wall of a building. I'm not sure I ever felt it when the other one tore my bag from off my shoulder. The next thing I knew, they were gone.

I was so shocked for a while I just stood there looking at the people walking by. It was like nobody even noticed. Then I got the shakes. I mean the shakes! I shook so hard, I thought I'd cry. I think I've never been so afraid of New York City in all of the nineteen years that I've lived here. Those two muggers have robbed me of more than just my money: they robbed me of my self-confidence.

In this case, the student's consciousness of her audience may have helped her to convey her experience in a more authentic voice than she might otherwise have used, in a voice that more thoroughly captured the range of her emotions. At first, you may feel intimidated by the recognition that you really do have an audience. But after writing several papers for a variety of readers, you should begin to sense how you can speak authentically and express your individuality to others in language that has the feel of a real person behind it.

SOME PRACTICE WITH VOICE

1. In the student's notes to Professor Ames above, how does the choice of words affect the overall tone of the language? For example, how do the words *departmental authorities* function in the first note? What words create a vague, ambiguous feeling in the second note? What words clear up this ambiguity in the third note?

2. What can you conclude about the intentions and the character of the voices in the following quotations?

    a. I have resolved on an enterprise which has no precedent, and which, once complete, will have no imitator. My purpose is to display to my kind a portrait in every way true to nature, and the man I shall portray will be myself. . . . I am like no one in the whole world. I may be no better, but at least I am different.

    —**Jean-Jacques Rousseau,** *Confessions*

b. When in the course of human events, it becomes necessary for one people to dissolve the political bands which have connected them with another, . . . a decent respect to the opinions of mankind requires that they should declare the causes which impel them to the separation.

—**Thomas Jefferson,** "Declaration of Independence"

c. Psychopathology: Aimed at understanding obsessions and phobias, including the fear of being suddenly captured and stuffed with crabmeat, reluctance to return a volleyball serve, and the inability to say the word "mackinaw" in the presence of women. The compulsion to seek out the company of beavers is analyzed.

—**Woody Allen,** "Spring Bulletin"

d. It is a truth universally acknowledged, that a single man in possession of a good fortune must be in want of a wife.

—**Jane Austen,** *Pride and Prejudice*

3. Select a popular newspaper or magazine with a distinctive voice. Write an entry in your journal on some commonplace event for that day, but try to narrate it in the voice of the magazine.

4. Write a brief advertisement for an expensive perfume, but use the voice you would expect to hear in a beer commercial. What kind of voice is usually used for these products? What are some words that would most likely appear in these commercials to create a distinctive voice?

5. Select sentences from your journal that don't really sound the way you think you sound, that seem to you to express an inauthentic voice. How do you account for this writing? Rewrite the sentences so that they seem to be more "truthful." What changes did you make?

6. Collect examples of newspaper and magazine advertisements that take on a voice that you find to be manipulative, deceitful, or dishonest. What kind of language do these voices use? What kinds of audiences are addressed by these advertisements?

7. Working against the expression of an authentic voice is the tendency of student writers to rely on clichés—secondhand thoughts and feelings. For example a reference at the beginning of the chapter to the "thrill of victory and the agony of defeat" suggests the abundance of clichés in the language of sports. Make a list of the sports clichés that you know. Collect clichés characteristic of other special-interest groups. What phrases can one substitute for the easily recognized expressions on your lists?

8. Change the following expressions into phrases that establish a more concrete voice in their description of objects or events:

   Example:
   Fantastically beautiful autumn woodland
   An October forest of red- and golden-leafed oak and maple trees

   a. Wonderful beach of sun worshipers
   b. Exciting marathon runners passing by
   c. Laughing students hanging out on campus
   d. Municipal hospital admissions room filled with people

9. Restore the common expressions disguised by an inflated voice in these sentences.

   Example:
   A rapidly accelerating glacial deposit accumulates zero spongy vegetation.
   A rolling stone gathers no moss.

   a. A military consortium peregrinates on its internal digestive organ.
   b. A feathered biped retained manually is cost-effectively superior to pairs inhabiting low-lying vegetation.
   c. Avoid enumerating domestic fowl prior to their postovum existence.
   d. Contemporaneously with the feline's exodus is experienced the diminutive rodent's ludic spontaneity.

TASK: WRITING AN ESSAY BASED ON YOUR JOURNAL

The task in this chapter is to write an essay based on information and ideas that you have generated by keeping a journal. By now you have used your journal to write about yourself in a number of different ways, narrating your experiences, recording your sense impressions, revealing your thoughts and feelings, experimenting with your voice. Now we will ask you to transform some of your journal materials into an expressive essay.

After reviewing a series of journal entries, write an essay about what the series reveals to you about yourself. This revelation should surprise you in some way: perhaps the entries confirm something that you already knew but that you did not realize you would focus so much on when you began keeping your journal; perhaps the entries indicate something new about you of which you were unaware.

The audience for this essay should be one sympathetic to your act of self-discovery. As you write, try addressing a group of readers who would be interested in your self-revelation because they, too, are involved in self-discovery.

If you find in reviewing your journal that there is a particular feeling or tone you can identify as your authentic voice, use that voice in writing the essay. On the other hand, you may find that you have written the journal entries in a less honest or "truthful" voice than you might have because you were too shy and reserved even in the privacy of your journal or because you were too imitative of the voices of others. If this is the case, aim for the sort of truthfulness that Macrorie advises you to seek, pointing out unexpected or opposing perceptions, and attempting through concrete words and details and short, narrative examples to help the reader know you as a person.

In the next section of this chapter, "Writing the Essay," we will discuss specifically how to use your journal as a source of material for this task, how to incorporate what you have learned about voice in selecting language and detail, and how to move through a rough draft and an evaluation of that draft to a finished product.

WRITING THE ESSAY

Using the Journal as a Source of Ideas

Reread your journal entries with an eye to those entries that contain information about yourself that you are surprised to find there. See if you can pick out a series of entries that contain similar information about you. To focus more specifically on the sort of information that you might write about, review the material that resulted from one or more of the exercises on pages 9–10. Were you surprised at what one of these exercises uncovered? Did you learn anything new about yourself? Did you show more interest than you suspected you would in something that you already knew about yourself?

Once you have a notion of what the pattern of feeling or the shape of thought in these entries might be, reread your entire journal, noting other entries that might have a bearing on the basic idea that this pattern reflects, on what we will call the *shaping idea*. Note those entries that give examples of behavior that contributed to your conclusions about yourself, those that explain the reasons for your behavior, those that seem to contradict it, and those that tell of the effects of it on you and others.

Hopefully, you now have several pages of raw material with which to work in writing an essay. Here are three entries a student chose that revealed to her how upset her life was making her and how irritable with other people she had become as a result:

September 8 Wednesday. Well, today started out pretty well, except that I was still tired. I picked up Liz and Sharon as planned. Amazing as it

was, I was even on time. At school, I got permission to enter two classes. That was the easy part. Liz and I went to registration to get the
classes officially. I can't believe the stupidity of those people. Unless
the computer tells them what to do, they cannot figure anything out. I
was so annoyed I wanted to drop all my classes and wait until next semester to register and start out fresh. Liz was there to try and calm
me down. Finally, she took all the papers for registration and dragged
me out of the building. Tomorrow she will register for me, as I will be
working.

This evening wasn't too bad. I had about three hours' sleep before I
had to teach the CPR class. I have a good group of students. They are
all interested in the subject and it shows. Almost all of them read the
chapters required and asked intelligent questions. The class went very
smoothly and it even ended early.

September 14 Tuesday. I can't believe how tired I am. I worked from
11:30 P.M. to 7:30 A.M. We had seven calls. Six were legitimate. One was
garbage. We got the call at 5:30 A.M.—a car accident on Queens Boulevard. The worst injury was a lacerated lip. When we finally rounded up
the "walking wounded," they treated the ambulance trip as a carnival
ride. One of the injured didn't want to get checked out but wanted to go
along for the ride. After a few statements, she decided to go along and
get checked out.

September 18 Saturday. Getting out of bed was almost impossible, even
with Cat swatting me in the face because she wanted to eat.

I met Mom, Celeste, the baby, and Helen for lunch. It wasn't bad until the baby tried to give me French fries covered with catsup. My shirt
will never be the same.

After lunch I stopped by the Ambulance Corps for a while. Kim
stopped by, so we went shopping. What better way to spend a Saturday
than to spend all my money.

Work wasn't that bad. We had seven or eight calls. The first one was
different—an overturned car on the Interboro Parkway. There were
more people there than you can imagine. The equipment was passed
over, around, under, and through us. One firefighter hit me twice with

the stretcher, but he smiled and apologized each time. Before we left, he asked me for my phone number. I didn't give it to him, but I regretted it later.

Developing Your Own Voice

Because you are seeking to develop the voice that is the most characteristic expression of yourself, you want to be as clear and "truthful" as possible. Try to avoid the pitfalls to which the best-intentioned writer can succumb: substituting other voices for your own, feeling intimidated by your audience, or using vague, overused words and omitting vivid detail.

As you begin writing the rough draft of this essay, attempt to work through these blocks to authentic writing. Strive for a voice that is your own, that is unaffected by what you have heard or what you think others want to hear. Remember, your audience for this task is a sympathetic group of people who are themselves interested in the process of self-discovery. Write for this audience, recalling and including vivid words and details that will involve them in your experience.

For example, the writer of the journal entries above includes some vivid details that encourage the reader to feel her fatigue and frustration, such as her annoyance at the registration workers, at Cat swatting her in the face to wake her up, at the catsup on her shirt, and at being hit by a stretcher. These are details that she should retain in the first draft of her essay.

She also uses words that convey her meaning specifically and vividly, such as *stupidity, dragged, garbage, lacerated,* and *carnival.* In other places, perhaps because she was too tired when writing, she does not convey her precise meaning and will want to do so when writing her rough draft. For example, "There were more people there than you can imagine" could be rephrased to convey more concretely the size of the crowd.

The writer has decided to choose as her subject her surprise at her irritability with other people. In her journal entries, she has concentrated on why she is frustrated; in her essay, she will also want to convey, honestly and in her own voice, the irritability that her frustration caused.

Arranging the Essay

Finding a Shaping Idea.   Now it is time to try to find a method of crystallizing exactly what you want to say in your essay: look for a sentence in the journal entries that captures the essence of your idea, or, after rereading your journal, pull together into one sentence what you have learned about yourself. At this point, it is important for you to clarify for yourself what specific idea will shape your writing. (See "Focus: Shaping Your Subject," pp. 25–27.)

You want to phrase this idea in a single declarative sentence (not a phrase, not a question) that contains both your subject and the main point that you are making about it. Your statement of your shaping idea should be precise, unambiguous, and gramatically correct. We advise that, as an apprentice writer, you place this statement in the first paragraph of your essay (although, as you will see, many skilled writers state the shaping idea elsewhere in the essay). By stating your main thought in one sentence and placing it at the beginning of your essay, you will be better able to keep focused during the drafting stages, and you also will give your reader a clear sense of the purpose of your essay at the outset.

Determining What You Want to Say About Your Subject.   What further ideas and information do your journal entries suggest you might develop about your subject, ideas and information that will help your reader understand your shaping idea more fully and completely? Have your journal entries provided reasons for, examples of, contrasts to, and the effects of the behavior or attitude or feeling that you are writing about? Try at this point to categorize the causes and effects of the behavior of the writer of the journal on pages 19–21. In her first entry for September 8, she contrasted the frustrating effects of school registration with the soothing effects of her CPR class in the evening. Each entry thereafter contains a discussion both of what provoked her response and of the response itself.

Once you have decided how each of your own entries might contribute to a discussion of your shaping idea, determine what you want to say about those entries that you intend to include. Also, where your journal entries do not supply the necessary information, make a note to develop it in your essay. For example, as it is quite likely that you wrote the journal for yourself, you may have to fill in background information for your reader, background that you did not find it necessary to include when writing for yourself.

Writing the Rough Draft

Here is the rough draft of an essay written by the student who recorded her frustration with other people in her journal entries.

THIS REALLY ISN'T ME

While looking over my journal, I was surprised to see how irritable my attitude was. I know I was extremely tired, but I thought I had handled it better. Most of the entries during the week showed anger, frustration, and annoyance at almost everything. The weekend entries, on the other hand, were happier and calmer.

During the week, I went to school five days, taught classes four nights, and worked four midnight shifts. I am the type of person who must have at least eight hours of sleep a night to act somewhat human the next day. I knew that with only four hours of sleep, I wouldn't win a personality contest, but I didn't expect to compete for grouch of the year. It seemed I was being sarcastic to everyone, and it carried through to the journal.

I think the best example of this (the so-so examples come later) was on September 8. I went to change my schedule and register for two more classes. The people at registration were as alert and helpful as usual. They couldn't figure out the overtallies, comprehend that one of my classes was canceled or even that I had paid for my other classes previously. Normally, I would have taken this in stride, but instead, because I was in such a great state of mind, I decided to drop all my classes. Thank God, Liz was with me. She grabbed my arm and dragged me out, although I was still complaining. The next day she made all the changes for me because I had to go to work. Looking back now, I realize how stupid I was. My brain must have been going in reverse if I thought I was teaching the people at registration by dropping out. I'm sure they couldn't care less one way or the other.

Another example was work. (I work on an ambulance that runs out of St. John's Hospital.) We responded to a car accident on Queens Boulevard about 5:30 in the morning. The cars were demolished, but the patients were walking wounded and slightly intoxicated. There were five in all, and needless to say, the ambulance was rather crowded. The girlfriend of one of the patients (she had a cut lip, probably requiring a stitch) wanted to go to the hospital with him, but not to be checked out. Normally, I would have explained that because we had so many people on the ambulance already, she could go only as a patient. Instead, I told her either she had to be looked at by a doctor at the hospital or she had to get out of the ambulance because we were overcrowded as it was. She decided to go and have her lip taken care of, which was the best thing for her to do, but I could have or, better still, should have been polite. (Her boyfriend, by the way, thought it was great that I took control of the situation and grabbed my thigh after his girlfriend left the ambulance.)

As I now know that my attitude is really that bad when I am tired, I
will have to think twice before saying or doing anything. There is no
reason for other people to take the brunt of my bad mood, especially
when they are my patients.

Notice that the writer has made definite choices of material from her journal
entries to include in her rough draft. Her first choice was to eliminate any material that did not contribute to her shaping idea, such as the evening of September 8, when her CPR class went well. Another choice was to eliminate all of the
material from the Saturday, September 18, entry, perhaps because, as she says
in her introduction, she was under the impression that she was calmer on weekends or perhaps because she felt she had already supplied enough examples for
her reader.

She has arranged her essay to include some background information about
her life as a means of explaining why she was so tired and therefore frustrated.
Furthermore she has used the two examples to form the body paragraphs so
that she can demonstrate what in the situations themselves further increased
her irritability and what the effects of that irritability were.

It is interesting to see what has happened to her voice in the essay as compared with the journal entries. In the essay, she has added the words *irritable*
and *grouch of the year* to describe her behavior. In doing so, she has achieved an
honesty or "truthfulness" about herself that her audience may appreciate. However, she has dropped many of the vivid words found in her journal, such as
stupidity, garbage, carnival, and *lacerated.* The reasons are intriguing: *stupidity* has
been replaced by *alert* and *helpful as usual,* indicating that the writer has adopted
a sarcastic tone. However, this tone has been dropped almost immediately in the
next paragraph, and the writer has become involved instead in explaining to her
readers a rather complicated event, omitting the language that might best have
helped to convey it. *Lacerated* has been replaced by *cut,* perhaps because the
writer is aware of being more educated than her audience—she teaches a class,
after all—and chose a simpler word.

In revising this draft, the writer will have to make further decisions about
adopting a unified tone—sarcastic or sincere—and about inserting or reinserting
more descriptive language.

Now, get ready to write your own rough draft.

First, like a professional writer, choose an appropriate time and place to
write. Set aside a specific place for writing: a quiet area of your home that has a
table or desk, a special part of your dorm room, or the least distracting desk in
your local or school library. Also set aside a block of two to three hours, possibly
the same time each day, when you do not have to worry about other responsi-
bilities. This kind of regularity—call it discipline, if you wish—can help you to

create a mood for writing. Now, all you need are the tools of the trade: lots of paper, pencils, pens, and/or a typewriter.

Once you have written through to the end of your first draft, stop writing and take a long break—twenty-four hours, if time permits.

FOCUS: SHAPING THE SUBJECT

When we begin to write we may think of ourselves as engines that need to be ignited by some mysterious spark before all our potential creative energy can be utilized. The time that elapses between our exploring a subject and our writing a first draft is often spent in confused mental conflict. During this time, we submit our topic to stern questioning. We turn it over and examine it from various angles. We try to establish its limits, even though we know that each thing we experience seems to overlap with and cast light on something else. We begin to carve from the stone of our subject a self-contained whole, a main idea that will give form or structure to our many thoughts by fusing them into a pattern of significance.

For this chapter's task, we asked you to use your journal as a source of ideas for an essay about yourself. To give the essay a focus, a main point around which to organize your ideas, we suggested that you look for a pattern of thought or feeling in your journals, then formulate a single statement expressing what this pattern is. Doing this, you are employing one possible strategy for developing a main or shaping idea.

Each of the sections on ''Writing the Essay'' that follows in this book will suggest other possible strategies for developing shaping ideas. Right now, we would like you to think a bit more about just what qualities a good shaping idea should have.

Let us say that you are looking for a topic to write on. Because your instructor has limited you to writing on some activity that you find beneficial, you begin to think about your summer hiking trip to New Hampshire and how much you enjoyed it. Perhaps, you decide to write in your journal each day for a week or two about this trip, your thoughts and feelings about it, experiences that you had while on it. Or, perhaps you decide to try some other means, such as free writing, to generate ideas about the subject. (We will introduce you in subsequent chapters of this book to a variety of ways to generate ideas.) Whatever strategy you use, you will want to select from the ideas you generate one, or a combination, that will form the best shaping idea for the essay.

Using your journal, you generate a number of thoughts about the benefits of your hiking trip. You did a lot of planning for the trip: mapping a route, taking the right clothing and equipment, conditioning yourself for the climate and terrain, and figuring the cost for yourself and your friends. You enjoyed the strenuous physical exercise, but you also became interested in the environment and how it should be preserved for future hikers. The following points seem to you to be the most important benefits:

1. Mountain hiking most exciting of outdoor activities.
2. Strenuous aerobic exercise good for entire body.
3. Developed mental skills of planning, analysis, powers of observation.
4. Put me in close contact with nature.
5. Taught me independence but also instilled need to cooperate with others.
6. Satisfied my need for overcoming challenges.
7. Freed me from difficult routine of work and school.
8. Stimulated my interest in history and tradition of the region.
9. Gave me a more mature perspective on human limitations.
10. Encouraged love of the environment and a desire to preserve it.

Which of these points or which combination of them might make a good shaping idea? Which will serve you best as a main point or "thesis" as some writers call it?

After sufficient time to think about your ideas, you begin to narrow your focus, to move toward a statement that will form the structural basis of your essay. For example, Statement 1 makes a broad value judgment that would be difficult to prove. Statement 4 might be better incorporated into Statement 10, since 10 points out the effects of this contact with nature. Statement 9 is an interesting idea, but it might be too ambitious a topic to include in a short essay. In addition, it seems closely related to what has already been said in Statement 5. This process of formulating a more exact view of the subject, then, reveals the close relationship of one statement to another. What may emerge from your perception of this logical bonding is the shaping idea of your paper.

The shaping idea states the subject, "mountain hiking," and then expresses a discovery that has resulted from your examination of the subject: "Mountain hiking has many benefits." This statement is accurate, according to the list of statements, but its conclusion seems obvious and tells the reader nothing that she or he probably doesn't already know. In order to create a sharper focus and a more challenging shaping idea for the reader, you need to make the subject more exact, more specific: not simply "mountain hiking," but perhaps the "benefits of mountain hiking." This shift of "benefits" from the part of the sentence that states discovery to the part that names the subject forces you to make a more specific commitment to your reader, providing him or her with a more vital and challenging view of your topic. The shaping idea that results from this shift, then, offers the reader a genuine insight and a unique angle of vision on your subject: "The benefits of mountain hiking changed me intellectually and emotionally as well as physically." By focusing on the unexpected discoveries of the writer, this improved version of the shaping idea reveals to the reader the surprising significance of what seems to be just another outdoor activity. It tells the reader what is to be said and why it is to be said.

SOME PRACTICE WITH SHAPING YOUR SUBJECT

1. From the following ideas, select the one that you think will create a sharply focused and organized essay and explain why you think so:

  a. Major league baseball is boring.
  b. Fast food is dangerous to your health.
  c. I don't like science fiction movies.
  d. My high-school biology teacher's persistent encouragement helped me to overcome my learning disabilities.

2. From the following related statements, form a clear shaping idea that will explain what they refer to:

  a. The neighborhood bars have been turned into "eating boutiques."
  b. Old, established small businesses have been driven out by high rents.
  c. Young executives and trendy singles have displaced the original ethnic mix of immigrant families.
  d. Tenements and row houses are being replaced by luxury high-rise condominiums.
  e. Schools and playgrounds are in need of restoration and expansion.
  f. Traditional political alignments are being revised.

3. Expand the following subjects to form shaping ideas. For example, "teenage alcoholism" to "Teenage alcoholism can be reduced if the drinking age is raised to twenty-one":

  a. Nuclear energy plants . . .
  b. The decline of the American automobile industry . . .
  c. Television soap operas . . .
  d. The nursing profession . . .

4. Select a topic that you are studying in another course. From your class notes or journal entries, write down several ideas that you have on this subject and begin to develop them into a shaping idea. For example, in business you are studying the Federal Reserve Board and its role in controlling the money supply. You might write down some of its duties and then formulate a statement that would work these ideas into a shaping idea ready to be developed into an essay.

REWRITING

Obtaining Feedback on Your Rough Draft

After you have written your rough draft and have "taken a break," you can resume the writing process by revising what you have written. Of course, you may already have made changes as you were writing the first draft, and, in fact, your copy may look much worked-over already. However, looking again at what you have written after a rest period will help you to read your paper as your audience will read it: more-or-less objectively.

In a sense, another self will take over, a self that may have been looking over your shoulder as you wrote the rough draft, keeping track of what you were doing, evaluating how each part fits in with the whole, noting problems and possible solutions, criticizing, and encouraging. This other self needs to be given full permission to comment at this point because it has a distance that you didn't have while immersed in the writing of the essay.

Your teacher may also wish to play the role of the "other self" at this point and to comment on your first try. And a third source of feedback is your peers. Your instructor may ask a group of your classmates to react to your paper, or if not, you may select a group yourself to do this job. Do not be afraid to show your work to your classmates. You can assume that most students have passed through similar periods of self-discovery and will be sympathetic to you.

Regardless of who provides the feedback—you, your instructor, your peers, or any combination—your paper should receive an evaluation that answers the following four questions of the "Audience Response Guide."

——— AUDIENCE RESPONSE GUIDE ———

1. **What does the writer want to say in this paper? What is his or her purpose in writing? What does he or she want the paper to mean?**
2. **How does the paper affect the audience for which it was intended?**
3. **How effective has the writer been in conveying his or her purpose and meaning?**
4. **How should the paper be revised to better fulfill its purpose and meaning?**

The following is a peer evaluation of the rough draft of the student essay "This Really Isn't Me" (pp. 22–24) in response to the four questions above:

1. The writer is explaining how grumpy she has been over the past week. The writer wants to change her attitude desperately, but we see that she is also overworked sometimes and seems not to be able to control herself.

2. We think the paper is honest in most areas, such as in admitting her faults. We are really sympathetic about her condition, but we are also happy that she has a desire to change.
3. We think that she is very effective in conveying her message. She went directly to the point. We also do not think that she is trying to cover anything but that she is honest about her feelings.
4. We think the purpose and meaning were being fulfilled in this paper, although she might have gone into more detail throughout.

Here is a revised version of ''This Really Isn't Me.'' Notice how the writer has responded to the group's suggestion that she include more details, as well as to her own sense of how the paper should be improved:

THIS REALLY ISN'T ME

As I looked over my journal, I was surprised to see how irritable I had been. I was aware of the fact that I had been very tired, but I did not think I had handled annoying situations so poorly. Most of the entries during the week showed anger, frustration, and extreme annoyance. On the other hand, the weekend entries were happier and calmer.

During the week, my schedule was very hectic. I went to school five days, taught classes four nights, and worked four midnight shifts. Because I am the type of person who needs at least eight hours of sleep a night to be somewhat human the next day, I had not expected to win a personality contest, but I certainly did not expect to be a runner-up for Grouch of the Year. It seemed I was sarcastic to everyone, and it even carried over to the journal.

I think one of the best examples was on September 8. I went to registration to change my schedule and add two classes. Of course, the people there were as alert and helpful as usual. They could not figure out the overtally, nor comprehend that one of my classes was canceled, nor that I had previously paid for the class I already had. Normally, I would have taken it in stride and attempted to communicate with the people, but instead, being in such a great mood, I became very sarcastic with them and decided to drop all of my classes. Thank God for Liz, who was with me. She grabbed my arm and dragged me out, although I was still complaining. Looking back, I realize how stupidly I was acting. My brain must have been working in reverse if I thought dropping classes was going to teach the people at registration a lesson. I am sure they could not have cared less if I went to school or not.

Another example happened at work. I work on an ambulance that runs out of St. John's Hospital. We responded to a car accident on Queens Boulevard about 5:30 A.M. The cars were demolished, but the patients were walking wounded who were slightly intoxicated. As there were five of them, the ambulance was overcrowded. One of the five, a girlfriend of one of the other patients, wanted to go along for the ride, but not to be treated at the hospital, even though she needed a stitch in her bottom lip. Instead of explaining that the ambulance was overcrowded and that we needed the room for patients with serious problems, I told her that she either had to be looked at by a doctor at the hospital or had to get out of the ambulance. She decided to go to the hospital and have her lip taken care of. Of course, that was the best thing for her to do, but I should have been polite. Her boyfriend, by the way, thought it was great that I took control of the situation and grabbed my thigh as soon as she left the ambulance.

Over the weekend, though, after I had adequate sleep, I was much more mellow. We responded to an overturned car on the Interboro Parkway. The patient had an avulsion between the thumb and the pointing finger and a laceration on his wrist. There were two ambulances, three police cars, and a firetruck, plus many nosey people who wanted to see how much blood and gore there was. Every time I turned around, there was someone in my way. I was stepped on, hit with various pieces of equipment, almost knocked over with the stretcher, and nearly run down by a car that ignored the flare cones. In the situation I remained calm. All treatment was given properly and politely. I did not yell or become rude. If I had been in my former mood, I probably would have started a riot.

Now that I know my attitude changes so dramatically, I will have to watch myself. It is bad enough that I am not happy at times, but it should not affect the way I treat other people, especially my patients.

The most obvious change that the writer made was to add the material from the Saturday entry, which supports her statement in her introduction that she is calmer on weekends. Initially, in the rough draft, that statement was left hanging. Notice that she has now changed *cut* in Paragraph 4 once more, this time to "she needed a stitch in her bottom lip," a vivid detail that improves not only on cut but also on *laceration,* which was used in the original journal entry. What other changes have been made for the better? Have any been made that do not improve the essay?

Once you have feedback from your other self, your instructor, or your peers, revise your rough draft.

The Final Product

Presentation. After a day, reread your revised essay for mechanical errors such as spelling, grammar, punctuation, and capitalization. (Refer to the Handbook on pages 359–421 if you are uncertain about how to correct a mechanical error.)

Neatness is the key at this final stage. Write neatly on good-quality lined paper, such as that from a loose-leaf notebook or a pad of lined paper. Do not write on spiral notebook paper.

Write on one side of the page, leaving two inches at the top of the first page for the title. Number the pages after page 1 in the upper-right-hand corner.

If you type your paper, choose a good-quality bond paper. Leave margins of one inch on all four sides. Type double-spaced on one side of the paper, again leaving room at the top of page 1 for your title and numbering the pages from page 2 on.

Your Title. A title fulfills two functions: it attracts your readers' attention and gives them some indication of your subject, although often the meaning of a title is not clear until the essay is read. And titles are fun to write; you can be as creative as you like.

In choosing a title, consider your shaping idea as the best source of the meaning of your title. Then, once the meaning has been established, use your creativity to devise a word or a phrase that conveys that meaning in an interesting way.

Proofreading. By now, you might expect that your work is over. Not quite. One final step is necessary. You must now proofread.

Proofreading is reading your final copy to check for mistakes, omissions, and typos that might have occurred in the transcription from the revised essay to the final copy that will be submitted to your instructor. This process is a tedious one and should be undertaken at a time when you are alert and calm. It is advisable, if time permits, to proofread some time after typing your essay; it is also advisable to proofread the draft at least three times. Make your corrections neatly and clearly.

1. Read slowly what is on the page, not what you think is on the page. Correct mistakes as you see them: spelling, punctuation, and so on.

2. Read again, out loud. Sometimes you will hear mistakes that you cannot see.
3. Read your essay backward from end to beginning, sentence by sentence. This procedure will relieve you of analyzing the content and will help you to focus on words and punctuation.
4. Skim from right to left and top to bottom, looking for misspellings and other errors.

BECOMING AWARE OF YOURSELF AS A WRITER

Make use of your journal to record your thoughts and feelings about the task in Chapter 1. As you write in your journal, consider the following questions:

1. What effect does writing a journal entry have on you? What value have you found in the process?

2. Do you think that a writer's journals should be read by others? How would you feel if others read your journals? How would the presence of others affect what you write?

3. What kinds of subjects make keeping a journal useful to you?

4. Which are your most interesting journal entries? Why do you think so?

5. What connection can you make between keeping a journal and writing an essay? What connection can you make between your journal and the essay you wrote?

6. How successful were you in conveying your authentic voice? What methods contributed to your success? What effect did writing for an audience have on your search for your authentic voice?

7. In what ways did your shaping idea affect what you said and how you said it? In what ways was your shaping idea effective or ineffective? What did it make your audience feel or do? Was this result intended by you?

2
WRITING ABOUT AN INCIDENT

PURPOSE

Seeking an authentic voice is one way you can learn how to express yourself more clearly and understandably as a writer. But it is not the only way, nor is it sufficient by itself. For one thing, your audience will probably never share your attitudes and perspectives completely. There will always be a gap between you and even your most sympathetic reader. Adjusting your voice to bridge this gap can be as important as discovering what your most authentic voice is.

This chapter will begin to introduce you to the different kinds of adjustments that a writer may make in his or her voice for different audiences. We will ask you in your writing for this chapter to order a series of impressions, a group of details about an important event in your life, so that a reader other than yourself can experience them in much the same way that you did.

If your reader is to understand an event you have experienced, you need to convey the facts of that experience, investigating them with the same sort of thoroughness that a journalist employs to report a news event. You also need to record your impressions, reactions, and interpretations vividly, concretely, and intelligibly enough so that your reader can see the event as you did and can share your responses with you.

In order to help your reader not only understand the event but see it from your point of view, you will want to consider your reader's point of view as well as your own, particularly as you try to determine what selection and arrangement of details will convey the essence of your experience of the event most effectively. But first you want to collect as many details as possible, to gather the facts. As one way of getting started, consider how, as an essayist, you can use the tools that a professional reporter uses when she or he investigates the facts of a newsworthy incident.

GENERATING IDEAS: THE JOURNALIST'S QUESTIONS

The news reporter often gets started on a story by asking six questions about whatever incident he or she is covering. The six questions are introduced by the following words:

who

what

where

when

how

why

If you examine the following article, which was taken from *The New York Times* of February 21, 1962, you will notice how the answers to the journalist's questions are integrated into it.

50,000 on Beach Strangely Calm as Rocket Streaks Out of Sight

---

"He's in Hands of the Lord Now," Woman Says—Hilarity Erupts at Word of Recovery—900-Pound Cake Is Cut

---

By Gay Talese
Special to The New York Times

COCOA BEACH, Feb. 20—At 9:47 A.M. today the rocket rose slowly over the beach like a high infield fly, but moments later it was streaking out of sight, leaving a thin, white and fluffy vapor trail.

Fifty thousand spectators stood along the beach watching the climbing Atlas carrying Lieut. Col. John H. Glenn Jr. into orbit. Some cheered, some clapped. An elderly woman said solemnly: "He's in the hands of the Lord now." Most remained silent.

They watched the sky until there was nothing left to see except pelicans and sea gulls, and until the rocket's vapor trail had lost its shape and become a floating, upside-down question mark.

Then they slumped on the beach to hear the rest by radio, or returned to homes, motels or taverns to watch on television, as millions were doing around the country.

Not until 3:01 P.M., when the astronaut had gone thrice around the earth and had been safely retrieved from the Atlantic by the destroyer Noa, did the hilarity begin. Faces lost their looks of concern.

Cheers Go Up

A 900-pound cake, the size and shape of the Mercury capsule, was sliced. And a huge movie-type marquee along the main road lighted up to say: "Our Prayers Were Answered."

There were cheers around poolsides when it was reported that President Kennedy would come here Friday to honor Colonel Glenn. By twilight, Cocoa Beach's jazz bands and cash registers were swinging and ringing in merry syncopation.

"Oh, he done it, buddy, he done it, so let's have a drink," John Godbee of Deland called to the crowd around him at the Vanguard Bar.

"I said 'go, go, go,' and seeing it go gave me a glorious feeling," John Pellegrino, the Vanguard's bass player, said.

"It was just undescribable," said Mrs. Thomas J. Knight of Baltimore, relaxing on the beach.

"Undescribable is right," Mrs. Howard Balliet of Orlando agreed with a nod.

Though the countdown was halted a few times, there was an undefinable feeling of optimism. People seemed to sense that this was finally the big day, that after ten postponements the orbital shot would leave the launching pad.

At 9:23, radios in cars, on people's shoulders and in their pockets could be heard everywhere saying, "T minus 22, and counting . . . T minus 20 minutes, and counting . . . T minus 17 minutes . . . T minus 13 minutes."

Now there was a vast quiet along the beach. People stood on sand dunes, motel porches, trucks and trailers, all with eyes fixed on the missile gantries, towering like a mirage eight miles north over the waves.

"Rosemary!" screamed a mother, almost hysterically, grabbing her fleeing child. "Get over here."

"T minus 3 minutes," went the radio. "T minus 30 seconds . . . 20 seconds . . . 10 seconds . . . 5 . . . 4 . . . 3 . . . 2 . . . . "

"Lift-off!" somebody yelled.

"Look, it's up!"

"Go, baby, go!" a man cried, clenching his fist.

But the great majority watched silently as the missile moved slowly skyward. There was a red flame behind it as it began to climb. Then it was just a blazing speck, rising higher and higher, with only the vapor trail marking the ascent for those without binoculars.

Pensiveness Noted

The lack of delirium, the pensiveness of the thousands who stared toward the sky were hard to interpret. The flights of Comdr. Alan B. Shepard and Capt. Virgil

I. Grissom here had brought rousing demonstrations. Each had evoked cheers usually heard after a game-winning world series home run.

Perhaps the crowd was quieter because it had been let down by the postponements, or maybe it thought there was no cause for cheering until Colonel Glenn was safely returned.

There was noticeable excitement at 2:30 P.M. when somebody at the Holiday Inn's television set shouted, "He's coming down, he's on his way down!"

Nine-year-old Michael von Fremd of Bethesda. Md., jumped up and down.

"I knew things would go right today," said Mrs. Marion Fega of Los Angeles.

A few hours later, the happy trailer caravans began to leave the beach, where some had been entrenched more than a week. The drivers shook hands and promised to write.

"Today was the highlight of my life," said Ernest Perkins, gunning his motor and heading back to Toledo.

We can reconstruct the six questions asked by the writer of this article, as well as the answers:

1. Who (or what) was involved in the incident? (Fifty thousand spectators and Lieut. Col. John H. Glenn Jr.)
2. What was the incident? (The lift-off of the Atlas rocket carrying Glenn into orbit; the journalist examines the reaction of the spectators.)
3. Where did the incident occur? (Cocoa Beach, Florida.)
4. When did the incident occur (February 20, 1962, at 9:47A.M.)
5. How did the incident occur? (The rocket rose slowly, then streaked out of sight; the spectators watched silently, for the most part, with looks of concern.)
6. Why did the incident occur? (The journalist speculates that the crowd might have been quiet because they had been let down by postponements or because they thought that there was no cause to cheer until Glenn had returned safely.)

Notice how the six questions generate additional questions, which contribute more details to the report:

1. Who were some of the spectators, by name and age?
2. What were the spectators doing during the liftoff? What did they do and say afterward?
3. Where did the spectators come from? Where did they go after the liftoff?
4. When did the crowd leave the beach?
5. How did the crowd's reaction compare to the reaction of the spectators at previous space shots? How did the crowd's reaction change after Glenn had landed?

Using the Journalist's Questions in Writing an Essay

The journalist's questions can be used for writing essays as well as newspaper or magazine articles. The responses of the essayist, however, may differ in form and substance from those of the journalist. Whereas the journalist usually writes under the pressure of a deadline, the essayist often has more time for contemplation and hence the opportunity to find longer and more fully developed answers to the six questions. Also, whereas a journalist is expected to record the facts as objectively as possible, an essayist is free to offer the most subjective insights into and interpretations of the facts.

The following questions are among those that an essayist may generate from the six basic ones:

Who   What must the reader know about the person or persons involved in order to understand what happened? What objective details must be included: age, appearance, social status, economic status, family relationships? What subjective elements about the person(s) should be supplied: background, philosophy, values, emotions?

What   What led up to the event? In what order did the stages of the event occur? Were there any foreshadowings of what was to come? What effect(s) did the event have, both immediate and long-range? What details must be included to convey the drama of the event to someone who was not there?

Where   How many locations are involved? How much description of the location(s) does the reader require? What details will convey the scene?

When   What time of day, what week, what year did the event occur? Of what significance was the date, the time of day, the weather?

How   In what way did the incident happen? How involved a description of the process is necessary? What details are required?

Why   Is the cause known for sure? Was there more than one cause? Was one person or thing more responsible than others? Can immediate causes be distinguished from distant ones? If there was no known cause, what interpretation can you bring to bear on the event? What general conclusions can be drawn?

Another major distinction between the essayist's responses and those of the journalist is the style in which they are written. The journalist tends to use a spare style, one stripped of those elements that personalize the essayist's work. Whereas the journalist tries consistently to sound direct, straightforward, and factual, the essayist may play more freely with such elements as tone of voice (see Chapter 1, pp. 11–18, and this chapter, p. 53); complex and varied sentence structuring (see Chapter 5, pp. 156–165, and Chapter 6, pp. 195–197); and comparisons such as metaphors, similes, and analogies (see this chapter, p. 50; Chapter 6, pp. 197–198; and Chapter 8, pp. 299–303; and Chapter 9, pp. 317–322).

Whereas the journalist, then, is usually concerned simply with reporting an event, the essayist may utilize fuller, more subjective responses and stylistic embellishments to dramatize the event, inviting the reader to participate in it vicariously. Put another way, whereas the journalist usually *tells* what happened, the essayist often *shows* what happened.

Finally, although in this chapter's task we will ask you to use the journalist's questions to report on an incident, you can also use these questions to develop ideas and information about many different topics. For example, if you were asked in an economics course to write an essay on a topic such as inflation, you might use the journalist's questions to develop information about what inflation is, who it affects and how, when and why it occurs, and so forth. Furthermore, although you may use all six questions in writing the narrative task for this chapter, other topics may require that you emphasize or focus on answers to only one or two of the questions. We encourage you, then, to use this method of generating ideas, along with others that we will introduce you to in later chapters, not only to complete the task at hand but also to develop ideas and information for other assignments in other courses.

SOME PRACTICE WITH THE JOURNALIST'S QUESTIONS

1. Read a newspaper article (preferably one that reports an event—a happening) and identify the answers to the journalist's six questions.

   a. Who?
   b. What?
   c. Where?
   d. When?
   e. How?
   f. Why?

2. a. Use the journalist's questions in order to gather information about an incident that you observed as an outsider rather than as a participant. Choose an incident that is limited in time and space, a distinct piece of action.
    b. Either with your class or on your own, analyze the details that you have gathered, How concrete, how specific, are they? Which aspect of the incident did you gather the most information about: The who? The what?

The where? The when? The why? Or the how? Are there any questions that you have left unanswered? Did you describe actions and objects only, or did you also describe thoughts and feelings?

3. Reread the article by Gay Talese and then analyze the reporter's impressions. Was his information about the thoughts and feelings of the spectators factual? To what degree did Talese include his own subjective thoughts and feelings in the article?

4. Using the journalist's questions, develop an account of an historical event. The event may have occurred in the recent past, such as the political turmoil in Central America, or at a distant time, such as the trial and sentencing of Socrates.

5. Using the journalist's questions, generate information that you might use in writing an account of your views on a topic that you are now studying in a class other than your English class.

ADDRESSING YOUR AUDIENCE: FRAME OF REFERENCE

Because the purpose of most writing, with the exception of the personal journal, is to communicate something to another person, you can write more effectively when you know, as well as you can, with whom you are communicating. Your audience—the people you write for—will in part affect both what you write about and the way in which you write about it. Just as you have attitudes toward your subject, so will your audience, and unless you consider your potential readers' attitudes as well as your own, you may be unable to keep your readers' attention; you might even offend them.

For example, pretend that you are going to write an essay entitled "The Facts of Life." Your audience is a class of first-graders and their mothers. What sort of essay would you write? What material would you include? What material would you exclude? What sort of tone would you adopt?

Now, change your audience. Pretend that you are writing the essay for a class of teenagers. Obviously, such an audience would be bored by the essay that you wrote for the class of first-graders. How might you write so as to capture the interest of the teenage students?

Your reader's attitudes should not affect the authenticity or truthfulness of your voice, of course, but rather should simply suggest adjustments in how you convey the truth of your subject. What these adjustments are and how they can be made is the subject of the "audience" section in Chapter 3 and of subsequent "audience" sections (see also in this chapter, pp. 49–50).

When you write, you are engaging in an activity that might be graphically portrayed as a triangle:

You are involved in both your own attitude and your reader's attitude toward the subject matter. These attitudes we will call *points of view*. In order to better understand each point of view, you will want to take into account what we will call the *frame of reference* both of yourself and of your reader.

The Writer's Frame of Reference

Whenever you write, you are discovering how you feel about your subject. How you feel and hence what you write are a reflection of who you are. You have a particular set of ideas and values because of where and how you have lived, whom you have known, what you have gone through, and what reading you have done. You come to your subject with a preconceived view of the world, and this view of the world, in turn, colors the way you perceive the subject: your *frame of reference* is your view of the world, which, in turn, determines your way of perceiving the subject, your *point of view*.

The way in which one's frame of reference influences one's point of view toward a subject can be illustrated by the following examples: If you are writing about space travel and are a socially concerned person, you might feel that tax dollars could be better spent on social programs. On the other hand, if you are a science major, you might support the point of view that space travel will contribute significantly to our expanding knowledge of the universe. Finally, if you are a science fiction fan, you might see space travel as providing an infinite range of exciting adventures. Your frame of reference will affect your view of your subject and hence how you write about it.

Or what if the topic is single parenthood? If you were a thirty-five-year-old divorced mother of three, had a very good job in a social service agency that was funding your education, loved your children and were too busy to marry again at the moment, your point of view might be that under favorable economic and emotional conditions, single parenthood is a viable option. On the other hand, if you were raised by one parent who worked a double shift to support the family and had no time or energy left over for personal contact with family members, you might feel that single parenthood is a burden to the parent and inadequate for the children.

The following ten questions will help you to determine your own frame of references:

1. How old are you?
2. Of what ethnic background are you? What economic or social class are you in?
3. Do you have a job or career? If so, what do you do? If not, what are your career plans?
4. Where were you born? Where do you live now?
5. What is your religious affiliation, if any?
6. Are you a member of a political party? If so, which one?
7. What roles do you play in your family?
8. What significant events have occurred in your life?
9. What are your hobbies or other leisure activities?
10. What are your goals for your life?

SOME PRACTICE WITH FRAME OF REFERENCE

How would your frame of reference, based on your answers to the above questions, affect your point of view on the following topics?

1. Single parenthood.

2. Chemical waste disposal.

3. Nuclear energy.

4. Nursing homes for the elderly.

5. The popularity of new religions.

SOME PRACTICE WITH POINT OF VIEW

1. a. Based on the details that you gathered by using the journalist's six questions (exercise 2a. on p. 38), write a one-paragraph description of the incident. Keep yourself completely outside the action. Just write what your sense impressions registered, what you saw and heard.
   b. Rewrite the paragraph, this time including your personal reactions, how you felt as an observer, and what thoughts went through your head.

    c. Rewrite the paragraph again, this time pretending that you were one of those involved in the incident.

    d. Either with your class or on your own, analyze the point of view of each paragraph. Why did you choose to write about certain details in the first paragraph? How did your frame of reference affect your point of view in Paragraph 2 as opposed to Paragraph 1? How did your attitude toward the incident change in the third paragraph, when you imagined yourself in the shoes of one of the participants?

2. Each of the following passages offers a different impression of the same incident. Describe the point of view that each writer took. What did the writers reveal about themselves in writing about the incident?

    a. This crazed maniac walked into the college cafeteria, picked up a boiling-hot plate of soup, and dropped it over the head of this gorgeous, innocent blond. Everyone was simply mortified by this sickie's routine. He should get twenty years.

    b. You should have seen the hysterical performance in the college caf yesterday. This clown poured some red stuff on his girlfriend's goofy bleached head and broke the whole place up. They should do their act on the stage—they were a riot.

    c. A riot call placed from the Holbrook College Cafeteria was responded to immediately by Patrolman Hodges, who found Jack Jenkins, the alleged perpetrator, with an empty plastic dish standing next to the plaintiff, Betty Lou Jones, a student at the college. Several witnesses were questioned. An investigation is under way.

    d. If you want some idea of today's college student, you should see what goes on in the cafeteria. Two students, I am told, acted in the kind of barbaric manner suggested in the movie <u>Animal House.</u> What can you expect with the kind of music they play over the loudspeakers there?

3. In the following paragraphs, part of an incident is described. Complete the narrative from the point where the performers begin to play:

The performers entered forty minutes late, buttoning their shirts and adjusting the slings on their instruments as they moved to center stage. They bowed nervously, turned awkwardly to one another, then got ready to play.

    The audience had restrained itself for the first thirty minutes but grew noticeably restless in the last few minutes before the performers appeared. Several people were throwing empty cans and boxes toward the stage. Others were standing, directing their boos and cries to the absent performers.

Several security police, hired for the occasion, paced the hall nervously, fearing an outburst of violence from the impatient crowd.

a. What does the ending that you have created reveal about your point of view toward the incident?

b. How might you have changed the ending you wrote if you were attempting to see the incident from the point of view of one of the performers, or of a member of the audience, or of a security police officer?

The Reader's Frame of Reference

Just as you have your frame of reference or set of attitudes, values, and beliefs, so do your readers. And your readers' frame of reference is probably different from yours. If you want to make sure that your essay communicates to them, that in some way it has meaning for them, you must set about purposefully to understand the frame of reference of your readers.

Knowing your readers' frame of reference, and hence their point of view on a subject about which you are writing, may result in many adjustments—some fine, some major—during the course of writing your paper. One student, about to write an essay for her classmates on her recently acquired ethnic pride in being a Lithuanian, came to realize that few of her readers had any notion of what this meant. She had to alter her expressive purpose by providing some exposition on what it meant to be Lithuanian. Because the class did understand what it meant to become aware of one's ethnic identity, the writer could use this frame of reference to build on, and she gained some new understanding of her experiences by learning how others had responded to theirs. Perhaps she learned more about her subject and its relation to her life by having to see it as others would. She was able to gain a certain distance from her subject, to see it from the perspective of others, and finally to see where she could meet her readers on a common ground. These are essential advantages in knowing your audience's point of view. They send you back to your writing with a sharpness and a clarity of purpose that you might not have gained otherwise.

Of course, even when you don't think about it consciously, you are making assumptions about your readers whenever you write. Take a look at the three descriptions of an incident that you wrote. What sort of unconscious assumptions did you make about your audience in each? Did you assume that they knew anything that, in reality, they might not? What details might you have explained more fully, so that someone who did not witness the incident could follow your description? Did the style and vocabulary of your descriptions suggest that you had a particular sort of reader in mind? Were you appealing more, for example, to your teacher or to your classmates?

There are a number of ways in which you can make yourself more conscious of the point of view of any potential reader of your work.

Interview

To discover your readers' frame of reference, and hence their point of view, you may interview them, asking them pertinent questions to elicit their frame of reference. The interview is useful when your reader is one individual who is available for questioning, such as a teacher or an employer or a small group of friends or classmates.

Interviewing often requires tact. You would not ask a teacher or your boss her or his age, for example. On the other hand, if your readers are your peers, to the extent that tact is not demanded, you can utilize the ten frame-of-reference questions in conducting your interview.

When tact is required, it is best to direct your questions toward the subject rather than toward the person. Appropriate questions for interviewing in this context, such as the following, although directed at the subject, will still tell you much about your readers' frame of reference:

1. What do you want to know about the subject?
2. What do you think should be stressed?
3. Is this a controversial topic in any way? If so, what do you think about the controversy?
4. What attitude do you have toward the topic?

SOME PRACTICE WITH INTERVIEWING YOUR READER

1. a. Choose a classmate and construct his or her general frame of reference by asking the ten frame-of-reference questions.
   b. From the answers that you receive, attempt to determine your classmate's attitude toward the five topics listed in "Some Practice with Frame of Reference" on page 41. If the answers are not helpful, perhaps they were not specific enough. You can extend the interview to include questioning the reader about his or her response to each topic, but as you become adept at interviewing, you will solicit answers to the ten questions that will give you a good clue to your reader's attitude toward almost any subject.

2. Because interviewing often requires tact, especially when you are interviewing an authority figure, choose a course you are taking this semester and phrase the set of questions that you would ask your instructor about a topic discussed in the course. Utilize the ten frame-of-reference questions and the above four subject questions in assembling your queries.

3. Using the information gathered when you interviewed your classmate, construct a brief biography of the classmate. If the responses to the frame-of-reference questions are not sufficient to construct a narrative, reinterview your subject in order to obtain fuller information. If necessary, prepare additional questions to ask.

Inference

A second way of discovering your readers' frame of reference is to make inferences. An inference is an assumption that you make about your reader, based on your observation of his or her appearance, conversation, or some other aspect of his or her behavior. Inference is particularly useful in writing to a large group of people, as you cannot possibly interview each individual. Inference is also helpful in filling in the gaps in the interview method: you can infer answers to questions that you cannot tactfully or practically ask.

With most groups of people, you can go a long way in inferring the answers to the ten frame-of-reference questions. You will, of course, have to generalize about the group and not record data about individual members. The general frame of reference of a group would include the following information:

1. Age.
2. Ethnic background, education, and economic and social class.
3. Occupation (or career plans).
4. Place of habitation
5. Religious affiliation.
6. Political affiliation.
7. Family structure.
8. Significant experiences (shared by the group).
9. Leisure interests and activities.
10. Goals.

SOME PRACTICE WITH INFERENCE

1. Using your class that has the largest enrollment this semester, infer the class's frame of reference. Then determine the point of view of the majority of the students on the following topics:

   a. Teacher–student relationships.
   b. Coed dormitories.
   c. The student newspaper.
   d. Abortion.

On what basis have you inferred the group's attitude in each case?

2. A certain student in your English class has freely voiced her opinions that children should be strictly disciplined, that marijuana use should remain illegal, and that juvenile offenders should be prosecuted as adults. Therefore it would be reasonable, if you were writing to her, to infer that she believes that society needs strict discipline. What do you think her point of view would be on the following issues? Formulate one or more statements on each topic that you think would represent her point of view:

   a. Alimony.
   b. A worker's right to strike.
   c. The draft.
   d. Children's rights.

Role Playing

Role playing may be a helpful technique for discovering and understanding your audience's point of view on your subject. This technique involves putting yourself in the shoes of your readers by assuming their frame of reference and then evaluating your subject from their point of view. Role playing is like acting in an improvisational theater; you may even wish to create a dialogue between you as writer and you as reader.

For example, if you were writing about an experience on an unemployment line to a group of people who have never lost a job, you might find it easy to construct their frame of reference but difficult to identify or empathize with their resulting point of view. By putting yourself in the place of your audience and looking at your experience in the unemployment line through their eyes, you may find a bridge between the varying points of view.

The following paragraph might result. In it, the writer compares the experience to one that the audience is more likely to have had:

My first experience on an unemployment line was unsettling, to say the least. "Nerve-wracking" describes it better. Not only were we middle-class kids who had never expected to be out of work, but it was also a blazing hot day in June, and the office was not air-conditioned. One of us even fainted, because he was so hot, tired, and emotionally upset. Compare the experience to being called into a hot, stuffy principal's office, unjustly accused but feeling claustrophobically guilty anyway, and you have some idea of how we felt that day.

SOME PRACTICE WITH ROLE PLAYING

1. Write a paragraph in which you express freely your point of view on one of the topics (alimony, a worker's right to strike, the draft, or children's rights) about which you formulated a statement in Exercise 2 of "Some Practice with Inference" (p. 46). If your point of view is different from that of the student who believes that society needs strict discipline, play the role of this student and criticize your own point of view. If your point of view is similar to this student's, play the role of a student who abhors strict discipline, and criticize your own point of view. In either case, develop a dialogue between your point of view and that of the student who is critical of it. Has the role playing you engaged in caused you to rethink your views on the topic in any way?

2. Write a paragraph in which you express freely your feelings about violence in sports. Now examine your point of view from the perspective of the following roles: the wife of a professional football player whose career was ended by an on-the-field injury; a college football player praised in the newspapers for his aggressive play; a high-school football coach.

3. Assume the role of someone who prefers reading the classics to watching television, who loves Mozart but finds rock-and-roll abominable, and who refuses to use a telephone because he so enjoys communicating by letter. In this role, freely express your thoughts about life in modern society. Either with a classmate or in your own imagination, develop a dialogue between a person in this role and a typical high-school student. What bridges can these two build at the end of their dialogue?

4. You can also learn to understand an audience's point of view by playing against your own role, that is, by expressing an idea or attitude that seems to contradict the expectations that an audience might have about you, given the role you are identified with. For example, a successful business executive writes to encourage students to pursue liberal arts courses in college; or a member of the National Rifle Association writes an article in favor of gun control. Choose a role, and then write a paragraph in which you express an attitude that plays against your role.

TASK: WRITING ABOUT AN INCIDENT

To begin the task for this chapter, search your memory for an incident that you observed or were involved in that abruptly changed your mood or your thoughts, that suddenly caused you to reassess your feelings toward or attitudes about something, and that thus in some way affected your life. This may be an event that impressed you when you were younger, or it may be a more recent event. Try to focus on an incident that occurred over the course of a few hours or a few days, but not beyond a week; then record the incident in detail, clarifying for the reader the important aspects of the experience, as well as what you think its significance was for you.

We suggest that you devote special attention to specific details in order to make your account of the incident vivid and authentic. The journalist's questions can help you to recall such details. Also, you will want to pay attention to the arrangement of your details, so that you can offer your readers a clear sense of the chronology of the incident, of the order in which the events of your story unfolded.

Your peers are the most likely audience for this essay. They may have experienced an incident similar to yours and therefore are likely to prove both interested and sympathetic readers. But even though you will be writing to an audience whose frame of reference is similar to your own, you cannot expect the group as a whole to understand all of your perceptions and feelings automatically. Subtle differences in point of view will have to be bridged, as they always must be, even between the closest of friends.

In the remaining sections of this chapter, we will discuss how to use the journalist's questions to generate ideas about your subject, how to build bridges between you and your readers, how to arrange the details of your incident, how to move into your rough draft, and how to revise your essay.

WRITING THE ESSAY

Using the Journalist's Questions

Once you have decided on an incident to write about, begin recalling and recording as much specific and related information as possible about your subject. Earlier in the chapter, you were introduced to the journalist's method of search and discovery, and you can use this method to discover relevant and telling details about the event that you have chosen as the subject of your essay. Apply the six questions of the news reporter to the event.

After you have generated information from the six basic questions, see if further questions arise, those subquestions that it is the luxury of the essayist to answer (see p. 37). Answer these as well. Do not worry if you seem to have a lot of information; when you begin to arrange your essay, you will probably discard some of it. If, however, you find that you lack specifics, that is cause for worry; you might need to go out and gather more information from other sources, such as relatives, friends, diaries, journals, photographs, and your own memories.

Determining Your Audience's Frame of Reference

As indicated in the description of the task (pp. 47–48), you are writing this essay to be read by your peers—probably the members of your freshman composition class.

An earlier section of this chapter discussed the importance of discovering the frame of reference of your audience. Now try using either direct questioning or inference (see pp. 44–45) to determine the frame of reference of your peers.

Having constructed your peers' frame of reference, you can determine their point of view on your incident. Role playing can help you here. Place yourself in the position of your audience and view your incident from their perspective. This new awareness should help you to write with your audience's point of view in mind.

Bridging the Gap Between Your Audience's Point of View and Your Own

Evaluating the point of view of your audience may lead you to explain things that you might have assumed were clear enough, had you not considered your reader(s). We will look into this subject at greater length in the "audience" sections of subsequent chapters. What we would like you to consider right now is how your knowledge of your audience's point of view may help you, when you are writing expressively, to show rather than simply to tell what your experiences, thoughts, and feelings are, to be, in Ken Macrorie's term, as "truthful as possible" (see Chapter 1, pp. 13–16).

For one thing, taking your audience and their perspective into account might lead you to describe details of an experience you are narrating that you otherwise might not have thought to describe. For example, it would be simple enough to *tell* your audience that an incident occurred on a romantic night. But if you want to *show* the audience how romantic the night was, you need to describe details that not only you but your readers will feel made the night romantic. The fact that it was the night of your senior prom might not touch a romantic chord in older readers, who probably are too far removed from their high-school days to share a senior's thrill over prom night. For such an audience, other details would have to be emphasized, perhaps the soft summer breeze and the clear, star-filled sky, to help them feel the romance of the evening.

Another way that you might use your knowledge of your audience to help them enter into an experience that you have had is to employ dialogue in your narration of the experience. Having imagined a dialogue between a reader and yourself may have helped you understand the reader's point of view better. Recreating in your narrative the details of a dialogue that occurred between you and someone whose point of view reflects thoughts and feelings that your audience might have should help your audience experience the incident more vividly.

Taking the point of view of your audience into account might also lead you to create analogies so that your readers can relate to your thoughts and feelings in terms of thoughts and feelings more familiar to them, and so that they can share your thoughts and feelings rather than simply being told about them. For example, what if you are a long-distance runner, and you want to show your readers—in this case your fellow students, many of whom are not athletes—what it felt like the first time you won a race? You might compare your feelings about winning to the sort of feelings many students have after a marathon study session that results in their scoring well on an exam.

Finally, your choice of words will be influenced by your knowledge of your audience. If you want to bridge the distance between your readers and you, if you want them to see as you saw and feel as you felt, you must be careful to employ language that they will understand and appreciate. Your peers may be drawn into your narrative if you employ the latest slang, but older readers may simply be put off. For some readers, you will use a more formal, sophisticated vocabulary; for others, a plainer, simpler one. Your analysis of your audience should help you to make adjustments not only in what you write but also in how you write it.

Answering the following questions of the "Audience Analysis Guide" will help you prepare to write for your audience:

AUDIENCE ANALYSIS GUIDE

1. **Who is my audience?**
2. **What is the frame of reference of this audience?**
3. **What point of view is my audience likely to have on my subject?**
4. **How do my own frame of reference and point of view differ from those of my audience?**
5. **How can I bridge any gap that exists between my audience's point of view and my own?**

Arranging Your Essay: Narration

Once you have discovered, through the journalist's questions, something to say about your subject and have formulated your answers to the "Audience Analysis Guide" you are faced with the problem of selecting and arranging the material in the order that best serves your purpose. You will want to formulate a shaping idea that indicates what significance the incident had for you. Then, in telling your story, you can select from the details that you have gathered those that are the most relevant and memorable and omit those that are unimportant and unnecessary. The next step is to arrange your material in such a way that you clearly convey the event to your readers, emphasizing its most important aspects and what it means to you.

Duration.   How do you decide on a particular order or arrangement of ideas for this chapter's essay? You are being asked to write about an event that took place in the past. You are being asked to elaborate on the journalist's question "What happened?" You can answer this question in several ways, depending on the purpose that you have in mind. First, you might decide to write a straightforward, chronological narrative that describes the event just as it occurred in time: an A-to-Z arrangement, with A as the beginning of the event and Z as the end. In the following selection, "The Angry Winter," Loren Eiseley used an A-to-Z arrangement, taking us through a series of steps in an incident that began when he laid a fossil bone on the floor of his study.

The Angry Winter

Loren Eiseley

> As to what happened next, it is possible to maintain that the hand of heaven was involved, and also possible to say that when men are desperate no one can stand up to them.   —XENOPHON

A time comes when creatures whose destinies have crossed somewhere in the remote past are forced to appraise each other as though they were total strangers. I had been huddled beside the fire one winter night, with the wind prowling outside and shaking the windows. The big shepherd dog on the hearth before me occasionally glanced up affectionately, sighed, and slept. I was working, actually, amidst the debris of a far greater winter. On my desk lay the lance points of ice age hunters and the heavy leg bone of a fossil bison. No remnants of flesh attached to these relics. The deed lay more than ten thousand years remote. It was represented here by naked flint and by bone so mineralized it rang when struck. As I worked on in my little circle of light, I absently laid the bone beside me on the floor. The hour had crept toward midnight. A grating noise, a heavy rasping of big teeth diverted me. I looked down.

The dog had risen. That rock-hard fragment of a vanished beast was in his jaws and he was mouthing it with a fierce intensity I had never seen exhibited by him before.

"Wolf," I exclaimed, and stretched out my hand. The dog backed up but did not yield. A low and steady rumbling began to rise in his chest, something out of a long-gone midnight. There was nothing in that bone to taste, but ancient shapes were moving in his mind and determining his utterance. Only fools gave up bones. He was warning me.

"Wolf," I chided again.

As I advanced, his teeth showed and his mouth wrinkled to strike. The rumbling rose to a direct snarl. His flat head swayed low and wickedly as a reptile's above the floor. I was the most loved object in his universe, but the past was fully alive in him now. Its shadows were whispering in his mind. I knew he was not bluffing. If I made another step he would strike.

Yet his eyes were strained and desperate. "Do not," something pleaded in the back of them, some affectionate thing that had followed at my heel all the days of his mortal life, "do not force me. I am what I am and cannot be otherwise because of the shadows. Do not reach out. You are a man, and my very god. I love you, but do not put out your hand. It is midnight. We are in another time, in the snow."

"The *other* time," the steady rumbling continued while I paused, "the other time in the snow, the big, the final, the terrible snow, when the shape of this thing I hold spelled life. I will not give it up. I cannot. The shadows will not permit me. Do not put out your hand."

I stood silent, looking into his eyes, and heard his whisper through. Slowly I drew back in understanding. The snarl diminished, ceased. As I retreated, the bone slumped to the floor. He placed a paw upon it, warningly.

And were there no shadows in my own mind, I wondered. Had I not for a moment, in the grip of that savage utterance, been about to respond, to hurl myself upon him over an invisible haunch ten thousand years removed? Even to me the shadows had whispered—to me, the scholar in his study.

"Wolf," I said, but this time, holding a familiar leash. I spoke from the door indifferently. "A walk in the snow." Instantly from his eyes that other visitant receded. The bone was left lying. He came eagerly to my side, accepting the leash and taking it in his mouth as always.

A blizzard was raging when we went out, but he paid no heed. On his thick fur the driving snow was soon clinging heavily. He frolicked a little—though usually he was a grave dog—making up to me for something still receding in his mind. I felt the snowflakes fall upon my face, and stood thinking of another time, and another time still, until I was moving from midnight to midnight under ever more remote and vaster snows. Wolf came to my side with a little whimper. It was he who was civilized now. "Come back to the fire," he nudged gently, "or you will be lost." Automatically I took the leash he offered. He led me safely home and into the house.

"We have been very far away," I told him solemnly. "I think there is something in us that we had both better try to forget." Sprawled on the rug, Wolf made no response except to thump his tail feebly out of courtesy. Already he was mostly asleep and dreaming. By the movement of his feet I could see he was running far upon some errand in which I played no part.

Softly I picked up his bone—our bone, rather—and replaced it high on a shelf in my cabinet. As I snapped off the light the white glow from the window seemed to augment itself and shine with a deep, glacial blue. As far as I could see, nothing moved in the long aisles of my neighbor's woods. There was no visible track, and certainly no sound from the living. The snow continued to fall steadily, but the wind, and the shadows it had brought, had vanished.

Eiseley narrated the incident in a step-by-step fashion. He omitted few steps between the beginning and the end, perhaps because the incident took a relatively short time. Are there moments in the incident that you would like to know more about? To what degree did Eiseley record objective facts? To what degree is the focus of his essay more on his subjective insights into and interpretations of the facts?

The longer the incident about which you are writing, of course, the more decisions you must make about which steps should be omitted from your narrative, which should be given only passing attention, and which should be emphasized with detail. Both your own point of view and that of your audience should be taken into consideration when you determine what parts of your narrative to emphasize or deemphasize.

What is Eiseley's shaping idea? Where does it occur in the essay?

What is Eiseley's point of view in his narrative? Is he serious, reasonable, scientific? Above all, is he authentic? How would you compare his voice to that of Gay Talese in his article about spectators who witnessed John Glenn's space shot? How do you account for any differences? What sort of assumptions did Eiseley seem to make about his audience's frame of reference and point of view?

Details.   As we have suggested, in writing your narrative it will help you to keep in mind that your readers want to become a part of what happened; they want to see and hear what you did. This is one reason for you to include memorable and relevant details conveyed in vivid language, including details of dialogue. Further, analogy should be used to help your readers share your thoughts and feelings about the incident.

Every detail included should contribute to what you want your readers to know and feel about the event. These details should elaborate the who, where, when, and how of your incident. The why and what may be answered through more direct statement. At the same time, irrelevant details should be omitted.

Reread the essay by Loren Eiseley, paying close attention to how the author used details to create the retelling of an event.

Now answer the following questions:

1. What role do the following details play in the essay?
   • winter
   • wind
   • fire and light
   • midnight
   • snow
   • shadows
2. The author mentioned in the first paragraph that the dog "glanced up affectionately." What role does this detail play in the story? Why did he add that the dog was big?

3. What details did Eiseley include to convey the dog's metamorphosis into a fierce beast? What further details dramatize the ambivalence that the dog feels about his new ferocity?

The following is the rough draft of a student's essay on an incident in which he was involved. Note that the student did not arrange the details of his narrative in strict chronological order from A to Z: rather, he referred at the start of the essay to the present, then moved in a flashback to the past. How effective is the student's use of details? Are there some details that need to be developed more fully? Are there any details that seem overemphasized?

SENSUOUS SOUNDS

Music allures me. I often sit and listen while sounds seem to whirl about and wrap me in silken robes whose fine textures are woven of the richness of a bassoon or the daintiness of a piccolo. Yet, until about four years ago, the sounds I was hearing were not those of a fine fabric, but of coarse burlap. The burlap was in the form of a two-hundred-dollar "stereo sytem" that veiled every musical delicacy. Like a deaf person who had never had the pleasure of hearing birds chirp or the din of a city street, so I felt. My first experience with truly lively sound is one I will not soon forget.

My brother-in-law, Mike, introduced me to high-fidelity audio equipment. One bright and sunny afternoon in January, when the few birds left from the autumnal exodus were singing, and the horns from nearby trucks were honking, Mike took me to Warren Street in downtown New York City. I walked into Great Sounds, a hi-fi store, and was immediately transported to another place; I felt like Alice in Wonderland. There I was, surrounded by state-of-the-art technology.

It was a classic case of love at first sight. There were amplifiers whose polished metal fronts looked like the surface of a delicate satin sheet. The lights from spectrum analyzers flashed and twinkled like a sequined dress worn by a shapely woman. The curvaceous knobs and buttons of various receivers, tuners, preamps, and tape decks called out to me, and the sounds they made were as beautiful as the placid silence one often hears in the country toward dawn.

I stood in awe for about one minute—or was it ten? I can't seem to remember now. As the feeling of euphoria that I was experiencing started to dissipate, I began roaming around the sound room. Enticed by the beckoning of all the machines, which seemed to have minds of their own, I gently turned, tugged, pushed, and pulled anything I could get my hands on. The equipment responded to my touch with blinking lights, rapidly pulsating needles, and sudden bursts of voluminous passion, as indicated by the garrulous speakers. They all seemed good enough to take home with me! But alas, I was in the awkward position of having to choose the best from all the wonderful varieties available.

Mike led me through three sound rooms. I listened with an open mind and an open ear. After all, I had to live for many years with whatever I chose. I could not base my decision solely on appearances—personalities counted for a lot. After about two hours, I found the equipment that appealed to me. It had a delicate balance of looks and sound. It was perfect in every respect.

As I prepared to leave the store, I glanced back one more time at the bevies of beauteous machinery. I winked seductively at them, and they blinked their lights back at me. Ah, to be young and in love.

Like the student who wrote this essay, you may not want to follow a strict chronological order from A to Z; instead, you may wish to heighten the drama of an event by using a flashback technique. In arranging the order of events, you may begin at the end or in the middle and flash back to earlier events. Thus you may go from Z to A to Z or from M to A to Z.

Why did the student employ a flashback technique? How would the effect have been changed by an A-to-Z arrangement or by an arrangement that began in the middle of the incident? How successful was the student in showing rather than telling? What might he have done to help his audience experience the incident more vividly?

Arranging the Details of Your Essay. Try the following procedure in organizing your essay: make a list of the stages in your incident, arranging them in the order that you think is most effective: A to Z, Z to A to Z, or M to A to Z; asterisk those aspects of the incident that you think are the most important; cross out those aspects that do not contribute much to what you wish to convey about your incident; beside each stage, jot down those details that you feel are necessary to convey the importance of each stage and the overall significance of the event.

Writing the Rough Draft

All of the preceding sections in "Writing the Essay" have prepared you to write your essay on an incident. It is now time to write it.

In Chapter 1, we suggested that different people go about writing in different ways. Just how you go about writing your rough draft, just what process you employ in getting the words down on paper, is a personal matter. Perhaps you are beginning to find that the words come more easily to you if you write freely at first, without stopping to edit your sentence structure or the arrangement of your details. Perhaps you do better if you focus on one paragraph at a time, working each paragraph into as final a shape as you can before moving on to the next.

Probably you will want to start your rough draft by writing down your shaping idea and then reviewing the list of concrete details that you put together by answering the journalist's questions. By now, you have also decided on a rough pattern of arrangement, both details and arrangement chosen with the audience's point of view in mind. Now place yourself in your chosen spot for writing, and begin.

Once you start, keep on going. Refer to your notes on details, audience, and arrangement as often as you need to. Bear in mind the need for chronological sequencing and specific details. Write through to the end in one sitting.

FOCUS: TRANSITIONS

Transitions are words and phrases that establish connections between words, sentences, and paragraphs. Through the use of transitions, the writer emphasizes the coherence of the essay for the reader. The most common form of transition is the conjunction. Conjunctions form such connections between thoughts as addition (*and*), contrast (*but*), comparison (*as*), causation (*for*), choice (*or*), process (*after*), and chronology (*before*). Transitional phrases can also be employed to make the same connections, for example, "in addition," "on the other hand," "as well as," "as a result," and "after a while."

A second means of creating transitions between thoughts is to refer to the shaping idea throughout the essay by repeating the key words that you have used to express it (or synonyms or pronouns clearly referring to it). The repetition of key words assures the reader of the unity of the paper and of its development of one main point.

In Passage 1 below, most of the transitions have been omitted. After reading the first passage, read Passage 2. Does the writing in the second version seem much clearer with the transitions (underlined) restored.

Passage 1

I think I was in the first press bus. I can't be sure. Pete Lisagor of the *The Chicago Daily News* says he was in the bus. He describes things that went on aboard it that didn't happen on the bus I went in. I think I was in the bus.

Confusion is the way it was in Dallas in the early afternoon of Nov. 22. No one knew what happened, or how, or where, much less why. Bits and pieces fell together. A reasonably coherent version of the story was possible. I know no reporter who was there who has a clear and orderly picture of the afternoon; it is a matter of bits and pieces thrown hastily into something like a whole.

Passage 2

I think I was in the first press bus. But I can't be sure. Pete Lisagor of *The Chicago Daily News* says he knows he was in the first press bus and he describes things that went on aboard it that didn't happen on the bus I was in. But I still think I was in the first press bus.

I cite that minor confusion as an example of the way it was in Dallas in the early afternoon of Nov. 22. At first no one knew what happened, or how, or where, much less why. Gradually, bits and pieces began to fall together, and within two hours a reasonably coherent version of the story began to be possible. Even now, however, I know no reporter who has a clear and orderly picture of that surrealistic afternoon; it is still a matter of bits and pieces thrown hastily into something like a whole.

—**Tom Wicker**, *Times Talk*, 1963.

In analyzing Tom Wicker's use of transitions in Passage 2, you might notice first that he used words like *but, and, or,* and *however* to form very specific connections (addition, choice, and contrast) between his words, phrases, sentences, and even paragraphs.

Second, as Wicker was narrating the events on the day of the assassination of John F. Kennedy, he used many conjunctive words and phrases that indicate chronology, thus clarifying the sequence of events: "at first," "gradually," "within two hours," "even now," and "still."

Finally, he inserted key words in every sentence. This repetition of key words builds bridges by establishing that his sentences and paragraphs cluster around his shaping idea, the confusion surrounding the president's assassination. This shaping idea is conveyed through the use of the key word *bus* in the first paragraph and the use of the word *confusion* and its synonyms *bits and pieces* and *surrealistic afternoon* in the second. Even the demonstrative adjective *that* is used several times to refer to the confusion of that afternoon. (The demonstrative adjectives *this, that, these,* and *those* also act as transitions.)

As a further example, notice the use of transitional words and phrases in the following paragraph:

<u>William Wolcott died and went to heaven. Or so it</u> — *Shaping key idea*
<u>seemed.</u> <u>Before</u> being wheeled to the operating table, he — *Conjunction indicating*
had been reminded that the surgical procedure would   *beginning of*
entail a certain risk. The operation was a success <u>but</u> just   *chronology*
as the anesthesia was wearing off, his heart went into fi-   *Conjunction establishing*
brillation <u>and</u> he died. <u>It seemed to him that he had</u>   *a contrast of ideas*
<u>somehow left his body and was able to look down upon</u>
<u>it, withered and pathetic, lying on a hard and unforgiving</u> *Repetition of key idea*
<u>surface.</u> He was only a little sad, regarded his body one
last time—from a great height, it seemed—<u>and</u> <u>contin-</u>   *Conjunctions and other*
<u>ued</u> a kind of upward journey. <u>While</u> his surroundings   *words that establish*
had been suffused by a strange permeating darkness, he   *chronology*
realized that things were <u>now</u> getting brighter—looking
up, you might say. <u>And then</u> he was being illuminated
from a distance, flooded with light. <u>He entered a kind of</u>
<u>radiant kingdom and there, just ahead of him, he could</u>
<u>make out in silhouette, magnificently lit from behind, a</u>   *Repetition of key idea*
<u>great godlike figure whom he was now effortlessly ap-</u>
<u>proaching. Wolcott strained to make out His face</u> . . .
   <u>And then</u> awoke. In the hospital operating room, — *Conjunction of*
where the defibrillation machine had been rushed to   *chronology*
him, he had been resuscitated at the last possible mo-
ment. <u>Actually,</u> his heart had stopped and, by some defi-   *Conjunctive word*
nitions of this poorly understood process, he had <u>died.</u>   *indicating contrast*
<u>Wolcott was certain that he *had* died, that he had been</u>
<u>vouchsafed a glimpse of life after death and a confirma-</u> *Repetition of key idea*
<u>tion of Judaeo-Christian theology.</u>
—**Carl Sagan,** "The Amniotic Universe," *Atlantic,* April 1974.

SOME PRACTICE WITH TRANSITIONS

1. Underline the transitional words in each of the following paragraphs. Indicate whether each word (or phrase) underlined is a conjunction or a key word. Be specific about what type of relationship each conjunctive word and phrase has formed (causal, contrast, and so on).

   In the cinders at the station boys sit smoking steadily in darkened cars, their arms bent out the windows, white shirts glowing behind the glass. Nine o'clock is the best time. They sit in a line facing the highway—two or three or four of them—idling their engines. As you walk by a machine may growl at you or a pair of headlights flare up briefly. In a moment one will pull out, spinning cinders behind it, to stalk impatiently up and down the dark streets or roar half a mile into the country before returning to its place in line and pulling up.

—*The Single Voice: An Anthology of Contemporary Fiction*, ed. Jerome Charyn.

Thus was born the original Women's Rights Movement, which became known as the Women's Suffrage Movement because the single great issue, of course, was legal political recognition. But it was never meant to begin and end with the vote, just as the abolitionist movement was never meant to begin and end with the vote. Somehow, though, that awful and passionate struggle for suffrage seemed to exhaust both the blacks and the women, especially the women, for when the vote finally came at the end of the Civil War, it was handed to black males—but not to women; the women had to go on fighting for 60 bitterly long years for suffrage. And then both blacks and women lay back panting, unable to catch their breath for generation upon generation.

—**Vivian Gornick,** "The Next Great Moment in History is Theirs," *Village Voice*, Nov. 27, 1969.

2. Combine the sentences below into one paragraph. Using transitional words and phrases, build bridges between the sentences, creating a paragraph unified in meaning.

   a. The most traumatic change now under way in American higher education is the shift from a seller's to a buyer's market.

   b. Many colleges now use promotional tactics that are downright dishonest.

   c. The most popular come-on is the so-called no-need scholarship, designed to lure academically able students.

   d. Promotional brochures are beginning to look like cigarette ads.

   e. One woman's college produced a brochure showing a girl with long blond hair lying in a field of flowers. "Especially for women," reads the caption, "because women are creative, intelligent and beautiful, resourceful and sweet and generally different from men."

   f. Entrepreneurs don't pussyfoot around with such indirect approaches. If freshmen are what you want, then that's what they deliver—at $250 a head and up.

   g. Serious problems are becoming apparent in the headlong rush to embrace the latest marketing strategies of the corporate world.

3. Insert transitional words and phrases in the following student essay:

THE HALLOWEEN PARTY

My friend decided to have a Halloween party on the Saturday before Halloween. I was invited. I had to decide on what costume I would wear. I went to Rubie's Costume Rental and picked out a Minnie Mouse costume.

I was especially excited about this party. Everyone would be wearing costumes. Costume parties always seem to be lively. The disguises are usually amusing, funny, scary, or creative, making the party interesting. It can be fun to be surrounded by imaginative figures. Each person's identity is disguised, and it's easy to play practical jokes on each other. My costume disguised me from head to toe. No one would know my real identity.

Saturday night came. I got dressed in my costume and headed over to the party. The house was full of people in their Halloween costumes. My friends could not recognize me under my mask. I had to identify myself to each one of them.

I noticed someone wearing a Mickey Mouse costume. He was taking pictures of some of the people at the party. He noticed me in my Minnie Mouse costume and motioned for me to come over. He handed his camera to someone wearing a Peter Pan costume so that Peter Pan could take a picture of Mickey and me together. After all, Mickey and Minnie Mouse are a pair. He thanked me for being in the photograph with him. I left the picture-taking scene to find my friends. I wondered who it was wearing the Mickey Mouse costume. He'd said only two words to me. I hadn't recognized his voice.

I saw an old friend of mine who happened to look really cute in a Little Bo-Peep outfit. I went over to talk to her for a while. We decided to look for more of our friends. We found them on the dance floor and joined them. Mickey Mouse happened to be dancing away on the dance floor. He spotted me, came over, and we danced together. Everybody was working up a good sweat. I got tired after dancing to a couple of songs. I went to get something to drink.

The movie Halloween was being played on a VCR in the TV room. I decided to watch it. By the time the movie was over, it had got rather late. I started to clean up the house while my friend broke up the party. I happened to turn around and catch Mickey Mouse without his mask on. He was saying goodnight to some people. To my surprise, I found that the man under the Mickey Mouse mask was my ex-boy-friend—the same ex-boyfriend that I usually feel so uncomfortable around and try to avoid.

Our relationship had been a good one until he had to move to Flori-da with his family. The day he left for Florida was a sad one. We wrote each other letters twice a week. We called each other on the phone at least once a week. After the first month, our communications grew less frequent.

Four months had passed. I had received only two short letters from him. Then I got a call from him. He told me that he would be moving back to New York within the next few months. I was extremely happy to think that I would be with him again. I counted the days until he moved back to New York.

After he had moved back here, I realized that our relationship had changed. He treated me as a friend instead of as a girlfriend. I realized that we no longer had a romantic realtionship. I felt foolish. I decided to avoid him whenever possible.

My experience with him at the Halloween party made me realize that there is no need for me to feel foolish or uncomfortable with him. The masks we wore helped me to relate to him as a person rather than as an ex-boyfriend. Feeling foolish was no longer an excuse for me to avoid him. It is okay to feel for him as a friend. I looked back at our relationship and was able to accept the change that had taken place.

Ending my relationship with him as a girlfriend did not end my re-lationship with him as a friend. I had not been a friend to him because of fear that rejection of me as a girlfriend had affected his attitude to-ward me as a person. It did not mean rejection of friendship. I now want a friendly relationship, like the one we had the night of the par-ty.

Images, impressions, fears, perceptions, and feelings toward others affect our relationships. We may see only one side of a situation or a person. The outside world can be very misleading about the real inside world that we live in and know. When we are disguised, our fears and anxieties, perceptions and worries, are put aside. We can be ourselves and learn to see another side of the world we live in or of the people we know. If we look closely enough, we can see ourselves.

REWRITING

Obtaining Feedback on Your Rough Draft

After you have written your rough draft, take a break for a period of time. This period should be long enough for you to be able to return to your essay refreshed. Once you have rested, your "other" self can emerge, the self that can see your essay objectively and make any necessary revisions.

You may also want to obtain peer feedback at this point. Because your peers are your audience for this essay, the responses of your classmates should be particularly useful in determining how well you have written for your readers.

Regardless of who provides the feedback—you, your instructor, your peers, or any combination—your paper should receive an evaluation that answers the four questions of the "Audience Response Guide."

——————— AUDIENCE RESPONSE GUIDE ———————

1. **What does the writer want to say in this paper? What is her or his purpose in writing? What does she or he want the paper to mean?**
2. **How does the paper affect the audience for which it was intended?**
3. **How effective has the writer been in conveying her or his purpose and meaning?**
4. **How should the paper be revised to better fulfill its purpose and meaning?**

Following is a peer evaluation of the rough draft of the student essay "Sensuous Sounds" (pp. 54–55). Compare your own evaluation of the draft to that of the peer group by answering the four questions of the "Audience Response Guide" yourself before reading their answers.

1. The group felt that the writer wished to convey his discovery of how much better music can be when heard on good hi-fi equipment as compared to when it is heard on cheap equipment.

2. The group liked the writer's use of detailed images, which helped them to share his excitement. The writing was witty, amusing, and imaginative. The analogy at the start between sounds and fabrics helped to convey the writer's feelings well.

3. Although the writer was effective in describing his experience, the group felt that he told more than he showed, particularly in the last three paragraphs. They did not feel that he helped them to hear what he heard.

4. They suggested that he go into more detail about the specific sounds he heard, perhaps further developing his use of analogy to convey his feelings in response to what he heard.

A revised version of "Sensuous Sounds" follows. How were the group's suggestions incorporated? What changes did the writer make himself? Why did he make these alterations? Why, for example, did he add the dialogue in the next-to-last paragraph?

SENSUOUS SOUNDS

Music allures me. I often listen while sounds seem to whirl about and wrap me in silken robes whose fine textures are woven of the richness of a bassoon or the daintiness of a piccolo. Yet, four years ago, the sounds I was hearing were not those of a fine fabric, but of a coarse burlap. The burlap was in the form of a two-hundred-dollar stereo system that veiled every musical delicacy. Like a deaf person who had never had the pleasure of hearing birds chirp or the din of a city street, so I felt. My first experience with truly lively sound is one I will not soon forget.

My brother-in-law, Mike, introduced me to high-fidelity audio equipment. One bright and sunny afternoon in January, when the few birds left from the autumnal exodus were singing, and the horns from nearby trucks were honking, Mike took me to Warren Street in downtown New York City. I walked into Great Sounds, a hi-fi store, and was immediately transported to another place—a place where machines spoke and sounds filled the air with life.

It was a classic case of love at first sight. There were amplifiers whose polished metal fronts looked like the surface of a satin sheet. The lights from spectrum analyzers flashed and twinkled like a sequined dress worn by a shapely woman. The curvaceous knobs and buttons of various receivers, tuners, preamps, and tape decks called out to me, and the sounds they made were as beautiful as the placid silence one often hears in the country toward dawn.

As the feeling of euphoria that I was experiencing started to dissipate, I began roaming around the sound room. One at a time I listened to the numerous sets of speakers that served as mouths for the many components. Among the various languages spoken by the speakers were Mozart, Mingus, and Moody Blues. I was amazed at the clarity and precision with which these "languages" were spoken.

The voices, much like human voices, sounded very different. Some were sultry and attractive, and others were raspy and repulsive; each had its own distinctive quality. The underlying message in all of the components seemed to be "Turn me on." I felt as if I were walking through a giant singles bar!

Finally, I approached an impressive-looking setup. I pressed the power button and turned it on. What happened next was unbelievable. The equipment blinked its lights and pulsated its needles, and in a sudden burst of passion, sounds emerged from everywhere. It was music to my ears.

"I'll take her. I'll take her," I shouted suddenly. The salesman who was standing nearby stared at me. "Pardon me, sir?" he asked. I checked myself abruptly and said, "I mean I'll take it."

As I walked out of the store, one box under each arm, I glanced back one more time at the bevies of beauteous machinery. I winked seductively at them, and they blinked their lights at me. Ah, to be young and in love.

Revising

Revising affects the content and organization of your essay. The revising that your "other self," your instructor, or your peer group suggests you do will no doubt be one or more of six activities; adding, rearranging, substituting, distributing, consolidating, or cutting. The peer group evaluating the essay "Sensuous Sounds" advised *adding* details and implied, at least, that some of the material that told rather than showed might be *cut*. Such revisions affect the meaning of the essay, some to a greater extent than others.

Each of these activities will receive a full discussion in a subsequent chapter, but in case when revising you wish to move ahead, we list the pages for each discussion:

Adding, below
Rearranging, pp. 97–98
Substituting, pp. 133–134

Distributing, p. 169

Consolidating, pp. 207–208

Cutting, pp. 247–249

Adding.   Adding—of words, phrases, or whole passages—is required when you neglect to put on paper information that the reader needs to know. Subconsciously, you may have assumed that because what you wrote was clear to you, it would be clear to the reader. Or some facets of your subject may simply not have occurred to you when you wrote your rough draft. However, your "other self," your peer group, or your instructor may now suggest that important additions be made.

Details may need to be added that will make your writing more concrete; perhaps you wrote something like "The experience was terrifying" without indicating to the reader what the terrifying elements of the experience were. Or perhaps you wrote something like "The situation impinged on the group in a negative fashion," thinking that you were writing impressively, but not realizing that your language was very abstract and did not present an actual picture to the reader of how the group felt about what was happening to them. By adding details, the writers of the two sentences above could create much more vivid writing: "Slipping into Professor Wout's class even one minute late turned my knees to jelly, my insides into a volcano, and my head into a pounding drum" and "Having been so eager to see the film, which was purported to be Woody Allen's best, my disappointed friends looked like their idol himself as they hunched sadly away from the darkened theater."

You may also need to add details that define the relationships between the ideas in your draft. Perhaps you wrote an essay on animals in comic strips and did not express clearly the differences between Garfield's and Snoopy's attitudes toward life. Finding even one word that crystallizes the view of each cartoon character may clarify this important point.

You may have neglected some important features of your subject and need now to expand your outline. Perhaps you wrote on the disappearing animal species of Kenya and neglected the elephant—a vital omission that you will now want to rectify.

In addition to considering the information that the reader needs to know, think also of his or her point of view on your subject. Does your voice build a bridge between your point of view and that of your reader, or should words and phrases be added that will create this rapport? For example, if you, as a college student, wrote to your younger brother about your new appreciation of Picasso and did not take into account his disparagement of those "funny figures" in Picasso's work, you might want to add phrases that would bring your attitude and his closer together. To the following sentence in your draft, "Picasso introduced the twentieth century to new perceptions of time and space," you might add, "as Einstein did in physics," as your brother is currently taking that subject in high school.

Whether you are adding information or building bridges between you and your reader, adding words, phrases, and even paragraphs is an important part of revision.

In adding to the rough draft of your essay for this task, decide whether you have enabled your audience to experience the incident as you did. If not, add details to make your narrative as vivid as possible, as did the writer of "Sensuous Sounds," or to enable your reader to see the relationships between your ideas. Also, if any important aspect of the incident has occurred to you belatedly, add that aspect. Finally, create a tone of voice that indicates that you are responsive to your audience by adding analogies or explanations that will encourage your reader to see your point of view.

Editing

Editing is different from revising in that revising affects content and organization, whereas editing affects the surface features of the essay, such as transitions, word choice, and mechanics. Editing should be done only when your revisions are complete. Editing changes include the same processes, however, as revisions: adding, rearranging, substituting, distributing, consolidating, and cutting.

Adding.   Add words that further clarify the meaning of your phrases and sentences. These words, such as adjectives and adverbs, can provide additional details as well.

Transitions.   Make sure to add transitions to your rough draft so that your peers can easily grasp the connections between your thoughts and also follow your chronological sequence. What transitions might the student who wrote "Sensuous Sounds" have added to his essay?

Mechanics.   At this point, forget *what* you are saying and concentrate on *how* you are saying it. Reread your first draft solely for mechanical errors such as spelling (use a good dictionary); grammar (refer to the handbook at the end of this text); punctuation (again, the handbook); and capitalization (handbook once again).

Now, revise and edit your rough draft.

BECOMING AWARE OF YOURSELF AS A WRITER

Make use of your journal to record your thoughts and feelings about the task for Chapter 2. As you write in your journal, consider the following questions:

1. How useful were the journalist's questions in generating ideas for the task? Did you rely on any other means of generating information? In what ways were these means useful?

2. Do you understand the concept of the audience's frame of reference? Under what writing circumstances do you think that you must analyze your audience's frame of reference?

3. Which method seemed most effective to you in trying to determine your audience's point of view? What are the limitations of interviewing, of inference, and of role playing? What are the advantages of each method?

4. How did you feel about writing for your peers? How helpful was it for you to evaluate the differences between their point of view and your own?

5. How did the writing process described in this chapter help or hinder the writing of your essay?

6. How helpful was the feedback you received on your rough draft? Did it lead to any significant improvements in your final draft?

7. What was the single most difficult aspect of the writing task for you? How did you resolve it?

3
WRITING ABOUT A PHASE

PURPOSE

In writing for yourself, as in a journal (see Chap. 1), you can develop a unique, personal voice. When writing for others (see Chap. 2), usually it is necessary for you to make adjustments—in what you say and in how you say it—in order to be understood by a reader whose point of view is different from your own. Now we want to examine the problem of how you can retain the sincerity of your most private, authentic voice at the same time that you modify it in order to communicate fluently and intelligibly to your audience.

Different readers, of course, require that you modify your voice in different ways. In a sense, as a writer you assume a different voice in relation to each audience that you address. For example, when you write a letter of advice to your younger brother, you may sound helpful, self-assured, and experienced; when you write to your friends, asking them to lend you some money, you might plead or reason. The voice you use as an older brother or sister is different from the voice you use as a friend because your role in relation to your audience is different.

The questions that this multiplicity of voices raises are complex. Can you express yourself freely and honestly and at the same time adopt a voice suited to your reader? To what degree can the voice that you adopt serve to bridge the gap between your point of view and that of your audience? These are questions addressed in Chapter 3.

Also in this chapter, you can experiment with the free-writing strategy that was introduced in Chapter 1 as a way to explore a personal experience as openly and as honestly as you can. We then ask you to identify a particular role that you played during or after that experience in order to see how writing in the voice of that role can be a means of accommodating yourself to your reader's point of view while still retaining your sincerity.

GENERATING IDEAS: FREE WRITING

Peter Elbow, in his book *Writing Without Teachers* (Oxford, 1973), explained what free writing is and how it can help you to find something to say about your subject. Free writing is writing about a subject without restrictions, writing whatever comes into your head, without concern for grammar, spelling, or organization. It is not prepared writing; it is not intended for a reader. Its only purpose is for you to explore on paper whatever thoughts and feelings you might have about your subject.

For example, the two students who wrote the following free-writing exercises were given a lemon and were asked to spend ten minutes in writing whatever came into their heads about it.

Writer 1

Lemon—a yellow lemon, the color of my bright yellow sweatshirt the color of yellow taxi cabs the color of the sun in a kid's coloring book my yellow paper on my test bananas are yellow. It feels smooth but has a soapy or waxy texture. The Lemon Ice King has good lemon ices. Lenny used to work at the Lemon Ice King, Lenny, Levy, and Mike used to rob a lot of money from Fat Pete. Lemons are yellow I had a yellow car that was a lemon. Bobby Pistilli's father used to call Bobby a lemon. He is a lemon driving in his Monte Carlo. I like lemons I hate the people who passed the lemon to me I don't want to see it. I like lemons, I like lemons in my iced tea, I like lemons over chicken cutlets, I like lemons raw, I like to take the lemon right out of the pitcher of iced tea and eat it raw. I love the sour taste, I love the expression on someone's face when they bite into a very sour lemon. I like lemon on seafood. My favorite is freshly squeezed lemon over freshly crumbed and baked shrimp or over fresh shrimp or over filet of any fish. Some lemons are round, others are oval-shaped—most lemons have a nipple at either end which is very small. One way to use a lemon (probably the most common way) is to slice it in half and squeeze it. Another way which is better is to first squeeze the lemon before you cut it open and roll it on a flat surface.

Notice how the first writer has relaxed and let his mind wander in any direction that the lemon has taken him; he touches on the appearance, the taste, and the feel of a lemon; its uses; and its emotional associations for him in the past and even in the present as he is writing. (Notice that he has omitted much punctuation, perhaps in order to encourage the flow of his thoughts.)

Past associations engulf the second writer as she relaxes and writes about her subject:

Writer 2

Sometimes when I see a lemon, it brings back memories of my childhood. I remember the lemon tree my family and I used to have in our backyard. There were other trees but the lemon tree was my favorite. No other house in our neighborhood had one. My mother had put nicely formed bricks around the trunk in a circle. It used to amaze me how those beautiful and nice-smelling flowers turned into lemons. This may sound ridiculous, but when I remember that lemon tree, it brings back nostalgic feelings. This may be because of how pleasant life used to be at that time.

SOME PRACTICE WITH FREE WRITING

1. As a way of getting started in free writing, begin with a subject that emphasizes a particular sense; for example, begin with the taste of a favorite food or dish and let go all your associations with it. Then, move on to the other senses—touch, sight, sound, smell—and write freely about the subjects and associations each evokes.

   As another way of stimulating free writing, write about one subject and try to include associations with all five senses.

2. Write for ten minutes about an impersonal object: a pencil, a pen, or a piece of chalk, for example. Then read the free writing that follows. Have you stretched your mind as much as or more than the student who wrote this piece?

Pen is an object, invented and created by man. It can make peace or start wars with just a simple wave from its point. It can teach people and help write important papers it can invent books, technology and create a picture of the universe. But yet we see what is a simple object which permits us to write as a worthless thing when really it holds the destruction of man or the creation of peace and love in the world in a small little tip. Down through time there have been different types of pens and pencils but all they did was to record our history and carry it down to each generation. A pen can be noble or very bad it all depends on who uses it. It has been called the sword of man or the staff of peace.

Free Writing as a Source of Ideas for Writing an Essay

Free writing can serve as a way of generating ideas once your imagination has really expanded, for you can discover ideas about subjects that you never realized were even in your mind. Peter Elbow said, "Free writing is a way to end up thinking something you couldn't have started out thinking." By examining your free-writing papers, you can find thoughts or feelings to expand into prepared essays.

For example, read over the following free-writing sample:

Well, trick or treat, it is Halloween today. How I used to love that saying. Well I guess that I am growing up because I really do not feel that way anymore. But of course that is normal.

The hoodlums on the corner were throwing eggs at everybody today. It was so much fun to observe the action. It was hilarious to see the dumb fools getting bombarded with eggs.

Nobody, of course, ever tried throwing an egg at me. If they had, I swear that I would definitely have flipped out. But I am a familiar face and one does not throw eggs at the people he knows.

At home, I packed the little candy bags and it was fun distributing candy to all the really cute little kids dressed in their costumes coming to the door. I felt sad for a while there, it reminded me of how much fun my sister and I used to have on Halloween.

Oh well, the advantages of being an adult beat anything—even the fun kids have on Halloween.

Well, it's Tuesday and it seems as though I am not going to go anywhere again. Last night I decided to sleep over at Aggie's house, me & that girl are so compatible that we have so much fun together.

I love Aggie, and she's been my best friend ever since I was little, and she'll always be. We have been friends ever since we were little and I have always thought of her as I would a sister.

Her parents really like me, they are always asking me about how I am doing and how my parents are doing. We've been through a lot of garbage together, and after all our messed-up years I really don't know how we are alive after all the drugs that we have done.

It is true that we had both flipped out once but now, thank god, we are all right.

Aggie though it seems to me is still a little shaky at times. I sometimes think that maybe the drugs did affect her more than any of us would ever care to admit to ourselves or of course to her.

Why do you think that the writer associated Halloween with her friendship with Aggie? What would you say was the primary topic, the main pattern of thought, that this writer had on her mind? What sort of thoughts and feelings might this writer expand into a formal essay, one that is organized, fully developed, and grammaticallly correct?

Free writing can be used to recall personal experiences, and it is also a good technique for getting down on paper all the material on a recently studied topic. It is a useful antidote to writer's block, or the "I don't know where to start" syndrome. If you have given considerable thought to, and perhaps even done some research on, an assigned topic but do not know where to begin in writing about it, free writing of your thoughts or your recollections of what you have read will get your material on paper. From this important first stage, you can move on to organizing what you have written.

MORE PRACTICE WITH FREE WRITING

3. Write freely for forty-five minutes about a holiday you went on and the memories that you associate with it. When you are finished, make a list of the aspects of your subject that you might develop into a prepared essay. How are these aspects related? What pattern of thought or feeling do they trace? Which of them fit the least well into the pattern? Might these latter aspects be the start of a different pattern?

4. Think of a subject that you have recently studied for one of your classes or one that you have read about rather extensively. Without thinking too hard about the subject, start writing freely about it. After writing for forty-five minutes, consider how many aspects of the subject you covered. Have you sufficient ideas for

an essay? What pattern do these ideas form? Now that you have taken stock of what you have written, would more free writing serve a useful purpose?

Free Writing and the Writing Process

Free writing can help you to locate worthwhile ideas for a prepared paper, and it can do so most effectively if developed through several stages. In order to generate a maximum amount of material with free writing, before moving on to work on the rough draft of an essay, Peter Elbow suggests completing two free-writing stages, each of which takes an hour.

Hour 1   Freely write on your subject for forty-five minutes. Sum up the pattern that emerges for fifteen minutes.

Hour 2   Freely write about the emerging pattern for sixty minutes.

The free writing that you practice in these two hours can then be shaped into the rough draft of an essay.

MORE PRACTICE WITH FREE WRITING

5. Hour 1   Using the topic about which you wrote freely in Exercise 3 or 4, sum up the pattern that emerges for fifteen minutes.

Hour 2   Freely write about the emerging pattern for sixty minutes.

Has the free writing that you produced in these two hours provided you with the material for a prepared essay? As a means of checking your answer, construct a rough outline for an essay.

ADDRESSING YOUR AUDIENCE: SELECTING A VOICE FOR YOUR READER

Selecting a Voice as a Means of Self-Expression

When we say that someone is playing a role, we usually mean that she or he is not being honest. When you played the role of the reader in Chapter 2, you presumably were stepping away from yourself and assuming someone else's identity. If your purpose was not to try to understand the other person's point of view but to deceive that person into believing that you were just like him or her, you would be dishonest. But sometimes, when we say that people are playing a role, we mean only that they are acting in a manner typical of a certain stage of life that they are in or a certain position that they hold. In this case, they *are* expressing themselves, telling us something true about who and what they are. The role they are playing is communicated through the voice they select.

We all select different voices during our lives, voices that are expressions of one or another aspect of ourselves. We are children and parents; we work for people and we hire people to work for us; we can be hosts or guests, friends or relatives or strangers. Because our lives have many aspects, we select different voices with which to speak at different times. A change in voice can reflect a change in our point of view, and often we change our voice any number of times in a single day. When we select among our various voices, we do not, however, lose our authenticity.

For example, consider a man who is both a father and a college student. At home, with his children, the man speaks knowledgeably, answering his children's questions with authority. At school, as a student, however, the man may speak less authoritatively; he may prefer asking questions to answering them; his manner, his tone of voice, the whole style with which he expresses himself may be different. Perhaps the man is more casual, more playful with his children, and more formal, more serious with his teachers. On the other hand, perhaps the man acts more seriously with his children than with his fellow students.

The fact that the man is selecting different voices does not necessarily mean that he is being insincere or dishonest about expressing himself. In fact, selecting a voice can be a most effective means of expressing one or another of the many sides of one's complex human character.

SOME PRACTICE WITH SELECTING A VOICE AS A MEANS OF SELF-EXPRESSION

1. Determine your point of view on each of the following subjects: The women's movement, military spending, the criminal justice system, the wisdom of adults, and the sexual revolution. Then determine the role you were playing as you thought about each subject. How many voices might you select in order to express the complexity of your feelings on each subject? Does any particular voice express your feelings more fully than others?

2. Review the free-writing exercises in which you wrote about a holiday or about a subject of study (see pp. 72–73). Can you identify a specific voice that you selected as you wrote? What role were you playing that influenced you to select this voice?

Selecting a Voice as a Bridge Between the Writer and the Reader

Because we do live out roles in life, selecting a voice to reflect each role can be a legitimate and honest means of expressing how we really feel and think. Also, because playing roles is a primary human experience, something that everyone does, selecting a voice to communicate a role can serve as a most effective bridge between a writer and a reader whose points of view may be quite different.

Consider the girl who wrote the free-writing exercise about Halloween. What sort of voice had she selected? What stage of life had she reached? Might an elderly or middle-aged person, one of her peers, and someone younger than she react differently to her attitude about "the advantages of being an adult"? Might she choose a different voice for each different audience?

For example, suppose the girl, after reviewing her free-writing exercise, decides that her focus seems to be her feeling that she is not a kid anymore, that she is growing up. How is she going to write convincingly about this feeling? If she is writing for her peer, Aggie, who might feel similarly, she might simply use the casual style of one friend to another. But what if she is writing for her English teacher? If she plays the role of student, she is likely to adopt a voice that sounds less like a grown-up and more like a subordinate than she, in fact, feels.

A primary reason for her feeling more adult is that, having passed through a period of time in which she was "flipped out" on drugs, she has learned how much better off she is without drugs. Perhaps she will be most understandable, as well as most convincing, if she writes in the role of a former drug user. She can speak from experience about the growing up that one does in passing through such a phase. She can explain her subject with authority, even expertise. She can adopt a more grown up voice if, as she writes, she thinks of herself in this role.

In doing so, she will be expressing her feelings honestly and reliably, even though her most private and authentic self is not identical with and is much more complex than the voice of a former drug user. Moreover, she will be giving her teacher a concrete image of the thoughts that she wishes to express.

The points of view of the girl and her teacher may be radically different. But the voice of someone who has recovered from a self-destructive habit is a typical voice in human experience, and even if the teacher has never adopted such a voice herself, it is likely to be familiar. Like most of the voices that we select in life, it is something of a stereotype. We can personalize any voice by the way in which we express it, even as we rely on its stereotypical nature to narrow the distance between us and our audience.

SOME PRACTICE WITH SELECTING A VOICE AS A BRIDGE BETWEEN WRITER AND READER

1. What sort of role and what corresponding voice might be most effective for you to assume if you want to express your point of view about violence on television to the sponsor of a particularly violent program? How might you alter your voice if, instead, you intend to address your eight-year-old nephew who enjoys watching the program? Might you select a different voice if you are writing to the star of the program, who happens to be one of your favorite actors?

2. What is your point of view on the Moral Majority? As a voter, how might you convey your point of view to a liberal Democratic member of Congress who is campaigning for reelection in your neighborhood? How might your voice change if, instead, you want to address your next-door neighbor, who is an ultraconservative Republican?

3. To what sort of audience might the voice that you adopted in the free-writing exercise on a holiday appeal? If you were to write an essay based on this exercise and the audience was to be your English teacher, would you change your voice in any way?

TASK: WRITING ABOUT A PHASE

The task for this chapter is to present an episode in your life that represented a break from your earlier behavior or outlook, either a phase you went through, a choice you made (or did not make), or advice you took (or did not take). We will ask you to record the episode in such a way as to indicate how it represented a break in your life, what happened during the episode, and what you think its significance has been for you.

To do this task, you will probably want to strike a balance between narration and exposition. You can employ chronological development to tell the story of what happened before, during, and perhaps after the episode; at the same time, you will need to explain just how and why the episode was a meaningful one.

As your audience for this task, we suggest your present English instructor. There is a practical reason for designating such an audience; probably you will be writing to teachers a good deal more than to anyone else over the next few years. But that is not the only reason that we ask you to address your instructor. Your instructor's point of view is bound to differ from your own in more ways than does the point of view of your peers. You will begin to learn here that you have a variety of options open to you that will help you bridge the distance between you and an audience whose perspective and ideas may be quite different from your own. Here, you can stress your voice as student, of course, and rely on your instructor's training and experience to narrow the gap between you. But you can also select a voice other than that of a student, a voice that more specifically expresses the role that you are playing, such as authority on a particular subject or someone sadder but wiser because of a particular choice.

In the remaining sections of this chapter, we will discuss how you can use free writing to generate ideas about your subject; how you can adopt a particular voice to express yourself intelligibly to your audience; how you can arrange your free writing to produce a rough draft of an essay based on both narration and exposition; and what considerations enter into the rewriting of this draft and its shaping into a final product.

WRITING THE ESSAY

Using Free Writing as a Source of Ideas

Earlier in this chapter, you were introduced to free writing and how it can help you discover what you think and feel about a given subject. Now you can try using the two stages of the free-writing exercise to develop what will become the first draft of your essay. Using Peter Elbow's two-step process, begin writing on an episode that represented a break from your past:

Hour 1 Write freely for forty-five minutes on the episode. Sum up the pattern that emerges for fifteen minutes.

Hour 2 Using the summing-up statement of Hour 1, write freely about your emerging pattern for sixty minutes longer.

At the end of this two-hour period, you will have two pieces of writing on the same topic. Hour 1 has hopefully produced a narrative culminating in a main point. Hour 2, on the other hand, has begun with the statement of the main point, and has then explained and discussed it. The next step will be to incorporate these two separate pieces into one piece of prose, thus producing a rough draft. That step is a long one and requires much thought; we will explore it in the section on arrangement.

Here is the work produced by one student in two hours of free writing on a phase:

Hour 1

The phase that I still remember is the one in which I was afraid of the devil. At that time, I was seven years old. I remember the bad dreams I had. I used to live in a small town with many superstitious people. They were talking to me of the devil as a red creature that likes bad boys and girls. I used to go to sleep with the light on because I was afraid of the dark. For me, darkness was the devil's hiding place. Once asleep, I used to dream of the devil coming at night to my town to take away bad children. I remember the dream that I had for so many nights. I was hiding in the basement of my house under three blankets, but still the devil found me and brought me into his world. There he cooked me, with some other boys and girls, for his daily dinner.

During that phase, many friends of mine used to invite me to the movies, but I always had an excuse to stay away. Frightening movies meant to me bad dreams and sleepless nights.

The devil was so impressed in my mind that when my father sent me into the basement to do something I almost cried. My grandfather used to tell me that there was a place in the valley where spirits and ghosts were having fun. The devil was their host. That statement always stood in my mind. The priest used to tell children that if they do bad things they will go to hell. I used to dream of hell as a place with flames where bad people suffered. They were surrounded by red creatures with horns on their heads and forks in their hands. I also dreamed I was on a high cliff where I was standing on the top and looking down in hell where many people were getting roasted. This phase lasted for more than two years.

Summary of Hour 1

I think this phase was caused by the community in which I was living. Also, I'm a very pessimistic individual now who always takes into consideration the negative aspects of life before the positive as a result of this experience.

But also, I'm a mature person. I try to obey my parents and respect other people, and I think this phase had a lot to do with making me that way.

Hour 2

Until I was fifteen I lived in a small town. I knew all the people who lived there. My community was like a big family. The people were very religious and superstitious. They believed in ghosts, devils, and spirits. They influenced my thinking very much. Many times I was told that the devil will take bad boys to hell. That statement stayed in my mind during my childhood and was the cause of many bad dreams. At night the town was very quiet and dark and very scary.

I'm a very pessimistic individual. Every time I watch a ball game, I think that my team is going to lose. Sometimes I even think of myself as a loser because I had so many painful experiences during my childhood.

But I'm not just pessimistic. I think this phase also had a positive effect on me because it made me more mature.

I think I became a more responsible person because of my phase with the devil. I tried to obey my parents and respect other people. When my father asked me to run an errand for him, it made me feel better about myself to do it.

This phase had a lot to do with making me that way. Now, I'm not afraid of hell or devils because I'm a secure individual with a future to think about.

The student now has a considerable amount of material with which to begin his work on a formal essay.

Selecting a Voice as a Bridge Between You and Your Audience

Your audience for this task is your present English instructor. Using inference and, if you like, role playing, try to determine what your teacher's point of view might be with regard to the episode that you will be writing about. Once you have done so, your next step is to consider what voice you might best select in order to bridge the gap between your point of view and your teacher's.

Of course, you can address your teacher simply from the point of view of a student. But you may wish to play a less traditionally subordinate role and to adopt a less formal voice. In writing about a break in your behavior or outlook, you are probably going to focus on a change from one sort of role that many people play in life to another. Perhaps you will be able to express your ideas and feelings about this episode most authentically if you select the voice expressing one of these roles, either the earlier one or the one developed by the change. Or perhaps you will do better to take a stance that represents the distance you have traveled since the episode, looking back on the episode from a role that you identify with now. In making the choice of voice, keep your teacher in mind. Which voice will most effectively communicate to your reader?

Once you identify your voice, review your two free-writing exercises. Where do you sound most in character? Are there thoughts expressed that seem out of character for the voice you wish to emphasize? Make whatever changes seem appropriate to the voice you have selected.

At this point, you might want to look back at the two hours in which a student wrote on his phase with the devil (pp. 77–79). What voice might the student select in order to present his experience more intelligibly? What would be the effect, for example, if he acted the pessimist who looks back on his phase with some resentment about the harm he experienced? How might the essay be different if he acted the secure individual who looks back on his childhood fears with a certain amusement? Which voice would appeal most to his reader?

You now want to continue to think and write as honestly and completely as you can in the voice you have selected, as you set about arranging your material into a rough draft.

Answering the following questions of the "Audience Analysis Guide" will help you to prepare to write for your audience.

——— AUDIENCE ANALYSIS GUIDE ———

1. **Who is my audience?**
2. **What is the frame of reference of this audience?**
3. **What point of view is my audience likely to have on my subject?**
4. **How do my own frame of reference and point of view differ from those of my reader?**
5. **How can I bridge any gap that exists between my reader's point of view and my own?**
6. **Which of my voices am I selecting as I write on this subject? How can the voice that I select bridge the gap between my audience and me?**

Arranging Your Essay: The Shaping Idea, Narration, and Exposition

Let's begin to shape the two pieces of free writing that you have produced into a rough draft of a prepared essay. At this point, you might focus on the problem of developing an effective arrangement strategy. You should try to come up with a shaping idea. You might also begin to decide at what points in the essay you will use narration to convey your experiences during the phase or episode and at what points you will use explanation to relate how these experiences represented a break from your previous behavior or outlook.

The Shaping Idea. In devising a shaping idea for this task (see Chapter 1, "Shaping the Subject"), one of the key questions that you need to address is "What is the particular significance of this episode?" Your statement of your shaping idea will embody the answer to this question.

To determine the answer, examine the two pieces of work produced in the two-step free-writing exercise. Do the following:

1. Examine your statement about the emerging pattern made at the end of Hour 1 and used at the start of Hour 2.
2. Identify a sentence that captures the unique quality (feeling, mood, tone, experience) of the episode.
3. If there is no such sentence, write a new sentence that does capture this unique quality.

4. Then, expand or refine the chosen sentence so that it includes (a) a clearly defined time period and (b) words that describe the significance of the episode.
5. Now check the sentence to see if it meets the other requirements of the statement of an organizing idea: precision, lack of ambiguity, and grammatical correctness.
6. Many writers do not know precisely how to organize their thoughts until after they have written the rough draft, and you may find that your shaping idea isn't clear to you until this later stage. The final version of your essay, however, should be clearly guided by one well-defined idea.

Now evaluate the following statements of the shaping ideas that some students used while writing drafts in the fulfillment of this task. Compare them with your own.

1. <u>Title:</u> My Dental Hygiene Phase

   <u>Shaping Idea:</u> Looking back on the years 1976–1978, I laugh when I remember the neurotic behavior that marked my dental hygiene phase.

2. <u>Title:</u> My Brief Career

   <u>Shaping Idea:</u> Years of listening to my mother's stories of her days spent in the theater launched me on my exciting but brief theatrical career.

3. <u>Title:</u> Learning to Live in New York City

   <u>Shaping Idea:</u> My trip from Bogota, Columbia, to Queens, New York, two years ago covered a distance I have only begun to take in stride.

4. <u>Title:</u> Two Generations Going Through Changes

   <u>Shaping Idea:</u> Psychologists say that girls experience tremendous changes in their lives between the ages of fifteen and sixteen and that women experience their change of life or menopause between forty and fifty-five; in my case, my mother's changes and mine clashed.

Narration and Exposition in the Service of Narration. Once you have identified and stated your shaping idea, a second key question in writing about an episode is "How do you order or arrange experiences that occurred over a period of time in such a way as to convey their realness to your audience, at the same time showing how they represented a break in your earlier behavior or outlook?'' In answering this question, you may employ at least two modes of writing: narration and exposition.

As we saw in Chapter 2, the narrative mode is a natural method of telling a story step by step. It is obviously a valuable mode to use in the retelling of experiences. An additional mode, exposition, will also be useful in writing this task. Exposition explains, summarizes, or interprets an experience. Because the task for this chapter is more complex than the task for Chapter 2, you will need to use exposition as well as narration.

In Chapter 2, you wrote about an incident of short duration. Here, you may be writing about a phase, a period of longer duration: three months, six months, even two years. You will want to decide when to come in for a close-up of a particular event or experience that occupies a short period within the episode and therefore to use narration. You must also decide when to move back for a wider view or when to plunge into a deeper examination, both of which require exposition. Narration expands time and provides emphasis; exposition contracts time and comments on significance.

Using Narration in Writing on a Significant Episode.   Review the section in Chapter 2 on narration (pp. 50–56). Now turn to the writing you produced during Hours 1 and 2 of the free-writing exercise. In all likelihood, the dominant mode of the work produced in Hour 1 is narrative. (This may or may not be true of Hour 2.) Hence, much of what you have already produced is arranged in chronological sequence. At this point, place the statement of your organizing idea at the top of a sheet of paper. Now do the following:

1. Read Hours 1 and 2 of your free-writing exercise.
2. Identify the narrative sections.
3. Check the chronology of the narrative sections for accuracy of sequence, effectiveness of writing, and time indicators (transitions, dates, and so on).
4. Consider your audience. Does your audience require a lot of background through a narrative account of the episode? Where is background most needed in the narrative?
5. Evaluate the narrated events. Are all the events of equal importance? If not, identify the events and experiences that you would like to zoom in on for a close-up, as well as those that might best be left in the background. This decision moves you toward identifying what should be narrated and what should be explained by exposition.
6. Now rewrite the ''close-up'' sections, providing them with vivid and concrete details.
7. As you rewrite, add time indicators (dates and transitions) to provide continuity.
8. Write on one side of your paper only.

Now, let's move on to the matter of exposition.

Exposition in the Service of Narration.   Unlike the purely narrative mode, the expository mode, when used in a narrative framework, does not recount events in chronological order; rather, it summarizes, explains, or interprets them. The skill that is required in the development of exposition in the service of narration is one that will test your ability to condense into a meaningful whole experiences that have occurred over long periods of time. Narration shows what your experience was like, and exposition tells about it. Both have their place.

The technique of summarizing is not something new to you. In our day-to-day activities, we all constantly condense experiences, conversations, and happenings because doing so allows us to extract the essence of an experience from all of the unnecessary details. Thus, when we summarize, we engage in heavy editing by asking ourselves, "What information can I omit without significantly changing the experience I am telling about?"

As an example, what is your favorite spectator sport? Have you ever noticed the difference between the sportscaster's on-the-air report on the action of a sporting event while it is occurring and the report of the event prepared for a newspaper the next day? The first is a blow-by-blow account, detailed and unedited, and if recorded, it would take up as much time as the game itself. The second account is condensed. It is likely to be heavily edited, with details only of highlights, and will probably also include interpretation or explanation. The impulse to comment (explain or interpret) is one that comes almost automatically from the writer's attempt to fuse highlights with selected details.

The opportunity to have some distance (time) between the actual event and the reporting of the event is valuable in the use of exposition for it forces you to ask yourself how you felt about the event when it happened and how you feel about it now. The differences between the two sets of feelings can provide the basis for a dynamic interpretation of the event. During narration, you are getting close to the action, capturing its immediacy through sensory details. During exposition, you are getting away from the action and applying your powers of interpretation and analysis to the event.

There are then several forms that exposition can take in the service of narration: (1) straight summary, which retains narration's effect of placing the reader in the scene and which is a condensed telling of what happened, and (2) explanation and interpretation, which remove the reader from the action and ask him or her to contemplate its meaning or singificance. Explanation and interpretation both clarify, increasing our understanding of an event; but the former is more emphatically objective and factual, whereas the latter tends to have a greater element of subjectivity and hence is more open to argument.

By way of example, think again of a sportswriter. If, when reporting on a track meet, the sportswriter tells you that Smith beat Jones in the mile, that the race was close, and that the winning time was 3:58, he or she is summarizing the event. If the sportswriter tells you that Smith, who was expected to break the record, failed, he or she is explaining. If the sportswriter suggests that the poor condition of the track was the main reason that Smith failed to set a new record, he or she is interpreting.

Following is the first draft of the essay written from the free-writing exercises on the student's phase with the devil. Notice how he has combined the two exercises in writing his draft (pp. 77–79).

MY PHASE WITH THE DEVIL

I still remember the days when I was afraid of the devil. During this period, I learned to be a responsible individual.

I lived in a small town with many superstitious individuals. I knew all the people that lived there. My community was like a big family that shared the good and the bad things in life. There, the old people influenced my thinking very much. They used to tell me stories about the devil that stayed on my mind for months. By the time I was seven, I had started to have bad dreams. I used to dream of the devil as a huge red creature, half human and half animal. I used to go to sleep with the light on because I was afraid of the dark. For me, darkness was the devil's hiding place. Once asleep, I used to dream of the devil coming at night to my town and taking away bad children. Some of the children in town were my best friends, and seeing them alive each morning was a great relief to me.

I remember a dream that I had for many nights. I was hiding in the basement in an empty barrel. The devil searched my house until he found me and brought me into his world of flames. There, he cooked me with some other boys and girls for his daily dinner.

During that phase, many friends used to invite me to the movies, but I always had an excuse to stay away from the theater. To me, horror movies meant dreams and sleepless nights. The devil was so impressed on my mind that when my father sent me to the basement to do something, I almost cried. My grandfather used to tell me that there was a place in the valley where ghosts were having fun. The devil was their host.

That story always stayed in my mind, and many times I dreamed about it. I dreamed of standing at the top of a high cliff and looking down into hell, a valley where many people roasted. The town priest used to tell children that if they did well they would end up in heaven. Otherwise, they would go to hell.

These dreams considerably affected my character. I became a more responsible individual. I tried to obey my parents and respect other people. I also became pessimistic, but in a positive way. What I mean is that I tried to do my best in defeating my pessimism. My dreams were very painful, but they helped me to become a mature person.

This period of unpleasant dreams ended when I was about ten years old. Now, I'm not afraid of hell or devils because I'm a secure individual with a future to think about.

Where in this draft did the student use narration? Where did he use summary or explanation or interpretation? How would you advise him to revise? Where does he need more detailed narration? Where does he need to explain or interpret more thoroughly?

Using Exposition in Writing on a Significant Episode.   Let's turn to the two hours of free writing from which you have already taken and rewritten your close-up narrative sections. Now you will want to identify the sections that summarize, explain, and interpret. If you started your writing in Hour 2 with a statement of the pattern that emerged in Hour 1, you will probably have in the Hour 2 material a fair amount of writing that already summarizes, explains, and interprets. The instructions that follow will serve as your guidelines for rewriting the sections from Hours 1 and 2 that have the expository impulse. Again, place the refined statement of your shaping idea at the top of a sheet of paper. Now, do the following:

1. Read Hours 1 and 2 of the work you produced by free writing.
2. Identify the sections with the expository impulse.
3. Evaluate these sections to see whether they (a) summarize narrative portions of the episode; (b) explain a particular action, conversation, or pattern of behavior that occurred during the episode; or (c) interpret any part of the episode. Note the specific function of each section of your free-writing in the margins.
4. Now evaluate also those sections that you decided during your narrative rewrite would serve you better as background. They too will be turned into expository sections.
5. Now rewrite all the identified sections of summary, explanation, and interpretation, using the refined shaping idea to get started. As you write these expository sections, remember that you are striving to summarize gaps of time not accounted for during the close-up sections; to explain specific situations; and to interpret individual experiences, conversations, events, and actions, as well as to interpret the significance of the episode

as a whole. Additionally each section should show its relatedness to your shaping idea.

6. Again, write on one side of your paper only.

Writing the Rough Draft: Cutting and Pasting

The next writing activity is not writing at all, but it is an integral part of the writing process. You can now literally splice the rewritten narrative sections and the rewritten expository sections to form the entire first draft. You do this splicing by cutting and pasting. You will need (1) your rewritten narrative and expository sections (put away your Hours 1 and 2 free writing but do not discard them); and (2) more paper, a pair of scissors, and some rubber cement or Scotch tape. You will also need all the courage you can muster, for many people are timid about cutting up their work. Do not be timid; out of this seeming destruction will emerge a new construction. Furthermore you can feel flattered that you are in the good company of many published writers who engage in cutting and pasting at some point in their writing process. Now do the following:

1. Read through the two rewritten sections, identifying and labeling potential parts of the essay, starting with the introduction and conclusion. Label them in the margins with a colored pencil. Use either letters or numbers to mark the sequence.
2. Decide what will follow your introduction, and label it in the margin also.
3. Continue this labeling process until you have labeled everything from these two narrative and expository sections. (This whole process requires a great deal of reading and rereading.)
4. Now that you have labeled all the sections numerically or alphabetically, cut out the introductory section and paste it on a new sheet of paper, which will become page 1 of your rough draft. Next, cut out the section labeled 1 or A, which is to follow your introduction, and paste it below, leaving three or four lines between the end of the introduction and the beginning of this new section. Continue in the same way until you have cut and pasted all the labeled sections through to your conclusion. You have now completed the first draft of your essay.

While you are taking a break between drafts of your own essay, read the following finished essay on a phase that a student writer went through. Notice his placement of his shaping idea and his blending of narration with exposition.

DAYDREAM BELIEVER

One of the advantages of youth is that you may indulge yourself in the wildest of fantasies. When I was young, I was an avid comic-book reader. You might say I was a fanatic. Wherever I went, my comics went with me. I anxiously awaited every new issue. My superheroes depicted adventurous deeds that I could easily identify with. Their experiences were for me, at the age of ten, very real. I portrayed, moreover, every character that I read.

Every one of them was capable of performing superhuman acts. Each was unique, possessing specialized powers. Some were able to fly, to become invisible, or to change their form, and some had strength far beyond that of mortals. Each superhero was easily identifiable by his name and costume, which added to the story line of the particular plot.

I remember one particular afternoon I was with my parents in the country. I was reading my favorite comic, Spider Man. Nearby some rocks towered above me. I instantly sensed danger and immediately scaled the rocks as the "wild web slinger." When I reached the top, my "spider sense" was tingling. I found myself face to face with my arch enemy, "The Lizard." We immediately became locked in a ferocious hand-to-hand, life-to-death struggle. A large crowd gathered below, watching in suspense. I blinded the reptilian creature with a face full of web. With a swift kick, I knocked him off the cliff in defeat.

It seemed as if I was continually reprimanded for living vicariously. My mother, as all mothers, was always concerned for my well-being. She apparently misconstrued my mysterious behavior. She also, however, seemed to possess the understanding and the realization that one day I would outgrow it.

All of my allowance was used to purchase comic books. On many occasions, I read my comic book in class. I would secretly place the comic in a text and read and dream while the class was in session. Although I managed to maintain a normal class standard, I had to expend more effort while dividing myself between two worlds. My teacher was suspicious of my actions and thus felt I was not giving my all. She felt I had a better academic potential than I was showing, and she periodically referred me to the dean for special counseling.

I recall that once in my sixth-grade math class I was very bored. In the next moment, I was Dr. Bruce Banner, walking the streets of New York. Suddenly people were running toward me in panic. They were screaming hysterically, fearing for their lives. They were running from a monster terrorizing the city. I, too, started to run away, but I was thrown to the ground by the crowd and lay helpless as the monster approached. With my heartbeat ever increasing, I knew that transformation would soon occur. In seconds, I was eight feet tall, with green skin and solid muscle. Dr. Bruce Banner once again became the Incredible Hulk.

In this period of my life, I did not have the same interests as my friends. As my friends emulated their sports heroes, I had my superheroes. Sometimes, in the midst of a game, I would be criticized for my lack of attention. I would let a ball slip by me, or I would miss a throw. This angered my teammates as it sometimes led to the loss of a game.

Despite any obstacles placed before me, I persevered. My world was filled with fantasy, and superheroes fired my imagination with adventure. Over the years, I have retained my vivid imagination. However, I now apply it to more practical ends.

What was the writer's attitude toward the daydream period of his youth? To what degree did he still identify with the role of "daydream believer"? To what degree had he distanced himself from that role? How would you describe the voice that he selected in order to write his essay?

FOCUS: PARAGRAPH STRUCTURE

Essays are divided into paragraphs as an aid to both the reader and the writer. The paragraph breaks in an essay help the reader to follow the flow of thought from point to point and of conversation from speaker to speaker. In addition, some paragraphs serve to emphasize for the reader the writer's major points by repeating a point developed in a previous paragraph.

Dividing an essay into paragraphs also helps the writer to develop his or her shaping idea sequentially throughout an essay and to emphasize special points. The writer of narrative may wish to use paragraph breaks to separate the major stages of the event, whereas the writer of exposition will use paragraphs to develop the primary aspects of his or her subject. Reexamine "Daydream Believer" in the previous section (pp. 86–88), for the paragraph structure. What rationale had the writer for his paragraph breaks?

Because of the importance of the paragraph, in writing your essay you will want to pay attention to the structure of each paragraph. Just as essays have a beginning, a middle, and an end, so most effective paragraphs have a beginning, a middle, and an end. You state the point of the paragraph in what can be called a *topic sentence* and then develop that point or topic in several other sentences. If the paragraph is sufficiently long, or if you want added emphasis, you may want a concluding sentence as well.

Notice in the following paragraph that the third sentence introduces the paragraph (after two initial background sentences), the next five develop the topic, and the last concludes emphatically by restating the topic sentence.

I have long wondered just what my strength is as a writer. I am often filled with tremendous enthusiasm for a subject, yet my writing about it will seem a sorry attempt. *Above all, I possess a driving sincerity, that prime virtue of any creative worker.* I write only what I believe to be the absolute truth—even if I must ruin the theme in so doing. In this respect, I feel far superior to those glib people in my classes who often garner better grades than I do. They are so often pitiful frauds, artificial, insincere. They have a line that works. They do not write from the depths of their hearts. Nothing of theirs was *ever* born of pain. *Many an incoherent yet sincere piece of writing has outlived the polished product.*

—**Theodore Roethke,** *On the Poet and His Craft*

The following paragraph begins with the topic sentence but has no conclusion, as the writer was more interested in the details of his day than he was in emphasizing the general idea of how he passed his time:

Do you want to know how I pass my time? I rise at eight or thereabouts—& go to my barn—say good-morning to the horse, & give him his breakfast. (It goes to my heart to give him a cold one, but it can't be helped.) Then, pay a visit to my cow— cut up a pumpkin or two for her, & stand by to see her eat it—for it's a pleasant sight to see a cow move her jaws—she does it so mildly & with such a sanctity.— My own breakfast over, I go to my workroom & light my fire—then spread my M.S.S. on the table—take one business squint at it, & fall to with a will. At $2\frac{1}{2}$ P.M. I hear a preconcerted knock at my door, which (by request) continues till I rise & go to the door, which serves to wean me effectively from my writing, however interested I may be. My friends the horse & cow now demand their dinner—& I go & give it them. My own dinner over, I rig my sleigh & with my mother or sisters start off for the village—& if it be a Literary World day, great is the satisfaction thereof.—My evenings I spend in a sort of mesmeric state in my room—not being able to read—only now & then skimming over some large-printed book.

—**Herman Melville**

In the following paragraph, the writer has only a conclusion, or one could say that he placed his topic sentence at the end. This arrangement creates a dramatic, climactic effect.

When I first began to describe the little world of yesteryear that lives again in my books, that small corner of a French province, scarcely known even to Frenchmen, where the vacations of my school days were spent, I had no idea that I would attract the attention of foreign readers. We are all quite convinced of our utter singularity. We forget that the books which we ourselves found enchanting, those of George Eliot or of Dickens, of Tolstoy or Dostoevsky, or of Selma Lagerlöf, describe countries very different from our own, people of another race and another religion; and yet we loved them, because we recognized ourselves in them. All humanity is in this or that peasant back home, and all the landscapes in the world coalesce in the horizons familiar to our childish eyes. The novelist's gift is precisely his power to make plain the universal quality concealed in that sheltered world where we were born, and where we first learned to love and suffer.

—Francois Mauriac

Joan Didion's topic sentence in the following paragraph asks a question, and her conclusion summarizes the answers given in the developing sentences. This arrangement also creates a climactic effect:

Why did I write it down? In order to remember, of course, but exactly what was it I wanted to remember? How much of it actually happened? Did any of it? Why do I keep a notebook at all? It is easy to deceive oneself on all those scores. The impulse to write things down is a peculiarly compulsive one, inexplicable to those who do not share it, useful only accidentally, only secondarily, in the way that any compulsion tries to justify itself. I suppose that it begins or does not begin in the cradle. Although I have felt compelled to write things down since I was five years old, I doubt that my daughter ever will, for she is a singularly blessed and accepting child, delighted with life exactly as life presents itself to her, unafraid to wake up. Keepers of private notebooks are a different breed altogether, lonely and resistant rearrangers of things, anxious malcontents, children afflicted apparently at birth with some presentiment of loss.

The following paragraph has no distinct topic sentence. The writer's point is understandable, however. Her topic sentence might have been, "Because the eyes can communicate in an instant, communication between two people in our fast-paced technological age is possible, but how can we learn to communicate in this way?" The topic sentence has been omitted because the writer was following a line of thought—delineating the aspects of a problem—rather than making a point:

Messages are conveyed by the eyes, sometimes by no words at all. It is no excuse to say that technology has accelerated our life to the point where we pass others without noticing them, without contacting, or without a real meeting. A real meeting can take place in one instant. But how does that come about? How do we reach a moment when in one instant we can communicate with another human being?

—**Marya Mannes,** "Television: The Splitting Image"

SOME PRACTICE WITH PARAGRAPH STRUCTURE

1. Three topic sentences are given for each of the paragraphs below. Can you decide which one is the actual topic sentence written by the author of the paragraph? Explain your choice in each case.

a. _____

_____

Where is Johnny? He is, you will recall, a college undergraduate, let's say a freshman. He has typically been exposed to a number of years of drill founded on a traditional and dubious grammar; he has done some writing of quite variable amount and character; he has read a few standard works of literature and probably a slender but startling miscellany of contemporary fare; he doesn't know how to pursue an idea through a piece of prose that has one; he concocts what he considers English for his English teacher and is shocked if anybody else expects this odd behavior of him; and, as there is no guarantee that he spells correctly, Professor Stackblowe is quite likely to be displeased with him. He has grown up believing that English means literacy because that is what he has been taught, and if it hasn't taken very well he is rather apologetic about it. Probably nobody has had time, strength, or inclination to help him very far toward competence. But, perhaps just because he is now eighteen or thereabouts, he can be helped toward competence and, if necessary, literacy into the bargain.

—"Why the Devil Don't You Teach Freshmen to Write?" *Saturday Review*

1. Literacy is the goal of Johnny's education.
2. Johnny has been given a incorrect definition of literacy.
3. The beginning of wisdom is to "take the student where he is."

b. From kids stealing candy bars to multi-million-dollar frauds, property crimes manifest a lack of concern for other people. _____

_____

Children living in places where people have no rights that they are capable of enforcing will rarely have a regard for rights of others. Since legal rights tend to reflect important values of society, such individuals have little regard for things society considers important. To know that police take bribes, the church treasurer ran off with the building fund, the construction contractor swindled your father out of the cost of new roofing, and three of your friends make more in a night stripping cars than you make in a week washing them is not conducive to respect for the law. Some finally rationalize that they would be fools to play it straight when everyone they know is on the make. The next step may be rolling a drunk. For suburban youth living in materialistic abundance the motivations for rapidly increasing property crime are different, diverse, and more difficult to identify. Neglect, anxiety, family breakup, emptiness, the loneliness of the individual in huge high schools and lack of identity contribute. Faceless youngsters of affluent families steal cars, burglarize suburban homes, and commit acts of malicious destruction most often because nothing else in their lives seems important.

—**Ramsey Clark,** "The Many Faces of Crime"

1. While the contributory factors are many and varied, crime is chiefly the result of poverty.
2. While the contributory factors are many and varied, the effects of property crimes cost billions annually.
3. While the contributory factors are many and varied, the capability for crime develops in early childhood when character is forming.

c. _____

_____

Deep-well disposal of chemical wastes by the U.S. Army near Denver led to earth tremors and small earthquakes as well as to contamination of the subsoil. The Navy dumps tons of raw sewage into offshore waters, and its facilities, such as the notorious Fire Fighting School in San Diego, throw off pollutants into the air. Vessels carrying herbicides to Viet Nam and other areas of the world could possibly provoke one of history's greatest catastrophes. Should one ship sink and should the drums containing the chemicals be ruptured, marine organisms for miles around would be destroyed, thus reducing the oxygen supply available to mankind. The transfer of these herbicides through food to humans is another specter, given the fantastic geometric progress of the concentration of these chemicals from plankton on up the food-chain to man himself. Municipal waste disposal practices are, for many towns and cities, primitive; and where waste is treated, effluents still upset the ecology of lakes, streams, and bays.

—from *Ecotatics*

1. Waste disposal is a great threat to mankind.
2. Government activity in sewage and solid waste disposal and in defense research has also burgeoned into environmental violence.
3. Governmental supervision of sewage and waste disposal is inadequate.

2. Write a topic sentence for each of the following paragraphs.

a. _____

_____

There were four of us in the long piroque, all of an age. For a long moment we were speechless. At last we said hello, and they answered in warm gay voices. We drifted the boat into the cove and began to speak to them. Two of the girls were sisters. The three of them had come to visit a relative who kept a fine summer lodge in the woods across the bayou from the camp. One of the sisters was fifteen and the others were seventeen. They were aglow with fresh and slender beauty, and their bathing suits were bright flags of color. Their impact upon us was overwhelming. We grew silly, tongue-tied, said foolish things we did not mean to say, shoved one another about in the boat, and finally overturned it. The loreleis laughed musical little laughs. They seemed unbearably beautiful. We had no idea what to do about it.

—**Thomas Sancton,** "The Silver Horn," *Harper's Magazine* (Feb. 1944).

b. _____

_____

For example, did they go to live in his father's castle? If so, how did she get on with the queen who was, incidentally, her mother-in-law? How many children did she have? Were they well adjusted or did she have to seek "professional help" for them? How did she handle the problem of sibling rivalry, which in this case may have been over no smaller a goal than the throne itself? How much did she see of her husband? Did wars, affairs or state, and commuting time ruin his family life? How could she possibly keep house without detergents? What did she do with herself when the children were all in school? She couldn't very well spend her time cleaning out the closets, as is sometimes the refuge of non-princesses. Did she grow old gracefully? Did she outlive her husband and, if so, by how many years? What kind of pension could she claim in an era that preceded the advent of Social Security? In short, what was it like to live happily ever after?

—**Juanita Kreps,** "What Was It Like To Live Happily Ever After?" *Vital Speeches* (Dec. 15, 1964).

c. _____

_____

We know that, far from attracting her, whiskers and mustaches only make her nervous and gloomy, so that man had to go in for somersaults, tilting with lances, performing feats of parlor magic to win her attention; he also had to bring candy, flowers, and the furs of animals. It is common knowledge that in spite of these "love displays" the male is constantly being turned down, insulted, thrown out of the house. It is rather comforting, then, to discover that the peacock, for all his gorgeous plumage, does not have a particularly easy time of courtship; none of the males in the world do. The first peahen, it turned out, was only faintly stirred by her suitor's beautiful train. She would often go quietly to sleep while he was whisking it around. The *Britannica* tells us that the peacock actually had to learn a certain little trick to wake her up and revive her interest; he had to learn to vibrate his quills so as to make a rustling sound. In ancient time man himself, observing the ways of the peacock, probably tried vibrating his whiskers to make a rustling sound; if so, it didn't get him anywhere. He had to go in for something else; so, among other things he went in for gifts. It is not unlikely that he got this idea from certain flies and birds who were making no headway at all with rustling sounds.

—**James Thurber,** "Courtship Through the Ages," *My World and Welcome To It*

d. _____

    _____

Consider the beer can. It was beautiful—as beautiful as the clothespin, as inevitable as the wine bottle, as dignified and reassuring as the fire hydrant. A tranquil cylinder of delightfully resonant metal, it could be opened in an instant, requiring only the application of a handy gadget freely dispensed by every grocer. Who can forget the small, symmetrical thrill of those two triangular punctures, the dainty pffff, the little crest of suds that foamed eagerly in the exultation of release? Now we are given, instead, a top beetling with an ugly, shmoo-shaped "tab," which after fiercely resisting the tugging, bleeding fingers of the thirsty man, threatens his lips with a dangerous and hideous hole. However, we have discovered a way to thwart Progress, usually so unthwartable. Turn the beer can upside down and open the bottom. The bottom is still the way the top used to be. True, this operation gives the beer an unsettling jolt, and the sight of a consistently inverted beer can might make people edgy, not to say queasy. But the latter difficulty could be eliminated if manufacturers would design cans that looked the same whichever end was up, like playing cards. What we need is Progress with an escape hatch.

—**John Updike,** "Beer Can," *Assorted Prose*

3. Which paragraphs in Exercises 1 and 2 have concluding sentences? Why has a conclusion been added in each case?

4. Develop the following topic sentences into paragraphs, experimenting by placing the topic sentence in different positions in the paragraphs. Use details or examples to support your point. Add a conclusion where you think one advisable.

   a. Registration for courses each semester is a hassle.
   b. Because of their desire for higher ratings, television news programs have become mostly entertainment.
   c. Instead of fulfilling their traditional role of providing fun, sports have deteriorated into hostile, often violent, competition.

5. Develop well-structured paragraphs based on the following topics. Word the topic sentence in each as clearly as possible. Add a concluding sentence if you think it effective.

   a. A free time pursuit.
   b. A recent observation of honesty.
   c. A current fad.
   d. The therapeutic value of a pet.

REWRITING

Obtaining Feedback on Your Rough Draft

Before you move into the revision of your first or rough draft, be sure that you have rested. Remember that you spent at least four hours moving through the rough draft, so if you worked continuously, take a break of twenty-four hours, unless, of course, the deadline is imminent. A break of a day can help to distance you from your work and can provide the objectivity that you will need in the reworking of your essay. You may also need this time for your peers or your instructor to evaluate your first effort. Before reading further, refer to the rewriting section in Chapter 2 for comments on adding and editing.

Your evaluators—yourself, your instructor, your peers—should organize their evaluations as before, according to the four questions of the "Audience Response Guide." Play the role of your intended audience (your instructor) as you read.

———— AUDIENCE RESPONSE GUIDE ————

1. **What does the writer want to say in this paper? What is his or her purpose in writing? What does he or she want the paper to mean?**
2. **How does the paper affect the reader for whom it was intended?**
3. **How effective has the writer been in conveying his or her purpose and meaning?**
4. **How should the paper be revised to better fulfill its purpose and meaning?**

Consider at this time the following peer evaluation of the rough draft of the student essay "My Phase with the Devil" (pp. 84–85). Compare your own evaluation of the draft with that of the peer group by answering the four questions of the "Audience Response Guide" before reading their answers.

1. The group felt that the writer wanted to convey how his fear of the devil had made him a more mature and responsible individual.
2. Playing the role of teacher, the group felt that the writer was writing as an adult who, perhaps like many adults, had matured because of a bad experience. His voice thus helped to create a bridge between him and his intended audience.
3. The group liked the writer's vivid use of detail, although they would have liked him to draw in closer to one of his dreams for a more thorough,

blow-by-blow account that might have let them experience his fear more fully.

4. The group felt that he could have explained more clearly just how the episode led him to become more responsible, because the connection between his pessimism and his responsibility was vague. As they felt the essay's organization was haphazard and did not seem to lead logically to the conclusion, they suggested that the writer rearrange his material by grouping together all of the stories told him by his elders, then all of his dreams, followed by their effects on him at the time they occurred, as well as their effects on him now.

Following is a revised version of "My Phase with the Devil." How well have the peer group's suggestions been incorporated? Did the writer make any additional changes himself? What additional changes might he have made?

MY PHASE WITH THE DEVIL

I still remember the days when I was afraid of the devil. Although this was a painful period for me, it helped me to become a more responsible individual.

I lived in a small town with many superstitious individuals. I knew all the people that lived there. My community was like a big family that shared the good and the bad things in life, including a belief in the devil.

The old people influenced my thinking very much. They used to tell me stories about the devil that stayed on my mind for months. My grandfather used to tell me that there was a place in the valley where ghosts were having fun. The devil was their host. Even the town priest spoke of the devil. He used to tell children that if they did well they would end up in heaven. Otherwise, they would go to hell.

My grandfather's story always stayed in my mind, and many times I dreamed about it. I dreamed of standing on a high cliff and looking down into hell, a valley where many people roasted. The devil was there, a huge red creature, half human and half animal. He stood over the people and laughed and stabbed their bodies with a pitchfork of flames.

I had other bad dreams as well. Sometimes I dreamed that I was hiding in the basement in an empty barrel. The devil searched my house until he found me and brought me into his world of flames. There, he cooked me with some other boys and girls for his daily dinner. I often dreamed of the devil coming at night to my town and taking away bad children. Some of them were my best friends, and seeing them alive each morning was a great relief to me.

Of course, I used to go to sleep with the light on because I was afraid of the dark. For me, darkness was the devil's hiding place. The devil was so impressed on my mind that when my father sent me to the basement to do something, I almost cried. And when my friends used to invite me to the movies, I always had an excuse to stay away from the theater. To me, horror movies meant bad dreams and sleepless nights.

These fears affected my character very much. I became a pessimistic individual. Every time I watched a ball game, I'd think that my team was going to lose. Sometimes I'd even think of myself as a loser because I had had so many painful experiences during my childhood.

But I tried to be pessimistic in a positive way. What I mean is that I tried to do my best in defeating my pessimism by working harder to make things turn out for the best. I became a more responsible individual because of my bad dream period. I tried to obey my parents and respect other people. My dreams were very painful, but they helped me to become a mature person.

This bad dream period ended when I was ten years old. Now, I'm not afraid of hell or devils because I'm a secure individual with a future to think about.

Rearranging

In revising your rough draft, you should decide whether the pattern of arrangement you have devised in the cutting-and-pasting stage of your writing process is effective. Start by testing your shaping idea once again. Does it suggest a pattern of organization for your essay, and if it does, does your essay's arrangement parallel the pattern it suggests? If it does not, rephrase your statement of your shaping idea so that it reflects the essay's arrangement pattern.

Next, examine the essay to see if the paragraphs follow each other in the most effective order. If sequences are askew, rearrange them.

Now, inspect the structure of your paragraphs. Does each have a topic sentence that is clearly related to the organizing idea of the essay? Do all the sentences in each paragraph develop the topic sentence? Is the topic sentence developed fully? Now rearrange any sentences that do not follow a logical pattern within your paragraphs. (Often narrative paragraphs do not have topic sentences because the subject is constantly changing through the passing of time.)

Finally, in completing the task for this chapter, evaluate the essay to see that it reflects an artful balance of narration, typified by specific details, and exposition, typified by summary, explanation, and interpretation. Evaluate the balance by counting first the paragraphs in which the dominant mode is narration and then those in which the dominant mode is exposition. If one or the other mode dominates overwhelmingly, ask yourself the following questions:

1. Have I included too many close-up narratives at the expense of the broader picture? If your answer is "no," do nothing and move on. If your answer is "yes," determine what close-ups can be omitted without damaging the essay and cut them out. Add the necessary exposition.
2. Have I tended to be too general, thus sacrificing the close-up? If your answer is "no," do nothing and move on. If your answer is "yes," determine what general exposition can be omitted and cut it out. Go into more detail to bring your narrative to life.
3. Have I written consistently in a voice that works as an effective bridge between my point of view and that of my reader? If your answer is "no," rephrase those passages in which you sound out of character.

Editing

Transitions.   The most well-organized paragraph may appear disorganized if transitions have not been used or if those used are imprecise. Effective transitions point out for the reader the essential unity of the sentence, the paragraph, and the essay. Reread the student essay "My Phase with the Devil" for the transitions that unify these various elements of writing. (For a review of transitions, read the discussion in Chapter 2, pp. 56–58.)

Topic Sentences.   Once again, review your topic sentences. Should transitions be added to relate the paragraph to the essay? Should any other words or phrases be added to make this important sentence as precise a summary of the paragraph as possible?

Mechanics.   Review earlier samples of your writing on which mechanical errors have been noted for guidelines to the spelling, punctuation, and grammatical errors common in your writing. Work with the handbook at the back of the book, if necessary, in making these corrections.

Finally, rewrite your draft, bearing in mind that even at this stage new material can be generated by the act of writing. In other words, do not mechanically rewrite or edit only, but continue to develop new ideas about your subject to include in your essay.

Now, revise and edit your rough draft.

BECOMING AWARE OF YOURSELF AS A WRITER

Now you might want to turn to your journal and write down your feelings about your progress as a writer, using if you like the following questions as guidelines:

1. Has free writing really "freed" you to think and write more clearly and fully about your subject? In what ways has free writing helped you in your writing thus far? In what ways might it be helpful in the future?

2. How easy was it for you to play a role as you wrote? Did the experiment of "selecting a voice" help you to express yourself more understandably? Would you be able to "select a voice" in another writing situation?

3. What new perspectives on yourself did you gain in writing about a significant episode in your life?

4. How did the writing process suggested in this chapter help or hinder the writing of your essay?

5. What was the single most difficult aspect of the writing task for you? How did you resolve it?

6. How much total time did you spend in the writing of the essay assigned in this chapter? Was this more time than you usually spend on an essay? How did you spend this time? Was this extra time beneficial?

7. Jot down below any additional observations you may have at this point about your behavior as a writer. Has your behavior been changed in any way by what you have learned so far?

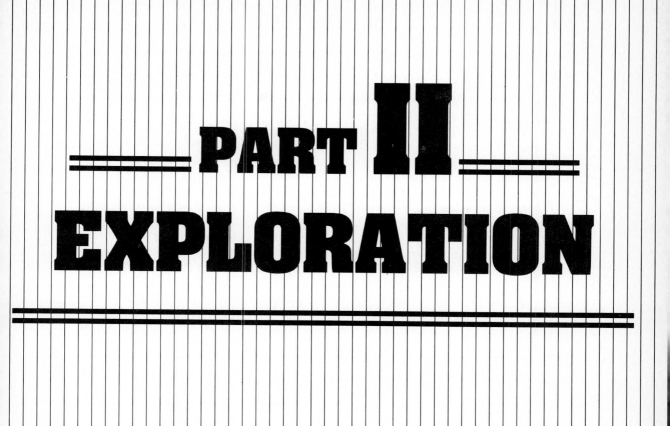

PART II
EXPLORATION

INTRODUCTION

It is a close play at the plate. The runner starts his slide just as the catcher gets the ball that has been thrown in from right field. The two players meet in a cloud of dust. The catcher is certain that he has tagged the runner out. The runner is equally certain that he has slid safely underneath the catcher's outstretched mitt. Each man looks toward the umpire . . .

Someone is likely to disagree with the umpire's decision. Whichever way he calls the play, someone in the stands or on the field is likely to say he is blind. Someone—the second baseman perhaps, or the manager in the dugout, or a fan in a box seat behind the first base—is likely to feel that the angle from which he or she saw the play gave him or her a clearer view of what really happened, a clearer view than the view that the umpire had in the midst of all the dust and confusion at home plate.

Yet the umpire's view is taken as final, because it is his role to play an objective observer. Unlike the fan or the manager or the second baseman, he has nothing to gain or lose as a result of his decision. His decision is always more impartial and less prejudiced, even if his perspective is often equally limited.

The umpire's view is limited; he attempts only to call the play *as he sees it.* Similarly, when you as a writer attempt simply to describe the world as you see it, as it appears from your personal angle of vision, you offer a limited perspective, a perspective that perhaps tells as much about you yourself as it tells about whatever you describe.

But what if you want to broaden your angle of vision and see the world more fully, not only as it looks to you but as it actually is in all its richness and complexity? What if you intend to write about the close play at the plate? Deciding whether, from your vantage point, the runner was safe or out, and thus whether you agree with the umpire's decision, may not be your first concern. You may be more interested in explaining why that decision is controversial, in comparing the play at the plate to other close plays you have seen, in speculating about the effect of the umpire's call on the outcome of the game, in evaluating the power of the right fielder's throwing arm or the agility with which the runner executed the mechanics of a slide into home plate. Of course, if you are watching the game on television, you may study videotaped replays of the tag as it is pictured by a variety of different cameras in different parts of the stadium. In each of these cases, you are exploring the world beyond any single self, any single perspective.

Your goal in the tasks that follow will be to explore the world from a perspective broader than that open to you when your concern is primarily self-expression, and then to inform your audience of the discoveries you have made.

The American writer Henry David Thoreau introduced his book *Walden* by writing, "I should not talk so much about myself if there were anybody else whom I knew as well. Unfortunately, I am confined to this theme by the narrowness of my experience." In Part I of this book, you were "confined" to the theme of yourself to some extent. Now we will ask you to escape this confinement by writing about the world as it may be experienced by others as well as by yourself.

4
WRITING ABOUT A PLACE

PURPOSE

In working through the tasks for the next two chapters, you will find that you are moving away from the type of writing you have been doing thus far. Rather than expressing the experience of the self, as in Chapters 1 through 3, you will begin to explore the world of experience beyond the self. Instead of asking, "What does this experience that I have had mean?" you will find yourself asking, "What do I perceive and how can I explain my perceptions as fully and richly as possible to others?" Your role will also shift from participant to interested observer, and your purpose will no longer be expressive but expository.

In moving on to this more objective, expository writing, you will continue to use, of course, the skills developed in the first three chapters, such as keen observation of what you see, a sense of ordering an experience chronologically, and an ability to analyze the significance of that experience. To these skills, now directed toward the world of others, you will begin to add other techniques, to be learned here, such as describing people, places, and objects and interviewing people to learn of their knowledge about your subject. Your focus will shift from narration and from exposition in the service of narration (Chapters 2 and 3) to exposition and narration in the service of exposition.

Because you will be seeking information about your subject, your method of generating ideas will be that of an explorer who asks, "How shall I learn about this subject?'' Your audience, too, will be seeking information, rather than your personal interpretation, and therefore the most important audience question for you to answer will become ''What information about my subject does my audience both want and need?''

Although the aim in expository writing is to explore (Chapters 4 and 5), inform (Chapters 6 and 7), and/or prove (Chapter 8), and the emphasis is therefore on the subject rather than on the writer, as in expressive writing, you as writer will not disappear from what you write. You will remain as both the guiding intelligence of what you write and a fervent believer in what you say.

GENERATING IDEAS: THE EXPLORER'S QUESTIONS

To generate ideas when exploring almost any subject, whether it is an object, a place, a person, an experience, or an idea, you can ask yourself the following five questions.

1. What features characterize it? In other words, what is it, and what does it look like?
2. How does it differ from others in its class? How is it similar to them?
3. How does it fit into larger systems of which it is a part: a larger category, an enterprise, a neighborhood, or a community?
4. How does it change? How has it changed since its inception? What was its high point? What will it be like in the future?
5. What are its parts, and how do they work together?

The first question asks for a description of the subject, whether it is a physical description of a place, an object, or a person, or the characterization of an idea or an abstract object, such as a poem. The intent in answering this question is to describe the thing in itself, the object in its unique existence. In describing a particular classroom on campus, for example, you might describe the old wooden desk tops on which past students have carved their initials, the poor ventilation that results in a stuffy atmosphere, the green color of the blackboards, and the other characteristics of this particular classroom.

Question 2 asks for a comparison of your subject with others like it—others in the same class. To continue with the example of the classroom, Question 2 asks how it compares with other classrooms, or perhaps with other places of study, such as a library. Is it a typical example of a classroom, or does it distinguish itself in some way? Is it, for example, smaller and more intimate than the typical classroom, perhaps having a large table around which students sit rather than individual desks? Or is it a room in which only science classes are held? Or is it a room in which you have been more bored or more stimulated intellectually than in other classrooms you have entered?

Question 3 wants to know about the many systems that most subjects fit into.

Any classroom fits into a number of different systems. It is a part of a campus building, a reflection of the architectural and engineering systems of the building. It is a part of an educational system, a reflection of the philosophy and techniques of educating students at a particular school. It is a part of a college community, a reflection of the professional and social relationships at the school, a place where learning occurs but also where friendships are formed, ambitions are tested, and so forth.

Question 4 investigates the subject as dynamic—as it changes or has changed or will change. A classroom may seem a very different place at different times of the day or of the semester. It ages, of course, over time and may be subject to renovation on occasion. Its high point might have been when it was brand new or when a particularly effective teacher taught in it. Its future may be dark or bright, depending perhaps on the fate of the school of which it is a part.

Finally, Question 5 asks how the subject works—what parts it is composed of, which together comprise its whole and perform its function. Classrooms are composed of tables, desks, chairs, blackboards, chalk, and erasers, of course, but also of books, students, teachers, and so forth.

To cite another example, let's look at an idea that might be discussed in a classroom. Suppose that in a political science class you are studying the constitutional principle of free speech. Finding answers to the explorer's questions can help you to learn and write about this principle.

What is this principle? It is a right guaranteed to Americans by the First Amendment. It prohibits the government from censoring or in any other way limiting our right to say what we think whenever and to whomever we want. But it does not give us blanket permission to speak out: the right to free speech does not include, for example, a sanction to shout "Fire!" in a crowded place when there really is no fire or a right to commit libel against someone else.

How does our right to free speech compare with other rights enjoyed by American citizens? It can excite as much controversy as our right to bear arms. It can conflict with our right to privacy. It also can be compared with the principle of free speech as practiced (or not) in other nations.

This principle is a part of the system of government by which we live, but it is also a part of other systems. You might write about the role that free speech plays in our philosophy of individualism, or in our capitalist economic system, or in our artistic community.

Although the actual wording that guarantees the right to free speech in the Constitution has not changed over time, our attitudes toward this right have changed. At some points in our history, for example, the Supreme Court has interpreted this right less broadly than at other times. Private attitudes toward this right, toward who should be allowed to speak freely about what, often change. Have Americans enjoyed this right more or less thoroughly in the past? How strong will this right remain in our future? Answers to these questions can help you explore the meaning of the principle, as can an examination of the parts that compose it.

Of what parts is a principle or an idea composed? The right to free speech is composed, to a degree, of the laws passed by Congress over the years to defend it. It is also composed of the moral and political ideals used by its defenders to justify their position.

SOME PRACTICE WITH THE EXPLORER'S QUESTIONS

1. Choose a simple object within view—a lamp, a book, a picture—and analyze it according to the explorer's five questions.

2. Recall a place that you visited recently where people were involved in some mutual experience or enterprise. Analyze this place using the five questions as your guide.

3. Using the five explorer's questions, construct a dialogue between two people whose questions and answers provide information about a subject. For example, in the following dialogue, one person is trying to learn about the other by asking these questions:

    Lou: Who are you? I've never seen you here before.
    Sue: That's for you to find out.
    Lou: That's pretty funny. It's dark in here. Do you have red hair or is that the lights?
    Sue: I'm six feet tall and look like Susan Anton.
    Lou: Are you like all the other girls who come to this place?
    Sue: Of course. They're beautiful and so am I. But I'm also brilliant.
    Lou: Boy, you're pretty high on yourself. What are you doing here if you are so terrific?

    Most likely, you can also guess where they are. In your dialogue, try to create a situation that will allow the characters to arrive at an understanding of a subject of your choice. Some suggestions: landing on the moon, the first day of the semester, choosing a teacher at registration, arguing about a team's prospects for the new season.

4. Create a riddle by having the subject define itself by giving information that answers that five explorer's questions. For example:

    I am long and blond, but that's not the point. Some think that I'm too soft, others think I'm hard enough but that I snap under pressure. Although I look like a lot of others in my class, I often have a distinctive name tatooed all over my body. Many people say I'm not as important as I was years ago, that I've been made obsolete. But let me tell you, buddy, I can still go a long way. Get the message?

    Answer: a pencil

5. You have been sent by your employer in marketing research to do some field research for Dr. Fu's Spicy Hot Chicken, a new fast-food chain that is thinking of opening up a new branch in your neighborhood. You are to do an analysis of their chief competitors, located across the street on a busy intersection in your community. Write a brief report using the explorer's five questions on two restaurants in your neighborhood that would be competitors for Dr. Fu's.

6. Select from one of your courses a topic that you have been asked to investigate. For example, in history you may have been asked to explain the changes in American attitudes toward politics in the 1960s. How could you use the explorer's questions to find an approach to this subject?

ADDRESSING YOUR AUDIENCE: DEPTH OF INFORMATION

As we have discussed already, an analysis of your audience's frame of reference and corresponding point of view makes it easier for you to plan and write an essay that bridges the gap between your point of view and that of your reader. In this chapter, we will discuss how knowing your audience's frame of reference can help you in determining how much and what kind of information to supply. We will discuss how to answer the question "What information about my subject does my audience both want and need?"

Some audiences require more information; some require different information. As we suggested in Chapter 2, if you were writing to a group of grade-school children, you would write differently from when you were addressing college students. Here are two passages on the same subject written for two different audiences, one (A) a class of college English students, the other (B) an English professor:

A. *Preparation.* For writers, there are probably two parts to the preparation stage. The first includes just about *everything* a person has engaged in before he or she starts on a writing assignment—education, personal experiences, sports, work, reading, family life. All these areas of one's life provide potential writing material, and the more alert and thoughtful one is about his or her experiences, the better prepared that person is to write.

The second part of the preparation stage in writing begins when the writer identifies the writing task. This stage may include choosing and narrowing a topic or clarifying an assignment made by someone else. It also requires identifying audience and purpose: for whom are you writing and why are you writing? When the writer has answered those questions, he or she can begin to employ various strategies for generating material. The writer may also start to develop it. The activity at this stage of the process might be compared to feeding information into a computer from which one will later write a program or solve a problem.

B. In preparation, the starting point for a writer is recognizing a problem worthy of honest inquiry. There must be reasonably substantial personal experience, observation, education, or reading to supply the subject matter or situation within which the student can recognize, formulate, and explore such a problem. Original thinking may grow out of recalling old and comfortable knowledge and integrating it with new or previously separate elements in a new combination. Students probably will demonstrate greater motivation and originality in their writing if they aim at something they find worth investigating on their own. But even that supposition needs qualifying, in that too many students seem conditioned to look for easy answers instead and avoid problems if they can. Students typically choose an idea acquired from someone else to write about, perhaps because they like it, not because there is any problem in it for them and not because they have anything original to say about it, at least at the moment of choosing. The most common curricular approach, to include challenging reading materials in a writing course, whether poetry by Dickinson and Plath or essays by Bruner and Eiseley, offers opportunities for problems, but only if the student reads attentively and competently enough to see the difference between a problem worthy of exploration and rather easily resolved factual ignorance. Richard Young, following John Dewey, suggests that the source of a problem lies in a clash of some sort contributing to an "uneasy feeling" in one's personal reaction to a situation. The clash may be explained as a logical inconsistency or a conflict with one's cultural values or educational training. But whatever the cause, awareness, curiosity, and a sort of discomfort usually stimulate strong motivation to correct or clarify the situation. The starting point, at any rate, is not with problems patiently waiting for any qualified researcher to come and seize them; rather it is with particular individuals recognizing and creating their own problems in the material they are working with. But students must not only be taught to look for problems; even at this early stage, they should define their problems so that the problems look potentially solvable and so that students will know when, and if, they have solved them.

—**David V. Harrington,** "Encouraging Honest Inquiry in Student Writing," *College Composition and Communication* (May 1979)

The first paragraph of Passage A, written for college students, roughly corresponds to Sentences 2 and 3 of Passage B, written for a professor. However, the second paragraph in Passage A offers much less information than the corresponding section in Passage B (the rest of the paragraph), which includes a more detailed discussion of selecting a writing task, generating material for writing about it, and planning the evolution of the paper. (Other characteristics of the two passages indicate their differing audiences as well, such as language level and paragraph length, but we are concerned here only with differences in depth of information.)

Here are two other passages written on the same subject—the Oedipus complex—for two different audiences, in this case, one a lay audience, the other a highly technical or professional one:

C. There is another typical dream dealing with the death of the father that we find particularly among young sons. We have to consider here the primitive state of the human being. There is always a rivalry between father and son for the love of the mother, and this, despite the fact that the father may love his boy very dearly. The son has learned that he receives much more attention and love from his mother, and is treated more leniently in the father's absence. In this type of dream, therefore, we see the desire on the part of the child to get rid of his father. It is really surprising to note how many boys dream openly as well as disguisedly of the death of their father. These dreams are even more common than those dealing with the death of the teacher, for the latter plays a smaller part in the child's psychic life than the father. For one thing, the teacher comes into his life at a later period, and as he is not surrounded with the halo of parental sanctity, hostile feelings against the teacher are generally quite conscious.

We call such dreams of the death of the father Oedipus dreams, because, according to Professor Freud, to whom we are indebted for the name, they bring to light an essentially human situation that has found most fitting expression in Sophocles's noted tragedy of *Oedipus Tyrannus.*

—**A.A. Brill,** from *Freud's Principles of Psychoanalysis*

D. Incest with the mother is one of the crimes of Oedipus and parricide the other. Incidentally, these are the two great offences condemned by totemism, the first social-religious institution of mankind. Now let us turn from the direct observation of children to the analytic investigation of adults who have become neurotic; what does analysis yield in further knowledge of the Oedipus complex? Well, this is soon told. The complex is revealed just as the myth relates it; it will be seen that every one of these neurotics was himself an Oedipus or, what amounts to the same thing, has become a Hamlet in his reaction to the complex. To be sure, the analytic picture of the Oedipus complex is an enlarged and accentuated edition of the infantile sketch; the hatred of the father and the death-wishes against him are no longer vague hints, the affection for the mother declares itself with the aim of possessing her as a woman. Are we really to accredit such grossness and intensity of the feelings to the tender age of childhood or does the analysis deceive us by introducing another factor? It is not difficult to find one. Every time anyone describes anything past, even if he be a historian, we have to take into account all that he unintentionally imports into that past period from present and intermediate times, thereby falsifying it. With the neurotic it is even doubtful whether this retroversion is altogether unintentional; we shall hear later on that there are motives for it and we must explore the whole subject of the "retrogressive phantasy-making" which goes back to the remote past. We soon discover, too, that the hatred against the father has been strengthened by a number of motives arising in later periods and other relationships in life, and that the sexual desires towards the mother have been moulded into forms which would have been as yet foreign to the child. But it would be a vain attempt if we endeavoured to explain the whole of the Oedipus complex by "retrogressive phantasy-making," and by motives originating in later periods of life. The infantile nucleus, with more or less of the accretions to it, remains intact, as is confirmed by direct observation of children.

—**Sigmund Freud,** from *A General Introduction to Psychoanalysis*

The first passage was written for an audience unfamiliar with psychology and its terminology. The writer, therefore, in simple language, explained first the causes and frequency of boys' dreams of the death of their fathers and then why Sigmund Freud termed these *Oedipal dreams*. In the second passage, the author, Sigmund Freud himself, was writing for other psychologists, explaining in depth the adult consequences of such dreams in highly technical terms (*totemism, neurotic, death wishes, retroversion*). Furthermore he assumed that the reader knows who Oedipus (and Hamlet) is.

In order to analyze the information needs for your audience, make an exhaustive list of the aspects of your subject. Then, using your audience's frame of reference as a guide, try to determine which aspects your audience is familiar with and which represent unfamiliar territory. Group those in the first category under the heading "Familiar" and the second under the heading "Unfamiliar." If you have more aspects grouped under "Familiar" than under "Unfamiliar," you know you are writing for an informed audience that will not require much in the way of a general introduction to your subject and that you can therefore concentrate on giving new, in-depth information about the unfamiliar aspects. If, on the other hand, you have very few aspects of your subject grouped under the heading "Familiar," your audience is uninformed, and you will give basic background on your subject and present little specialized information.

For example, the author of Passage C above went into depth at some points but skimmed over others. Outlined, his passage looks like this:

Background:
1. A young boy dreams of the death of his father.
2. The reason is that his mother gives him more attention and treats him more leniently.
3. These dreams are called *Oedipal dreams* because Sophocles wrote about this situation in a tragedy called *Oedipus Tyrannus.*

New Material:
1. It is really surprising to note how many boys dream openly, as well as disguisedly of the death of their father.
2. This dream is even more common than that of the death of the teacher.

Passage D, if outlined, would look like this:

Background:
1. Incest with the mother is one of the crimes of Oedipus and parricide the other.

New Material:
1. Adult neurotics were themselves Oedipuses.
2. The adult Oedipus complex is enlarged and accentuated by retroversion.
3. The infantile nucleus also remains in adulthood.

As we have seen, the writer of Passage C was writing to an audience that was unfamiliar with this subject, and he therefore found it necessary to give a lot of background information. The writer of Passage D, whose readers were more informed, was able to discuss the Oedipus complex in some depth after giving only the briefest of introductions.

SOME PRACTICE WITH AUDIENCE DEPTH OF INFORMATION

1. You are a carpenter and have been asked to write an article for homeowners on how to build wooden shelves. You have been told that the publication for which you are writing appeals mostly to young couples. What would be the proportion of familiar to unfamiliar or new material? Would the article include more background or more new information?

    You are later asked to write on the same subject for a journal called *Craftsmanship*. Those who subscribe to this journal are craftspeople of many trades, not only carpentry. What would be the proportion of new material to background material? How would the proportion compare with that in the first article above?

2. You are the head of the art history department at your school, and one art history course is required in the first semester for all incoming freshmen. However, most freshmen are not art majors, and you want to write them a letter at the end of the first semester, hoping to get them interested in taking other courses besides the required one. How much depth of information would you include? You want to write a letter to declared art majors at the same time informing them of second-semester course offerings. How would this letter differ in depth of information?

3. Prepare to write two letters on some aspect of college life, one to your college classmates and one to some friends still in high school. How do the frames of reference of the two audiences differ? With what aspects of your subject is each group familiar? Unfamiliar? What background information must you give each group? What new material can you present? Once you have determined the answers to these questions, write the letters.

TASK: EXPLORING A PLACE

The task for this chapter asks you to visit a place closely or tangentially related to your major, to a hobby, or simply to an interest, a place you have not visited before, one that you know about only through the opinion of others. This should be a place for which you have high regard because of its reputation. You will want to observe its appearance and what is going on there, and to interview the people you meet there so that you can come to some overall impression of the place that does or does not justify your initial good opinion.

The purpose of this assignment is to give you the opportunity to explore a place about which a myth may have been created for you by others. Essentially, you will be answering the question "What do I perceive and how can I explain my perceptions to others as fully and richly as possible?" Do this by asking yourself a more specific writing question: "Is this place as vital as everyone led me to believe?" or "What can I discover about this place that will either support or negate my earlier opinion?"

You might, for example, plan to be a children's librarian, and you may always have wanted to visit the main branch of the public library in your city. The local librarians have cited as their models the procedures followed in the main branch, and you wish to visit to see if efficiency does indeed reign there. Or, as a future aerospace engineer, you may have read about Grumman or Boeing or McDonnell Douglas as the giants in the field. A visit might confirm your sense of admiration, but the industry is facing strong competition from abroad, and a visit might also explain why the once-proud aircraft industry is faltering. By asking yourself the question "Does this place justify my regard?" you leave yourself open to an honest evaluation of what you have discovered.

The audience for this task should be someone like you who is interested in your findings about this place, so we suggest that you write for a group of like-minded people, such as a class in your curriculum or a group of people who share your hobby or interest. This audience will know more about your subject than either a random selection of college students or your English class or possibly your English teacher. By adopting the explorer's questions, you can amass information about this place, and by evaluating the depth of information needs of your audience, you can determine what about your subject the audience needs to know.

The next section, "Writing the Essay," will help to answer the arrangement question, "How can I weave chronology, description, exposition, and dialogue together to create an overriding impression of my subject?"

WRITING THE ESSAY

Using the Explorer's Questions

To generate information and ideas for this assignment, try using your powers of observation to answer as many of the explorer's questions as time and access permit. You may need help in answering all of the questions fully, however, and that is why we suggested in the task that you interview people in the place you visit. The explorer's questions may, in fact, form the basis of several interviews.

Some questions may generate fuller answers than others, and some may be more crucial to the particular place you are writing about than others. For example, a place not similar to others in its class may require more description than a place comparable to others. A unique place will demand the most description of all.

Ask yourself which questions are the most important in writing about your place, which you can answer yourself, which you will need to interview people to answer, and how full an answer you require in each case. Note that you may want to reshape the five questions to elicit the most appropriate information about your subject. You may want to add questions, make them more specific, or redirect them in some way.

Following is the approach of a student who plans to write about the geology exhibit of a museum.

Question 1
What does this geology exhibit look like?

Question 2
How does it differ from the other exhibits in the museum? Why has the museum arranged it in this way? How does it compare with other geology exhibits I have seen?

Question 3
How does it fit into the layout of the museum? As this is a museum of natural history, how does a geology exhibit fit into the overall purpose of the place? What role does the exhibit play in the education of those who view it?

Question 4
How has the exhibit changed since the museum first created it? How will it change in the future, based on what I know or can learn about geological findings? Was the acquisition of moon rocks the high point of the exhibit? If not, what was?

Question 5
How is the exhibit arranged? What specific categories are there? What special exhibits exist?

Like this student, you may need to reshape the explorer's questions to suit the needs of your task.

Audience Depth of Information

You will want to compose a frame of reference for your audience and analyze how much depth of information your audience will need. Answer the questions "What points can I skim over?" "What knowledge can I take for granted?" and "Where and how much can or should I go into depth?"

In answering these questions, refer to the material you have generated through the explorer's method of inquiry. Ask yourself if any of the answers to the explorer's questions, or parts of the questions, should be given to your audience as necessary background. If so, should the answers be detailed or brief? Which questions, or parts of questions, should be answered in depth for this audience? How much depth can the audience absorb?

For example, the student writing about the geology exhibit composed the following frame of reference for her audience:

- **Audience:** A Geology I class.
- **Characteristics:** Interested in geology, although not necessarily planning to major in it.
- Did well in high-school science courses.
- Two are creationists; the rest are evolutionists.
- Most have not visited the geology exhibit.

The frame of reference helped her to understand the depth of information that her audience required:

Background (Brief)
1. What does the exhibit look like?
2. How does it differ from the other exhibits in the museum? From geology exhibits in other museums?
3. How does it fit into the museum? Into the interests of geologists and geology students in the area?

New Material (in Depth)
4. How has the exhibit changed over the years since it was first introduced into the museum? What was its high point? How might it change in the future?
5. What method of arrangement has been used? What special exhibits are there?

Answering the following questions of the "Audience Analysis Guide" should help you to write more effectively for your audience.

——— AUDIENCE ANALYSIS GUIDE ———

1. **Who is my audience?**
2. **What is the frame of reference of this audience?**
3. **What point of view is my audience likely to have on my subject?**
4. **How do my own frame of reference and point of view differ from those of my reader?**

5. How can I bridge any gap that exists between my reader's point of view and my own?

6. Which of my voices am I selecting as I write on this subject? How can the voice that I select further help me to bridge the gap between my audience and me?

7. How much depth of information does my audience need and want on the background of my subject? On the new material I wish to present?

Arranging Your Essay

As you answer the explorer's questions, you will find yourself using different patterns of paragraph development. Question 1 calls for description; Questions 2 through 4 suggest patterns of exposition, such as comparison, contrast, classification and analysis; and Question 5 requires a form of narration that describes a process. You will therefore be weaving together patterns of narration, description, and exposition.

Narrative Patterns.   Although in this chapter you are writing about a place involving others, you should not disappear from the essay entirely, as you have chosen this place to write about because of its vital interest to you. As an observer of the place and the activities there, you can put yourself in the essay by giving a chronological account of your visit as an unobtrusive narrative framework to the essay. The question of arranging the essay then becomes "How can I frame the essay with a narrative account of my visit so that I can convey my considerable interest and at the same time keep the atmosphere and action of the place in the foreground?"

One way to answer this question is to develop a second narrative that, in answer to the fifth question of the explorer's method of inquiry, relates the process by which the systems of the place work together. Process analysis is a type of chronology that indicates how a person or mechanism accomplishes a task from the beginning of the operation to its completion. Whenever one discusses how anything works—from a simple can opener to the writing of an essay—one is dealing in time: in beginnings, middles, and endings.

A narrative account of the operation may be most effective in answering the question "How does this place operate?" The period of time covered, of course, will depend on the cycle or cycles of operation. Processes can be completed in an hour, in a day, on a weekly basis, monthly, annually, or seasonally. Once you have determined what processes need explanation, the objective is to narrate them sequentially (see Chapter 5, pp. 151–152, for more on process analysis).

Here is an example of a process:

It's seven in the morning and the day shift is starting to drift in. Huge tractors are backing up to the big-mouth doors of the warehouse. Cattle trucks bring tons of beef to feed its insatiable appetite for cargo. Smoke-covered trailers with refrigerated units packed deep with green peppers sit with their diesel engines idling. Names like White, Mack, and Kenworth are welded to the front of their radiators, which hiss and moan from the overload. The men walk through the factory-type gates of the parking lot with their heads bowed, oblivious of the shuddering diesels that await them.

Once inside the warehouse they gather in groups of threes and fours like prisoners in an exercise yard. They stand in front of the two time clocks that hang below a window in the manager's office. They smoke and cough in the early morning hour as they await their work assignments. The manager, a nervous-looking man with a stomach that is starting to push out at his belt, walks out with a pink work sheet in his hand.

—**Patrick Fenton,** "Notes of a Working Stiff"

Patterns of Exposition.   The answers to the explorer's Questions 2, 3, and 4 call for exposition. As we saw in Chapter 3, exposition is the presentation and explanation of ideas. In contrast to narration, which presents the world of time, and to description (which we will discuss below), which presents the world of space, exposition presents the world of the mind as it exists apart from time and space and interprets their relationships and analyzes their meanings.

The ideas presented by exposition may be concrete: an analysis of a beaver dam, a comparison of race tracks, a classification of the foods eaten by the athletes in various sports. They may also be abstract: a classification of the psychologies of different groups in America, an analysis of the international banking system, a comparison of Eastern and Western philosophies of religion. Whether concrete or abstract, or a mixture of the two, exposition classifies, analyzes, and compares ideas about ideas, objects, places, and emotions. (These and other purposes of exposition will be explained more fully in subsequent chapters.)

In fulfilling the task for this chapter, you will want to use exposition in answering the explorer's Question 2, which asks you to compare your subject with others like it; Question 3, which asks you to analyze what larger systems it is a part of; and Question 4, which requires you to analyze how it has changed, does change, and will change.

Understanding the differences between comparison and analysis will help you to organize your answers. Comparison and its corollary, contrast, ask you to point out the similarities and differences between two objects or among three or more objects. You can do this either (1) by presenting the similarities and then the differences or (2) by comparing and contrasting your subject point by point (see Chapter 5, pp. 150–151, for further discussion of comparison and contrast). An example of comparison and contrast follows. Which method of arrangement does it use, (1) or (2)?

We know from our work hundreds of outstanding competitors who possess strong character formation that complements high motor skill. But we found others who possessed so few strong character traits that it was difficult on the basis of personality to account for their success. There were gold-medal Olympic winners at Mexico and Japan whom we would classify as overcompensatory greats. Only magnificent physical gifts enabled them to overcome constant tension, anxiety, and self-doubt. They are unhappy, and when the talent ages and fades, they become derelicts, while someone like Roosevelt Grier just goes on to bigger mountains. We often wonder how much higher some of these great performers might have gone if they had, say, the strong personality structure that characterized our women's Olympic fencing team.

> —**Bruce C. Ogilive and Thomas A. Tutjo,** "Sport: If You Want to Build Character, Try Something Else"

Analysis calls for a breaking down of the subject into parts. It calls for probing beneath a solid surface to discover what a thing is composed of or how it changes (has changed or will change). Analysis also seeks to discover the larger pattern to which a thing belongs. The arrangement pattern of analysis is the presentation of the parts in a systematic order. What parts does the author of the following passage delineate in the origin of *Y'know?*

We know less about the origin of Y'know than about the origin of Boola boola, but there is some reason to believe that in this country it began among poor blacks who, because of the various disabilities imposed on them, often did not speak and for whom Y'know was a request for assurance that they had been understood. From that sad beginning it spread among people who wanted to show themselves sympathetic to blacks, and among those who saw it as the latest thing and either could not resist or did not want to be left out.

> —**Edwin Newman,** "A Protective Interest in the English Language"

Patterns of Description.   Description presents the appearance of things that occupy space, whether they be objects, people, buildings, or cities. The aim of description is to convey to the reader what something looks like. It attempts to paint a picture with words.

In order to clarify the appearance of your subject for your reader, you should develop the tools of the visual artist and describe shapes, colors, positions, and relationships. Following a particular order—left to right, top to bottom, inside to outside—also aids the reader. Selecting your details with an eye to creating a main impression simplifies your task and at the same time enhances the description.

The question to be answered in description is "How can I best describe my subject so that my readers can visualize what I want them to see?"

Here is an example of description:

In winter, the warehouse is cold and damp. There is no heat. The large steel doors that line the warehouse walls stay open most of the day. In the cold months, wind, rain, and snow blow across the floor. In the summer, the warehouse becomes an oven. Dust and sand from the runways mix with the toxic fumes of forklifts, leaving a dry, stale taste in your mouth. The high windows above the doors are covered with a thick, black dirt that kills the sun. The men work in shadows with the constant roar of jet engines blowing dangerously in their ears.

Description may be used as an end in itself but it often serves other purposes. In fulfilling this task, in fact, you will describe your place in answering Question 1, but you will combine description with process narration in answering Question 5, as the reader will better understand the process if she or he knows what the machinery, equipment, props, uniforms, and so on look like.

Dialogue.   *Dialogue* literally means the conversation of two people. In fulfilling this task, you will be interviewing one or more people in the place visited, and therefore dialogue will be a part of your arrangement. In writing the paper, you may want to include part of an exchange you had with someone, or you may want simply to quote the person interviewed. Your guide will be to select comments that highlight an aspect of your subject. The question you will be answering is "What comments were made that are particularly useful to my purposes because they succinctly state the answers to the explorer's questions?"

Following are two examples of quotation, one including only one speaker, the second the dialogue of two speakers. Notice the use of paragraphs for each speaker in the dialogue and the use also of quotation marks:

"Some of these activities are very, very appealing to people who've been turned off by team sports," William H. Monti, a physical education reform leader at San Rafael High, explained. "A number of students who rebelled against all forms of physical education have gravitated toward rock climbing. These were the types who said that they didn't like team sports of any kind. Later, of course, they found out that rock climbing involves as much teamwork as the traditional team sports, or more. They still love it."

—**George Leonard,** *"Why Johnny Can't Run"*

Banke, a red-haired, red-faced man, takes a special interest in the Elmhurst tanks because he lives in Maspeth, which borders Elmhurst.
    "This is a natural landmark," he said. "It's our version of the Statue of Liberty."
    "Anything that goes wrong here, I yell at him," said Trieste.
    "I get the neck of the chicken," said Banke. "But, being a local resident, I make sure things go right."

—"Tanks," *The New Yorker*

The Overriding Impression.   So far you have been asking and answering questions about the parts of this task: the five explorer's questions, the four types of arrangement spelled out. You now need to ask, "What is my overriding impression about this place? What ties all these parts together?" Included in your overriding impression will no doubt be an answer to the specific question of the task: "Is this place as vital as everyone has led me to believe?" A sentence clearly stating this impression will serve as the shaping idea of your essay (see Chapter 1) and will help you write the rough draft.

Following is a professional essay that attempts to answer the same questions that you are answering in terms of the description of place, narration of visit and the place's processes, and exposition of the more abstract facts about systems and dynamics, including dialogue between the observer and people in the place. Most important, the author, Saul Bellow, explored the question "How vital (and how safe) is a kibbutz?"

Developed in Israel, the kibbutz is an autonomous, self-sustaining communal settlement usually engaged in agriculture. All its members participate in the many duties of the kibbutz, even the elected leaders. The children are generally reared and educated apart from their parents, although recently this practice has changed in many kibbutzim.

On a Kibbutz
Saul Bellow

On a kibbutz.

Lucky is Nola's dog. John's dog is Mississippi. But John loves Lucky too, and Nola dotes on Mississippi. And then there are the children—one daughter in the army, and a younger child who still sleeps in the kibbutz dormitory. Lucky is a woolly brown dog, old and nervous. His master was killed in the Golan. When there is a sonic boom over the kibbutz, the dog rushes out, growling. He seems to remember the falling bombs. He is too feeble to bark, too old to run, his teeth are bad, his eyes under the brown fringe are dull, and he is clotted under the tail. Mississippi is a big, long-legged, short-haired, brown-and-white, clever, lively, affectionate, and greedy animal. She is a "child dog"—sits in your lap, puts a paw on your arm when you reach for a tidbit to get it for herself. Since she weighs fifty pounds or more she is not welcome in my lap, but she sits on John and Nola and on the guests—those who permit it. She is winsome but also flatulent. She eats too many sweets but is good company, a wonderful listener and conversationalist; she growls and snuffles when you speak directly to her. She "sings" along with the record player. The Auerbachs are proud of this musical yelping.

In the morning we hear the news in Hebrew and then again on the BBC. We eat an Israeli breakfast of fried eggs, sliced cheese, cucumbers, olives, green onions, tomatoes, and little salt fish. Bread is toasted on the coal-oil heater. The dogs have learned the trick of the door and bang in and out. Between the rows of small kibbutz dwellings the lawns are ragged but very green. Light and warmth come from the sea. Under the kibbutz lie the ruins of Herod's Caesarea. There are Roman fragments everywhere. Marble columns in the grasses. Fallen capitals make garden seats. You have only to prod the ground to find fragments of pottery, bits of statuary, a pair of dancing satyr legs. John's tightly packed bookshelves are fringed with such relics. On the crowded desk stands a framed photograph of the dead son, with a small beard like John's, smiling with John's own warmth.

We walk in the citrus groves after breakfast, taking Mississippi with us (John is seldom without her); the soil is kept loose and soft among the trees, the leaves are glossy, the ground itself is fragrant. Many of the trees are still unharvested and bending, tangerines and lemons as dense as stars. "Oh that I were an orange tree/That busie plant!" wrote George Herbert. To put forth such leaves, to be hung with oranges, to be a blessing—one feels the temptation of this on such a morning and I even feel a fibrous woodiness entering my arms as I consider it. You want to take root and stay forever in the most temperate and blue of temperate places. John mourns his son, he always mourns his son, but he is also smiling in the sunlight.

In the exporting of oranges there is competition from the North African countries and from Spain. "We are very idealistic here, but when we read about frosts in Spain we're glad as hell," John says.

All this was once dune land. Soil had to be carted in and mixed with the sand. Many years of digging and tending made these orchards. Relaxing, breathing freely, you feel what a wonderful place has been created here, a homeplace for body and soul; then you remember that on the beaches there are armed patrols. It is always possible that terrorists may come in rubber dinghies that cannot be detected by radar. They entered Tel Aviv itself in March 1975 and seized a hotel at the seashore. People were murdered. John keeps an Uzi in his bedroom cupboard. Nola scoffs at this. "We'd both be dead before you could reach your gun," she says. Cheerful Nola laughs. An expressive woman—she uses her forearm to wave away John's preparations. "Sometimes he does the drill and I time him to see how long it takes to jump out of bed, open the cupboard, get the gun, put in the clip, and turn around. They'd mow us down before he could get a foot on the floor."

Mississippi is part of the alarm system, "She'd bark," says John.

Just now Mississippi is racing through the orchards, nose to the ground. The air is sweet, and the sun like a mild alcohol makes you yearn for good things. You rest under a tree and eat tangerines, only slightly heavy-hearted.

From the oranges we go to the banana groves. The green bananas are tied up in plastic tunics. The great banana flower hangs groundward like the sexual organ of a stallion. The long leaves resemble manes. After two years the ground has to be plowed up and lie fallow. Groves are planted elsewhere—more hard labor. "You noticed before," says John, "that some of the orange trees were withered. Their roots get into Roman ruins and they die. Some years ago, while we were plowing, we turned up an entire Roman street."

He takes me to the Herodian Hippodrome. American archeologists have dug out some of the old walls. We look down into the diggings, where labels flutter from every stratum. There are more potsherds than soil in these bluffs—the broken jugs of the slaves who raised the walls two thousand years ago. At the center of the Hippodrome, a long, graceful ellipse, is a fallen monolith weighing many tons. We sit under fig trees on the slope while Mississippi runs through the high smooth grass. The wind is soft and works the grass gracefully. It makes white air courses in the green.

Whenever John ships out he takes the dog for company. He had enough of solitude when he sailed on German ships under forged papers. He does not like to be alone. Now and again he was under suspicion. A German officer who sensed that he was Jewish threatened to turn him in, but one night when the ship was only hours out of Danzig she struck a mine and went down, the officer with her. John himself was pulled from the sea by his mates. Once he waited in a line of nude men whom a German doctor, a woman, was examining for venereal disease. In that lineup he alone was circumcised. He came before the woman and was examined; she looked into his face and she let him live.

John and I go back through the orange groves. There are large weasels living in the bushy growth along the pipeline. We see a pair of them at a distance in the road. They could easily do for Mississippi. She is luckily far off. We sit under a pine on the hilltop and look out to sea where a freighter moves slowly toward Ashkelon. Nearer to shore, a trawler chuffs. The kibbutz does little fishing now. Off the Egyptian coast, John has been shot at, and not long ago several members of the kibbutz were thrown illegally into jail by the Turks, accused of fishing in Turkish waters. Twenty people gave false testimony. They could have had a thousand witnesses. It took three months to get these men released. A lawyer was found who knew the judge. His itemized bill came to ten thousand dollars—five for the judge, five for himself.

Enough of this sweet sun and the transparent blue-green. We turn our backs on it to have a drink before lunch. Kibbutzniks ride by on clumsy old bikes. They wear cloth caps and pedal slowly; their day starts at six. Plain-looking working people from the tile factory and from the barn steer toward the dining hall. The kibbutzniks are a mixed group. There is one lone Orthodox Jew, who has no congregation to pray with. There are several older gentiles, one a Spaniard, one a Scandinavian, who married Jewish women and settled here. The Spaniard, an anarchist, plans to return to Spain now that Franco has died. One member of the kibbutz is a financial wizard, another was a high-ranking army officer who for obscure reasons fell into disgrace. The dusty tarmac path we follow winds through the settlement. Beside the undistinguished houses stand red poinsettias. Here, too, lie Roman relics. Then we come upon a basketball court, and then the rusty tracks of a children's choo-choo, and then the separate quarters for young women of eighteen, and a museum of antiquities, and a recreation hall. A strong odor of cattle comes from the feeding lot. I tell John that Gurdjiev had Katherine Mansfield resting in the stable at Fontainebleau, claiming that the cows' breath would cure her tuberculosis. John loves to hear such bits of literary history. We go into his house and Mississippi climbs into his lap while we drink Russian vodka. "We could live with those bastards if they limited themselves to making this Stolichnaya."

These words put an end to the peaceful morning. At the north there swells up the Russian menace. With arms from Russia and Europe, the PLO and other Arab militants and the right-wing Christians are now destroying Lebanon. The Syrians have involved themselves; in the eyes of the Syrians, Israel is Syrian land. Suddenly this temperate Mediterranean day and the orange groves and the workers steering their bikes and the children's playground flutter like illustrated paper. What is there to keep them from blowing away?

1. Bellow provided a loose narrative framework by telling the story of his morning tour of the kibbutz. What features of the kibbutz did he describe during his ex-

ploration? How complete a picture did he paint? Did he offer any points about
the philosophy on which the kibbutz operates?

2. Bellow did not compare this kibbutz to others that he may have visited. Where
   did he make comparisons that help us to understand the nature of life on this
   kibbutz better? What do you make, for example, of the opening contrast that he
   draws between the two dogs?

3. How does the kibbutz fit into the larger system of Mideast politics? How did the
   answer to this question alter Bellow's view of the kibbutz?

4. In what ways have the kibbutz and the life of its inhabitants changed over time?
   What do the answers to this question reveal about the inhabitants of the kibbutz?

5. What overriding impression of the kibbutz did Bellow finally offer? How does
   the dialogue in Paragraph 5 contribute to this impression?

Writing the Rough Draft

The question at this point is how to weave together the various answers to the
explorer's questions and the elements required by the task: narration, exposition, description, and dialogue.

One approach, of course, is to use the explorer's questions as an outline for
your essay, working description in naturally in answering Question 1, exposition for the answers to Questions 2 through 4, and process narration for Question 5. Appropriate dialogue or quotations can be tucked in at any point. And
the chronological account of your visit can frame the essay, providing the content of the introduction and the conclusion.

Or you can follow the method of Saul Bellow and weave a more intricate
design by interspersing the elements throughout the essay. Notice, however,
that Bellow did use a narrative framework.

To begin organizing your essay, write down the overriding impression that
you wish to convey about the place you visited. This shaping idea may also suggest a pattern of arrangement. If not, this pattern will occur to you as you forge
an outline before beginning to write, or you may need actually to immerse
yourself in writing for a pattern to emerge. Regardless of your method—preout-
lining or immersion outlining—you will want to arrive at a coherently presented essay.

Here is one student's rough draft. What patterns of arrangement did the student use?

THE ASSEMBLY-LINE METHOD OF REPRODUCTIVE HEALTH

The walk from the subway seemed long. A strong, cold wind was at my back, pushing me down Twenty-third Street. It was a nice part of the city. There were lots of auxiliary cops around because I was near the Police Academy. I noticed lots of kids with portfolios who were coming from the School of Visual Arts. The wind kept pushing me towards Second Avenue. From a distance, I could see my destination. A dirty blue and white banner hung from the second story of 380 Second Avenue, proudly announcing the Margaret Sanger Center of Planned Parenthood, New York City.

Planned Parenthood has quite a reputation. It is where young girls can go to get information about birth control, pregnancy, abortion, and venereal disease. The outstanding feature is the clinic's promise of confidentiality. The organization is funded by private donations, and federal subsidies make up less than 15 percent of its budget.

I entered the reception area and asked for an appointment. Without looking up, the secretary said, "Go down the hall, turn right, and pick up one of the beige phones to make an appointment." Although I was taken aback by her indifference, I did as she said. The woman on the phone said I could have an appointment that morning, and she sent me back to the reception desk.

This time the woman looked up. She gave me forms to fill out and said that I would have to pay in advance. A pelvic exam was fifty dollars. I filled out the form, paid the fifty bucks and waited.

The waiting room was comfortable. There were eight loveseats arranged in a rectangle with small tables at the corners. Five women hid behind magazines and newspapers. One guy sat staring out the window. I was the only person who wasn't nervously puffing away at a cigarette. It was uncomfortably silent. Nothing happened for half an hour. Then my name was called.

A robot of a woman directed me to a laboratory. My urine was tested for sugar and my blood for iron. The robot directed me to another waiting area, and once again I was told to listen for my name to be called. I sat and waited in disgust. There wasn't a friendly face around. My finger was bleeding from the blood test. I hadn't realized it, so there was blood on my purse and my notebook. It was embarrassing, and I could feel the heat in my face as I blushed. My stomach was queasy, and I hoped it would not take much longer.

The girl across from me offered me a tissue. Finally, I thought, a human! I asked her what she thought of the place, and she said exactly what I expected: "It's not cheap, the people aren't very nice, and I can't wait to get this over with." Other women in the room were listening to us and agreed with a chorus of "Me, too" and "They're too slow."

I waited for over twenty minutes before I was called. A very young girl led me to her office. We went over my family's medical history and she took my blood pressure. She seemed nice, but she was in a hurry. She led me to a changing room and told me to don the traditional paper robe and slippers. Then, I couldn't believe it, another waiting room!

This room was a small cubicle with chairs lining the walls. There were three women already waiting there, dressed as I was and looking very silly. Again, I asked opinions about the clinic. One woman complained that she had been there for over an hour—so had I. Another girl said she'd been to better clinics—so had I. We all agreed that fifty dollars for a pelvic exam was not the going rate. My clinic, the Flushing Women's Health Organization, charges forty dollars on the first visit and thirty dollars every time after. This wait was the longest. We talked for over half an hour.

When the doctor called me, I sighed with relief. She introduced herself as Irma and smiled. We discussed the advantages and disadvantages of different methods of birth control, and I began to feel at ease. I told her how disappointed I was with Planned Parenthood and she didn't seem surprised. She said that up until a year ago, they had heard no complaints, but because they've become increasingly popular, they've had more patients than they're equipped to handle. "Yet," she defended, "we do our best."

Given a choice, I would go to my usual doctor. It is closer to home, cheaper, and much faster. I spent over two and a half hours at Planned Parenthood—I'm not impressed.

Now begin writing your rough draft. When you have completed it, take a day's rest.

FOCUS: PARAGRAPH DEVELOPMENT

Whether writing an essay or a paragraph, the writer is faced with the same questions: How do I develop my subject? What do I say? The ways of generating ideas that are useful for the essay are also useful for the paragraph: the journalist's questions or free-writing or the explorer's questions.

Another way of generating ideas results from examining the structure of most paragraphs, for just as sentences either coordinate ideas or subordinate them, so do most paragraphs. Coordination occurs when two or more equal ideas are enumerated or an idea is repeated for emphasis. Subordination offers one idea in explanation of another. Coordination enumerates or emphasizes; subordination explains. In developing your topic sentence, therefore, determine the needs of your readers. Do they require you to enumerate or list points about your subject, or do they need an explanation of it? This method of inquiry should help you to develop any topic into a paragraph once you have determined your readers' needs.

For example, the following paragraph utilizes coordination:

When a society's values and institutions are seriously questioned, life transitions become anxious and traumatic. What does it mean to face the time of marriage when divorce is so common and alternative living arrangements, such as communes and cohabitation, are so widely explored? What does it mean to choose a vocation when all forms of work, and the idea of work itself, are so severely criticized? What does it mean to grow up when adulthood implies being locked into support of a violent, directionless culture? What does it mean to grow old when old people are isolated, put off by themselves in "homes" or institutions, apart from family and ongoing community? What does it mean to die when science has challenged sacred religious beliefs and in the place of spiritual comfort has left only the "scientific method"?

—**Robert Jay Lifton and Eric Olson,** "Death—the Lost Season," from *Living and Dying*

An outline of this paragraph would look like the following:

Topic sentence: When a society's values and institutions are seriously questioned, life transitions become anxious and traumatic.

1. What does it mean to face the time of marriage when divorce is so common and alternative living arrangements, such as communes and cohabitation, are so widely explored?
2. What does it mean to choose a vocation when all forms of work, and the idea of work itself, are so severely criticized?
3. What does it mean to grow up when adulthood implies being locked into support of a violent, directionless culture?
4. What does it mean to grow old when old people are isolated, put off by

themselves in "homes" or institutions, apart from family and ongoing community?

5. What does it mean to die when science has challenged sacred religious beliefs and in the place of spiritual comfort has left only the "scientific method"?

Note the use of the repetitive "What does it mean" phrase to emphasize the equality of all five points. Coordination often employs repetition, thus creating a dramatic effect.

The following is an example of subordination, in that Sentence 3 develops the topic sentence by explaining why the order of the city streets is complex, and Sentence 4 compares city-street life to a ballet, explaining the topic sentence further. Sentence 5 continues the analogy:

Under the seeming disorder of the old city, wherever the old city is working successfully, is a marvelous order for maintaining the safety of the streets and the freedom of the city. It is a complex order. Its essence is intricacy of sidewalk use, bringing with it a constant succession of eyes. This order is all composed of movement and change, and although it is life, not art, we may fancifully call it the art form of the city and liken it to the dance—not to a simple-minded precision dance with everyone kicking up at the same time, twirling in unison and bowing off en masse, but to an intricate ballet in which the individual dancers and ensembles all have distinctive parts which miraculously reinforce each other and compose an orderly whole. The ballet of the good city sidewalk never repeats itself from place to place, and in any one place is always replete with new improvisions.

—**Jane Jacobs,** *The Death and Life of Great American Cities*

Outlined, the paragraph looks like this:

Topic sentences: Under the seeming disorder of the old city, wherever the old city is working successfully, is a marvelous order for maintaining the safety of the streets and the freedom of the city. It is a complex order.

I. Its essence is intricacy of sidewalk use, bringing with it a constant succession of eyes.
   A. This order is all composed of movement and change, and although it is life, not art, we may fancifully call it the art form of the city and liken it to the dance—not to a simple-minded precision dance with everyone kicking up at the same time, twirling in unison and bowing off en masse, but to an intricate ballet in which the individual dancers and ensembles all have distinctive parts which miraculously reinforce each other and compose an orderly whole.
      1. The ballet of the good city sidewalk never repeats itself from place to place, and in any one place is always replete with new improvisions.

Most paragraphs are a mixture of coordination and subordination because most lists need explanation and explanations often require lists of examples. In the following paragraph, subordination follows coordination, as the first four sentences are coordinate, and the fifth is subordinate to the fourth.

This man made no flourishes to attract anybody. He never drove a fast horse. He never wore trousers with checks any larger than an inch square—which, for the time, was conservative. His house never got afire and burned down just after the fire insurance had run out. Not one of his boys and girls ever got drowned or run over by the steamcars. The few that died growing up died of diphtheria or scarlet fever, which were what children died of then, the usual ways.

—**Robert P. Tristram Coffin,** "My Average Uncle," from *Book of Uncles*

An outline of Coffin's paragraph clearly shows the mixture of subordination with coordination:

Topic sentence: This man made no flourishes to attract anybody.

1. He never drove a fast horse.
2. He never wore trousers with checks any larger than an inch square—which, for the time, was conservative.
3. His house never got afire and burned down just after the fire insurance had run out.
4. Not one of his boys and girls ever got drowned or run over by the steam-cars.
   a. The few that died growing up died of diphtheria or scarlet fever, which were what children died of then, the usual ways.

The following paragraph, on the other hand, illustrates the mixture of coordination with subordination. Two parallel examples in Sentences 4 and 5 provide the coordination in an otherwise subordinate organization:

I have an increasing admiration for the teacher in the country school where we have a third-grade scholar in attendance. She not only undertakes to instruct her charges in all the subjects of the first three grades, but she manages to function quietly and effectively as a guardian of their health, their clothes, their habits, their mothers, and their snowball engagements. She has been doing this sort of Augean task for twenty years, and is both kind and wise. She cooks for the children on the stove that heats the room, and she can cool their passions or warm their soup with equal competence. She conceives their costumes, cleans up their messes, and shares their confidences. My boy already regards his teacher as his great friend, and I think tells her a great deal more than he tells us.

—**E. B. White,** "Education," from *One Man's Meat*

Again, an outline reveals the pattern:

> *Topic sentence:* I have an increasing admiration for the teacher in the country school where we have a third-grade scholar in attendance.

> I. She not only undertakes to instruct her changes in all the subjects of the first three grades, but she manages to function quietly and effectively as a guardian of their health, their clothes, their habits, their mothers, and their snowball engagements.
>   A. She has been doing this sort of Augean task for twenty years, and is both kind and wise.
>   1. She cooks for the children on the stove that heats the room, and she can cool their passions or warm their soup with equal competence.
>   2. She conceives their costumes, cleans up their messes, and shares their confidences.
>   a. My boy already regards his teacher as his great friend, and I think tells her a great deal more than he tells us.

When composing a paragraph, of course, a writer is also choosing a pattern of exposition. In a coordinate paragraph, he or she may be listing reasons, examples, definitions, or effects. In a subordinate paragraph, he or she may also use definition, example, cause, and effect to explain the points. And in a mixed paragraph, lists and explanations may be based on any combination of patterns (see Chapter 5, p. 149–154, for further discussion of patterns of exposition).

For example, Robert Jay Lifton's coordinate paragraph above lists causes, or reasons why; Jacobs used analogy to explain her point; Coffin used a list of examples followed by a contrastive explanation; and White combined a cause-and-effect explanation ("She has been doing this sort of Augean task for twenty years, and is both kind and wise") with a list of causes and concluded with an explanation that is an example.

SOME PRACTICE WITH DEVELOPING PARAGRAPHS

1. Analyze the following paragraphs to determine whether their organization is coordinate, subordinate, or mixed. Outline the paragraph, if an outline is helpful.

   a. Besides, aren't commercials in the public interest? Don't they help you choose what to buy? Don't they provide needed breaks from programming? Aren't many of them brilliantly done, and some of them funny? And now, with the new sexual freedom, all those gorgeous chicks with their shining hair and gleaming smiles? And if you didn't have commercials taking up a good part of each hour, how on earth would you find enough program material to fill the endless space/time void?

   > —**Marya Mannes,** "Television: The Splitting Image," from *The Saturday Review of Literature* (Nov. 1970)

b. The mother wasp goes tarantula-hunting when the egg in her ovary is almost ready to be laid. Flying low over the ground late on a sunny afternoon, the wasp looks for its victim or for the mouth of a tarantula burrow, a round hole edged by a bit of silk. The sex of the spider makes no difference, but the mother is highly discriminating as to species. Each species of Pepsis requires a certain species of tarantula, and the wasp will not attack the wrong species. In a cage with a tarantula which is not its normal prey, the wasp avoids the spider and is usually killed by it in the night.

—**Alexander Petrunkevitch,** "The Spider and the Wasp," from *Scientific American* (Aug. 1952)

c. Tell General Howard I know his heart. What he told me before I have in my heart. I am tired of fighting. Our chiefs are killed. Looking Glass is dead. Too-hoolhoolzote is dead. The old men are all dead. It is the young men who say yes or no. He who led on the young men [Ollokot] is dead. It is cold and we have no blankets. The little children are freezing to death. My people, some of them, have run away to the hills, and have no blankets, no food; no one knows where they are—perhaps freezing to death. I want to have time to look for my children and see how many of them I can find. Maybe I shall find them among the dead. Hear me, my chiefs! I am tired; my heart is sick and sad. From where the sun now stands I will fight no more forever.

—**Chief Joseph,** U.S. Secretary of War Report, 1877.

d. It is thus no exaggeration to say that Americans have taken to mechanical cooling avidly and greedily. Many have become all but addicted, refusing to go places that are not air-conditioned. In Atlanta, shoppers in Lenox Square so resented having to endure natural heat while walking outdoors from chilled store to chilled store that the mall management enclosed and air-conditioned the whole sprawling shebang. The widespread whining about Washington's raising of thermostats to a mandatory 78°F suggests that people no longer think of interior coolness as an amenity but consider it a necessity, almost a birthright, like suffrage. The existence of such a view was proved last month when a number of federal judges sitting too high and mighty to suffer 78°F, defied and denounced the Government's energy-saving order to cut back on cooling. Significantly, there was no popular outrage at this judicial insolence; many citizens probably wished that they could be so highhanded.

—**Frank Trippett,** "The Great American Cooling Machine," *Time* (1979)

2. What patterns of exposition—definition, contrast, comparison, exemplification, cause and effect, analogy, and so on—did each writer of the paragraphs above use?

3. Develop the following topic sentences into paragraphs. Write for a reader unfamiliar with the subject. Decide before writing whether you wish to proceed through coordination, subordination, or a combination of the two:

a. Sports figures are admired by everyone.

    b. Many young children understand the computer better than most adults.

    c. You can tell a person's lifestyle by the tee-shirt he or she wears.

What pattern of arrangement did you use in each paragraph you wrote?

REWRITING

Obtaining Feedback on Your Rough Draft

By now, you should have developed one or more successful channels for obtaining responses to your rough draft: your "other self," your peers, or your teacher. Again, use these channels for obtaining answers to the "Audience Response Guide" about your draft of your essay on a place.

——— AUDIENCE RESPONSE GUIDE ———

1. **What does the writer want to say in this paper? What is his or her purpose in writing? What does he or she want the paper to mean?**
2. **How does the paper affect the reader for whom it is intended?**
3. **How effective has the writer been in conveying his or her purpose and meaning?**
4. **How should the paper be revised to better fulfill its purpose and meaning?**

The following is a peer evaluation of the rough draft of the student essay "The Assembly-Line Method of Reproductive Health," in response to the four questions above:

1. The writer wants to convey her disappointment with the Planned Parenthood Center. She feels that she could have received as good if not better treatment from her own doctor, who would not have charged her as much or kept her waiting as long.
2. A reader can identify with the writer's feelings about the way patients are treated in a health clinic, particularly with her complaints about the indifference of some of the employees and the amount of time she had to wait. A reader who is interested in going into the health care profession might want to know more about how the clinic is run.
3. The group felt that the writer had been quite effective. She might, however, have tried to show in more detail what the other patients were like and

what they were feeling. Also, the group felt that the writer did not give enough information to account for the clinic's popularity.

4. The group suggested that the writer include more dialogue between herself and the other patients. They also suggested that more details about the positive aspects of her experience might help complete the picture.

Here is a revised version of "The Assembly-Line Method of Reproductive Health." How has the writer responded to the group's suggestions that she add more dialogue and more details? What other changes has she made?

THE ASSEMBLY-LINE METHOD OF REPRODUCTIVE HEALTH

The walk from the subway seemed long, and a strong cold wind was at my back, pushing me down Twenty-third Street. It was a nice part of the city, however, as there were lots of auxiliary cops around from the nearby Police Academy, and lots of kids with portfolios were coming from the School of Visual Arts. The wind kept pushing me toward Second Avenue. From a distance, I could see my destination. A dirty blue and white banner hung from the second story of 380 Second Avenue, proudly announcing the Margaret Sanger Center of Planned Parenthood.

Planned Parenthood has quite a reputation. It is where young women and men can go to get information about birth control, pregnancy, abortion, and venereal disease. The outstanding feature is its promise of confidentiality. Although other women's health organizations also offer confidentiality, Planned Parenthood was the first to do so.

I entered the reception area and asked for an appointment. Without looking up, the secretary told me to "Go down the hall, turn right, and pick up one of the beige phones on the wall to make an appointment." Although I was taken aback by her indifference, I did as she said. The woman on the phone said I could have an appointment that morning and told me to return to the reception desk.

This time, the woman looked up. She gave me forms to fill out and said I would have to pay in advance. A pelvic exam would be fifty dollars. I filled out the forms, paid the money, and waited.

The waiting room was comfortable. There were eight loveseats arranged in a rectangle with small tables at the corners. Five women hid behind newspapers and magazines. One man sat staring out the window at the street below. I was the only person who was not puffing away nervously at a cigarette. The silence was uncomfortable.

Nothing happened for twenty minutes, and then my name was called. A robot of a woman directed me to the laboratory, where my urine was tested for sugar, and my blood was examined for iron. The robot then directed me to another waiting area, and once again, I was told to wait, and listen for my name to be called. I sat and waited in disgust. There wasn't a friendly face to be found. My finger was bleeding from the blood test, and I hadn't realized it, so there was blood on my purse and my notebook. It was embarrassing, and I could feel the heat in my face as I blushed. I reached into my purse for a tissue but didn't find one. I felt very uneasy, and I hoped it wouldn't be much longer before I was through.

The girl across from me offered me a tissue. Finally, I thought, a human! I asked her what she thought of the place, and she said exactly what I expected: "It's not cheap, the people aren't very nice, and I can't wait to get out of here." Other women in the room were listening to us and agreed with what she said. Another girl spoke up, "I think their prices are pretty good. My abortion would cost more anywhere else." All the other women said they were there for mere pelvic exams and seemed to feel sorry for this woman. She explained, "I already have two children and my husband can't find a job." We talked for over twenty minutes. She said she would love to have the child if she thought she could offer it a decent life. "Times are tough," she said. When she left, the room became quiet again. It was sad to watch her walk away.

I waited for another twenty minutes until my name was called. A very young girl led me to her office on the other side of the building. We went over my personal and family medical history, and she took my blood pressure. I asked her who pays for the organization and found out that most of its funding comes from private donations. Federal subsidies make up only 15 percent of its budget. She said that if proposed legislation by the government was passed, they could use the federal money only to service women over eighteen. They are well prepared for anything that the laws may do to stop them from helping minors, however. This consultant was obviously interested in her work but couldn't talk long because of her busy schedule. She led me to a dressing room to don the traditional paper robe and slippers and then—I couldn't believe it—another waiting room!

This room was a small white cubicle with chairs lining the walls. There were three women already waiting there, dressed as I was and looking, as I did, very silly. Again, I asked for opinions about the clinic. One woman complained that she had had been there for over an hour—so had I. Another girl said she had been to better clinics—so had I. We all agreed that fifty dollars for a pelvic exam was not the going rate. My clinic, the Flushing Women's Health Organization, charges forty dollars for the first visit and thirty dollars for every visit after that. One middle-aged woman said that it wasn't so bad a year ago. She said that it had never taken more than one hour as long as you had an appointment. By the time I was called by the doctor, I had already been there two hours!

When the doctor called me in, I sighed with relief. She introduced herself as Irma and smiled. We discussed the advantages and disadvantages of different methods of birth control, and I began to feel at ease. I then told her of how disappointed I was with Planned Parenthood, and she didn't seem surprised. She said that up to a year ago they had heard no complaints. However, as they've become increasingly popular over the past year, they have more patients than they're equipped to handle. "Yet," she defended, "we do our best."

Given a choice, I would go back to my usual doctor. He's closer to home, cheaper, and much faster. I spent over two and a half hours at Planned Parenthood—I'm not impressed.

Revising: Substituting

A third method of revision, in addition to adding (pp. 65–66) and rearranging (pp. 97–98), is substituting. Substituting means trading words, phrases, and/or whole passages that do not contribute to the meaning of your essay for those that do.

Substitutions may be desirable for several reasons. One is that a word you have used may seem, when you are reading your essay over, to be not concrete enough: Why say the sky is gray when you can say it is leaden? Another is that a word may be inexact: you may have told your parents that your campus is far from the airport, leaving them to draw their own conclusions as to how much time they should leave for the taxi drive; to say that it is thirty minutes away is much more exact. You may also decide that one word conveys your tone of voice more successfully than another: "Teachers are stern" may convey the tone you want to establish more successfully than "Teachers are mean."

You may also want to substitute details if you find that your original detail does not create the impression that you wish to convey of your subject to your audience: When you are delineating the problems you are having with your car, its good features are out of place and should be replaced with further complaints, especially if your audience is the mechanic whom you paid to fix the car in the first place.

The structure of your essay may require substitutions as well. Whole paragraphs may be substituted if you discover that one point serves your purpose better than another. An item erroneously classified, for example, may be replaced with an item that does belong in the class you are writing about: Were you to classify the Kodak Instamatic as one of the types of 35mm cameras and omit the Leica, then a substitution would clearly be in order.

The student writer of "The Assembly-Line Method of Reproductive Health" has substituted some extensive dialogue in her revised version for the brief dialogue offered in her rough draft. Compare the revised version with the rough draft that appeared on pages 123–124. Can you point out other substitutions that the writer has made, more exact for less exact words, for example, or more appropriate for less appropriate details?

In writing the task for this chapter, you may want to substitute some dialogue that is especially pertinent for some that is lackluster. Some description may be extraneous to the operation of the place, and you may want to trade that for description that clarifies the process of the place. Or perhaps you have included too much narration of your visit and wish to substitute more information about the place.

Editing

Substitutions.   Substitutions can also be made when you are editing. A word or a phrase can be traded for another word or phrase for a number of reasons: more formal language is needed, more precise words are available, more colorful expression is desirable, or a different grammatical construction is required.

Transitions.   You are now combining your sentences nicely with conjunctions and conjunctive words and phrases. Scan your draft for these transitions. Are you using too many *and*'s and *but*'s? Try substituting more precise transitions—those that convey the exact relationship between ideas. *And* and *but*, particularly, are easily overdone.

For this particular assignment, substitute transitions of place when you are describing: "in the right-hand corner," "above me," "to my left," "on top." These prepositional phrases visually orient your readers and lead them from space to space.

Paragraphs.   Although rewriting paragraphs is usually a revising chore affecting meaning, paragraphs can also be edited. On the surface, in other words, does each paragraph have a clear structure, or does the topic sentence need a few additions or substitutions to clearly characterize the content of the paragraph? Are transitions included between thoughts? Are they, moreover, precise?

Mechanics.   By now, you know what mechanical errors you are inclined to make. Proofread your rough draft for these habitual mistakes and for any others that may have crept in.

Now revise and edit your rough draft.

BECOMING AWARE OF YOURSELF AS A WRITER

1. How did the explorer's method of inquiry aid you in thinking about your subject? For what other subjects might this be a useful inquiry method?

2. How did writing for a class in your curriculum differ from writing for your peers in general (or your English class) in the task for Chapter 2? How did it differ from writing for your instructor in the last chapter? To what extent do you think your audience affects the way you write?

3. Was interweaving the exposition, narration, description, and dialogue difficult for you? Do you understand the differing functions of exposition, narration, and description? Can you think of other writing assignments in which you have interwoven or might interweave the three?

4. What more have you learned about your own writing process from completing the task in this chapter? For example, are you more comfortable outlining before writing, or does an outline emerge only after you have completed your rough draft? Or does some other method of arranging your essay work for you?

5. What did you learn from writing about a place that was meaningful to you when you began the assignment? How did exploring the subject affect your perception of the place? What other subjects might you explore in the same way?

6. What kind of feedback are you receiving from your evaluators? Is it helpful? How could it be more helpful? What role do you play in its helpfulness?

7. How are you as an evaluator of the writing of others? To what extent does your reading of the writing of others affect your own writing?

8. What problems are you facing as a writer at the present? What steps have you plotted to solve them?

9. What are you satisfied with in your writing?

5
WRITING A CASE

PURPOSE

In this chapter, you will continue the activity of the previous chapter: exploring a question. Whereas in Chapter 4 you asked the question "Is my visit to this place going to corroborate the high opinion others have of it?" here you will be asking, "After frequent observation of a situation which I have prejudged, will I prove my prejudgment or prejudice to be, in fact, an accurate evaluation, or will I find that I must discard it in favor of a new conclusion?"

Observing a situation—an ongoing event or a person—over a period of time is called *casing the subject*, much as, in the popular use of the term, a thief "cases a joint" before breaking in to determine employee or resident patterns of behavior, or police "case" a location to catch criminals. Probably the most common use of the term *case* is found among social workers, who write case studies about the families they visit to explain their financial, physical, and emotional needs. And psychiatrists use the term to refer to their written narratives about the lives of their patients. The task for this chapter will be to observe a situation of some kind over a period of time and to write your own case study.

The main thrust of the chapter lies in testing a prejudice by acquiring facts about the subject. Prejudice is by definition an evaluation arrived at before one knows the facts of a situation. Although we form these hasty conclusions all too often throughout our lives, thoughtful people attempt to decrease their tendency to prejudge and attempt instead to form a conclusion based on a thorough examination of the subject.

In the first four chapters, we presented four methods of generating ideas: the journal (Chapter 1), free writing (Chapters 1 and 3), the journalist's questions (Chapter 2), and the explorer's questions (Chapter 4). In this chapter, we are going to present another series of questions, the classical questions, as further probes into your material.

The classical questions were devised by Aristotle during the Classical Age of Greece. As Athenians needed material for oral presentations at court and on ceremonial occasions, Aristotle devised a list of "topics" that would provide various ways of looking at any subject and generating ideas about it. These classical topics have been used in the study of rhetoric—both speech and writing—ever since. They have thus influenced Western patterns of thought for over two thousand years.

As you observe your situation, you may find some of the classical questions helpful in generating material for your case study. These questions, as used over the years, have also generated corresponding methods of arrangement of the material they generate, and they thus become a primary tool for the writer at various stages in the writing process.

After testing a prejudice through actual and frequent observation, and after writing about it with the aid of the classical questions, you should consider publishing your essay. The audience section in this chapter discusses writing for the common reader, that vague audience addressed by most publications to whom you might submit your essay. By selecting the audience that would be most interested in the outcome of your case and by finding an appropriate vehicle for publishing your findings, you may affect others' opinions about the situation you have observed.

GENERATING IDEAS: THE CLASSICAL QUESTIONS

Ten of the questions that Aristotle and other classical rhetoricians devised to generate ideas are the following:

1. What is it?
2. What class does it belong to, or what classes can it be divided into?
3. How is it like or unlike other objects, events, or ideas?
4. What caused it?
5. What did (will) it cause?
6. What process does it go through (has it gone through)?
7. What has been said about it by others?
8. What general ideas and values does it exemplify?
9. What examples are there of it?
10. What can be done about it?

In this chapter, we will consider Questions 3 through 6. (Questions 1 and 2 overlap with two of the explorer's questions discussed in the last chapter, and we will treat Questions 7 through 10 in subsequent chapters.)

In order to develop your topic fully, you will want to inquire into your subject at as many points as possible. Therefore, by forming subquestions about each of the classical questions, you can generate fuller answers. Some possible subquestions for Questions 3 through 6 are these:

III. How is *X* like or unlike other objects, events, or ideas?
    A. Am I equally interested in the other objects, events, or ideas, or am I using comparison and contrast as a device to describe *X* alone?
    B. If I am interested in all, then what points do they have in common? How are they different?
    C. If I am interested in describing *X* alone, then what objects, events, or ideas can I compare it with?
        1. Is there an analogy that usefully conveys *X?*
        2. How is *X* like *Y,* or like *Y* and *Z?*
    D. What can I contrast *X* with? How are these objects or ideas unlike *X?*

IV. What caused *X?*
    A. What is the most probable cause(s)?
    B. How far can I push the cause-and-effect relationship without committing one of the following logical fallacies (see also Chap. 8, pp. 275–277):
        1. Oversimplification
            a. Is it reasonable to assume *X* caused *Y?* Am I linking *X* and *Y* only because *X* happened just before *Y?*
            b. Is *X* the only cause of *Y?*
        2. Scapegoating
            a. Am I unfairly blaming an individual or a group for causing an effect that they did not actually cause?

V. What will *X* cause?
    A. Is the effect inevitable?
        1. Will *X* lead to this effect and this effect, alone?
        2. Has *X* been the only cause of this effect?
    B. What reasonable effect(s) can I postulate?
    C. What analogies can I devise to show what the outcome might be?

VI. How does *X* work?
    A. What does *X* do?
    B. How is *X* put together?
    C. What was *X* intended to do?
    D. How well does *X* fulfill its intention or purpose?

To best illustrate how the classical questions can be applied to a subject, let us compare and contrast them with the explorer's questions from Chapter 4. What material, for example, would the classical questions generate about a classroom as compared with the material that results from the explorer's queries?

What can a classroom be compared to? The explorer's questions asked how a classroom compared and contrasted with others in its class. The classical questions would also generate this material but would allow for analogy as well, for going outside the class of schoolrooms or, more broadly, places of study altogether for sources of comparison. Analogy discovers the similarities between two dissimilar things. It suggests that two unlike things are, in fact, alike in some important characteristics; for example, a classroom might be called a kind of mental gymnasium because it is a place where people exercise and develop their mind. Analogy may even be used to argue that dissimilar objects with some apparent similarities may also be similar in less apparent ways. By comparing Rome and America, both powerful nations, historians also argue that like Rome, America will become corrupt and decline. One could very well argue that as the gym has become more mechanized with the introduction of such bodybuilding equipment as the nautilus machine, so the classroom will become more mechanized with the development of computerized educational techniques.

What caused it? The explorer's questions do not search for a causal relationship. They do not ask about the forces that brought the classroom into existence. The classical questions not only ask what immediate force caused the classroom, such as the construction workers who built it, but also about ultimate causes, in this case the human need for a formal education outside the home or workplace, for a place where the student can concentrate on learning for the sake of learning.

What will it cause? Again, the explorer's method does not look for effects. The classical answer might be that a classroom causes learning, which, in turn, allows people to develop intellectually and perhaps socially and economically as well.

How does it work? Here the classical and the explorer's questions are very close (just as the classical questions "What is it?" and "What class does it belong to?" are very close to two of the explorer's questions).

Explorer's	*Classical*
• What larger system is it part of?	• What was it intended to do?
• How do the parts work together?	• What does it do? How is it put together?

The classical approach also adds an evaluative dimension in asking, "How well does it fulfill its intention or purpose?"

From the comparisons and contrasts between the two sets of questions, their differing thrusts should be clear: the explorer's questions seek out new facts about the subject—as a static entity, as a dynamic entity, and as part of a larger system—whereas the classical questions relate the subject to past or current knowledge and values by comparing and contrasting it with unlike subjects, by explaining its causes and effects, and by evaluating it. Both sets of questions, used separately or together, can aid you in generating an almost infinite number of ideas about your subject.

SOME PRACTICE WITH THE CLASSICAL QUESTIONS

1. Identify the logical fallacies of the following causal statements. Which are examples of oversimplification and which of scapegoating?

   a. The size of Cleopatra's nose caused the fall of the Roman Empire. If her nose had been longer, she would have been less beautiful, and Marc Antony would not have fallen in love with her. He would not then have neglected his military duties and lost the battle of Salamis, thus setting in motion the decline in might and authority of Roman rule.

   b. Johnny caused his teacher to go crazy. When he accidentally hit her with a board eraser he had thrown across the room, Mrs. Gorp became hysterical and had to leave school. She never returned. It was later reported that she had been institutionalized.

   c. The headline read, ''Pac Man Kills. Enraged Youth Kills Friend After Losing at Video Game.''

   d. The student was asked, ''Why did you fail math?'' The student replied, ''Because the teacher was boring. If the class had been more interesting, I'd have been more attentive to my work.''

2. Which pairs of items seem most promising as subjects for comparison or contrast? Explain why some are promising but not others. How do comparison and contrast help you to understand each item in the pair better than if it were described alone?

   a. *E.T./The Wizard of Oz*
   b. *The Empire Strikes Back/M.A.S.H.*
   c. The Beatles/the Marx Brothers
   d. Video game arcades/assembly lines
   e. NHL hockey games/street fighting
   f. Cigarette smoking/drug addiction

3. Complete the following statements by devising an analogy to fit each example. How does each analogy help to describe the subject?

   a. My love is like . . .
   b. This politician was as smooth as . . .

c. He captained the basketball team like . . .
d. Her hamburger tasted like . . .
e. He strode down the street like . . .

ADDRESSING YOUR AUDIENCE: THE COMMON READER AND WRITING FOR PUBLICATION

When writers write for publication, they usually write for one of two audiences. Either the magazine or journal is directed toward a very specific audience, or it has a general readership. In the last chapter, we discussed writing for a specific audience, one that is interested in your subject matter and knowledgeable about it. In this chapter, we are going to discuss how to write for a very general audience, the one often known as the common reader, an audience that may or may not be interested in your subject and may or may not know much about it.

The writer who writes for a common reader usually writes for a large audience that is comprised of many different groups of people. She or he must therefore extrapolate those interests and qualities that these readers share and use this composite frame of reference in deciding how to write for this audience. How this can be done is the subject of this section.

No matter what magazine or newspaper you may read, none is written for everyone, no matter how unspecialized the content may appear to be. Each publication has a readership that can be fairly well defined, even though it may not be a technical journal, an entertainment rag, or a musician's bible. The common reader of one publication is not necessarily the common reader of another.

Think, for example, of the newspapers that are sold on the newsstands in your town. Newspapers with national circulations like *The Wall Street Journal* and even *The New York Times* have audiences that can be fairly well defined. Businesspeople probably read *The Wall Street Journal,* and many people who buy *The New York Times,* with its sections on cultural affairs and informed opinion, are college-educated. Consider next the paper with the largest distribution in your state. Its readership may include these two audiences, but it may also number many who read neither *The Journal* nor *The Times.* And when you add your local neighborhood daily or weekly to the list, you find still another common reader emerging, one who may read none of the other newspapers, one interested only in news that is close to home, like local marriages and births, sports, and politics. Finally, the common reader of your college newspaper is still another composite based on the interests and knowledge shared by the students on your campus.

How does one determine the frame of reference of the readership common to a particular publication? The following aspects of the publication should provide some guidelines: the types of subjects covered, the depth of the information given, the editorial perspectives delineated, the level of vocabulary used, the number and type of visuals printed (such as photographs and comics), and the advertisements included.

Take *The New York Times*, for example, which is available in all college libraries if not on your local newsstand. Why do we assume that it is for a common reader who has a college education? Look first at the subjects covered. We find in Section 1 world and U.S. news and two pages of editorials, usually of a liberal bent, and informed opinions; in Section 2, we find extensive treatment of the stock market; and there are various daily supplements on sports, business, science, education, and entertainment. Although the types of information do not necessarily set *The Times* aside as aimed at the educated reader, the depth of information clearly does so. Also, the vocabulary level is high (it is estimated to be at a 12th-grade reading level). The number and type of visuals are a further indication because the headlines are small, the pictures are few, and no comic strips are included. And although middle-priced items are advertised in its pages, luxury items tend to predominate.

At the other extreme are the tabloids. The topics covered in their pages are news, sports, and entertainment, with an emphasis in each case on the sensational aspects. The size of the headlines is very large, as are the pictures. The articles, on the other hand, are very short, and their depth of information is shallow. They are written on about an 8th-grade reading level. The advertisements are for products that are in a low to middle price range.

Once a writer has scanned his or her chosen publication from these angles, he or she can begin to assemble a reader frame of reference. The typical reader of the tabloid, we can assume, has perhaps a high-school education but often less; has a lower to middle income; is interested in the easily understood, often flamboyant aspects of the news rather than an in-depth analysis; and spends as much time on the sports, human interest, and comic sections as on the news. The reader of *The New York Times*, we can assume, not only is educated but is also inclined to be fairly prosperous, interested in understanding the news as well as in keeping abreast of it, liberal in political views, and willing to read the news on a daily basis. Anyone writing for either publication must take all of these factors into account if he or she wishes to reach the intended readership.

Of course, a writer does not always know what publication a given piece of writing should best be directed toward. Often one must select a publication after a piece has been written. The question then becomes "What publication has an audience similar to the one I have written for?" The first step in the process of finding an appropriate home for your writing is to make a list of the publications with which you are familiar. In addition to newspapers on the national, state, local, and campus levels, consider newsletters as a likely vehicle for publication. Newsletters are published by most agencies—by libraries, schools, department stores, homeowners' associations, athletic associations, and theater groups. The advantages of writing for a newsletter are many: the audience in most cases is specialized, and if you are yourself familiar with the specialization, their frame of reference will be easy for you to discover. Also, newsletters will be more like-

ly than a more professional publication to publish the work of a beginning writer. Finally, the editor might work with you in shaping your piece for
publication.

After you have considered the likely vehicles for the publication of your essay, such as newspapers and newsletters, begin to think of magazines that might
publish your work. If you are serious about being published, think realistically
about which magazines, such as small specialty magazines, might be likely to
publish the work of a student writer. You can arrive at the frame of reference of
the readers common to magazines by analyzing the same features as were analyzed above for newspapers and newsletters.

SOME PRACTICE WITH WRITING FOR THE COMMON READER

1. Analyze the audiences of the following publications written for a so-called common reader. What groups in America are excluded by the audience appeal of
   any of these magazines? Which magazines are addressed to the same audiences?

   Life Magazine

   Time Magazine

   National Enquirer

   Reader's Digest

   TV Guide

   People Magazine

   Atlantic Monthly

2. Compare the audiences of *The New York Times,* your state's largest daily newspaper, and your hometown newspaper. To what extent do their audiences overlap? How are they different?

3. Take the frame of reference assembled above for the readers common to *The
   New York Times* and determine how they would best be approached on the following topics in terms of their attitude toward the subject, the depth of information they would require, and your role in relation to them:

   The CIA in Central America

   Poland

The New York Yankees

Disarmament

Princess Di

Unemployment

4. Select one of the following topics, find a shaping idea for it, and determine what audience you would best like to reach. Then choose a publication that reaches that audience, explaining why you think it does:

The American auto industry

Cable television

The value of an education in America

Young people and the job market

Automation

5. Analyze the frame of reference of the audience for your college newspaper suggested by a perusal of a few issues. How similar is this frame of reference to that you devised for your peers in Chapter 2? On the basis of any dissimilarities, what suggestions would you make to the editors about the appropriateness of the newspaper for its audience?

TASK: WRITING A CASE

As the writing task for this chapter, choose an ongoing situation—an event, a person, a process, or a condition—about which you have made a prejudgment of some sort, and through a series of visits, observations, and/or interviews, write a case study in which you test your prejudgment or prejudice against the information that you have amassed. Your subject must be one that you have not observed sufficiently to form a legitimate conclusion about and that you have prejudged for one reason or another, either from past experience with similar subjects, because of hearsay, or because you judged hastily. This subject must be one that you can frequently observe while you are preparing to write the essay.

Logical areas in which to search for the subject of your case study are school, work, or your neighborhood. You might, for example, observe a sports team at practice or in the first two weeks of play to determine if the players are as bad as your prejudice tells you they are; a class after a difficult exam to determine if they will, as you suspect blame only the teacher; a new arrangement at work that you believe will prove counterproductive; a noisy group in the local library who you think cannot possibly be accomplishing any work; public transportation that you have always assumed to be ineffficient although you have never used it; or a person with whom your first encounter was unpleasant.

In order to successfully test your prejudice, you will want to observe your situation frequently and with objectivity. You will be following much the same procedure that a scientist engages in when testing a hypothesis: through the gathering of many facts, she or he either corroborates the hypothesis or rejects it. Because a prejudice, like a hypothesis, precedes the acquisition of actual knowledge, testing both is absolutely essential for the thoughtful, educated person. As you embark on this task, play the role of the scientist—that of a disinterested, objective observer who is always willing to reject her or his own hypothesis if the facts demand it.

Use the questions of the classical method of inquiry in generating material for your case study. Different questions will be useful for different topics, so you will want to choose those that seem like they are going to prove most useful for you in gathering information and evaluating your reaction.

Obviously, other people may share your prejudice about your subject, and you may want to prove to them that you and they have been either wrong or completely justified. Choose a publication whose readership would be interested in your case study and that would actually consider publishing your essay. You might try for the school newspaper, for example, or a newsletter at work or the neighborhood weekly. Because most of such publications are addressed to a common reader, the discussion of writing for the common reader above should be helpful in determining what your readers' background and point of view are and what depth of information they require. If you are not serious about publication at this point, then select any magazine that you are familiar with, and do your best to analyze and write for its audience.

In the sections that follow, we will discuss how to choose the most appropriate classical questions for your topic, how to construct a frame of reference and evaluate the depth of information needs of the reader common to a particular publication, and how to arrange your essay according to the arrangement patterns that correspond to the classical questions you have asked.

WRITING THE ESSAY

Generating Ideas with the Classical Questions

Before beginning the observations of your subject, you might want to review the classical questions discussed in the first section of this chapter as a way of deciding what to look for while you observe. Although all of the listed questions are at your disposal, and all subjects will answer some questions better than others, four seem to be most useful in completing this task. Each of these four questions generates others in responding to the task in general and may generate still others in response to your particular subject:

1. *How is it like or unlike other objects, events, or ideas?*
   How is it like or unlike other similar situations?
   How is it like or unlike the ideal of its situation?
   How is it like or unlike what I thought of it before observing it?
2. *What caused it?*
   What brought about the situation or an aspect of the situation?
   What caused the prejudice that I originally had (or the conclusion I still have) about the situation?
3. *What did (will) it cause?*
   What effect(s) has this situation I am observing caused?
   What effect(s) do my observations suggest it might cause in the future?
4. *What process does it go through (has it gone through)?*
   What process is the situation going through as I am making my observations?
   How is the situation changing from observation to observation?

Jot down any other variations on these questions that occur to you to ask about your subject. A student writing about the Soho Soccer Club, a team based in Manhattan, which he felt lacked cohesion, asked the following questions:

1. *How is it like or unlike other objects, events, or ideas?*
   How does the Soho Soccer Club compare and contrast with a professional soccer team?
   How does their coach compare with professional coaches?
2. *What caused it?*
   Why does the team lack cohesion?
   Why is the coach unable to achieve this cohesion?
3. *What did (will) it cause?*
   Will the team improve in the next two weeks under this coach's supervision?
   Will the team suffer loss of morale?
   Will team discipline be affected?
   Will the team have a losing season?
4. *What process does it go through (has it gone through)?*
   What will the coach encourage his team to do in the practices I observe?
   Will he teach transition before he teaches the proper passing techniques?
   Will he teach them how to kick properly?
   Do his players like and respect him?

Addressing the Reader Common to Your Publication

Think of a publication that might conceivably publish your essay, such as your college newspaper, a neighborhood weekly newspaper, a newsletter connected in some way with the situation you have chosen to write about, or some similar journal. Although actually publishing an essay is worth trying and would certainly be rewarding, if no such publication occurs to you then choose any publication whose readers you think would be interested in your subject matter.

If you are not well versed in the particulars of your publication, then browse through it at some length now, looking at the types of articles and reading some of them to determine the depth of information they contain; examining the editorials, if any, for the editors' point of view; noting the products advertised and any other visuals (how large are the headings, are pictures or photographs included, are there any cartoons, and, if so, of what nature: political, comic strip, other?); and surveying the feature columns for subject and focus. Ask yourself throughout this get-acquainted period whom each article and editorial is intended for: Is the reader being addressed educated, and if so, how much? Is a special hobby or career being presupposed? What social class does the publication seem aimed at? Is religion or sex or political persuasion being appealed to?

Once you have a knowledge of the publication you are writing for, answer the questions of the "Audience Analysis Guide" developed for this task.

———— AUDIENCE ANALYSIS GUIDE ————

1. **What is the frame of reference of the readers common to this publication for which I am writing?**

2. **What will be their point of view on my subject? Will they share my initial prejudice?**

3. **What voice am I selecting as I write this essay? How can or will my voice selection affect my audience's point of view? If through observation I have decided that I no longer believe what I once did about my subject, but I suspect that my audience is still prejudiced about it, what voice can I use to bridge the gap?**

4. **What depth of information about my subject does my audience need and want: (a) are they prejudiced as I was; (b) have we both observed the situation sufficiently to form a valid conclusion; or (c) have they formed no opinion on my subject at all. In each case, a different depth of information will be needed: the first reader will need much depth of new material gleaned from your observations, the second reader will be interested both in why you formed the prejudice in the first place (background), and in why you subsequently changed your mind (new information), and the third reader will need to know both what the situation is and why you formed a prejudice about it (mainly background).**

For example, a student interested in the Thalia Spanish Theater wrote about its "innovative" director, who "encourages the creativity of the actor." The publishing "home" for his essay was the Thalia Program, which audiences receive at the beginning of each performance. He decided that the frame of reference of his readership was that they were Catholic, were of Spanish descent (although some might be simply devotees of the Spanish theater), were middle-class, had received a secondary education in their native countries or had a background in the performing arts, and were of both sexes and all ages.

He felt that his audience loved the theater and would share his excitement about the director. The role he was playing was that of a student of the Spanish theater who hoped one day to be a leading actor in the Thalia Company. He felt that the audience would respond to the voice of someone who shared their love of the theater and knew something about it.

Because his audience was familiar with his subject, at least in its general outlines, he knew he could devote his essay to an in-depth discussion of the techniques employed by the director.

Arranging the Essay

The Shaping Idea.   Several arrangement patterns may be used in fulfilling this task: cause and effect, comparison and contrast, and process analysis. These may be used separately or in combination, depending on the shaping idea that you have chosen for your essay. If you have not yet chosen a shaping idea, you will want to compose one now, one that reflects the situation that you are casing, your prejudice toward it, and the classical questions that you chose to answer in generating ideas for your paper. Here are some examples of students' shaping ideas:

1. I have heard that the process of creating a character is always challenging when working with Mr. Davila, who has developed a number of innovations on the Stanislavsky method that have proven stimulating to the creativity of the actor.

2. Although some of the players have a good sound knowledge of the game, the team lacks cohesion because of the coach's poor tactical methods.

3. I have always thought that the public library is like a zoo and that students cannot accomplish very much there.

The student writing on the first shaping idea will no doubt discuss the process that Mr. Davila goes through in directing his actors, perhaps also discussing why this approach is so stimulating to the actors, and perhaps comparing him with other directors as well. The second shaping idea calls for a discussion of the coach's poor process of teaching tactical methods, of the effects of this process on the players, and of the ways in which he compares with other coaches. The last shaping idea intends to present the effects on students of studying in the public library and perhaps to contrast this place of study with other, quieter ones.

These classical questions all have corresponding patterns of arrangement, and we will now discuss cause and effect, comparison and contrast, and process analysis.

Cause and Effect.   The pattern of arranging your material when discussing causes and effects depends entirely on your subject matter and how many causes and effects you are discussing. The basic patterns are these:

- A caused B (and C and D, depending on the number of effects).
- A is caused by B (and C and D, depending on the number of causes).
- A caused B, B caused C, and C caused D.

These patterns can be used to apply to a single paragraph or to an entire essay. When applied to a paragraph, A, B, C, and D may each be contained in one or two sentences; when applied to an essay, each letter may be the subject of an entire paragraph. Here is a student paragraph developed according to one of these causal patterns:

Eight books were assigned from the course, and I found myself reading from four at a time. As if that wasn't difficult enough, the reading material never seemed to be fully explained in class. Something was always left hanging. For a while, I figured that perhaps it was just I who was having difficulty and that I wasn't putting enough effort into my work. No one asked questions as "Mrs. Doe" went along through the battles between lords and vassals, popes and kings. Thus I figured that everyone else understood the work, and that I just had to devote more time and effort to my studies. So read and study I did, until I was down to four hours' sleep per night.

Comparison and Contrast.   Two basic patterns are available when you are comparing and contrasting subjects. One is the "whole-by-whole" method, in which each subject is presented separately, and then comparisons and contrasts are delineated; the other is the "part-by-part" method, in which the two subjects are compared and contrasted point by point throughout the paragraph or essay.

When applied to a paragraph, the whole-by-whole method requires that two or three sentences at the beginning of the paragraph be devoted to the first subject, two or three in the middle deal with the second subject, and the final third of the paragraph point out the similarities and differences. The part-by-part method for a paragraph calls for every sentence to explore a different point at which the two subjects either compare or contrast.

When applied to an entire essay, the whole-by-whole method would suggest that the first section of the essay discuss one subject, the middle section present the other, and the final section directly compare and contrast the two. In using the part-by-part method for an essay, one would probably assign to each paragraph a different point on which the two subjects would be compared and/or contrasted.

Below are two student paragraphs illustrating these two methods of comparison and contrast:

Part-by-part

The roles of the candidates' wives finally convinced me who would win. Louise Lehrman sent a "woman-to-woman" message telling of the faith she had in her husband. This may have been a good idea, but unfortunately Matilda Cuomo beat her to the punch. Days earlier, Mrs. Cuomo was seen on TV giving virtually the same message. Matilda Cuomo was on the campaign trail with and without her husband. Louise Lehrman's lack of involvement in her husband's campaign may have hurt him very much.

Whole-by-whole

When the public library is busy, which is most of the time, all the tables are full, and the majority of people are engrossed in conversation. The smaller kids are running around wildly. High-school kids are noisily putting the books back on the shelves. The elderly talk louder because many of them are hard of hearing. Long lines have formed at the reference desk and checkout counters. On the other hand, the library at the local college has lots of space for students who want to study. It is equipped with several small, comfortable, soundproof rooms for people who need peace and quiet. These rooms have glass all around them, and you can see people talking but you can't hear them. The college library is more spacious, more quiet, and more accommodating.

Process Analysis. Process analysis combines elements of narration and exposition: narration because a process usually occurs in chronological order, exposition because one is explaining how something is done. The logical pattern for process analysis is to break up the stages of a process into their proper or logical order: Step A, Step B, Step C, Step D, and so on. If one is describing a process that others must attempt to follow, one cannot take too much care in presenting the correct order of the steps in the process as well as in describing what takes place at each step.

Again, as in the cause-and-effect and the comparison-and-contrast patterns, if one is writing a paragraph on a process, each sentence will depict a different step; if one is writing an essay, each paragraph will describe a step or a unified series of steps. Here is a paragraph developed according to the process pattern:

Our defense is an intelligent and coordinated one. I drop back ten yards to break up a pass over the middle. Danny Romero, a solid defensive player, moves to the deep right side as safety. Left-side safety Eddie Dietrick, who leads the team in interceptions with four, tears across his side of the field. Short left-side safety Jimmy White, who has the reactions of a cat, watches the opposing quarterback intently. On the short right-hand side, John Sullivan, the most physical player on the team, prepares for a receiver foolish enough to run into his orbit. Jeff Marconi and Frank Roberto, two solid backup defensive players, dig their cleats and tense their bodies. This is the way our shifting zone defense works.

Model Essay.   The essay that follows, from *Pilgrim at Tinker Creek* by Annie Dillard, exemplifies the chapter task in many ways. The author "stalked" (or cased) muskrats over a short period of time (one summer, although she says it took her years to become completely successful at it), and although from her experience and her reading, she had decided that "muskrats were almost impossible to observe," through persistence she proved this prejudgment wrong.

Stalking Muskrats
Annie Dillard

Learning to stalk muskrats took me several years.

I've always known there were muskrats in the creek. Sometimes when I drove late at night my headlights' beam on the water would catch the broad lines of ripples made by a swimming muskrat, a bow wave, converging across the water at the raised dark vee of its head. I would stop the car and get out: nothing. They eat corn and tomatoes from my neighbors' gardens, too, by night, so that my neighbors were always telling me that the creek was full of them. Around here, people call them "mushrats"; Thoreau called them "Musquashes." They are not of course rats at all (let alone squashes). They are more like diminutive beavers, and, like beavers, they exude a scented oil from musk glands under the base of the tail——hence the name. I had read in several respectable sources that muskrats are so wary they are almost impossible to observe. One expert who made a full-time study of large populations, mainly by examining "sign" and performing autopsies on corpses, said he often went for weeks at a time without seeing a single living muskrat.

One hot evening three years ago, I was standing more or less *in* a bush. I was stock-still, looking deep into Tinker Creek from a spot on the bank opposite the house, watching a group of bluegills stare and hang motionless near the bottom of a deep, sunlit pool. I was focused for depth. I had long since lost myself, lost the creek, the day, lost everything but still amber depth. All at once I couldn't see. And then I could: a young muskrat had appeared on top of the water, floating on its back. Its forelegs were folded languorously across its chest; the sun shone on its upturned belly. Its youthfulness and rodent grin, coupled with its ridiculous method of locomotion, which consisted of a lazy wag of the tail assisted by an occasional dabble of a webbed hind foot, made it an enchanting picture of decadence, dissipation, and summer sloth. I forgot all about the fish.

But in my surprise at having the light come on so suddenly, and at having my consciousness returned to me all at once and bearing an inverted muskrat, I must have moved and betrayed myself. The kit—for I know now it was just a young kit—righted itself so that only its head was visible above water, and swam downstream, away from me. I extricated myself from the bush and foolishly pursued it. It dove sleekly, reemerged, and glided for the opposite bank. I ran along the bankside brush, trying to keep it in sight. It kept casting an alarmed look over its shoulder at me. Once again it dove, under a floating mat of brush lodged in the bank, and disappeared. I never saw it again. (Nor have I ever, despite all the muskrats I have seen, again seen a muskrat floating on its back.) But I did not know muskrats then; I waited panting, and watched the shadowed bank. Now I know that I cannot outwait a muskrat who knows I am there. The most I can do is get "there" quietly, while it is still in its hole, so that it never knows, and wait there until it emerges. But then all I knew was that I wanted to see more muskrats.

I began to look for them day and night. Sometimes I would see ripples suddenly start beating from the creek's side, but as I crouched to watch, the ripples would die. Now I know what this means, and have learned to stand perfectly still to make out the muskrat's small, pointed face hidden under overhanging bank vegetation, watching me. That summer I haunted the bridges, I walked up creeks and down, but no muskrats ever appeared. You must just have to be there, I thought. You must have to spend the rest of your life standing in bushes. It was a once-in-a-lifetime thing, and you've had your once.

Then one night I saw another, and my life changed. After that I knew where they were in numbers, and I knew when to look. It was late dusk; I was driving home from a visit with friends. Just on the off chance I parked quietly by the creek, walked out on the narrow bridge over the shallows, and looked upstream. Someday, I had been telling myself for weeks, someday a muskrat is going to swim right through that channel in the cattails, and I am going to see it. That is precisely what happened. I looked up into the channel for a muskrat, and there it came, swimming right toward me. Knock; seek; ask. It seemed to swim with a side-to-side, sculling motion of its vertically flattened tail. It looked bigger than the upside-down muskrat, and its face more reddish. In its mouth it clasped a twig of tulip tree. One thing amazed me: it swam right down the middle of the creek. I thought it would hide in the rush along the edge; instead, it plied the waters as obviously as an aquaplane. I could just look and look.

But I was standing on the bridge, not sitting, and it saw me. It changed its course, veered towards the bank, and disappeared behind an indentation in the rushy shoreline. I felt a rush of such pure energy I thought I would not need to breathe for days.

That innocence of mine is mostly gone now, although I felt almost the same pure rush last night. I have seen many muskrats since I learned to look for them in that part of the creek. But still I seek them out in the cool of the evening, and still I hold my breath when rising ripples surge from under the creek's bank. The great hurrah about wild animals is that they exist at all, and the greater hurrah is the actual moment of seeing them. Because they have a nice dignity, and prefer to have nothing to do with me, not even as the simple objects of my vision. They show me by their very wariness what a prize it is simply to open my eyes and behold.

1. How does Dillard's use of comparison and contrast help the reader to understand what a muskrat is?

2. What other comparisons did Dillard use in this essay? Did she use analogy? What do you think is her most effective comparison?

3. How does Dillard's initial process of searching for the ''kit'' muskrat compare and contrast with the process she later developed for searching for muskrats? What do we learn about the processes that muskrats engage in?

4. What is the cause of the muskrats' avoiding being seen, according to Dillard? What effect did seeing them have on her?

5. What publication might Dillard be writing for? What sort of reader might be common to a publication that would print Dillard's essay?

Writing the Rough Draft

Once you have made your observations with the aid of the classical questions, have decided what common reader you are addressing, and have planned what arrangement patterns you will use, you are about ready to begin your rough draft. At this point, if you have not already done so, you will also want to decide whether your observation of your subject has supported your prejudice. Although your shaping idea has announced your prejudice, it will not necessarily indicate your final decision about it, especially if you have changed your mind in the course of your observations. Your verdict can emerge in your essay at various junctures: in the introduction, in the course of presenting your observations, in your conclusion, or in all three. As we have seen in discussing the effect of writing for a common reader, knowing your verdict about your situation is important before beginning to write: whether or not your reader agrees with your prejudice will shape what you say and how you say it.

Following is the rough draft of a student's essay in fulfillment of this task. Where did she state her shaping idea? At what point do you know whether she felt her initial prejudice was justified or not? What questions did she ask in generating material? How did she arrange her paragraphs? Her audience was other New York City parents who were on the verge of becoming disillusioned with the public schools. She addressed them in the local *Parent-Teacher Association Newsletter*. Did she address them effectively?

YOUR RIGHT TO A GOOD EDUCATION

Recently, I was informed that my daughter GeriAnne was having difficulty in school. Her trouble stemmed from her inability to grasp learning how to read by the use of phonics. My initial reaction was to take the child out of public school and place her in a private school. I always believed that the teachers employed by the New York City Board of Education were only overpaid and overglorified baby-sitters.

Through speaking to one of the mothers, I found out that the school was equipped to handle children with learning disabilities in a place called the "resource" room. This room is equipped with games and toys geared especially for children who have problems learning. There is also a teacher who is specially trained in this area to handle these children. The children are taught in small groups of a maximum of five children.

The problem with the system is that just any child cannot qualify for the resource room. Because of the limit placed on the number of children in a group and lack of funds to pay for additional teachers, only a select few can benefit.

Immediately, I made an appointment with Mrs. Schwartz, the principal, and she agreed that GeriAnne might be a candidate for this program, but I would have to sign some forms before she could be tested. She also told me that the resource room was the least she could do to help GeriAnne.

A couple of days later, I received a letter giving me an appointment with Mrs. Linden, a social worker, to explain what the tests entailed. I then met Mrs. Shulman, another social worker, who interviewed me about my background and about GeriAnne's previous experiences in school. Sometimes a learning disability can be passed on genetically. I was then informed that the tests would have to be given within a period of thirty days of my signing for them.

Three days ago, GeriAnne was given her first series of tests. First, a child psychologist interviewed her to evaluate her emotional state and to determine if her problem was caused by an emotional upset. After her interview, she was given a test to detect if there is a malfunction in her visual perception. She was given a series of blocks in a certain sequence and asked to duplicate it. Sometimes a child suffers from a vision problem in which her eyesight reverses the lettering, giving the child difficulty in seeing and forming words. Another test was performed to detect visual problems through hand-and-eye coordination.

So far, these have been the only tests given to GeriAnne, but I have been made aware that there are still more in the series.

Since our first phone conversation, GeriAnne's teacher has called me in the evening at least seven times to report her progress.

I was also informed that an equivalent test is given at Long Island Jewish Hospital for a fee of $750.

I do not know if GeriAnne's problem can be solved by this program, but I do know that I now believe that the taxes I am paying in New York City are not just being wasted in overpaying teachers, and that the city school system is still, as far as I'm concerned, one of the finest you could ask for.

Now write your rough draft.

FOCUS: SENTENCE COMBINING

The sentence, like the paragraph, is a basic unit of thought. How one phrases one's sentences—their language, their structure, their punctuation, and even their length—indicates one's level of maturity as a writer. In this section, we suggest exercises that will help you to improve the structure and therefore the maturity of your sentences by giving you options for shaping them with which you may be unfamiliar. The first exercises work with the simple base sentence. These exercises gradually lead into longer, combined sentences. Other exercises show the relationship of punctuation to sentence structure. Still others show how sentence structure can help build transitions between thoughts, on both the sentence level and the paragraph level.

The Base Sentence

The base sentence is a simple sentence that includes a subject, a verb, and often either an object, a predicate nominative, or a predicate adjective. Examples of these four base sentence patterns are the following:

The girl cried. (SUBJECT AND VERB)

The girl takes calculus. (SUBJECT, VERB, AND OBJECT)

The girl is a mathematics major. (SUBJECT, VERB, AND PREDICATE NOMINATIVE)

The girl is smart. (SUBJECT, VERB, AND PREDICATE ADJECTIVE)

SOME PRACTICE WITH BASE SENTENCES

1. Write a paragraph on any subject, using only simple sentences. Base your sentence patterns on the four base sentences above.

2. Rewrite the paragraph from Exercise 1 placing each sentence on a separate line and leaving three spaces between each sentence. Then list three adjectives, three adverbs, and three prepositional phrases that will add information to each base sentence. Finally, combine all the new elements into each simple sentence and rewrite the four sentences as a paragraph.

> *Example:*
> *Base sentence:* The boy eats chocolates.
> *Adjectives:* plump, young, expensive
> *Adverbs:* slightly, hastily, greedily
> *Prepositional phrases:* in the cafeteria, of his school, during lunchtime
> *Combined:* The slightly plump young boy hastily and greedily eats expensive chocolates in the cafeteria of his school during lunchtime.

3. Write a second paragraph on any subject. Again, write in simple sentences based on the four simple patterns above. Combine two or more base sentences with coordinating conjunctions such as *and, or, but, for,* and *yet,* adding adjectives, adverbs, and prepositional phrases where appropriate as you go along (see Handbook, pp. 361–375).

Subordinate Clauses

You can turn a base sentence into a subordinate clause by adding subordinating conjunctions before it, such as *although, as, because, since, when, that, after, before, how, if, though, unless, until, what, where, while, in order that, provided that, as long as, as though,* and *so (that)*.

Example:

Base sentence 1: Television is no longer slavishly watched.

Base sentence 2: The network executives are becoming worried.

Combined: Because television is no longer slavishly watched, the network executives are becoming worried. (The addition of the subordinating conjunction *because* creates a subordinate clause out of the first base sentence, and the second sentence remains "independent." Note: subordinate clauses cannot stand alone as sentences; they must be joined to an independent base sentence for the completion of their meaning.)

SOME PRACTICE WITH SUBORDINATE CLAUSES

4. Combine the sentences in the paragraph in Exercise 3 so that some base sentences become subordinate clauses.

Example:

Base Sentence 1: The husky coach calmly and quietly announced the lucky winner of the first prize for boxing at the college.

Base sentence 2: My usually courageous brother shook.

Combined: As the husky coach calmly and quietly announced the lucky winner of the first prize for boxing at the college, my usually courageous brother shook.

Free Modifiers

Base sentences can also be turned into "clusters" of words that act as free modifiers coming before, after, or in the middle of base clauses and set apart by punctuation. These clusters can act as nouns, verbs, adjectives, or adverbs in reference to another base sentence.

Noun Cluster

Example:

Base sentence 1: Wally is a jokester.

Base sentence 2: He finds that his pranks are funny only to him.

Combined: A jokester, Wally finds that his pranks are funny only to him.

Verb Cluster

Example:

Base sentence 1: Wally hooted with laughter at the absurd dilemma of his friend.

Base sentence 2: He was not appreciated.

Combined: Hooting with laughter at the absurd dilemma of his friend, Wally was not appreciated.

Adjective Cluster

Example:

Base sentence 1: Wally is disliked.

Base sentence 2: Most of his fraternity brothers avoid him whenever possible.

Combined: Disliked, Wally finds himself avoided by most of his fraternity brothers whenever possible.

Adverb Cluster

Example:

Base sentence 1: Wally is scarcely aware of their antipathy.

Base sentence 2: This is hard to believe.

Combined: Unbelievably, Wally is scarcely aware of their antipathy.

Subordinate clauses are also free modifiers.

When two or more free modifiers modifying the same word are used in a sentence, they should be in the same or parallel form.

Example:

Base sentence 1: The April sun shone *weakly.*

Base sentence 2: *Intermittently,* the sun shone.

Base sentence 3: The sun, *while the rain fell,* shone.

Base sentence 4: While storm clouds threatened to eclipse it, the sun shone.

Combined: Weakly and intermittently, the April sun shone while the rain fell and storm clouds threatened to eclipse it.

SOME PRACTICE WITH FREE MODIFIERS

5. Write three sentences, each of which contains parallel free modifiers. Use a different type of free modifier in each sentence.

6. Rewrite the paragraph from Exercise 3, turning each subordinate clause into another type of free modifier.

Example:

Subordinate Clause: Because television is no longer slavishly watched, the network executives are becoming worried.

Verb Cluster: Noticing that television is no longer slavishly watched, the network executives are becoming worried.

7. Write as long a sentence as you can by adding all types of free modifiers to the base clause. Remember to keep the free modifiers in parallel form. Structure the sentence so that it does not sound strung together. As an example, examine the sentences in the paragraph that follows, some of which continue for five or six lines, but none of which sounds tedious or run-on:

> About ten years ago a well-known literary critic and essayist, a good friend of long standing, told me that a wealthy widely-circulated weekly pictorial magazine had offered him a good price to write a piece about me—not about my work or works, but about me as a private citizen, an individual. I said No, and explained why: my belief that only a writer's works were in the public domain, to be discussed and investigated and written about, the writer himself having put them there by submitting them for publication and accepting money for them; and therefore he not only would but must accept whatever the public wished to say or do about them from praise to burning. But that, until the writer committed a crime or ran for public office, his private life was his own; and not only had he the right to defend his privacy, but the public had the duty to do so since one man's liberty must stop at exactly the point where the next one's begins; and that I believed that anyone of taste and responsibility would agree with me.
>
> **—William Faulkner,** ''On Privacy,'' *Harper's Magazine,* July 1955.

Varying Sentence Length and Rhythm

Base or simple sentences need not always be combined; they remain useful to the mature writer, usually to introduce a new topic or to emphasize a point or to make a dramatic statement. Examine the use of varying sentence structures in the following paragraphs, paying attention to the rationale with which the writers used simple sentences as well as combined sentences. How are both sense and rhythm affected in each case?

> It is the traffic that makes it all unique. A traffic in trams grinding round corners, a traffic in approximately London buses whose radiators seem ready to burst, in gypsy-green lorries with ''Ta-ta and By-by'' and other slogans painted on the back, in taxis swerving all over the road with much blowing of horns, in rickshaws springing unexpectedly out of sidestreets, in bullock carts swaying ponderously along to the impediment of everyone, in sacred Brahmani cows and bulls nonchalantly strolling down the middle of the tram-tracks munching breakfast as they go. A traffic, too, in people who are hanging on to all forms of public transport, who are

squatting cross-legged upon the counters of their shops, who are darting in and out of the roadways between the vehicles, who are staggering under enormous loads, who are walking briskly with briefcases, who are lying like dead things on the pavements, who are drenching themselves with muddy water in the gutters, who are arguing, laughing, gesticulating, defecating, and who are sometimes just standing still as though wondering what to do. There never were so many people in a city at seven o'clock in the morning. Patiently the driver of the limousine steers his passage between and around them, while they pause in mid-stride to let him through, or leap to get out of his way, or stare at him blankly, or curse him roundly, or occasionally spit in the path of his highly polished Cadillac. Presently, and quite remarkably, he comes to the end of the journey without collision and deposits the traveler and his luggage upon the pavement in front of an hotel. And here the traveler has his first encounter with a beggar. He had better make the best of it, for beggary is to be with him until the end of his days in Calcutta.

—**Geoffrey Moorhouse,** *Calcutta*

Now when I had mastered the language of this water and had come to know every trifling feature that bordered the great river as familiarly as I knew the letters of the alphabet, I had made a valuable acquisition. But I had lost something, too. I had lost something which could never be restored to me while I lived. All the grace, the beauty, the poetry, had gone out of the majestic river! I still kept in mind a certain wonderful sunset which I witnessed when steam-boating was new to me. A broad expanse of the river was turned to blood; in the middle distance the red hue brightened into gold, through which a solitary log came floating, black and conspicuous; in one place a long, slanting mark lay sparkling upon the water; in another the surface was broken by boiling, tumbling rings that were as many-tinted as an opal; where the ruddy flush was faintest was a smooth spot that was covered with graceful circles and radiating lines, ever so delicately traced; the shore on our left was densely wooded, and the somber shadow that fell from this forest was broken in one place by a long, ruffled trail that shone like silver; and high above the forest wall a clean-stemmed dead tree waved a single leafy bough that glowed like a flame in the unobstructed splendor that was flowing from the sun. There were graceful curves, reflected images, woody heights, soft distances, and over the whole scene, far and near, the dissolving lights drifted steadily, enriching it every passing moment with new marvels of coloring.

—**Mark Twain,** *Life on the Mississippi*

SOME PRACTICE WITH SENTENCE LENGTH AND RHYTHM

8. Now write a paragraph, again on a subject of your own choosing, in which you use a variety of sentence structures: simple sentences, sentences with a variety of free modifiers, including subordinate clauses, and base sentences joined with coordinating conjunctions. What function does each type of sentence play in conveying the meaning of the paragraph?

Punctuation

Once you understand the concept of base clauses, subordinate clauses, and verb, noun, adverb, and adjective clusters, the punctuation of sentences becomes much clearer. Below are four rules for sentence punctuation.

1. A comma either separates elements in a series or sets off a base clause from a free modifier. With a conjunction, it can separate two base clauses.

   Examples:
   The rain, fog, and humidity did not deter them from making the trip.
   Quietly and furtively, he approached the abandoned car.
   Children are growing up very fast, and their parents must be partly responsible.
   Because children are growing up very fast, their parents must be partly responsible.

2. A semicolon can separate two base clauses.

   Example:
   Children are growing up very fast; their parents must be responsible.

3. A colon can appear only at the tail end of a base clause; it introduces either a list or a restatement of the base clause.

   Examples:
   The economy has been sluggish in many ways: employment, construction, and trade.
   I would like to invite you to dinner: I would like to see you very much.

4. A dash acts as a strong comma, setting off middle- and final-position free modifiers from a base clause.

   Examples:
   The man left the office—at once.
   The man—who could scarcely wait to don his coat—left the office.

Transitions

Free modifiers are also useful as transitions between thoughts, whether these thoughts occur in sentences or in paragraphs. When placed at the beginning of a sentence, the free modifier connects the sentence to the preceding one.

Example:

Farm prices are down from what they were five years ago. As a result, farmers are angry.

Notice in the following paragraphs the use of free modifiers to connect thoughts between parts of sentences, between sentences themselves, and between paragraphs.

Why is that woman laughing so early in the morning? I keep trying to put myself in her place, but she always surprises me. From somewhere else in the building, sound waves echoing around the courtyard to disguise their origin, comes a brutal argument. So I must wonder what makes that couple fight so furiously and, even more, what makes them continue living together despite their rage.

I live in an apartment, but not totally apart. I can tell a body not to enter my space, but I cannot command the sound waves. They enter as they will. And not only that, but they force their way into my head and, with no regard for my own volition, tie me into the lives of my neighbors.

Accosted also by sounds from the street, I am pulled into the activity there. A youngster tries to call his friend down from a high floor, and calls and calls his name, unaffected by lack of response. Soon I yearn for Henry to come down as much as the caller does. A transistor blares with a volume that bothers my ears. Drawn to the window, I marvel that the teenage boy, dancing alone on a stoop, can stand it right beside him. The sound must anesthetize like a drug. Now someone double parked is blocking a man who wants his car out. He honks, and makes me turn from whatever I'm thinking about to share his frustration, which is intense.

Back inside, I hear a young woman in an apartment next to mine practicing her clarinet. She is pretty good, beginning a professional career, I've learned, getting jobs with an orchestra here and there. Her practice hours give the building a cool, classical sound. I'm also brought into the anxieties of her young career. I hear the answering machine she has installed, asking whoever it is please to leave a message. Maybe it will mean another break for her.

—**Tracey Early,** "Sounds That Bring Us Closer Together," *Christian Science Monitor,* Jan. 1980

SOME PRACTICE WITH SENTENCE COMBINING

9. Write two paragraphs in which you use free modifiers to connect the thoughts within sentences, between sentences, and between paragraphs. Use the appropriate punctuation.

10. Combine the following sentences into an effectively written essay. The breaks between sentence groups represent paragraphs in the student's original essay, but ignore them if you think it advisable. Add words when necessary to combine the sentences but do not change the meaning:

Imaginary Jane

1. I moved into the house I am living in now.
2. I was only three years old.
3. We bought the house from my grandfather.
4. We have been living there for about fifteen years now.
5. There were no other children on my block.
6. There were no children to play with.
7. The other families were mostly old people.
8. The other families lived on my block.
9. Their children were already grown up.
10. This left me with no choice.
11. I had to play by myself.

12. I found many things to do on my own.
13. I would play house alone and dolls alone also.
14. I played with my parents.
15. My parents were often too busy.
16. The day was really long and boring.
17. This went on for a couple of years.
18. Then kindergarten started.

19. School was a relief.
20. I made new friends.
21. I had a lot of classmates.
22. This did not, of course, help me with my problem of staying alone.
23. I continued to stay by myself at home.

24. I became six years old.
25. A little girl named Diane moved next door.
26. I did not like to play with her.
27. I was so used to staying alone.
28. I did not want her to touch any of my things.
29. I was afraid.
30. She was going to take my toys away from me.

31. Staying alone was not such a good idea.
32. I started to make things up.
33. I started to pretend.
34. I had an imaginary friend.
35. My friend's name was Jane.
36. I have no idea where the name came from.
37. I do not know anyone with that name.

38. Jane lived in the bathroom and in many of the closets around the house.
39. I used to talk to her.
40. I pretended that she answered me.

41. We would play house together.
42. My mother used to give me cookies and milk.
43. I, of course, ate my cookies.
44. So did Jane.
45. I ate her cookies.
46. I pretended she ate her cookies.
47. This went on for about a whole year.
49. I would play with Jane.
50. I went to bed in the evening.

51. My parents began to get worried.
52. They asked my doctor about Jane.
53. They asked my doctor about this imaginary friend.
54. The doctor said it was normal.
55. A lonely child creates an imaginary friend.
56. He made a recommendation.
57. I should play with a real friend.
58. I should play with Diane.

59. My mother would make me play with Diane.
60. I would call for Diane.
61. Diane and I would play together.
62. We would play for a little while.
63. I forgot about Jane little by little.
64. I played with Diane all the time.

65. This was not an unusual phase to go through.
66. This went on for a whole year.
67. I rarely thought about Jane again.
68. That is, until now, for this essay.

REWRITING

Obtaining Feedback on Your Rough Draft

In order to give you the proper response to your rough draft, your evaluators will want to role-play the common reader to whom your essay is directed. Your "Audience Analysis Guide" should give them sufficient information about your audience to successfully look at your essay from its point of view. If you yourself are evaluating your rough draft, then you too will want to role-play your audience as you do so.

The "Audience Response Guide" can then be filled in.

——— AUDIENCE RESPONSE GUIDE ———

1. **What does the writer want to say in this paper? What is his or her purpose in writing? What does he or she want the paper to mean?**
2. **How does the paper affect the audience for which it was intended?**
3. **How effective has the writer been in conveying his or her purpose and meaning? Explain.**
4. **How should the paper be revised to better fulfill its purpose and meaning?**

Below are two peer responses to the rough draft of "Your Right to a Good Education" (pp. 155–166). Each evaluator responded to the four questions of the "Audience Response Guide."

Question 1.

Evaluator A: The writer wishes to convey that the prejudice she had was wrong because the school system is better than she thought.

Evaluator B: The writer now believes that the public schools are not as bad as people make them out to be.

Question 2.

Evaluator A: It is interesting because she conveys that she is impressed by the amount of special attention that her daughter is being given.

Evaluator B: It helped change some ideas I had about the public schools.

Question 3.

Evaluator A: The writing is effective but it should include more detail about GeriAnne.

Evaluator B: The writer is very effective in conveying her purpose through her examples and the process through which she went with the teacher's help.

Question 4.

Evaluator A: The paper should include more information about GeriAnne and the writer's role in her education. With the mother going to school herself, it must be difficult for her to help GeriAnne at school.

Evaluator B: There should have been a little more explaining of the report on the progress of her daughter.

The two evaluators both agreed that the writer's purpose was to indicate that a prejudice of hers was not justified by what she actually experienced. In answering Question 2, Evaluator A did not indicate exactly how the audience was affected, but Evaluator B stated very succinctly what the writer's effect would be on a parent. Evaluator A was very clear, however, in answering Question 3 by saying that more information is required. Both evaluators, in answering Question 4, wanted more information about (1) GeriAnne; (2) the progress she is making in school; (3) the writer's role in her progress.

Here is the revised version of the student's essay.

YOUR RIGHT TO A GOOD EDUCATION

Recently, I was informed that my seven-year-old daughter, Geri-Anne, was having difficulty in school. Her trouble stemmed from her inability to grasp learning how to read by the use of phonics. My initial reaction was to take the child out of public school and place her in a private one. I had always believed that the teachers employed by the New York City Board of Education were only overpaid and overglorified baby-sitters. This idea was reinforced when I visited my daughter's class last year, and the teacher calmly walked out of the class to go to the bathroom, neglecting to separate two little boys who had their hands around each other's throats.

Through speaking to one of the mothers, however, I found out that the school was equipped to handle children with learning disabilities in a place called the "resource" room. This room is equipped with games and toys geared especially for children who have problems learning. There is also a teacher who is specially trained to handle this type of situation. The children are taught in small groups of five, and each child is given individual attention.

The problem with this system is that just any child cannot qualify for the resource room. Because of the limit placed on the number of children in a group and the lack of funds to pay for additional teachers, only a select few can benefit.

Immediately, I made an appointment with Mrs. Schwartz, the principal, and she agreed that GeriAnne might be a candidate for this program, but I would have to sign some forms before she could be tested. She also told me that enrolling her in the resource room was the least she could do to help GeriAnne.

A couple of days later, I received a letter giving me an appointment with Mrs. Linden, a social worker who would explain what the tests entailed. I then met Mrs. Schulman, another social worker, who interviewed me about my background and about GeriAnne's previous experiences in school. Ironically, as a child I also had difficulty in learning how to read, and Mrs. Shulman explained that sometimes this type of problem can be inherited. I was then informed that the tests would be given within a thirty-day period and that the results were to be available to me.

Three days ago, GeriAnne was given her first series of tests. First, a child psychologist interviewed her to evaluate her emotional state and to determine if her problem was caused by an emotional upset, because if a child has a high anxiety level, she will sometimes test poorly. After her interview, GeriAnne was given a test to detect if there is a malfunction in her visual perception. She was given a series of blocks in a certain sequence and was asked to duplicate it to detect if there is a reversal in her seeing the letters, which would give her difficulty in seeing and forming new words. Another test was performed to diagnose any visual problems through hand-and-eye coordination.

So far, these have been the only tests given to GeriAnne, but there are still more in the series. I was also informed that an equivalent test is given at Long Island Jewish Hospital for a fee of $750.

Since our first phone conversation, GeriAnne's teacher has called me in the evening at least seven times to report her progress.

I do not know if GeriAnne's problem can be solved by this program, but I do know that I now believe that the taxes I am paying in New York City are not just being thrown away on overpaid teachers and that the city school system is still, as far as I am concerned, one of the finest you could ask for.

Distributing

The writer of this essay responded to the urging of her evaluators that she add information about her own role in her daughter's progress by distributing this information throughout her essay. Distribution is a form of addition in which material on one aspect of your subject is added to more than one segment of the original draft. The writer added to the first paragraph one of the sources of her original prejudice and added to the fifth paragraph the information that she herself had had reading problems and that perhaps the problem was hereditary.

You may also find other instances in which distribution is called for in revising, usually as a means of achieving unity. A key word may bear repeating (see Chap. 2 on Transitions, p. 56). By distributing words like *GeriAnne, tests,* and *this program* throughout her essay, the writer of "Your Right to a Good Education" provided bridges between thoughts that unified the essay.

By examining the early paragraphs of a piece that you are writing, you may discover structures that should be distributed throughout; for example, a metaphor worked out early in the essay might well be extended throughout in order to create a coherent and unified pattern. If at one point in your essay, you compare your car to an old friend because it is so reliable, you might consider extending the comparison to your entire description of your car.

In general, do not start an approach to your subject and then drop it. Rather, distribute that approach throughout your work. If the smell of a place overwhelms you, then that odor should permeate your entire essay. If your tone of voice is playful in your introduction, then the words and details that support that tone should be distributed from beginning to end, unless, of course, you have a reason for changing your attitude and indicate that reason to the reader.

Editing

Once you have gone through the steps of revising your essay—adding (Chap. 2); rearranging (Chap. 3); substituting (Chap. 4); or distributing (above)—you should turn to editing to determine correct word choice and grammatical precision.

Distributing.   Distributing can be an editing exercise also. For example, if you decide to alter your word choice, you may decide to distribute that alteration throughout the essay wherever you have used that word. Or you may need to distribute a change in verb tense or pronoun reference. Distribution, whether in revising or in editing, asks that you look at the larger picture, at the total essay, rather than tinkering with isolated parts only.

Sentence Combining and Transitions.   A very important part of editing, as we have stressed in each chapter so far, is the use of transitions. To combine sentences is another way to establish connections between thoughts. Sentence combining also keeps your essay from having the "choppy" rhythm of strung-together simple sentences and achieves instead the flowing rhythm of the mature combined sentence. Reviewing your writing from the point of view of sentence combining is one of the most important of the editing techniques.

Paragraphs.   Continue to regard your paragraphs closely. Are they structured tightly around some clearly defined unit of thought? Have you developed them with sufficient coordinate accumulation of detail or subordinate provision of example and explanation? Review as often as you need to the paragraph sections in Chapters 3 and 4.

Mechanics.   What mechanical errors of grammar or spelling have persisted in your writing? Perhaps it is time now to make a list of those errors that have constantly defied your attempts to correct them. Now turn this list into a chart by indicating next to each error a definition of the problem and then a method of solution. Finally, in a fourth column, analyze why the method of solution has escaped you. As you go about editing the rough draft for this task, develop this analysis further in the hope of finding a way of implementing the solution.

Now, revise and edit your rough draft.

BECOMING AWARE OF YOURSELF AS A WRITER

1. In what future situations can you foresee writing cases? What appear to be the important features of case writing?

2. Do you feel satisfied that you know how to analyze the frame of reference and the point of view of the readers common to a particular publication? When in the future can you imagine yourself writing to the common reader of another publication? How did you analyze your reader's frame of reference when you wrote the essay for this chapter?

3. How useful is the sentence-combining approach to your own writing? Are your ideas combined already, or do you feel that you need to pay attention to this aspect of your writing?

4. Did you "enjoy" learning about your subject as you tested a prejudice while writing? How important do you think writing is or should be as a way of learning, as well as of expressing what you already know?

5. How often in the past have you used the classical questions without being aware of having used them? Have you observed others using them? The explorer's questions have been devised in this century out of a need to supplement the classical ones. What roles can you foresee both sets of questions playing in your thinking and writing?

PART III
EXPLANATION

INTRODUCTION

Writing as an interested observer, you invited your readers to explore a subject along with you, to experience your own curiosity and the broader perspective that it led to. Now we are going to ask you to write instead as an instructor, to explain a subject to your readers that you have already explored yourself.

The difference between exploration and explanation is subtle. It is a difference, in part, of tone and emphasis. In the former case, you are likely to adopt the attitude of a peer as you share your discoveries with your audience. In the latter case, you may take on a more knowledgeable, authoritative tone, drawing conclusions based on your broadened perspective and offering information that has a general application and validity.

Your own ideas about a subject may gain more validity the more you take into account the ideas of others who are knowledgeable about the subject. To explain a subject well, it is often helpful to inform your audience not only of your own explorations but of the explorations and discoveries, the observations and conclusions of others. As the explorer of a place, you may have interviewed people whom you met there in order to evaluate and understand the place better. But to see the place from the broadest possible perspective, and to explain its significance as fairly and fully as you can, you also want to take into consideration the views of others who have made similar explorations.

As an instructor who provides information about and an explanation of a subject, you are likely to investigate the information that others have gathered before you, to study the explanations others have offered, and to observe not only the world outside yourself but the views of that world that others have taken. The most obvious way to gather a wide range of such information is to read what has been written by others about your subject. The more you learn of what others have said about a subject, the more informed you make yourself, and hence the more informative your explanations become.

In the next two chapters, we will ask you to write in as informative a manner as you can.

6
WRITING ABOUT WHAT YOU KNOW

PURPOSE

To the extent that your discoveries as an explorer of the world beyond yourself broaden your perspective on that world, you may earn a greater capacity to understand and appreciate widely different patterns of behavior and thought. In a sense, you learn to look with new eyes, to comprehend what once might have puzzled you, and to see the value in what you once might have thought valueless. It is a natural impulse to seek to teach others what you have learned in this fashion. In this chapter and the next, we would like you to act on such an impulse, and to write as an instructor, informing your readers, broadening their knowledge, and explaining a subject to them so that they understand and appreciate it more fully than they otherwise might.

To instruct or explain effectively, you can continue to rely on your personal experiences and observations in order to gather information. You may also want to begin calling on memorable reading or other media experiences that you have found instructive. In either case, you will want to generalize, to point out the broader, more universal interest inherent in your specific observations and explorations. We will suggest in this chapter that you attempt to answer the classical questions "What has been said about my topic by others?" and "What general ideas and values does my topic exemplify?" (see Chap. 5, pp. 138–139).

The belief that any idea has a general application and validity rests on the assumption that people share certain values. For example, when you see a film that you like, you tell your friends to see it, too, because you assume that they will agree with you that the film has merit. You are relying on a sense of values that you and your friends share.

Because writers cannot know their audience's values as intimately as they know those of their friends, they often rely on the set of values traditionally deemed appropriate in the classroom: education is an experience shared by all. A writer, for example, may use methods of generating ideas and patterns of arranging these ideas that have been used for centuries in many fields of study. In doing so, she or he is appealing to a conventionally educated audience. In this chapter's task, we are going to ask you to appeal to such an audience as you explain the results of your exploration.

GENERATING IDEAS: THE CLASSICAL QUESTIONS

You already know that how you select and present information is a key factor in determining whether your reader will accept your information as holding validity and relevance. Information selected and presented with an expressive purpose has less general validity and relevance than that presented with an exploratory aim. Now you can experiment with ways of further broadening your angle of vision and of lending a more authoritative, knowledgeable tone to your writing.

By answering the classical questions "What has been said about my topic by others?" and "What general ideas and values does my topic exemplify?" you can gather additional information on a topic by considering that topic from a multiple rather than a single perspective. Your answers to the first question will add the perspective of informed people other than yourself. Your answers to the second question will invite your readers to understand the broader implications and significance of your information.

"What Has Been Said About My Topic by Others?"

In order to present information credibly, it is necessary to be well enough informed to know what you are talking about. A scientist, for example, earns credibility by conducting his or her own experiments and by engaging in extensive research into the work of other scientists. Developing a degree of scientific, scholarly expertise through inductive reasoning and research is a cogent way of gathering and presenting instructive information (see Chap. 7). But for most everyday occasions, you can be less formal in considering how the ideas of others will help you to convey information that may have a generally recognized validity.

How often have you found yourself explaining to someone else a piece of information that you learned by going to a class, or by reading a book or a magazine or a newspaper, or by listening to the radio or watching television? "Do you know what I found out today?" you say, and suddenly you find yourself in the role of instructor. Obviously, the more informed you are, the more classes you have attended, the more books you have read, the more instructive your conversation may prove to be. Similarly, your writing may prove to be more informative for your reader if you introduce into it the ideas of others that you yourself have found instructive.

The problem that many students face is how to go about locating sources of information that will be relevant to a particular writing topic. If you are writing on a topic about which you are already well informed, the problem is simply one of selecting the most factual, knowledgeable commentators to refer to. If you are writing on a topic about which you have little information from others, you must begin by discovering the sources of relevant information that are readily available to you.

In the first case, you really need only exercise your own good judgment. If you know a good deal about what others have said on a topic, you will refer to the most authoritative commentators, to those who have respectable credentials, who demonstrate a firm command of the most reliable facts and the most current issues, and who speak or write in a manner that you find consistently intelligent and convincing.

If you are writing on a topic about which you have little information, you must select particular commentators to evaluate. You can engage in library research, although often that is not necessary. Sometimes a teacher, a fellow student, or a friend can suggest an article to read or a program to tune into. Sometimes you can solve the problem by exercising a bit of imagination and attempting to discover how information that you already command may prove relevant to a topic that you are writing on.

Course work in one class, for example, may provide information relevant to a writing assignment in another class; thus students in a literature class may find that a course they have taken in psychology provides them with information about the motives of characters in a play or a novel. A book, an article, or a program with which you are familiar may hold information worth citing in a paper that is ostensibly about a very different subject; thus a television documentary on the aborigines of Australia provided one student with information on tribal behavior that was useful in a paper on peer-group pressure at the student's college.

Many times, of course, you may be gathering information before you decide to write about a subject. Then, an article in a magazine or a documentary on television or a lecture in a class may stimulate you to write. In this case, you still may want to seek out and examine other sources of information before you write your paper. But at least you have a head start.

It is important, then, that you begin to familiarize yourself with a variety of information available from others, with observations and insights and ideas beyond your own. The more you do so, the more informative your own writing will become.

SOME PRACTICE WITH READING AS A WAY OF GENERATING IDEAS

1. Write down the information about one news event that you learn by watching the evening news on television. Discuss in class how you might gather additional information that would increase your understanding of the event.

2. Read an editorial in your local newspaper; then seek out additional sources of information on the subject so that you can discuss in class whether the opinions expressed in the editorial are reliable.

3. Find three sources of information on a contemporary figure of public interest (an entertainer, a politician, a criminal); then write a paragraph explaining which of the three sources seems the most credible to you.

4. Review a paper that you wrote earlier this semester. Since writing the paper, have you encountered a book or an article, a program or a class, to which you might have referred in order to make the paper more informative? If not, try, either with the help of your classmates or on your own, to find one.

5. Discuss in class how a memorable reading experience that you have had might substantiate one of your ideas very effectively or might be a good starting point for a paper.

"What General Ideas and Values Does My Topic Exemplify?"

A new student enters a class, sits in the back of the room, seems not to pay attention, and does not participate in class discussion; when the teacher asks him a question, the student mumbles that he doesn't know the answer. What are we to make of the student's behavior? There may be specific reasons for his acting as he does: he may be naturally shy, or the teacher may be difficult to understand, or the classroom atmosphere may be unfriendly. But whatever the specific reasons, we also realize that the student's actions form one sort of behavior pattern that is typical of people when they enter a new situation. We can probably understand the student better if we keep in mind that his actions, beyond what they indicate about his personality and the atmosphere of the class, are significant for what they indicate in general about how individuals interact with groups.

An ability to explain the general significance of information is important to a writer who would instruct his or her readers. For one thing, it is often intelligent generalization that sparks interest in a subject. When you evaluate information in order to draw a generalization about how to interpret it, you are helping a reader appreciate the relevance and value of that information.

Suppose, for example, that a teacher asked you to read the following passage from an essay called "Coon Tree," by E. B. White:

> I am not convinced that atomic energy, which is currently said to be man's best hope for a better life, is his best hope at all, or even a good bet. I am not sure energy is his basic problem, although the weight of opinion is against me. I would feel more optimistic about a bright future for man if he spent less time proving that he can outwit Nature and more time tasting her sweetness and respecting her seniority.

Would your interest in the passage be sparked if the teacher explained that White was pessimistic about the value of atomic energy? Would you be learning much either about White or about why his work might be worth reading? Such a summary statement would tell you little more than you have probably observed yourself. Students might legitimately expect their instructor to teach them something more about the general meaning and importance of White's remarks.

The instructor might observe that White was not only doubtful about the value of atomic energy, he was concerned about human disrespect for nature. Further, White seemed to feel that "the weight of opinion" was against him, and that he represented a minority position. Putting all this together, the instructor might generalize that White was an environmentalist who was perhaps somewhat old-fashioned in his preference for nature over scientific progress.

White's position raises questions about human attitudes toward nature and science in today's world, as well as about the values that such attitudes reflect: Is our ecology the victim of our concern about energy? Is this a reason to feel pessimistic about our future? What values does the environmentalist favor, and how do they conflict with the values of those who favor the development of nuclear energy? To answer these questions is to draw broad generalizations about the significance of White's position. By coming up with answers to such questions, you generate material for an essay, material in this case that might help others understand and appreciate White better.

There are three things to keep in mind when you generalize about the significance of information you are presenting:

1. You want to collect a sufficient amount of information before you begin to generalize. Avoid making unfair, inaccurate assumptions based on a lack of knowledge. How often, for example, do we regret having misjudged another person because we failed to take the time to understand that person's attitudes

or behavior fully? It is difficult to draw intelligent generalizations if you are poorly informed about your subject.

2. You want to keep in mind that some generalizations are of more universal, less personal interest than others. For example, in an essay explaining the problems caused when one becomes sexually involved at a young age, a student wrote, "Imagine the unhealthy results when a teenage girl is constantly worried about being pregnant." The general idea that sexual involvement is not for the young because they should not have to worry about pregnancy is one of immediate personal interest to the student, herself an eighteen-year-old.

Compare the following idea from an essay about the same topic, "From Popping the Question, To Popping the Pill," by the anthropologist Margaret Mead: "As we seek more human forms of existence, the next question may well be how to protect our young people from a premature, pervasive insistence upon precocious sexuality, sexuality that contains neither love nor delight." Note how Mead maintained a more objective distance from her subject than the young student. She was older and her primary concern was with improving—"humanizing"—the quality of life in general. Her disapproval of premature sexuality was thus a matter of less immediately personal interest to her, and she disapproved for a less narrowly defined reason that the student. There may be any number of reasons, in fact, that she felt that premature sexuality "contains neither love nor delight," one of which might have been her sympathy for those young people troubled by the fear of pregnancy on which the student focused.

3. You want to be reasonable about whatever generalizations you make, to be sure that your topic really does exemplify the ideas you say it does. For example, consider the historian Arnold Toynbee's attitude toward premature sexuality as expressed in the essay "Prolonging Sexual Innocence":

I admire the nineteenth-century West's success in postponing the age of sexual awakening, of sexual experience and sexual infatuation far beyond the age of physical puberty. You may tell me that this was against nature; but to be human consists precisely in transcending nature—in overcoming the biological limitations that we have inherited from our pre-human ancestors.

Toynbee was probably reasonable in asserting that postponing sexual experience "far beyond the age of puberty" transcends nature; but was he still reasonable when he went on to generalize that acting "against nature" is valuable because "to be human consists precisely in transcending nature"? Does one really overcome "biological limitations" by postponing sexual experience, or was Toynbee making too much of the conservative attitude of the nineteenth century?

If your generalizations are unreasonable, the validity of the information you are presenting may be doubted. The more reasonable you are in evaluating the general significance of the information you have gathered, the more credible an instructor you may prove to be (see Chap. 8, pp. 264–280).

SOME PRACTICE WITH GENERALIZATION AS A WAY OF GENERATING IDEAS

1. Discuss in class the difference between the general value that Toynbee found in delaying sexual involvement and the general value that Mead found. Which author appeals to a value system that would be most readily embraced by E. B. White?

2. Read every article on the front page of your daily newspaper; then write a paragraph about one general condition of contemporary life that the information you have read illustrates. In what way might information from other sources change the generalization that you have made?

3. Make a list of books and articles that you have read, television programs that you have seen, and classes that you have attended, each of which you think would be of interest to your English class. What does the list reveal in general about your interests? What does it reveal about your view of your English class?

4. Joan Didion generalized about John Wayne that he symbolized "the inarticulate longings of a nation wondering at just what pass the trail had been lost." What specific things do you know about Wayne that might support this generalization? What general ideas and values does Wayne symbolize in your eyes?

5. Ben Franklin, writing in his *Autobiography* about his difficulty in correcting his moral faults, compared himself to a man who goes to a blacksmith to buy an ax. The man, Franklin wrote,

> desired to have the whole of its surface as bright as the edge; the smith consented to grind it bright for him if he would turn the wheel. He turned while the smith pressed the broad face of the ax hard and heavily on the stone, which made the turning of it very fatiguing. The man came every now and then from the wheel to see how the work went on; and at length would take his ax as it was, without further grinding. "No," says the smith, "turn on, turn on; we shall have it bright by and by; as yet 'tis only speckled." "Yes," says the man, "*but I think I like a speckled ax best.*"

What generalizations about human nature might you draw from Franklin's tale of the man and his ax? How might you incorporate the general ideas represented by the tale into a paper of your own?

ADDRESSING YOUR AUDIENCE: A SHARED SENSE OF FORM AND VALUE

One of the widest possible audiences open to any writer may be that composed of readers who share with the writer a similar level and quality of education. People who are different in many other ways have often been educated in much the same manner. The conventions of the classroom and particularly the memories of teachers who embodied these conventions link heterogeneous groups of students together. Long after they are through with school, members of these groups may find most instructive the writer who employs the methods and reflects the values once shared in the classroom.

Many readers, for example, associate the classical methods of arrangement with the formal instruction that they experienced throughout their school years. The writer who analyzes cause and effect or explains a process or offers illustrative examples is likely to remind such readers of the teachers whom they learned from.

It is helpful to remember that conventions are not, of course, hard-and-fast rules. Teachers and students expect different things from one another in different eras and in different settings. For example, the classroom atmosphere in most schools today is less tightly disciplined than in the past. Because conventions are flexible and changing, there are likely to be different types of educated readers, just as there are different types of common readers. If you set out to write for an educated audience, you will probably be most successful in appealing to readers whose level and quality of education match your own. You cannot expect all college graduates, for example, to have read the same books or to have studied the same subjects. Even in the same class, different students learn different things in different ways. In a country like our own, where education is widespread and open to many different groups, the conventions of the educational process are apt to be anything but uniform.

Nevertheless there are certain patterns of thought and expression that seem so basic to the teaching process that they may hold a traditional appeal for most college-educated readers. By generalizing about our own educational background, we can try to draw up a partial list:

1. In order to present us with information that is new to us, a teacher must know more about a subject than we do. In general, we expect teachers to explain and evaluate their own knowledge of a subject, particularly their knowledge of what has been said about that subject by others.
2. A teacher tends to go over in detail each step of the thinking process that leads to a certain conclusion. In general, we expect teachers to explain or argue each point that they make with a reasonable degree of step-by-step, logical completeness.

3. A teacher also aims for unity and emphasis. A good teacher keeps to the subject and knows which points to emphasize and which to treat as supporting details.
4. A teacher uses an acceptable style of speaking and observes standard grammatical forms.
5. A teacher who employs specialized or technical terms tends to define those terms for us in nonspecialized, nontechnical language. In general, we expect teachers to instruct us in the language of their subject or discipline.
6. A teacher, traditionally, does not impose his or her own most private values on us. In general, we expect teachers to be somewhat open-minded, and to analyze with objectivity the relative merits and limitations of any particular ethical, religious, or philosophical position.

The conventions we are listing suggest, then, that the writer who would appeal to an educated audience should be well informed, reasonably logical, and articulate about her or his subject, reflecting values such as literacy, thoroughness, and rationality. A writer who breaks these conventions may, of course, prove as instructive as one who observes them. But the latter, by reflecting the sense of form and value often deemed most appropriate in the classroom, may appeal to the broadest possible spectrum of educated readers.

SOME PRACTICE WITH A SHARED SENSE OF FORM AND VALUE

1. Discuss in class what other patterns of thought and expression you might add to our list of those that seem basic to the teaching process. Generalize about your own educational background in order to add to the list.

2. Discuss in class the difference between a convention and a rule. Explain the difference by comparing concrete examples of each. Are there rules that apply to writing, or simply conventions?

3. The programs on the public broadcasting station on your television are often perceived as having a greater appeal to the more highly educated viewer than those on the networks. Discuss in class why the programs on public television (PBS) have this reputation. Does PBS actually appeal only to the well educated? If not, which of its conventions appeal to the less educated?

4. Examine the opinions expressed in class by a teacher whom you consider particularly informative. Generalize about the values that the teacher holds, given his or her opinions. What sort of value system does the teacher seek to impress on the class?

TASK: WRITING ABOUT WHAT YOU KNOW

The task for this chapter is to write about some special knowledge that you possess that others might not know about as fully as you do. This knowledge might be about an attitude that you have, an activity that you engage in, a belief that you hold, or an idea that you think important. Because your audience does not share your knowledge, they may have a misconception about your subject, or they may regard it as unbelievable, unrealistic, or inconsequential. Explain what generally understandable and acceptable value lies behind the subject that you are writing about. Offer information from your reading or other media experience that demonstrates how the activity or belief has a general value that your readers can understand.

In writing this essay, you may find yourself seeking a balance between the broad generalizations and the specific information that you offer to explain your point of view. A pattern of arrangement may emerge from this alternation of the general with the specific, or one or more of the classical patterns of arrangement may prove an effective way of developing your explanation (see Chap. 5, pp. 149–152).

Your audience for this task would most likely be a group of readers who have an educational background similar to yours, but who do not share your understanding of the particular subject. Write, if you like, for members of your English class who will not share your thoughts about your subject although they are on the same level of education; or choose another audience with a similar educational background that is unlikely to share your position, for example, the members of an older or a younger generation. Your audience may be composed of a rather mixed group, as long as their education has given them a similar respect for certain broad, general values of expression, of logic, and of morality—a value system that you can call on to bridge the distance between your point of view and theirs.

In the remaining sections of this chapter, we will discuss how you can use Questions 7 and 8 from the list of classical questions to generate ideas about your subject; how you can use a shared sense of form and value to write for an educated audience; how you can arrange your information to explain your point of view to your audience; what you can do to clarify your style of expression; and how to revise and edit your rough draft.

WRITING THE ESSAY

Using Your Reading or Other Media Experience as a Way of Generating a Subject and/or Generating Ideas

You may come up with a subject for this essay by reviewing your journal for experiences you have had, conversations you have enjoyed, or subjects that you can write about. Or you may find your subject in a book that you have been reading or a class that you have been taking.

Should you decide to choose your subject from reading or the media, there are any number of ways you might react to the attitudes and ideas you meet with in books, magazines, newspapers, and other sources of information, such as radio, television, and the classroom lecture. You might agree or disagree with the ideas of the other person. You might feel respect or contempt for a belief. You might be puzzled or angered or pleased by an attitude or an action. In seeking a subject for this chapter's task from your reading, you will be looking for a statement or a story that you find reasonable yourself but that you realize others may not. Perhaps you have something in mind already, something you read in a magazine or saw on television or learned from a textbook. If not, you may find it helpful to seek out an article to read or a documentary to watch or a lecture to attend that may stimulate you to write on a particular topic. Whether your reading helps you to generate a subject or you have drawn your subject from your own thinking, use your reading as a means of generating ideas about which to write.

As an example, the following passage from an essay by E. B. White called "On a Florida Key" was discussed in a student's English class:

There are two moving picture theaters in the town to which my key is attached by a bridge. In one of them colored people are allowed in the balcony. In the other, colored people are not allowed at all. I saw a patriotic newsreel there the other day which ended with a picture of the American flag blowing in the breeze, and the words: one nation indivisible, with liberty and justice for all. Everyone clapped, but I decided I could not clap for liberty and justice (for all) while I was in a theater from which Negroes had been barred. And I felt there were too many people in the world who think liberty and justice for all means liberty and justice for themselves and their friends. I sat there wondering what would happen to me if I were to jump up and say in a loud voice: "If you folks like liberty and justice so much, why do you keep Negroes from this theater?" I am sure it would have surprised everybody very much and it is the kind of thing I dream about doing but never do. If I had done it I suppose the management would have taken me by the arm and marched me out of the theater, on the grounds that it is disturbing the peace to speak up for liberty just as the feature is coming on. When a man is in the South he must do as the Southerners do; but although I am willing to call my wife "sugar" I am not willing to call a colored person a nigger.

Although the student found White's response to his situation quite reasonable, many of her classmates felt that White should have acted on his feelings in some way and should have registered his protest more forcefully. This reaction prompted the student to write an essay in which she explained the general value of White's position. In the essay, she called on additional reading that she had done, as well as on her personal experiences, to help explain her attitude.

Here is what she wrote:

ON CIVIL DISOBEDIENCE, WITH DISCRETION

In totalitarian countries the ordinary citizen has no problem dealing with his government, he simply does what he is told. Paradoxical-
ly, in a free society, one is often worried and frustrated by government
policy. For E. B. White in 1941, the issue was segregation; for Henry
Thoreau in 1845, it was slavery and the war in Mexico; and for me today, it is Central America. Thus two essays, White's "On a Florida Key"
and Thoreau's "On the Duty of Civil Disobedience," held a special impact for me, leading me to decide that discretion is the better part of
valor.

Discretion is what E. B. White used when he encountered segregation while vacationing in Florida. He went to the movies at a theater
from which black people were barred. When the American flag and the
words "with liberty and justice for all" appeared on the screen, he did
not join in the applause. Instead, he tells us,

> I sat there wondering what would happen to me if I were to jump up and
> say in a loud voice: "If you folks like liberty and justice so much, why do you
> keep Negroes from this theater?" . . . it is the kind of thing I dream about
> doing but never do.

If Henry David Thoreau had been White's companion at the movies
that day, he would certainly have stood up, proclaimed his beliefs, and
marched out of the theater, taking as many people from the audience
as he could muster. This is a reasonable assumption, based on Thoreau's theory of civil disobedience. To protest slavery and the Mexican
War, Thoreau suggested that a thousand men not pay their tax bills.
"This is, in fact," he says "the definition of a peaceable revolution." The
practicality of such action is highly debatable, even though the tax col-
lectors of 1845 must have been like Santa Claus in comparison to our
IRS. The thousand men would certainly have landed in jail, as Thoreau
himself did when he refused to pay his poll tax. An anonymous friend

paid the tax, and the experiment turned out to be a lark.

My own brief encounter with civil disobedience was not a lark. I took part in protest marches in two different cities and felt dreadful on both occasions. This feeling of shame arose not because I was showing open disagreement with the people surrounding me, but because of my method of dealing with my elected government, which would have been justified were I living in an occupied country. I felt as though I were marching against my own family, and I doubt if anything would motivate me to do it again.

A method of expressing dissent is incorporated into our American democratic government, and that is why I endorse E. B. White's way of holding fire and influencing public opinion by his writing.

By contrasting White's position with Thoreau's and then with her own, the student helps us to understand the general value that she finds in White's response to segregation. But was she as informative as she might have been? Her peers felt that she could have explained in more detail what general value discretion holds for any man or woman, rather than placing as much emphasis on her personal views about it. She did not, they felt, instruct them as thoroughly or objectively as a teacher might.

Do note that the student was careful in her essay to state specifically what the sources of her information were. Like her, you can use what others have said not only to come up with a topic but also to gather information relevant to a discussion of your topic: factual data, examples, explanations of others that you can incorporate into your paper along with your own observations. Whenever you incorporate someone else's material into an essay, be sure to specify the source of that material. If you quote directly from someone else, indicate that you are doing so by using quotation marks or by indenting and single-spacing the quotation. If you summarize someone else's position, or even if you just mention an idea or a fact that you took from someone else, tell your readers who your source is. Not to do so is to be guilty of plagiarism, that is, of presenting someone else's material as if it were your own (see Chap. 7, pp. 241–246).

Now you should take some time to investigate possible sources of information for this chapter's task. Look not only for an activity, an attitude, or an idea or a belief that you find of general value, but also for supportive material. Try to be as imaginative as possible in seeking out relevant information. Remember that a book or a lecture or some other source that is concerned with a subject different from the one that you are writing about may still contain information that can help you to explain your ideas.

Using Generalization as a Way of Generating Ideas

Once you have selected a particular statement or story to explain and to make more understandable for your audience, you should clarify for yourself what its general significance or value might be. You may draw a generalization quickly, as an immediate reaction to your subject; or you may find it necessary to collect more information first.

The student who wrote about E. B. White, for example, might have come up right away with the general idea that the value of White's response was in its discretion. But is discretion always valuable? Obviously not. By collecting more information about how others had responded to a desire to protest, the student narrowed her generalization to focus on the value of discretion in a democratic country. Do you think that she collected enough information from her reading and her personal experience to make her generalization a reasonable one?

Decide now whether you have enough information to make an intelligent and reasonable generalization about your subject. If not, seek more information before you attempt to explain the general value of the particular attitude or idea or belief that you have decided to write about. Keep in mind that you may not come up with any firm sense of the general ideas and values exemplified by your topic until you have gathered a good deal of information. Or you may come up with an initial generalization only to find yourself altering it based on information that you subsequently gather.

Using a Shared Sense of Form and Value in Addressing Your Audience

One way you can appeal to an audience of educated readers is to use conventions of presenting information that your readers may have become accustomed to during their college years. Place yourself in the role of an instructor who wants to answer the question "What range of information and what general values can I call on to bridge the gap between my audience and me?" Try to be as informed, logical, and thorough as you can. Take an open-minded, objective attitude about not only the merits but also the limitations of your position. Note that, like many good teachers, you are trying to broaden the understanding of your audience, not to convince them that your view is right and theirs is wrong.

Before you begin to work on the rough draft of your essay, take a few moments here to review the "Audience Analysis Guide."

———— AUDIENCE ANALYSIS GUIDE ————

1. **Who is my audience?**
2. **What is the frame of reference of this audience?**
3. **What point of view is my audience likely to have on my subject?**
4. **How do my own frame of reference and point of view differ from those of my audience?**

5. How much depth of information does my audience require?
6. What range of information and what general values can I call on to bridge the gap between my understanding of this subject and the lack of understanding of my audience?

Arranging Your Essay: The Shaping Idea, Generalization, and Specification

At this point, you should have an idea or an attitude or an action or a belief that you intend to explain. Hopefully, you have come up with information from further reading and/or from your own observations and experiences that will help you to develop your explanation and one or more generalizations about the significance of your information.

The Shaping Idea.   Your shaping idea may come from a portion of the material that you have gathered, or it may emerge as a summary statement about the overall significance of this material. If you find that there is one general value of major importance that you intend to focus on, as the student who wrote on E. B. White focused on the value of discretion, a statement about that value may work well as a shaping idea for the essay. If, on the other hand, you find that there are a number of understandable values exemplified by the idea or the attitude that you are explaining, you may want to develop a shaping idea that will generalize about them in a summary fashion. In one way or another, though, your shaping idea should provide your readers with an overall sense of how the information you are presenting will help them to understand the value of a position that they might find unreasonable.

Generalization and Specification.   Once you have determined what your shaping idea will be, you may decide to begin your essay with it, to focus on it in your introduction, and then to present the information you have gathered step-by-step, perhaps in ascending or descending order of importance, explaining at each step how a particular piece of information is related to the shaping idea. Or you may decide to begin with a description of the source and the substance of the idea or attitude or belief you intend to explain, and then to offer in detail the information that your readers need in order to broaden their understanding of the subject, in which case your shaping idea could appear in the middle or even at the end of your essay.

In either case, the arrangement of this essay should reflect a balance between your generalizations and the specific facts, ideas, and explanations that lead up to or illustrate and clarify each generalization. You may find it helpful to adopt the following strategy as you work through your rough draft: each time you write about a specific piece of information, follow it with a comment on what general point in your overall subject it helps to explain; each time you offer a generalization about your subject, follow it with specific information that illustrates or clarifies it. You might follow this procedure in some sort of outline before you write your rough draft, or you might do it as you write out the draft.

Take one more look at the essay on E. B. White, and note how the student writer followed this sort of strategy. After introducing her subject, dissent in a democracy, she began with a generalization about the value of discretion, then used the passage about the movie theater to illustrate her generalization; she next explained how another piece of information, on Thoreau, had led her to another general observation, about the ineffectiveness of his brand of civil disobedience; she continued with a specific example from her own experience of the value of discretion and then concluded with a final piece of information meant to help us perceive the reasonableness of White's position.

You may, of course, seek a tighter pattern of arrangement. You should feel free, at this point, to use any of the patterns we have introduced in previous chapters. Perhaps you will prefer to write a narrative of how you came on your subject and then gathered the information that led you to your overall conclusion; or you may choose to make use of one or more of the classical patterns introduced in Chapter 5, explaining, for example, what causes led you to conclude that a particular idea is reasonable, or comparing, like the student who wrote on E. B. White, an action you see as valuable to actions that seem less valuable to you.

Now take a look at an essay by E. B. White in which he explained why Americans seem to prefer white eggs to brown ones. Can you detect an easily definable pattern of arrangement in this essay?

Riposte

E. B. White

Allen Cove, December 1971

To come upon an article in the *Times* called "The Meaning of Brown Eggs" was an unexpected pleasure. To find that it was by an Englishman, J. B. Priestley, gave it an extra fillip. And to happen on it while returning from the barn carrying the day's catch of nine brown eggs seemed almost too pat.

Why is it, do you suppose, that an Englishman is unhappy until he has explained America? Mr. Priestley finds the key to this country in its preference for white eggs—a discovery, he says, that will move him into the "vast invisible realm where our lives are shaped." It's a great idea, but one seldom meets an American who is all tensed up because he has yet to explain England.

Mr. Priestley writes that "the weakness of American civilization . . . is that it is so curiously abstract." In America, he says, "brown eggs are despised, sold off cheaply, perhaps sometimes thrown away." Well, now. In New England, where I live and which is part of America, the brown egg, far from being despised, is king. The Boston market is a brown-egg market. I note in my morning paper, in the Boston produce report, that a dozen large white eggs yesterday brought the jobber forty-two cents, whereas a dozen large brown eggs fetched forty-five cents. Despised? Sold off cheaply? The brown egg beat the white egg by three cents.

"The Americans, well outside the ghettos," writes Mr. Priestley, "despise brown eggs just because they do seem closer to nature. White eggs are much better, especially if they are to be given to precious children, because their very whiteness suggests hygiene and purity." My goodness. Granting that an Englishman is entitled to his reflective moments, and being myself well outside the ghettos, I suspect there is a more plausible explanation for the popularity of the white egg in America. I ascribe the whole business to a busy little female—the White Leghorn hen. She is nervous, she is flighty, she is the greatest egg-machine on two legs, and it just happens that she lays a white egg. She's never too distracted to do her job. A Leghorn hen, if she were on her way to a fire, would pause long enough to lay an egg. This endears her to the poultrymen of America, who are out to produce the greatest number of eggs for the least money paid out for feed. Result: much of America, apart from New England, is flooded with white eggs.

When a housewife, in New York or in Florida, comes home from market with a dozen eggs and opens her package, she finds twelve pure white eggs. This, to her, is not only what an egg should be, it is what an egg is. An egg is a white object. If this same housewife were to stray into New England and encounter a brown egg from the store, the egg would look somehow incorrect, wrong. It would look like something laid by a bird that didn't know what it was about. To a New Englander, the opposite is true. Brought up as we are on the familiar beauty of a richly colored brown egg (gift of a Rhode Island Red or a Barred Plymouth Rock or a New Hampshire) when we visit New York and open a carton of chalk-white eggs, we are momentarily startled. Something is awry. The hen has missed fire. The eggs are white, therefore wrong.

"The English prefer the brown egg," writes Mr. Priestley, "because it belongs to the enduring dream of the English, who always hope sooner or later to move into the country." Here I understand what he's talking about: the brown egg is, indeed, because of its pigmentation, more suggestive of country living—a more "natural" egg, if you wish, although there is no such thing as an *un*natural egg. (My geese lay white eggs, and God knows they are natural enough.) But I find the brown egg esthetically satisfying. For most of my life I have kept hens, brooded chicks, and raised eggs for my own use. I buy chicks from a hatchery in Connecticut; by experimenting, I have found that the most beautiful brown egg of all is the egg of the Silver Cross, a bird arrived at by mating a Rhode Island Red with a White Plymouth Rock. Her egg is so richly brown, so wondrously beautiful as to defy description. Every fall, when the first pullet egg turns up on the range, I bring it into the living room and enshrine it in a black duckshead pottery ashtray, where it remains until Halloween, a symbol of fertility, admired by all. Then I take it outdoors and, in Mr. Priestley's memorable phrase, I throw it away.

A neighbor of mine, a couple of miles up the road, is planning to go the brown egg one better. He dreams of a green egg. And what's more, he knows of a hen who will lay one.

Where did White state his shaping idea? How well did he support his generalizations with specific instances? What sort of audience did he seem to be writing for? How well informed was he? How reasonable? What values did he appeal to in order to explain his own preference for brown eggs?

Writing the Rough Draft

It is now time to write your rough draft. Once you have completed it, take a break. Before you begin to think about rewriting, look at the following essay written by another student in response to this chapter's task:

HORRORS

The evolution of horror films certainly doesn't compare to the wondrous and lengthy evolution of humankind. In fact, horror films might merely be a reflection of the twentieth-century's ever-changing morals, values, and fears. Indeed, horror films have certainly changed over the years; however, whether yesteryear's horror films are better than today's is as arguable as stating that modern humans are better than their ancestors. Do we not commit the same atrocities (rape, thievery, murder) that our ancestors did?

The year 1931 marked the coming age of the horror genre. Although there had previously been scattered examples of films that dramatized the horrible and the grotesque, the horror film did not flourish until the high-budgeted Frankenstein, based loosely on Mary Shelley's novel, was released by Universal amid tremendous fanfare.

Audience reaction proved so favorable that the major Hollywood studios (chiefly RKO and Universal) loosely adapted many other classic horror novels and certain legends to the silver screen in films such as Dr. Jekyll and Mr. Hyde (with Spencer Tracy as Robert Louis Stevenson's schizoid novel creation); Dracula (with Bela Lugosi as the irrepressible count of Bram Stoker's novel); Island of the Lost Souls, (with Charles Laughton in this adaptation of H. G. Wells's novel); The Mummy (Karloff in tape); The Invisible Man (with Claude Rains); The Wolf Man (with Lon Chaney, Jr.); and King Kong. Not only was this new genre very successful, but it spawned a plethora of new stars who would become known as "horror stars" (such as Karloff, Lugosi, and Chaney, Jr.).

Curiously, Dracula, Frankenstein, and other assorted monsters achieved a weird kind of commercial immortality with their sudden success. It was necessary to resurrect them, no matter how thoroughly they had been killed off in the preceding film. They returned as themselves or as "sons," "daughters," and "ghosts" in such films as Son of Kong, The Invisible Man Returns, The Mummy's Ghost, and The Bride of Frankenstein.

However, there's a limit to human invention, if not human credulity. Horror films came out with the regularity of a monthly magazine. By the mid-1940s, Hollywood had gorged the public past horror satiety. In a desperate attempt to rejuvenate horror's sagging box office, Hollywood united horror filmdom's monsters (Frankenstein Meets the Wolf-Man), a move that slowed down the erosion of box-office dollars but didn't stop it. Feeling that the imaginary horror of a film couldn't possibly compete with the true horror tales of Nazism and World War II circulating in the United States, Hollywood lamely blamed World War II for the continuing plummet of horror's box-office popularity. Finally, horror expired in self-parody as it was exploited for cheap laughs: Abbott and Costello Meet Frankenstein, The Dead End Kids Meet the Spook, and so on. Ironically, a genre in which death was a constant staple had died the most unkind of deaths itself by 1945.

In 1952, like a Phoenix rising from its own ashes, the horror genre entered its second cycle, but it took on a vastly different appearance. With the major studios generally abandoning horror, the small, independent film companies (ranging from the fairly big American International Pictures to the ultracheap Astor) became the most consistent suppliers of horror films. These independents specialized in making quick, contemporary horror films, all of which had assured profit potential because of minuscule budgets and sensationalized advertising. Indeed, AIP, in many cases, just made up an advertising campaign, and if they liked the campaign's look, they would make the film in three to six days.

From old myths of vampires, werewolves, and inhuman monsters, the horror genre veered into new angles as it married with science fiction in such films as I Married a Monster from Outer Space, It Conquered the World, and The Incredibly Strange Creatures Who Stopped

Living and Became Mixed-Up Zombies. If one replaces the words <u>monster</u>, <u>zombie</u>, and <u>it</u> with <u>Communist</u> and the words <u>outer space</u> with <u>Russia</u> in the preceding film titles, it becomes evident that with these films, the independents shrewdly exploited the prevalent fear in the United States of being "taken over" by subversives.

The public's fear of imminent nuclear disaster was also skillfully exploited. Thus were born the "atomic age monsters," who were either normal living organisms turned into mutants by incessant human dabbling in the atomic field (<u>Colossal Man</u>, <u>Attack of the Crab Monsters</u>) or supposedly extinct dinosaurs unleashed from their "dormancy" deep below the oceans or ice caps because of atomic testing (<u>The Beast from 20,000 Fathoms</u>). The independents also keenly sensed that with the advent of fast cars and rock 'n' roll, the mood of its basically youthful audience was shifting. Thus began the recycling of old horror monsters into romantic villains (<u>I Was a Teen-Age Werewolf</u>, <u>I Was a Teen-Age Frankenstein</u>)—misunderstood and inarticulate but sympathetic to the underdogs (i.e., the young audience) and irritants to authority (i.e., the establishment).

It was during this reincarnation of "old-time" monsters that the genre was ushered into its third cycle as it looked on its old saviors to return it to the prosperity that it had once tasted. In 1958, Hammer Films, a small, fledgling independent film company, released <u>Horror of Dracula</u> (with Christopher Lee and Peter Cushing). It was essentially a remake of the 1932 <u>Dracula</u> with an authentic gothic look (which became a Hammer trademark). Buoyed by the film's enormous success, Hammer recycled other horror films of the 1930s (<u>Evil of Frankenstein</u>, <u>Curse of the Mummy</u>, <u>Curse of the Werewolf</u>). AIP also delved into gothic horror with the release of <u>The Pit and the Pendulum</u> (very loosely based on Edgar Allan Poe's story and featuring Vincent Price) as a counterpunch to Hammer. The success of this movie compelled AIP to go through a wild rummage of Poe: <u>Masque of the Red Death</u>, <u>The Oblong Box</u>, <u>The Raven</u>, and others (all with Price). Interestingly, horror was once again spawning its own stars, as the names of Price, Lee, and Cushing became synonymous with horror.

Besides Hammer's "British invasion" (which, incidentally, was not only similar in popularity to the Beatles' but preceded them by six years), Japan sent us Godzilla, who was actually a remnant of the "atomic-age monster" period. Released in 1958, the film did so well that Godzilla returned in numerous sequels with a slew of foes and allies to accompany him. The Japanese even reincarnated King Kong, who inevitably did battle against Godzilla.

It was during the third cycle that the major studios returned, opting for a more bold type of horror, which often paralleled reality—Whatever Happened to Baby Jane? (mental illness), The Collector (sexual perversion), and Repulsion (sexual obsession)—rather than the costumed period pieces of the independents. It was also during the third cycle that blood and fairly explicit violence were used or, as director Don Sharp said in a recent interview on the subject of Hammer Films, "They'd got into the pattern of making each film a bit bloodier than the one before it." It was with Alfred Hitchcock's Psycho in 1960 that horror achieved a new permissiveness in the limits on screen violence, as that film would forever shatter the invisible line of what was and was not acceptable on the screen. In 1968, that line was further annihilated when a small independent, Lavrel, released the ultragraphic Night of the Living Dead, a film which was unrated by the Motion Picture Association of America.

This film signified the beginning of the fourth cycle, a period in which both the major studios and the independents prospered and screen violence was given a new definition because the newly imposed film ratings freed movies from their hitherto self-imposed censorship. The major studios continued to reject such previously traditional subjects as vampires, werewolves, and mad scientists and now relied on common earth critters to provide ample terror (Jaws, Orca, The Swarm) and became fixated on the supernatural (The Exorcist, The Omen, Carrie). The burgeoning expansion of independents also continued in the fourth cycle, as they forayed into the unusual (Ilsa: She-Wolf of the SS, Gore, Gore Girls, I Dismember Mama). It was in 1974, as the independents continued to create unusual formulas for success, that the highly successful ultraexplicit Texas Chainsaw Massacre was released. This film not only set a new precedent in screen violence but created a formula (the indestructible killer) that still saturates the independent horror-film market today (<u>Friday the 13th</u>, <u>Maniac!</u>, <u>Madman</u>). Today independents in the fourth cycle continue to follow the "deranged slasher" theme (affectionately dubbed <u>splatter film</u> by its fans), while the major studios continue to opt for new formulas. In recent years, the major studios have returned to their "bankable stars," as can be witnessed by the current spate of werewolf movies (<u>The Howling</u>, <u>American Werewolf in London</u>) and vampires (<u>The Hunger</u>). It is evident that, like most of their monsters, horror films never die.

What reading and media experiences provided both the subject and the ideas for this essay? What was the writer's shaping idea? How did he move between the general and the specific? What shared conventions did he use in writing to his reader?

FOCUS: STYLE

The Components of Style

A writer's style, according to E. B. White, might be defined as "the sound his words make on paper." Writers may sound proper and formal or relaxed and colloquial. They may write lyrically and poetically or logically and scentifically. Their words may seem simple and forthright or satirically double-edged. Although one's style changes, clarity is most often the key to an intelligent style in any age. The question for writers is rarely whether they want to be clear or unclear, but whether they want to achieve clarity through simplicity or complexity, through plainness or eloquence. In *The Elements of Style,* White advised inexperienced writers to write about their subject as directly, simply, naturally, and sincerely as they can. By doing so, they may develop a clarity of expression often sacrificed by those who use the extremes of ornate, pretentious locution or breezy, offbeat slang.

Style is shaped by the writer's purpose in writing and by his or her audience. For example, a writer who has information to convey is likely to seek a plainer, less eloquent style than one who is writing to entertain or to argue. Thus, the author of a cookbook would be well advised to avoid writing like a poet: telling a reader to bake a cake in an oven "as hot as a jealous heart" would create pointless confusion. At the same time, a writer who is attempting to explain Einstein's theories of relativity will need to sound more erudite, and perhaps more poetic as well, than one who is explaining how to bake a cake.

Style is also shaped by the audience. For example, writing for a young, uneducated audience will affect the "sound your words make on paper" in a different way from writing for a peer audience (see Chap. 2) and from writing for an instructor (see Chaps. 3 and 9). Your style in writing for a sympathetic audience would be different from your style in writing for an unsympathetic audience.

Perhaps, the key word is *adjust.* Writers do not usually use radically different styles in different situations; rather they make subtle adjustments in the style that comes most naturally to them. They try to be a bit more concrete for one audience, a bit more abstract for another. Often a writer is wise to introduce some variety, a simple sentence in a paragraph of complex ones, a metaphor in a sea of scientific facts.

Ways of Adjusting Style

What sort of adjustments in sentence structure and diction can one make in order to simplify or embellish the sound of one's prose? Perhaps we can seek a few basic answers to this question.

Often simplicity of style stems from concreteness, complexity from abstraction.

Adjusting for Concreteness.   To simplify your style and to make it easier to follow, write about your subject in concrete, specific terms. You may try using a narrative mode, for example, even when you are explaining a principle or a concept, as a dramatic situation is often more accessible than an abstract explanation. Compare the following two passages, each of which explains why Thoreau, the author of *Walden,* chose in 1845 to leave his home in the town of Concord, Massachusetts, and to go off to live alone in a hut in the woods by Walden Pond:

> The principle of turning one's back on unpleasant facts—unpleasant, because they were so deeply inessential, so foreign, in a way, to our essential Nature—is one *naturally* congenial to the American mind. Thoreau gave this principle its classic utterance. In his spirit, if not in his name, we still take to such woods as we can find.

> I think one reason he went to the woods was a perfectly simple and commonplace one . . . (He was a) young man, a few years out of college, who had not yet broken away from home. He hadn't married, and he had found no job that measured up to his rigid standards of employment, and like any young man, or young animal, he felt uneasy and on the defensive until he had fixed himself a den. Most young men, of course, casting about for a site, are content merely to draw apart from their kinfolks. Thoreau, convinced that the greater part of what his neighbors called good was bad, withdrew from a great deal more than family.

The second passage, by White, is a bit easier to follow than the first, by Wright Morris, because White dramatized the ''principle of turning one's back on unpleasant facts.'' At the same time, in writing more abstractly, Morris offered a more cogent summary statement of the general significance of Thoreau's action.

The Verbal Sentence.   When you narrate in order to explain, you involve your reader in an action that illustrates the ideas you want your reader to understand. You also write more concretely when you employ short sentences that emphasize persons or things as their subject and active verbs as their predicate. Look at the following three sentences:

> The boy knew every trick.
>
> He grew up in the ghetto.
>
> He was tough and streetwise.

Each one is what we call a verbal sentence: the focus is on a subject that is an actor, a verb that tells what the action is, and modifiers that tell something more about who the actor is and/or what he is doing. Each one is in the active voice, which many style manuals argue is more direct than passive constructions, in which the actor becomes the object of the sentence and the verb is turned into a past participle ("Every trick was known by the boy"). You may not necessarily write more clearly if you favor short, active, verbal sentences, but your style will sound simpler and more concrete.

Of course, a piece of writing composed only of short, simple sentences is apt to be choppy and monotonous. Even the most concise and direct stylist wants to include longer, more complex sentence structures in her or his writing. In the "Focus" section of Chapter 5, you received some practice in sentence combining as a way of making your style more complex. A possible combination of the three sample sentences might be "Growing up tough and streetwise in the ghetto, the boy knew every trick." In this sentence, the noun *boy* is modified by the cluster "Growing up tough and streetwise in the ghetto," a cluster in which the verbal component "Growing up" is itself qualified by "tough and streetwise in the ghetto."

Adjusting for Abstractness.   In the combined sentence above, attention has been directed to the ghetto toughness of the boy. The sentence is thus more abstract, focused as much on a concept, "ghetto toughness," as on an action. By modifying a noun or a verb, either with a string of adjectives and/or adverbs or with clusters of subordinate clauses, you draw the reader's attention to the distinctive qualities of the subject and/or the action you are writing about.

The use of modifiers and of long, involved sentences will not guarantee an intelligently complex style. But, especially in the service of abstract explanation, these rhetorical tools can lend clarity to the expression of complicated ideas. Thus, in the first sentence of the passage about Thoreau by Wright Morris, the subordinate clause, with its modifying adjectives *inessential* and *foreign,* does help to explain the concept of *unpleasant facts* and thus clarifies a reader's understanding of the subject of the sentence, the "principle of turning one's back on unpleasant facts."

The Nominal Sentence.   Let's take the combined sentence about the boy in the ghetto and make one more alteration: "His growing up tough and streetwise in the ghetto is what taught the boy every trick." Note that "the boy" is no longer the subject of the sentence. We have nominalized the verbs and adjectives of the modifying cluster; that is, we have turned them into nouns that can function as the subject.

Nominal sentence structures, because they tend to create abstract subjects of verbs and adjectives, can be effective tools for the stylist interested in analyzing ideas. If you change the verbal construction "He loved the woods and felt free there and so went camping often" into a nominal construction, "His love of the woods and the freedom he felt there led him to go camping often," you are directing the reader's attention more emphatically to the idea that explains why the person went camping.

If you work in a more abstract, idea-oriented style, however, your writing will not necessarily be more profound than if you write in a more concrete, verbal style. Nor will you necessarily sound more eloquent. You may, in fact, choose plain, direct words because you want to explain a complex idea as clearly as you can.

How to Write More Eloquently

Whether your style is simple or complex, concrete or abstract, there are a few guidelines you might follow in attempting to write with more eloquence.

Balanced Phrasing.   Balanced phrasing is an effective means of lending an eloquent sound to your style. "He ate scrambled eggs, buttered toast, and fresh-squeezed orange juice" would sound less polished if it were written, "He ate scrambled eggs, toast with butter, and orange juice that had been freshly squeezed." Particularly when you are writing long, complicated sentences, phrasing similar grammatical units and similar ideas in similar ways is an important means of achieving clarity. Note how repetition lends balance to the following sentence: "The difference between living today and living at any time in the past is the difference between living in fear of nuclear destruction and living free of such fear." This would be a more difficult sentence to understand without such a balanced effect: "The difference between living today and at any time in the past is fear of nuclear destruction."

Loose and Periodic Sentences.   As you seek balance in your phrasing, seek variety in your sentence structuring. It is sometimes argued, for example, that periodic sentences, in which the modifiers precede the base, sound somehow better than loose sentences, in which the modifiers follow the base. But writing only periodic sentences is as dull as writing only short, simple sentences. The periodic sentence "Having gone to the woods, he camped out" does place more dramatic emphasis on the subject than would a loose version of the same sentence, "He camped out, having gone to the woods." But there is really no justification for preferring one type of sentence over the other. A loose sentence may prove as effective as a periodic sentence, depending on what element in the sentence a writer wishes to emphasize and whether the emphasis will be best achieved by the placement of that element first or last. The context must always be taken into consideration.

Figurative Language.   Skillfully and judiciously used, similes, metaphors, irony, understatement, and similar figures of speech will lend eloquence to your style.

A metaphor is an implied comparison between dissimilar things. To write "Our world is a ship without a helmsman on the dark sea of space" is to imply that our world, like a ship drifting on the sea, needs someone to guide and steer it. In a simile, the comparison is made explicitly by the use of *like* or *as*.

There are a number of dangers in using metaphors and similes. They may end up sounding trite, as does the example above. If they are used too frequently, they may actually distract a reader's attention from the point that the writer wishes to make instead of making the point more memorable. Also, novices who try to extend a metaphor often mix it up, with ludicrous results. Thus, if the writer who compared the world to a ship goes on to write, "If we are not careful, our ship may sink in the flames of a third world war," the "sea" has gone through a most awkward transformation. In general, use the occasional metaphor that comes to you naturally in the course of writing.

Irony.   Irony involves undercutting a reader's expectations. To write "After Adam and Eve ate the apple, they found life a bit tougher" is to create an ironic effect through understatement. The reader expects you to say and knows that you mean that Adam and Eve found life very much tougher. Like any form of verbal humor, irony requires subtlety. The ironist is always in danger of falling flat on his or her face. Irony should not be overdone.

You may find yourself most eloquent when your language is as simple and direct as you can make it. Take the following advice from E. B. White:

The beginner should approach style warily, realizing that it is himself he is approaching, no other; and he should begin by turning resolutely away from all devices that are popularly believed to indicate style—all mannerisms, tricks, adornments. . . .

Style takes its final shape more from attitudes of mind than from principles of composition, for, as an elderly practitioner once remarked, "Writing is an act of faith, not a trick of grammar." This moral observation would have no place in a rule book were it not that style *is* the writer, and therefore what a man is, rather than what he knows, will at last determine his style.

—**Strunk and White,** *Elements of Style.*

SOME PRACTICE WITH STYLE

1. Identify each of the following sentences as verbal or nominal. Restructure each verbal sentence into a nominal one, each nominal sentence into a verbal one:

    a. You take the high road, I'll take the low road, and I'll get to Scotland before you.

    b. Keeping physically fit has become a major preoccupation of many people today.

    c. Our capacity for wonder at the news has been lost because of television.

    d. I like the essay, have always liked it, and even as a child was at work, attempting to inflict my young thoughts and experiences on others by putting them on paper.

2. Identify each of the following sentences as periodic or loose. Recast each periodic sentence into a loose one, and each loose sentence into a periodic one. What are the differing effects?

    a. Having a thick coat of fur, the animal survived.

    b. Mercilessly goading the bully, our hero saved the day.

    c. Snowstorms make driving hazardous and thus endanger lives, even as they give countless children hours of gleeful play.

    d. Newsmagazines are popular, offering an artful combination of news, popular opinion, and gossip.

3. Identify each of the following sentences as active or passive. Restructure each active sentence into a passive one, each passive sentence into an active one:

    a. Paradoxically, in a free society, one is often worried and frustrated by government policy.

    b. The house was torn apart by the swirling winds of the tornado.

    c. The hard day's work at the factory tired him out.

    d. Don't count your chickens before they hatch.

4. Simplify the style of the following paragraph by rewriting in order to dramatize its central idea:

> The mass of men lead lives of quiet desperation. What is called resignation is confirmed desperation. From the desperate city you go into the desperate country and have to console yourself with the bravery of minks and muskrats. A stereotyped but unconscious despair is concealed even under what are called the

games and amusements of mankind. There is no play in them, for this comes after work. But it is a characteristic of wisdom not to do desperate things.

—**Henry David Thoreau**, *Walden.*

5. Write a paragraph of abstract generalizations that summarize the significance of the passage by E. B. White about the movie theater episode.

6. Analyze the following passages for their style: identify sentences as verbal or nominal, periodic or loose, simple or complex; indicate whether verbs are passive or active; determine how phrasing has been balanced, what figures of speech have been used, and if irony is a component. Finally, has clarity been maintained throughout? What would you say is the chief means by which the writer's style gave eloquence and meaning to each passage?

Springtime in the heyday of the Model T was a delirious season. Owning a car was still a major excitement, roads were still wonderful and bad. The Fords were obviously conceived in madness: any car which was capable of going from forward into reverse without any perceptible mechanical hiatus was bound to be a mighty challenging thing to the human imagination. Boys used to veer them off the highway into a level pasture and run wild with them, as though they were cutting up with a girl. Most everybody used the reverse pedal quite as much as the regular foot brake—it distributed the wear over the bands and wore them all down evenly. That was the big trick, to wear all the bands down evenly, so that the final chattering would be total and the whole unit scream for renewal.

The days were golden, the nights were dim and strange. I still recall with trembling those loud, nocturnal crises when you drew up to a signpost and raced the engine so the lights would be bright enough to read destinations by. I have never been really planetary since. I suppose it's time to say good-bye. Farewell, my lovely!

—**E. B. White**, "Farewell, My Lovely!"

In a newsreel theater the other day I saw a picture of a man who had developed the soap bubble to a higher point than it had ever before reached. He had become the ace soap bubble blower of America, had perfected the business of blowing bubbles, refined it, doubled it, squared it, and had even worked himself up into a convenient lather. The effect was not pretty. Some of the bubbles were too big to be beautiful, and the blower was always jumping into them or out of them, or playing some sort of unattractive trick with them. It was, if anything, a rather repulsive sight. Humor is a little like that: it won't stand much blowing up, and it won't stand much poking. It has a certain fragility, an evasiveness, which one had best respect. Essentially, it is a complete mystery. A human frame convulsed with laughter, and the laughter becoming hysterical and uncontrollable, is as far out of balance as one shaken with the hiccoughs or in the throes of a sneezing fit.

—**E. B. White**, "Some Remarks on Humor"

7. Take a passage from your journal or from an essay that you have written, and recast the sentences to make your writing more abstract and complex. Assume, for example, that you are writing for *The New York Times*. If your original passage was a narrative, you can summarize it as an abstract statement. You might recast your sentences into the nominal form and combine the various elements into sentences of greater length. Do not, of course, sacrifice clarity in your revision.

8. Now, revise the passage again, this time aiming for concreteness. You might begin by developing a narrative to support the main point of the piece. Employ any figures of speech that seem to you to add vividness. Balance your complex sentences with shorter verbal structures in the active voice that give emphasis to the action.

9. Examine the passage for ways in which you can make your writing more eloquent. What balanced phrasing can be added, and what variations in sentence structure, to achieve both periodic and loose sentences? Would it be possible to revise your passage once again, aiming for an ironic slant toward your subject?

REWRITING

Obtaining Feedback on Your Rough Draft

Once you have taken sufficient time away from your rough draft so that you can review it with a measure of objectivity, turn to one or more of the channels you have developed for obtaining feedback on what you have written: your "other self," your peers, or your teacher. Again, use these channels for obtaining answers to the "Audience Response Guide" about your draft.

———— AUDIENCE RESPONSE GUIDE ————

1. **What does the writer want to say in this paper? What is his or her purpose in writing? What does he or she want the paper to mean?**
2. **How does the paper affect the audience for which it is intended?**
3. **How effective has the writer been in conveying his or her purpose and meaning?**
4. **How should the paper be revised to better fulfill its purpose and meaning?**

Consider at this time the following peer evaluation of the rough draft of the student essay "Horrors." Compare your own evaluation of the draft to that of the peer group by answering the four questions of the "Audience Response Guide" before reading their answers.

1. The readers disagreed on the purpose of the essay. One felt that the writer intended to give a historical survey of the development of horror films and its later offshoots, but the other said that the purpose was unclear, that the paper provided a lot of information but failed to explain why it was doing so.

2. The first reader believed that the paper was intended for an uneducated film audience—one that had not seen most of these films and wasn't aware of the horror film's origins. The other reader felt a bit overwhelmed by the information.

3. Both readers agreed that the essay included too much information and too little assimilation, and that the information lacked supplemental explanations of its intended purpose. Both were very impressed by the extent of the writer's knowledge.

4. The readers agreed that the writer should narrow his focus, concentrate more on some representative films, and explain his purpose further.

Here is a revised version of "Horrors." How well were the readers' suggestions incorporated? Did the writer make any additional changes himself? What additional changes might he have made?

HORRORS

The evolution of horror films certainly doesn't compare to the wondrous and lengthy evolution of humankind. Horror films are, however, a vivid reflection of the twentieth century's ever-changing morals, values, and fears. Although horror films have certainly changed over the years, saying that yesteryear's horror films are better than today's is as arguable as stating that humans are better now than they were a half century ago. Do we not commit the same atrocities (rape, thievery, murder) as our grandparents or our greatgrandparents did?

The year 1931 marked the coming of age of the horror genre. Although there had previously been scattered examples of films that dramatized the horrible and the grotesque, the horror film did not flourish until Universal released <u>Dracula,</u> featuring Bela Lugosi as the irrepressible Transylvanian count of Bram Stoker's classic novel; shortly after, Universal released <u>Frankenstein,</u> featuring Boris Karloff as Mary Shelley's monstrous novel creation. As the genre prospered, in 1932 Karloff appeared in <u>The Mummy;</u> in 1933 Claude Rains was <u>The</u>

<u>Invisible Man</u> and <u>King Kong</u> made a monkey of himself; and in 1940 Lon Chaney, Jr., was transformed into <u>The Wolf Man</u> to add to horror's growing assemblage of monsters and spooks. Interestingly, this new genre, in which all of the major Hollywood studios were involved, spawned a plethora of new stars who would become known as "horror stars" (such as Karloff, Lugosi, and Chaney, Jr.).

The horror genre's sudden success was indeed puzzling because these films succeeded during the economic depression that occurred after 1929. In fact, audiences relentlessly flocked to this macabre new genre. Perhaps the audiences of that era equated the grim stories of countless people and villages being destroyed by various creatures with the Great Depression, which in reality destroyed many people and cities. Perhaps they hoped that, like the films in which the creature dies at the end and a sense of balance is restored to the village, the poverty and despair induced by the Depression would also be conquered and a sense of order would be restored.

Curiously, Dracula, Frankenstein, and other assorted monsters achieved a weird kind of commercial immortality with their sudden success. Thus the studios set out on a steady and profitable progress through a series of sequels in which the creatures returned as themselves or as "sons," "daughters," and "ghosts" in such films as <u>Son of Kong</u>, <u>The Invisible Man Returns</u>, <u>The Mummy's Ghost</u>, and <u>The Bride of Frankenstein</u>.

However, there's a limit to human invention, if not human credulity. Horror films came out with the regularity of a monthly magazine. By the mid-1940s, Hollywood had gorged the public past horror satiety. In a desperate attempt to rejuvenate horror's sagging box office, Hollywood united horror filmdom's monsters (<u>Frankenstein Meets the Wolf Man</u>), a move that slowed down the erosion of box-office dollars but didn't stop it. Feeling that the imaginary horror of a film couldn't possibly compete with the true horror tales of Nazism and World War II circulating in the United States, Hollywood lamely blamed World War II for the continuing plummet of horror's box-office popularity. Finally, horror expired in self-parody as it was exploited for cheap laughs: <u>Abbott and Costello Meet Frankenstein</u>, <u>The Dead End Kids Meet the</u>

Spook, and so on. Ironically, a genre in which death was a constant staple died the most unkind of deaths itself by 1945.

After the war, little was heard of horror until the advent of science fiction in 1950 when the genre, like a Phoenix rising from its own ashes, entered its second cycle. With the big Hollywood studios generally abandoning horror like a wounded, dying animal, various small, independent film companies, ranging from the fairly big American International Pictures to the ultracheap Astor, became the most consistent suppliers of horror films. The independents shrewdly manipulated and exploited the prevalent fears and changing values of that era. The independents' skillful exploitation of the public's fear of imminent nuclear destruction, for example, gave birth to the "atomic-age monsters," who were either normal living organisms, transformed into mutants by incessant human dabbling in the atomic field (in such films as Colossal Man and Attack of the Crab Monsters), or supposedly extinct dinosaurs unleashed from their centuries' long "dormancy" deep below ocean floors or ice caps because of atomic testing, as in Beast from 20,000 Fathoms.

More subtle was the independents' shrewd, artful exploitation of McCarthyism for a generally unknowing audience. Such films as The Incredibly Strange Creatures Who Stopped Living and Became Mixed-Up Zombies, It Conquered the World, and I Married a Monster from Outer Space, although seemingly only crude productions dealing with aliens conquering us and/or infiltrating our very human existence, purposely paralleled (if somewhat indiscreetly) the shocking real-life aspects of McCarthyism. Indeed these films' menacing fictional aliens served as metaphors for the McCarthyite vision of Communists infiltrating and conquering our land.

The second cycle of horror was a time of high exploitation as the independents specialized in making quick contemporary horror films, all of which had an assured profit potential because of minuscule budgets and sensationalized advertising. In fact, American International Pictures, in many cases, just made up an advertising campaign, and if they liked the campaign's look, they then made a film (usually in three to six days) pertaining to the poster's theme. As noted film historian Leslie Halliwell claimed, in The Film Goer's Companion, "Such crude and shoddy productions cheapened the genre considerably." Perhaps they were "crude and shoddy," but they were attuned to their audience's whims, and the independents keenly sensed that with the advent of fast cars and rock 'n' roll, the mood of its basically youthful audience was undergoing a drastic shift. Thus began the recycling of familiar horror-film monsters into "romantic villains" in such films as I Was a Teen-age Werewolf and I Was a Teen-age Frankenstein, whose heroes were misunderstood and inarticulate but, not uncoincidentally, sympathetic and identifiable to these films' chiefly youthful audiences, who had the same problems as these monsters; even less uncoincidentally, these monsters were irritants to authority, just as their youthful audiences were. By shrewdly exploiting this new significance of the teen-ager, these independents helped establish the now famous "youth market."

It was during this reincarnation of "old-time" monsters that the genre was ushered into its third cycle as it looked on its old saviors to return it to the prosperity that it had once tasted. In 1958, Hammer Films, a small, fledgling independent film company, released Horror of Dracula (with Christopher Lee and Peter Cushing). It was essentially a remake of the 1932 Dracula with an authentic gothic look, a bold style, and a new permissiveness in "screen blood." Buoyed by the film's enormous success, Hammer recycled other horror films of the 1930s (Evil of Frankenstein, Curse of the Mummy, Curse of the Werewolf). AIP also delved into gothic horror with the release of The Pit and the Pendulum (very loosely based on Edgar Allan Poe's story and featuring Vincent Price) as a counterpunch to Hammer. The success of this movie compelled AIP to go through a wild rummage of Poe: Masque of the Red Death, The Oblong Box, The Raven, and others (all with Price). Interestingly, horror was once again spawning its own stars, as the names of Price, Lee, and Cushing became synonymous with horror. An explanation for this new and sudden fixation on "old" values might be linked to the presidency of that era. Just as America saw in the JFK administration the past pleasant virtues of Camelot, so may people have sought in Hammer's films the past virtues of the old horror "look."

It was during the third cycle that the major studios returned, opting for a more bold type of horror that often paralleled reality—<u>Whatever</u> <u>Happened to Baby Jane?</u> (mental illness), <u>The Collector</u> (sexual perversion), <u>Repulsion</u> (sexual obsession)—rather than the costumed period pieces of the independents. It was also during the third cycle that blood and fairly explicit violence were used or, as director Don Sharp said in a recent interview in <u>Fangoria</u> on the subject of Hammer Films: "They'd got into the pattern of making each film a bit bloodier than the one before it." It was with Alfred Hitchcock's <u>Psycho</u> in 1960 that horror achieved a new permissiveness in the limits on screen violence, as that film would forever shatter the invisible line of what was and was not acceptable on the screen.

In 1968, that line was further annihilated when a small independent, Laurel, released the ultragraphic <u>Night of the Living Dead</u>. This film, which went unrated by the Motion Picture Association of America, signified the beginning of the fourth cycle, a period in which both the major studios and independents prospered and screen violence was given a new definition because the newly imposed film ratings freed movies from their hitherto self-imposed censorship. Perhaps this new permissiveness mirrored the fact that our society at the time equated carnage with horror, what with television daily invading living rooms showing the grisly effects of the Vietnam war. After seeing such real-life bloody carnage in their homes, perhaps the public could no longer accept the quaint gothic horrors of the past.

During the mid-1970s, the major studios seemed intent on reflecting our ecological worries in such tales of ecological revenge as <u>Jaws</u>, <u>Orca</u>, and <u>The Swarm</u> and became fixated on the supernatural (<u>The Exorcist</u>, <u>The Omen</u>, <u>Carrie</u>). Meanwhile the independents successfully forayed into a variety of unusual subjects, including the return of Dracula and Frankenstein in the most unlikely of vehicles, such as <u>Blacula</u>, <u>Andy Warhol's Frankenstein</u>, and other film oddities such as <u>Gore Gore Girls</u>, <u>I Dismember Mama</u>, and <u>Ilsa: She-Wolf of the SS</u>. It was in 1974, as the independents continued to create unusual formulas for success, that the highly successful, ultraexplicit <u>Texas Chainsaw Massacre</u> was released. This film not only set a new precedent in screen violence but created a formula (the indestructible killer) that still saturates the independent horror-film market today (<u>Friday the 13th,</u> <u>Maniac!, Madman</u>). This type of film has been affectionately dubbed <u>splatter film</u> by its fans, for obvious reasons.

One thing is certain: whether the monsters come from graveyards, outer space, or oceans or are just plain homicidal psychotic killers, horror films, like the monsters they dramatize, will not die, and as the twentieth century continues to evolve, horror films will reflect our changing preoccupations.

Consolidating

Words, sentences, and whole passages often need consolidating to make a stronger impact. Consolidating occurs when the writer brings together ideas that in the rough draft were scattered throughout a sentence, a paragraph, or the entire essay. This scattering weakens the effect that the writer wishes to make by diluting the impact, whereas consolidating the material strengthens it by creating a concentrated effect.

Consider this sentence: "The health effects of all the different chemicals ingested by animals are well documented by impartial M.D.'s, so this is not just hearsay from ASPCA people or the like." This is not a bad sentence as it is, but consolidating the two clauses on the health effects creates a more focused effect: "That animals' health is affected by all the different chemicals they ingest is not just hearsay from the ASPCA but is well documented by impartial M.D.'s." (Refer also to the section on sentence combining on pp. 156–165 for the different ways in which sentence elements can be consolidated.)

Consider the following introductory paragraph to an essay on fraternal orders:

As a youngster, I remember watching such shows as <u>The Honey-</u> <u>mooners</u> and <u>The Flintstones</u>, during which, on many occasions, the main characters tried to deceive and lie to their wives in order to go bowling or play cards with their brother lodgemen. The lodges or fraternities that these men belonged to had funny names like "The Raccoons," which Ralph belonged to in <u>The Honeymooners</u>, and "The Loyal Order of Waterbuffaloes," which Fred was a member of in <u>The Flint-</u> <u>stones.</u> All the members wore funny hats and had ridiculous handshakes. Unfortunately, that is where my education and that of many others about fraternal organizations began.

Although this first version presents some effective details, consolidating the information makes a stronger impact on the reader:

In order to go bowling or play cards, Fred Flintstone lied to his wife about his destination. Then he donned a funny hat and, with a ridiculous handshake, joined his brother lodgemen at "The Loyal Order of Waterbuffaloes." Ralph, in The Honeymooners, also had to stoop to deceit in order to participate in the activities of "The Raccoons." Unfortunately, these shows were where my education and that of many others about fraternal organizations began.

Look again at the final draft of "Horrors," the student essay on pp. 202–207. Although on the basis of his peer-group analysis, the writer had consolidated much of the material that appeared in his rough draft (pp. 190–194), what additional consolidation might he have made? What segments of his sentences, paragraphs, and the whole essay might he have brought together to make his point more strongly?

Editing

Consolidating.   Consolidate words and phrases that ramble aimlessly in order to achieve a stronger impact. Why say "thin and sickly" when you can write "emaciated"? Or why write "Carrying the football, I lunged forward, the ball tucked snugly under my arm," when "I lunged forward, the football tucked snugly under my arm" consolidates your material for a sharper effect?

Style.   Review your essay with an eye to adjusting your style so that you have presented your ideas as clearly as possible. Are there sentences or phrases or words that you need to simplify? Might you turn a verbal sentence into a nominal one in order to focus your reader's attention on an abstract point? If you have employed figurative language, have you done so judiciously?

Mechanics.   Once again, review earlier samples of your writing in which mechanical errors have been noted, then check your draft for spelling, punctuation, and grammatical errors common to your writing. Work with the handbook in the back of the book, if necessary, to make corrections.

Now revise and edit your rough draft.

BECOMING AWARE OF YOURSELF AS A WRITER

You might want to make use of your journal to record your thoughts and feelings about the task for this chapter. As you write in your journal, consider the following questions.

1. How did you use your reading in generating ideas for this essay? If you chose some other source of information (a documentary, a lecture, or a film), why did you make such a choice and how did the material help you?

2. Was the information you provided sufficient for your audience to understand your subject? What kind of information could you have added? If you had offered more information, how would it have helped your audience?

3. Did you find that the ability to generalize was of help to you when you sought to convey information to your audience? What purpose did the generalization serve?

4. What would you say is the primary difference between learning about something and teaching someone else about what you have learned?

5. How specifically were you able to support the generalization on which you based your essay? What concrete examples or details did you use?

6. How would you characterize the style of writing that comes most naturally to you? Did you find it necessary to make adjustments in your style in order to write an effective explanatory essay? What kind of adjustments did you make?

7
WRITING ABOUT RESEARCH

PURPOSE

You enter a large room. You observe that approximately thirty males and females, mostly between the ages of eighteen and twenty-one, are seated facing a wide wall with a gray slate board mounted on it. In front of the wall, an adult male is seated behind a wood-grained metal desk. The young people in the room are looking directly at the seated male, who is speaking to the entire group. Occasionally an arm rises, followed by a comment from the person whose arm was raised. After about an hour, the adult male stops speaking, begins to collect his books and papers from the desk, and stands. Shortly after, the young people stand and walk toward the door.

Because these observations are so familiar, you don't have to think long before deciding on a generalization that explains the situation just described. Somewhere during your reading of this paragraph, the details cohered into a single conclusion: this is a description of a class. The process of reasoning that leads us to this conclusion is called *induction*. Induction is one of the major methods through which we arrive at the meaning of our observations and experience, providing us with a technique for verifying what we decide is the factual truth. Scientists in the laboratory and in the field use induction to arrive at conclusions about phenomena in nature and in society.

In this chapter, we will ask you to write with the specific purpose of explaining to your reader the nature and meaning of scientific conclusions on a topic of your choice; that is, we will ask you to write on interpretations of certain observed phenomena that can be accepted as valid because they have been verified by the experimentation of scientists and are convincingly explained according to the standards of accepted scientific discourse. Your task will be a research paper on a scientific subject organized according to the principles of inductive reasoning. Inductive reasoning relies on the assumption that collected data—the products of observation or experimentation—can produce reliable explanations of the physical world, provided that the data are relevant to the problem under consideration. The writer who wishes to provide valid scientific explanations must be able to produce evidence and to draw conclusions from it that the reader will recognize as "scientific" and thus will accept as valid explanations.

In fulfilling the writing task in Chapter 5, you relied solely on your own powers of observation to give you authentic information on a place or an ongoing event. And what gave power to these observations was the use of the classical questions. These questions provided you with a mental framework on which you could construct your case. In this chapter, your emphasis will be on the implications for scientific inquiry contained in the questions "What examples are there of it?" and "What conclusions can we draw from these examples?" Whereas, in Chapter 6, you also responded to these questions, there you cited examples to support a generalization about the value of some knowledge that you possess. Here we will ask you to discuss scientific ideas arrived at by the scientific method. You will want to explain both examples and conclusions in a way that gives credibility to your method of investigation. You also will want to present a hypothesis or explanation that is meaningful, one that does not conflict with the accepted scientific model of the physical world. You could not expect to offer convincing evidence that there are unicorns in the municipal zoo or that the sun will literally rise or set tomorrow. Following from your reasonable hypothesis, you will need to provide, through your research, examples of investigations or experiments performed by scientists that pertain to your subject and that, taken together, prove your hypothesis. You will also want to know the methods that are used to create a piece of scientific research: finding and evaluating information; arranging materials into a meaningful, logical form; employing the conventions of scientific documentation; and using the voice and tone of objective discourse.*

Although your emphasis will be on using scientific materials, the methods of research that you employ to investigate your topic can be applied to many other

---

*We are using the term *research* in two not unrelated ways: one refers to your research into the work of others, or academic research, and the other refers to the research of scientists in the laboratory or field. Essentially your task will be to research the research that scientists have done, and to use the inductive method in your presentation.

subjects. Many subjects are assigned in college with the assumption that the student has the knowledge and the skill to apply certain methods of investigation to solving problems. A knowledge of the process of induction can lead you to insights in unexpected areas. One of these areas is simply your own personal observation. Although this is not on the same conceptual level as research performed in a laboratory, your informed observation of, for example, students applying for jobs at the college employment office is a method of arriving at an inductive understanding of the job prospects for potential college graduates. Similarly, an interview with the employment counselor, in which you learn that employment opportunities for liberal arts graduates have declined by 20 percent in the past five years, will give you inductive evidence for coming to a conclusion about where the future job opportunities will be found. You can then support these findings with the research you have done in books and periodical articles that investigate the topic of employment opportunities for college graduates. Through the combined use of library research, observation, and interview you can arrive at a conclusion that is the result of original investigation.

Our brief discussion of the kind of discourse we recognize as scientific implies the existence of an audience for whom this discourse is intended. A scientific audience may be one that is interested primarily in the practical application of scientific principles (as in magazines like *Popular Mechanics* and *Popular Electronics*), or one interested in the explanation of current research and scientific theory for the science-educated nonspecialist (as in *Scientific American* or *Science*), or the audiences for the many specialized and highly technical publications in which such professional scientists as nuclear biologists or enzyme chemists report the results of their experiments. As we move up the pyramid of complexity, the audience becomes smaller and smaller, so that at the highest levels of abstraction only a relative handful of readers is capable of evaluating and validating the writer's conclusions. In the audience section of this chapter, we will discuss the kinds of audience to whom you might direct your investigation, as well as the nature of the discourse that you will want to adopt.

When you write in order to explain, you want to take into account other important elements of the writing process. In dealing with a large number of ideas or relevant examples, you are faced with the need to organize your materials and to form a preliminary framework on which to arrange them so that they can be presented most logically and efficiently. This outline also functions as a kind of screen on which you project the order of your evidence and the conclusions that result from it. You can then begin to see the emerging direction of your paper. The result of this process can be a paper that is credible and convincing. Although you will not be expected to make an original scientific discovery, you can, through the act of synthesizing (or combining already existing materials into a new arrangement), create a discourse that has the authority of skillful, objective research. You can lead your reader to a new insight.

GENERATING IDEAS THROUGH INDUCTION

In a sense, induction is not really a formal method of inquiry but an ongoing process of perception that gives us knowledge of the external world by imposing an order on the rush of sensations that we constantly experience. The more experiences we have and then file away in our active memories, the more order and understanding we can bring to bear on future experiences. Further experiences cause us to test the validity of our past experiences, and if necessary, we revise our mental maps to take into account new or additional information. Just as physical sensations must leap across nerve cells before they can be transmitted to our brains, experiences must undergo a kind of "leap," an inductive leap, before we can arrange them into a pattern of meaning.

If, during several days of going from a dimly lit building into bright sunshine, you found the bright light dazzled you each day in succession, the chances are quite good that it will continue to do so unless you prepare for it in advance. One day you get the idea to put on your sunglasses just before you emerge from the building. You have reasoned from particular experiences and arrived at a general conclusion: sunlight dazzles. Further observations may cause you to refine your conclusion: some days the sky is cloudy and the sun shines through only intermittently; if you leave the building on such a day, you might not need sunglasses. Or you calculate that if you leave after a certain hour, the sun will have shifted and will no longer dazzle your eyes when you emerge from your usual exit. In fact, there seems to be an endless number of variables that affect your actions, many of which you don't even give conscious thought to because they are so habitual.

Of course, we base our conclusions on a certain degree of probability. Although we cannot be absolutely certain that the sun will emerge tomorrow, we can be pretty sure that it will and that it will appear to rise in the east and set in the west. Our reasoning requires that we base our inductive leap on a limited but *adequate number of examples*. You can't be sure that the last pair of pants on a department-store clothing rack has a price tag on it, but if the other twelve pairs on the rack have such a tag, you can reasonably expect the last pair to have a tag. After you noticed that the first eight or ten pairs of pants had a price tag, you reasoned inductively and concluded, "All these pants have price tags." If you then decided to generalize further, claiming, "Every item in this store has an attached price tag," you would be guilty of making a *hasty generalization*. How can you be sure that every item has a price tag attached? Would you check every item in the store, spending the next two years of your life moving from department to department? Well, certainly not, but you might decide to check a number of items in every department, taking what you estimate to be a *representative sampling* of items in the store. And you must not avoid counting departments like fine china or baked goods, where you suspect that many dishes and pastries don't have attached price tags, for such an omission would indicate a tendency on your part to exclude *unfavorable evidence that would negate your conclusion*. You don't want to *distort or falsify your evidence* either, for again, that would put your conclusion in question. Finally, you must *evaluate your evidence for the reliability of its sources* to determine whether your conclusion is based on reliable information.

One source of evidence that would seem reliable is our own power of observation. But as was suggested earlier in the example of the "rising" and "setting" of the sun, personal observation is full of pitfalls, offering little assurance that we can always believe what we observe. Consider the account of an early-twentieth-century attempt to demonstrate that animals could perform human mental operations such as counting. Michael Polanyi, in his book *Personal Knowledge*, related the story of the horse "Clever Hans":

The horse . . . could tap out with his hoofs the answer to all kinds of mathematical problems, written out on a blackboard in front of him. Incredulous experts from all relevant branches of knowledge came and tested him severely, only to confirm again and again his unfailing intellectual powers. But at last Mr. Oskar Pfungst had the idea of asking the horse a question to which he, Pfungst, did not know the answer. This time the horse went on tapping and tapping indefinitely, without rhyme or reason. It turned out that all the severely sceptical experts had involuntarily and unknowingly signalled to the horse to stop tapping at the point where they—knowing the right answer—expected him to stop. This is how they made the answers invariably come out right.

In this incident, we see how strongly observers can influence the results of observation by the strength of their own desire to have an experiment mean what they want it to mean, in effect to "prove" what they already believed at the outset of their scientific inquiry. This example suggests that scientific objectivity—the total impartiality of the observing scientist—is never a simple, unambiguous given that we can assume as the guiding principle of all scientific research, but that it is an ideal (some would say a myth) that needs to be understood in advance by the researcher who uses scientific evidence. Having acknowledged this fact, however, how are you, the student writer—lacking the technical knowledge or the scientific authority to evaluate your sources—to determine whether these sources have a definite "axe to grind"? To a large extent, you cannot. You must rely on the reputation of the authorities—the institution, the author, or the periodical—that stand behind the published results. And you can use the knowledge that you have of the reasoning process to aid you in determining how reliable a given source is, whether it is yourself, someone you interview, or sources that you locate in the library.

SOME PRACTICE WITH INDUCTION

1. Use your journal to record observations that are as objective as possible. Select a place from which to begin observing and recording examples, for instance, the student cafeteria, a bench in front of a bus stop, or the window in your room that overlooks the street. Record the details observed from this vantage point over a period of several days. Try observing the same object but from a different observation point. You might take a photograph of the scene or even tape-record the sounds that you heard for a limited period of time. What generalizations can you make from your observations? Was there any discernible pattern that emerged from these observations?

2. Assume you are a social anthropologist, one who observes the practices of cultures that are strange to us and tries to understand their meaning. Select some ritual of daily life that goes largely unnoticed, for example, a gathering of students at the campus lounge. Write down your observations very carefully, trying not to impose your views on what is taking place. Some other rituals that you might observe are lunchtime at a fast-food establishment or the behavior of customers in a supermarket. After gathering sufficient examples of behavior, arrive at a conclusion about the meaning of the ritual or the pattern of behavior observed.

3. Select a topic about which to poll student attitudes on campus. Prepare a series of questions. Determine what would be an adequate sampling of views and how the respondents should be selected. Next, conduct your poll, collecting answers to your questions from selected students. Evaluate your collected data and make some generalizations about the views of the students who contributed opinions. To what extent are your results accurate as a representation of student opinion? What criticisms might be made of your method of questioning or your sampling of opinions?

4. Basing your opinion on the evidence supplied, explain whether the generalizations in the examples below are valid:

   a. Everyone in the class has had at least one unpleasant experience in dealing with bureaucracies. The class overwhelmingly concludes that bureaucracies are terrible and should be abolished.

   b. In Steve's survey of students who smoke, 67 percent in two classes of business majors smoke, whereas only 48 percent of the students in two classes of English majors smoke. Steve concludes that business majors smoke more than English majors.

   c. When asked by a local newspaper, ten out of ten members of the college administration state that the evening students on campus are satisfied with the college's evening program, as enrollment has gone up from last year. The newspaper says that the unanimous agreement of the administration is conclusive evidence that they are right.

ADDRESSING YOUR AUDIENCE: THE LAY READER

On one of his morning television programs, Phil Donahue had as guests two of the most widely read scientist-writers of our time, Carl Sagan and Stephen Jay Gould. Here were two highly trained, technically skilled university professors explaining theories of evolution to a large television audience. Pointer in hand and standing before a large TV graphic, Sagan explained that all of geological time could be understood if we thought of it as if it were only a one-year calendar. According to this analogy, humankind makes its first appearance about December 25, almost at the very end of the "year." In this way, Sagan tried to show how recently our species had arrived on the planet. It was an imaginative comparison, one that his audience could grasp far more easily than if he had said that the evolutionary process was of several billion years' duration. Certainly Sagan would not have used this analogy if he were addressing a convention of the American Association for the Advancement of Science or a graduate seminar on the origins of the solar system. But for an audience of the scientifically unschooled, this was a highly effective learning device.

As this textbook is being prepared, the public consciousness of science is undergoing a minor revolution. Much of it may be due to the rise of the computer sciences and their startling grasp on the popular imagination. In addition, there are exciting discoveries that have altered our view of human genetics and its effects on the human species.

You need look no further for evidence of this ferment in scientific exploration and discovery than your nearest newsstand. Here are some of the many science magazines now being directed to relatively large audiences:

The Sciences	*Natural History*
Science 83	*Scientific American*
Omni	*Nature*
Science News	*Discover*
American Scientist	*Psychology Today*

Each of these magazines differs somewhat in style and substance. Some are weighted more heavily toward the behavioral and life sciences. Others, intended for a large reading public, are heavily illustrated and tend to focus on the future implications of scientific technology. *Scientific American* and *Nature* make rigorous demands on the reader and often report important new discoveries. All of these periodicals are aware of the level of interests and scientific abilities of their readers.

At the same time that more people are becoming interested in science, the technical language of scientific explanation is becoming more remote from the understanding of the ordinary—even if scientifically educated—reader. Thus the need exists for writers who can explain and interpret the world of scientific discourse in ways that are interesting yet not patronizing to their readers. Stephen Jay Gould, a professor of biology and geology at Harvard University, writes a monthly essay on a variety of biological topics for *Natural History,* a widely circulated magazine published by the American Museum of Natural History in New York. His writing is a combination of human curiosity and penetrating intelligence, supported by a fine writer's eye for the unexpected analogy and the offbeat allusion:

When I was 10 years old, James Arness terrified me as a giant, predaceous carrot in *The Thing* (1951). A few months ago, older, wiser, and somewhat bored, I watched its latest television rerun with a dominating sentiment of anger. I recognized the film as a political document, expressing the worst sentiments of America in the cold war: its hero, a tough military man who wants only to destroy the enemy utterly; its villain, a naively liberal scientist who wants to learn more about it; the carrot and its flying saucer, a certain surrogate for the red menace; the film's famous last words—a newsman's impassioned plea to "watch the skies"—an invitation to extended fear and jingoism.

Amidst all this, a scientific thought crept in by analogy and this essay was born— the fuzziness of all supposedly absolute taxonomic distinctions. The world, we are told, is inhabited by animals with conceptual language (us) and those without (everyone else). But chimps are now talking. All creatures are either plants or animals, but Mr. Arness looked rather human (if horrifying) in his role as a mobile, giant vegetable.

Either plants or animals. Our basic conception of life's diversity is based upon this division. Yet it represents little more than a prejudice spawned by our status as large, terrestrial animals. True, the macroscopic organisms surrounding us on land can be unambiguously allocated if we designate fungi as plants because they are rooted (even though they do not photosynthesize). Yet, if we floated as tiny creatures in the oceanic plankton, we would not have made such a distinction. At the one-celled level, ambiguity abounds: mobile "animals" with functioning chloroplasts; simple cells like bacteria with no clear relation to either group.

Taxonomists have codified our prejudice by recognizing just two kingdoms for all life—Plantae and Animalia. Readers may regard an inadequate classification as a trifling matter; after all, if we characterize organisms accurately, who cares if our basic categories do not express the richness and complexity of life very well? But a classification is not a neutral hat rack; it expresses a theory of relationships that controls our concepts. The Procrustean system of plants and animals has distorted our view of life and prevented us from understanding some major features of its history.

The style and tone of Gould's essay assumes that a reader interested in the subject of evolution and biological taxonomy (classification) need not possess a highly specialized vocabulary nor a graduate degree in order to understand and appreciate the subject. Gould began by recollecting a movie that terrified him as a child. It now suggested to him an analogy of how we divide living things into either plants or animals. This is a "Procrustean system," that is, a limited way to "express the richness and complexity of life." The last sentence points ahead to Gould's main intention: to show how our method of classifying living things prevents us from understanding their real nature.

Although he began with references to himself, Gould's purpose was not to draw attention to the terrors of his childhood or to his taste in films. He was simply using these references as an interesting, colorful introduction to the scientific ideas that are brought into the second paragraph. The author's main purpose was expository, not expressive. He was soon engaged in a serious discussion of the implications of scientific classification. As a scientist, he freely used the language of scientific discourse (*macroscopic organisms, functioning chloroplasts, taxonomists*), yet the overall voice in his language is that of a literate, interested writer making contact with a reader of similar qualities who can also perceive that his is a topic of importance. Both author and reader meet at a level of special knowledge and range of reference that should not be very difficult for a college student to attain.

In discussing a scientific topic in language that will be understandable and interesting to a lay audience, your writing will require the synthesis, or combining, of scientific knowledge into a coherent discussion that presents this knowledge in a convincing way. The language of your discussion must be adapted to the knowledge of the subject that your audience can reasonably be expected to possess. As Gould's writing shows, this approach does not have to result in oversimplification or in trivialization of the subject matter. You should see yourself as the reader's guide through a densely wooded forest, where your familiarity with the trails is the important factor that ensures everyone's safety.

SOME PRACTICE WITH WRITING FOR A LAY AUDIENCE

1. Select three of the science magazines listed in the audience section. Write an analysis of each magazine's intended audience. Does each magazine address its audience successfully? Which is the most successful and why? What changes in each publication would you recommend? How does the format of each magazine (layout, length of articles, amount of advertising, illustrations, special features, and so on) reveal a particular intended audience? How is the language different?

2. Select an author of one of the articles featured in any science magazine named above whose other works are named in the magazine. Look these up in your college library. Write a brief analysis of the differences between the author's treatment of the same (or different) scientific subject in the magazine article and

in the book or more specialized publication in which the writer's other work appeared. What differences in audience do you notice? What differences in research techniques do you notice?

3. College textbooks are excellent examples of how specialized technical material is adapted for a large audience. Analyze your own textbook from one of the natural, physical, or social sciences with regard to the methods it uses to teach technical material to a college audience. How has the author tried to interest students? Has the author been successful? Would you read this book if you were not a student? Contrast this text with another on the same subject and determine which is the more successful. Write a brief report for the department chairman on the book, either recommending it for further adoption or urging that it be dropped.

4. Prepare an outline describing a proposed college science magazine or newsletter. Organize your outline under the following headings: advertising techniques and products; general format of publication; and special features. Briefly explain how this magazine would have special interest and appeal for a college-aged population.

TASK: WRITING ABOUT RESEARCH

Your task for this chapter is to investigate a subject, in either the natural or the social sciences; to analyze and interpret the materials you find; and to convey your information as a discovery that you have made. You will not yourself experiment with a hypothesis. But your synthesis of the findings of others, recorded in books and periodicals, and of information that you gather through your own observations and from interviews with others who are capable of providing you with authoritative comment on your subject can result in evidence and a conclusion that may not be found in this same form anywhere else.

In this act of informing your readers by interpreting your findings and those of others, you are engaging in the activity of research. Although this process is one we undergo everyday—say, in the gathering, interpretation, and evaluation of the information needed to find a suitable gift for a friend or to buy a used car—in the more formal discourse of the college and professional worlds, research implies a specific kind of mental activity and a specific form for presenting this effort to others. In many of your college classes, you may be asked to write a paper showing that you understand how to use the methods and forms of academic research.

As a possible approach to the research task for this chapter, you might begin with your experiences with your cousin, who suffers from anorexia nervosa, and then explain the causes of the illness. In order to do so, you will need to gather outside information on the subject, to interpret your sources to find scientifically convincing and acceptable statements on the causes of the illness, and to present your findings in a clear and accurate manner so that your readers will have learned something new, just as you have. Or, if you are interested in writing about the controversy that has centered on the late Margaret Mead's early research in Samoa and her classic work *Coming of Age in Samoa,* you might include in your essay the results of an interview with a member of your college's anthropology department, as well as the information that you acquire from the printed sources.

When you are writing such a paper, it is helpful to imagine an audience that would profit from your findings. An audience of your peers, readers of a college publication, for example, would be interested in the research activity of other students. And a publication that shares the results of such exploration with others would be a genuine source of information that others would profit from. For this task, try writing your researched essay as an article for a college magazine that presents the work of students exploring the natural and social sciences: your audience will be interested in your findings and will profit from them but will be essentially a lay or nonscientific audience.

The extent of this article is something that your instructor will most likely wish to discuss with you. An investigative paper of approximately five to eight pages, using at least six printed sources, should provide you with an adequate introduction to the methods of inductive research.

In the "Writing the Essay" section that follows, we discuss how to generate ideas, find a topic, gather sources, take notes, organize your evidence, consider your audience, and finally put the paper together.

WRITING THE ESSAY

Using Induction as a Means of Generating Ideas

In writing your paper, it will help to make use of the classical questions "What examples are there of it?" and "What conclusions can we draw from these examples?" Not only will your task require you to provide examples of your topic through the research techniques of personal observation, interview, and library investigation, but you will also want to make some conclusions about the material you have presented.

The personal observation that you want to include may occur before you begin your paper. In fact, your topic may emerge from this observation: you may have observed a natural phenomenon, such as a shooting star or an illness or a social phenomenon such as the behavior of a group, and you may have decided to investigate further. You may also want to set about gaining such a personal experience after selecting your topic. Your observation may occur, of course, in conjunction with your interview: if you plan to interview a coach for an essay on the group behavior of athletes, you may observe her or his team in action before or after the interview.

In seeking an interview, you need to decide who might be considered an authority on your subject who would also be available for an interview, for example, a professor, a doctor, or a social worker.

We discuss how to obtain print sources in following sections, but in all cases—observation, interviews, books, and periodicals—you will want to apply the principles of valid induction to the data that you compile. You need, in other words, to gather examples that will constitute a sufficient sampling of evidence (avoid making hasty generalizations) and that will also constitute a representative sampling (do not ignore unfavorable evidence). Furthermore you will want to use reliable sources that, to the best of your knowledge, do not have an "axe to grind," or if all your sources do appear to have subjective or at least differing attitudes, then you will want to make sure to present both or all approaches to the evidence (it is wishful thinking to assume that all scientific research can be interpreted in only one way).

You can then synthesize these data and arrive at your own conclusion, one that may or may not correspond to the conclusions of the experts.

Because you have already written essays in which you gathered information, interpreted its significance, and presented your results to an audience, you have already acquired much of the experience necessary for taking on the research paper. The major difference is that, in writing this article, you will derive much of your material from sources written by others.

Finding a Topic

Although your purpose is to write an article for a school publication, your topic should be one that interests you as well as others. Will you be able to learn from your topic in the process of explaining it to others? There is little point in writing on a topic that you yourself find uninteresting. But if you have been wondering for some time whether nuclear reactors are really safe, or if animals can really think, this might be a good place to begin.

Quite possibly you may be drawn to a topic because you have heard a lot about it, have seen it featured on TV, or have read about it in a magazine or newspaper. Topics like these are often controversial as well; they provide the writer with a certain advantage in catching the attention of an audience. For the researcher, however, controversy poses some difficulty: some topics are so timely that you might have difficulty finding any information other than newspaper stories and a few scattered magazine articles. A subject needs to seep into the public consciousness and to be studied over a period of time before reasoned, reliable books begin to appear. You might be better off writing on a topic that has been the subject of considerable study. Here are some topics that you might find interesting and about which you should be able to find ample recent investigations. Some are fairly broad and need to be narrowed before they can be used. Discuss them with your instructor or suggest your own topic:

Sciences

1. AIDs syndrome
2. Herpes simplex
3. Anorexia nervosa
4. Genetic engineering
5. Animals threatened with extinction
6. Toxic wastes
7. Organ transplants
8. The artificial heart
9. Animal intelligence
10. The aging process
11. The discovery of DNA
12. Cancer and diet
13. The debate over cholesterol and the heart
14. Vitamins and health
15. Nuclear power and the environment
16. Hypertension
17. Toxic shock syndrome
18. New diagnostic tools in medicine
19. The origins of the universe
20. Harnessing the sun's energy
21. The future of artificial satellites
22. Applications of laser technology
23. Microchips and semiconductors
24. Halley's comet

Social Sciences

1. Occupational health and safety
2. Measuring human intelligence
3. Computer and child learning
4. Religious cults
5. Changing roles of men and women
6. The new immigration
7. The rise of the Sunbelt
8. Child abuse
9. The Japanese worker
10. Violence in sports
11. Creationism and the schools
12. The attack on psychoanalysis
13. Nursing homes
14. Nurse practitioners
15. Women executives
16. Children of divorce
17. Urban gentrification
18. Phobias: their causes and effects
19. The effect of video games on children
20. The battered-wife syndrome
21. The job outlook for the 1990s
22. Sex stereotypes on TV
23. The value of the hospice
24. Physical fitness: fad or revolution?

Your first attempt to find a topic will often begin with a question: What do I know about the extinction of the great whales? Why are some people subject to severe phobias? What are the most successfully treated malignancies? Not only can a question help to point you to a topic that interests you, it can also guide you through your first crucial choice: selecting a topic that is limited enough so that you can explain it in a short article. Once you have done this, either by your own investigation or by discussing it with your instructor, you are ready to begin the exploratory part of your research.

Gathering Sources: Preparing a Preliminary Bibliography

Gathering sources—for many writers the most interesting part of the research process—takes you to the library and sends you through its vast maze of printed materials. Intimidating as it first is for many students, the library soon becomes a place where you feel more confident as you grow to have more and more authority in using its resources.

You might begin by looking at one of the magazines named in the audience section of this chapter. It may give you an insight into a topic that you are curious about or may lead you to a topic that you hadn't really been aware of. To find more magazines, often with more information, consult *The Readers' Guide to Periodical Literature.* For many years, this source has been an indispensable starting point for researchers. Arranged by author and subject, *The Readers' Guide* lists articles in more than 150 periodicals read by a relatively wide audience. For example, if you are interested in the subject of the brain, you will want to begin by looking at recent entries:

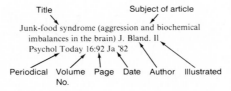

In addition to *The Readers' Guide,* there are a number of reference works that list more specialized articles in periodicals for particular fields in the sciences and the social sciences, such as:

Applied Science and Technology Index
Biological and Agricultural Index
Consumers' Index
Educational Index
General Science Index
International Index
Social Sciences and Humanities Index
Social Sciences Index

For recent developments and past events, a good place to begin is *The New York Times Index,* where you will find, listed by subject, summaries of news articles that have appeared in this important newspaper. Most college libraries have the *Times* in microfilm. Check yours to see if this service is available.

Once you begin to explore sources on your subject, you will need a method for recording essential information identifying those sources from which you will take your data. Although any scrap of paper will do for scribbling down a few words, such as *"Scientific American* May 1980," a more efficient method includes at least a full reference to the author, the title of the book or of the periodical, the title of the article, its date and pages, and some comment briefly stating the contents of the work, along with any identifying number for locating this source in the library. Having this information handy can save you additional trips to the library, especially once you have already begun to prepare your paper. A convenient way to record this information is to write all the important bibliographic data on a separate slip of paper or an index card. These separate bibliographic cards will—along with your note cards (see below)—contain the results of your investigations in the library stacks and periodical sections. Later, you can use these cards to prepare the final bibliography for your completed paper. At this stage of your research, your main concern is to acquire a sufficient number of sources from which to draw your information.

For an article of five to eight pages, you might begin with twenty or more periodicals and books. After some broad reading in your sources—skimming, in the case of books, to find usable material—you will most likely depend mainly on six to eight sources in preparing your article. If you use considerably more than this number, your topic is probably too broad, and you may not be able to organize your information coherently. If you are too dependent on one or two books or articles, you probably will write more of a summary or a report than a paper that investigates a variety of sources and synthesizes information to form

> Rorvik, David M. *Your Baby's Sex: Now You Can Choose.* New York: Dodd, Mead & Co., 1970.
>
> — background of preselection
> — research of L. B. Shettles
> — effects on population control
>
> QH 309
> R 54

BIBLIOGRAPHY CARD

a new whole. There is no formula for determining the right number of sources to use, but too many or too few tend to produce an uninteresting and unsatisfying paper.

Taking Notes

Taking notes from your sources is one of the most important steps in preparing your paper. Not only are you recording information, but by turning another writer's language into your own, you are also selecting, analyzing, and interpreting this material with an eye to how it will be made into your own continuous discussion. You need to decide as you are reading over your material what is likely to be important to your topic. You can't always be certain that a particular passage will be of value, but it is better to take more notes than you will actually need than to realize later that some material that you decided not to take down was quite important. Nor can you rely on the duplicating machine to do your note-taking for you. Certainly duplicating is useful if you want to spend more time with materials like periodical articles or reference books that you cannot ordinarily take out of the library. But you will then still want to take notes from your information: underlining or annotating the text of an article cannot substitute for extracting specific passages for quotation or summary and arranging them under subject headings that will later become the organizing plan of your article.

For your notes, you will want separate slips of paper or index cards. Because you will already have written the complete bibliographic information on a sepa-

New developments on the horizon

Ray, 76.
   Scientists experimenting with pills that stop one type of male sperm production

Rorvik,
   Shettles is experimenting with insemnation high into the cervical canal. The more motile male sperm reaches the egg first. He feels he can achieve a 90% success rate. Female sperm can be preselected since they are stronger and survive after aging for days in a petri dish.

Values to preselection

Ray, 77

   Couples can limit family size to the children they desire. They can have only one girl if they so choose. This element of choice has important implications for limiting population growth.

---

rate card, you will need only to write some identifying word, usually the author's last name, on your note card. You can leave room at the top of the card for a subject heading if you aren't sure at this time what your headings will be. If you are quoting directly, you can write the page number(s) next to your quotation. The quotation must be exact. If you wish to omit words or sentences that

---

Sperm separation

Pinkel, 904

   "The only . . . difference on which to base sperm separation is chromosomal constitution." In mammals, sperm with X chromosomes result in females; Y chromosomes in males.

---

are unnecessary for your purposes, you can show this through the use of the ellipsis, (see Handbook, pp. 400–401).

A note card is more effective if it is limited to a single note. Even if you are taking notes from the same page of an article or the same chapter of a book, the quoted information may actually pertain to more than one of the main subjects of your paper. If you remember that you are always trying to anticipate how you can have ready access to your information when you are writing your paper, you will not bury a note in such a way that it will be difficult to find later. Efficient notes, for example, cannot be lumped together on a large notebook page. Also, because you will be taking notes from many sources, you will probably not want to copy lengthy quotations from all of them.

You will want to make sure to quote carefully and exactly the text you wish to use. Sometimes you may want to quote an author who has narrated a distinctive anecdote or has summed up his or her main purpose clearly and succinctly. Or perhaps an author has made a far-reaching conclusion that you would like to use as part of your closing paragraph. These are legitimate uses for quotations. Most of the time, however, it is best to use direct quotations—especially extended ones—sparingly. Therefore you may find it useful to develop the habit of combining these methods of taking notes: quotation, summary, and paraphrase. A summary is a substantially reduced note that records information that you may want to include in your paper but that you don't think is necessary to quote directly. A paraphrase, like a summary, is written in your own words, but, unlike a summary, it approximates the form and content of the original. Whether you quote, summarize, or paraphrase, it is essential to refer to the source of your information in your footnotes, so you will want to be sure to take down the page numbers of all such material that comes from your sources. Failure to provide such required documentation is plagiarism, a practice that many students imperfectly understand.

Many students feel that direct quotations are evidence enough that they have used specific sources. Actually this is not true. Anytime you use information that is not your own, you must credit your source. Paraphrasing or summarizing outside source material accurately (making sure to note the specific source and page numbers of your information) is one way to avoid using others' writings as if they were your own. In response to the student who asks, "You mean my whole paper will be continuous footnoting, as everything in it comes from others sources?" the answer is, "Yes, you will obviously need a large number of footnotes, but every statement or sentence need not be footnoted individually. Often one footnote will do for a series of sentences from one source." Remember also that your task for this writing assignment makes use of your own direct observations, interviews, or surveys of others who can provide you with information. This material also requires documentation, which will be discussed in the "Focus" section of this chapter.

Working through this stage in your task, you will accumulate a substantial number of notes, with some direct quotations that you think are highly informative, distinctively worded, or illustrative of some main idea that you intend to explain. Your next task will be to examine your notes and subject headings to see how they can be organized into a meaningful plan or outline. This plan, which forms the skeletal structure of your paper, will then be followed as you begin your first draft.

Outlining

An outline is the pattern of meaning that emerges from the body of notes you have taken. After you have given much thought to your notes and the main ideas under which you arranged these notes, you will begin to see how these main ideas are related to one another and which main ideas should precede or follow others. In other papers that you have written, you performed the same kind of organizing operations. But in a research paper, with its larger number of facts and statements, the need to organize is much more essential. During the course of your research, you may find it helpful to make several outlines, beginning with a broad overview of your topic and ending with a more detailed plan once the direction of your investigation becomes clearer. At first you might write a broad outline such as this:

Topic: Choosing the sex of an unborn child

    I. Introduction

   II. X and Y chromosomes

  III. Recent experiments

  IV. Effects on society

After you have organized your notes, perhaps even gathering more information to fill what you think are gaps in your research, you will want to prepare a more detailed outline. This outline, listing the main topics of your article, as you foresee them emerging during the course of your writing, actually shows you what the paragraph structure of your paper will be. Each main topic or subtopic of your outline shows you that one paragraph or more will be needed to explain this idea. And the words that you use in your outline to describe each topic can later become the topic sentences for these paragraphs. Thus, when you prepare a fairly detailed outline, you are actually beginning the first draft of your paper.

Here is a more detailed version of the previous outline, revealing a more advanced stage of a student's plan:

CHOOSING THE SEX OF AN UNBORN CHILD

I. Introduction
   A. Couples have always desired to choose the sex of their child
   B. Values to society of preselection
   C. Failed methods

II. Methods for choosing the sex of an unborn child
   A. The basis of all theories of sex determination: X and Y chromosomes
   B. The research of L. B. Shettles into X and Y chromosomes
      1. Differing sizes of X and Y sperm cells
      2. Need for ways to separate boy sperm from girl sperm
   C. R. J. Ericsson separated sperm for the first time
   D. S. Langendoen developed dietary programs for women prior to conception
   E. Selective abortion

III. New frontiers in the science of preselection

IV. Conclusion: Effects of preselection on society.

In this outline the student has divided her plan into four main sections. Part II, the longest part of her paper, has been divided into five subtopics, one of which has been subdivided into two parts. Notice that each time you create a subheading, you need to supply two subtopics. For every A, there must be a B; for every 1, a 2. Notice also that each major division is indented to show that it is subordinate to the topic above. This student may yet modify her outline as she continues to organize her information and revise the plan of her article. But in preparing a fairly detailed outline, she has begun her next step, writing the first draft of her paper.

Considering Your Audience

When you begin to write your first draft you will need to remind yourself that your audience comprises the teachers and students of your college. Although some of them may be quite well informed on your topic, many of them will not know the more detailed information that you present to them. In addition, you are including in your paper personal observations and interviews (possibly with some of these very same faculty) that will make your article an original piece of research.

This inclusion of your own experience, however, can create a difficulty when you address an audience for the task in this chapter. In earlier chapters, you were encouraged to write about yourself and your observations in a vivid, often imaginative style. In this chapter, however, you will need to restrain your expressive language, writing instead in a more objective, expository manner. Your purpose is to let the force of your material, gathered inductively, convey to your audience the importance of your subject and the validity of your conclusion. Although you may wish to explain scientific or psychological concepts that you have obtained from technical or specialized sources, you will want to explain these ideas to your audience in as nontechnical a way as possible, but without simplifying the material to the point where your audience will find your discussion superficial. You will want to avoid the use of jargon terms but to recognize also that there may be no substitute for some of the language of your sources. Most important, your purpose is not to try to direct attention to yourself. Because you are writing to inform your audience on a subject that they will find worthwhile, they will tend to believe what you say if you appear to be an objective, informed guide to the material you present.

SOME PRACTICE WITH RESEARCH METHODS

1. To write a paraphrase of this paragraph, fill in words that would adequately substitute for those in the original source.

> The fast-growing field of research has even been given a new name—psychoneuroimmunology—and is finally beginning to win the respect of the modern medical establishment, which despite physicians like Dr. Osler had scorned or ignored previous suggestions of a strong mind–body link. Many of the studies are now being supported by various branches of the National Institutes of Health. More and more, as Dr. Osler recognized, the emotions are being considered necessary components of the cause as well as the treatment of most illness.

The quickly developing area of _____ has been _____ psychoneuroimmunology and is at last starting to _____ of today's medical _____ who had criticized or _____ former _____ of a _____. Much of the research is being _____ by _____ of the National Institutes of Health. Increasingly, as Dr. Osler _____, the _____ are _____ important _____ of the cause and _____ of most _____.

2. Write a summary and a paraphrase of the following paragraphs of an article written by Jane Brody that appeared in *The New York Times,* May 24, 1983.

> Nearly a century after some leading physicians first recognized the powerful role of the mind in health and healing, scientists have begun to decipher exactly how stress and other emotional states can influence the onset and course of disease.
>
> Aided by new biochemical techniques and a vastly expanded understanding of immunology and neurochemistry, their studies show that emotions, acting through the brain, can affect nervous system function, hormone levels and immunological responses, thereby changing a person's susceptibility to a host of organic ills.
>
> Depending on the circumstances, animal and human studies have revealed that emotional reactions can suppress or stimulate disease-fighting whiteblood cells and trigger the release of adrenal gland hormones and neurotransmitters, including endorphins, that in turn affect dozens of body processes.

3. Compare the original source with the summary that follows. Did the student fail to change the original wording adequately? How effective will these notes be when the student prepares the paper?

> Although the influence of mind on body was well known to ancient healers and has dominated folklore to the present day, "scientific" medicine has until recently focused almost exclusively on physical causes for bodily illness. Only a few so-called psychosomatic diseases, such as asthma and ulcers, were said to have an emotional basis.
>
> The new studies strongly indicate, however, that virtually every ill that can befall the body—from the common cold to cancer and heart disease—can be influenced, positively or negatively, by a person's mental state. By unveiling the mechanisms behind these effects, the studies point to new ways to prevent and treat some of the nation's leading killing and crippling diseases. They strongly suggest that psychotherapy and behavioral techniques should be an integral part of preventive and therapeutic medicine.

> *Summary:* "Brody states that although the influence of mind on body was well known to ancient healers, modern medicine has given attention only to the physical causes of bodily illnesses. New research shows that almost all illness is affected by a person's psychological condition. By unveiling the mechanisms behind these effects, the studies point to new methods of stopping the country's leading illnesses. They show that psychotherapy and behavioral techniques should be considered essential to preventive and therapeutic medicine."

4. Read an article in one of the periodicals named in the audience section. Take notes from this article, making sure to provide complete bibliographic information and subject headings on your note cards.

5. Select one of the topics listed in this chapter and do the following:

   a. Prepare three questions that would give a focus to someone planning to investigate it.
   b. Develop a tentative shaping idea for the topic.
   c. Prepare a broad outline of a paper on this topic.

6. Select one of the topics listed in this chapter and explain how you would begin to investigate it in your library.

7. Prepare a preliminary bibliography of at least six items for the investigative paper that you are writing. Write each source on a separate index card or slip of paper.

8. Select a paragraph from one of your sources. Write a paraphrase and then a summary. How are they different? Compare your paraphrase with the original. Did you change the language sufficiently?

Putting Your Notes Together

In writing the rest of your paper, you will want to take your collected notes and work them into a continuous discussion of your own, based on your outline. It is important to avoid an unbroken chain of quotations, for they will require the reader to sort out the crowd of voices in such a paper. Try instead to turn these other voices into your single voice. That is, clarify in your own mind the relationships among your notes of quotations, summaries, and paraphrases, in order to transform them into sentences and paragraphs that will blend smoothly into a single, coherent discourse.

Here is one student's use of quoted material:

When alcohol begins to take effect in small amounts, feelings of happiness and lightness may occur, depending on the personality, mood, and expectations of the user. Alcohol offers an escape from the pressure and tension of everyday society. As the drinking continues, drowsiness, extreme boisterousness, or depression may occur, along with physiological discomfort. "Most people don't drink because they like the taste or smell of alcohol: they drink because they have been taught to do so by the advertisements and the examples of those around them."[3]

This student's use of quotation is inadequate. The student has not introduced the quotation or shown why it is important. If it were not quoted material but an original sentence, it would simply be incoherent, having no connection to the rest of the paragraph. Furthermore, the information conveyed in the quotation does not seem particularly noteworthy, as its main point—that drinkers are affected by outside influences—seems obvious.

Another student's paragraph reveals other problems in the use of quotations:

"Supporters of lie detector methods insist that the technique is more than 90 percent accurate, that it is difficult for most offenders to deceive an experienced polygraph operator."[4] "Others contend that the polygraph has never been accepted by the scientific community, and libertarians question the fairness of the lie detector, arguing that it unjustly robs a person of his innermost secrets."[5] But its main function is to clear the wrongly accused innocent, not to convict the guilty.

This writer relied on a quotation to provide a main idea sentence for the paragraph. Beginning a paragraph with a quotation leaves it up to the reader to determine what the paragraph is to be about and why the quotation is important. And using quotations in sequence without even a minimal bridge between them creates a paragraph of little value because the relationship of its parts is not made clear, nor is its connection with the rest of the essay clarified.

In the following paragraph, the writer tried to avoid direct quotation, using it only once, but failed to work the rest of her material into effective original sentences. The footnote after almost every sentence shows that the writer did not really assimilate the source material, and the sentences don't follow each other very clearly. The paragraph is mainly a series of loosely related facts:

This pill works after egg implantation and technically produces an abortion.[6] Louise Tyrer, M.D., says that "people should be aware of this."[7] Although this would not be a problem for a majority of people, some would not feel comfortable with it.[8] This four-day pill does not regulate the hormonal cycle.[9] Instead it makes it temporarily impossible for the uterus to absorb progesterone.[10]

In the next example, written by a professional writer, the author has skillfully worked other material into a continuous discourse. Most of the paragraph is quotation, but through the use of ellipses and by carefully selecting the quoted material, the author has made it part of the structure of his own sentences:

> The persistent objective of Coleridge's formal philosophy was to substitute "life and intelligence . . . for the philosophy of mechanism, which in everything that is most worthy of the human intellect, strikes *Death*." And the life transfused into the mechanical motion of the universe is one with the life in man: in nature, he wrote in 1802, "everything has a life of its own and . . . we are all *One Life*."[75]
>
> —**M. H. Abrams,** *The Mirror and the Lamp*

Writing the Introduction

Once you have organized your information and prepared a working outline, you will be ready to begin writing your paper. As you did in the essays that you wrote in previous tasks, you will need to provide an introduction for your reader. The introductions to your other essays probably began with general approaches to your subject and concluded with your shaping idea. In a research paper, you may have to provide a more extensive introduction for your reader as you move from the general to the specific. Perhaps two or three paragraphs might be necessary to state your topic, to give some necessary information to the uninformed reader, and to tell your reader what the plan of your paper will be. How you introduce your subject often determines how much confidence and belief your reader will have in your research. An introduction that makes the subject interesting, gives the reader an overview of the subject, and tells the reader how you are going to present your material will establish your credibility and give authority to your research.

To introduce your subject, you must first identify it, either directly or indirectly. Some questions you might ask yourself when preparing your introduction are

1. Why is my subject important?
2. What has been said about it?
3. What will I limit myself to?
4. How am I going to investigate it?
5. What idea or conclusion am I going to prove or set forth?
6. How might my subject change in the future?

It is often the practice of a writer to answer these questions in the introduction to his or her investigation. If you can answer them clearly and briefly in the opening paragraph of your article, you will be able to write the rest of your investigation confident that you will be informing your reader in an interesting and persuasive way.

Writing the Rough Draft

After you have outlined your topic, have arranged your notes in a meaningful order, and have considered the information you wish to convey to your reader, begin your first draft. Make sure that you have exact references for all the sources you wish to cite. If you wish to use direct quotations, be certain that you have copied down the precise words and punctuation of your source. Remember also to use transitions as you move from one section of your article to another.

It is not necessary to divide your paper into sections or "chapters." Because you are writing a relatively short paper, you will be able to write a continuous prose discourse, moving clearly and efficiently from one main idea to the next. You might find it convenient, however, to work on one main section of your paper at a time. This procedure will gradually get you through the paper and give you the feeling of having completed something even though you still have more to accomplish.

Following is a student's rough draft of her research paper. As you read through the paper, you will want to determine whether the writer has used her sources effectively. There should be a smooth transition from the sources to the author's own writing. Paragraphs especially need smooth transitions from one major idea to another. Most important, the paragraphs should flow from the author's own mastery of her sources and information rather than being a string of notes pieced together to form pseudoparagraphs. No less than in the other tasks that you have completed, the voice in the research essay should emerge as coherent, authoritative, and interesting.

ACHIEVING A TIE SCORE: ONE BOY TO ONE GIRL

The gender of an unborn child is often the most prevalent thought on the minds of the prospective parents. Although baby doctors universally believe that the unborn child has an equal chance of being a boy or a girl, having the power to choose the sex has been a thought-provoking issue, an issue that has plagued the minds of the prospective parents for ages.

Crude forms of preselection were practiced as far back as the Middle Ages. In order to produce a son, a woman drank a mixture of wine and lion's blood. While an abbot prayed, the couple made love under a full moon. At least five hundred formulas of one kind or another have been concocted and recorded through the ages.

Besides the obvious, satisfying the parents' curiosity simply to know the sex of their unborn child, there are other values to preselection that should be considered. If, like my husband and me, parents have always wished for a little girl, and what they have are three boys, they could limit family size from the start by choosing first to have the girl. Ultimately sex preselection would be most useful in limiting not only family size, but population growth as well.

It would be a very simple task if we were all green turtles. In conservationists' efforts to raise the turtles and save them from extinction, they found that the temperatures in the hatcheries had a direct correlation to the sex of the baby turtle. When incubator temperatures were cold (that is, 28°C and below), almost no female turtles were hatched, statistically zero to 10 percent. When temperatures rose above 29.5°C, 95 to 100 percent of the offspring were females. A similar phenomenon was found in some other reptiles, including the American alligator, but in the reverse: 30°C and below produced exclusively females, whereas 34°C and above produced all males.

Unfortunately these methods have not been found to work for human beings, as temperature level has no relation to the sex of the yet-to-be-conceived child. All theories of sex determination in humans are based on the fact that there are two types of sperm: one carries the X chromosome, which determines females; and one carries the Y chromosome, which determines males.

This fact was first discovered by Dr. Landrum B. Shettles, now an associate professor of obstetrics and gynecology at Columbia University's College of Physicians and Surgeons. He is recognized universally for his discovery and identification of male- and female-producing sperm. One night he viewed liver sperm in a phase-contrast microscope, an instrument that throws halos of light over dark objects. He noticed that sperm cells came in two distinct sizes. After examining approximately 500 specimens, he hypothesized that the small, round-headed sperm were the Ys (males) and the larger, oval sperm were the Xs. He sought rare specimens, where almost all sperm were of one type. That father had children all of one sex. Doctor Shettles thought that there must be other differences besides shape. It seemed certain that the female-producing sperm were stronger, by virtue of their size. By conducting sperm counts, he found that there were approximately twice as many male sperm as female sperm; yet there are not twice as many men on earth as there are women. He was convinced that some substance slaughtered the male-producing sperm. He began studying the uterus and its secretions and watching sperm activity in the secretions. Shettles filled capillary tubes with vaginal secretions, taken from various points in the woman's menstrual cycle. He added sperm at the tops of the tubes and monitored their activity. The female-producing sperm fared better when the solution was more acidic; their greater bulk rendered them feistier in the bath, and they lived longer. When the cervical mucus was taken very close to the time of ovulation, the woman's most fertile, most favorable time for conception, the smaller, faster male-producing sperm fared better. He therefore deduced that the time of intercourse was crucial to determining the sex of the child: two to three days before ovulation for a girl, when the uterus is slightly acidic, and at ovulation, when the environment is most favorable and alkaline, for a boy.

Dr. Shettles determined the time of ovulation either by using a temperature chart or by using Tes-Tape paper, which measures pH balance in the mucus of the uterus. Primarily used to determine sugar levels in diabetics, the paper turns darkest when the woman is just about to ovulate. Dr. Shettles also recommends douching before intercourse to reconstruct the acid–alkaline environment of the uterus. A vinegar douche will induce a girl, and baking soda will give the uterus a more alkaline environment, resulting in a boy. By combining douching with timing the intercourse for around the time of ovulation, Dr. Shettles believes that we can all expect to get the sex of our choice 80 percent of the time.

When it became obvious that there are two types of sperm, other scientists searched for ways to separate the boy sperm from the girl sperm, so that the chosen specimen could be introduced into the uterus.

In 1974, R. J. Ericsson and his co-workers at the A. G. Schering Company in Berlin separated the sperm for the first time. Volunteer sperm were collected and diluted in Tyrode's solution; then they were placed on top of a column and set loose in a solution of bovine serum albumin. Those that did not penetrate the solution were separated from those that did. The more motile sperm, the ones that made it through the solution, were determined to be mostly male, whereas the less motile sperm remaining in the solution were mostly female. Once they were separated, the desired sex sperm sample could be inseminated in the mother-to-be.

It has also been established that sperm can be separated on the basis of chromosome level. There is a 3 to 4 percent difference in the DNA content between the male and female sperm. Techniques known as <u>flow cytometric</u> are precise enough to resolve the proportion of X to Y with respect to their DNA content. Flow-sorting instruments can be used to separate sperm according to DNA content. A liquid suspension of single cells stained with fluorochrome intersects a beam of excitation light. Optical detectors convert fluorescent flashes into electrical signals, which are then analyzed with an instrument called a <u>multichannel analyzer</u>. The cells are compared by the analyzer with respect to the number of cells versus the brightness per cell. When duller versus brighter cells are 3 to 4 percent apart in count, observation with respect to male and female <u>sperm</u> can be made without resolution. This method is used by scientists who prefer to discount Dr. Shettles's theories based on shape.

Another method practiced by R. J. Ericsson is called the <u>sperm-separation</u> method, which only increases the chance of having a son. As mentioned earlier, Ericsson separates the sperm, and the resulting, unharmed sperms are all males, as the females are left in the solution. Ericsson then monitors the mother's early-morning temperature for two months in order to pinpoint her ovulation time and to determine the best day for conception. On that day, the male sperm are inseminated. Any possible harm to the fetus is denied, as theoretically only the stronger sperm are able to survive the procedure, and a healthier child may possibly result. So Ericsson uses a combination of three methods: separation, time of ovulation, and insemination.

Another idea has been established by Sally Langendoen, a registered

nurse, who has based her theories on the work of Dr. Joseph Stolkowski of the University of Pierre, of Marie Curie in Paris, and of Dr.
Jacques Lorrain of the Sacre-Coeur Hospital in Montreal. Stolkowski
and Lorrain determined that eating foods high in sodium and potassium, and low in calcium and magnesium, results in male births, whereas the reverse gives females. They practiced this dietary program with
260 women, achieving an 81 percent success rate. Ms. Langedoen has
created two eating regimes to be followed by women for the four to six
weeks before conception tries. Husbands may join with their wives in
this diet for moral support, but their cooperation is said to have no effect on the end result. When the woman has become pregnant, there is
no need for her to continue dieting. For girls, the diet consists of salt-
free foods, lots of milk, and very few meats, such as chicken, steak, or
lamb. Emphasis is placed on foods low in potassium, and on fruits and
vegetables such as pears, peaches, apples, beans, and peas. The diet for
boys includes having no milk products, and sticking to salty meats,
such as bacon, sausage, and ham. Fruits and vegetables such as oranges, grapefruits, bananas, potatoes, artichokes, and mushrooms
should be eaten. The boy diet is high in salt, so hypertensive mothers-
to-be should check with their physicians before trying it. Theory has it
that the diet must alter either the membrane around the egg or the environment around the uterus to favor male or female sperm, although
no one knows the actual explanation.

The most accurate method of sex preselection is selective abortion.
Via amniocentesis, an injection into and withdrawal of amniotic fluid
from the uterus, the sex of the fetus can be determined. The option of
abortion is therefore available to the parent on the basis of the sex of
the fetus. The idea of abortion flitted through my mind last year after
amniocentesis indicated that I was pregnant with my third boy, but
my gynecologist advised me that neither society nor the profession
was ready to consider selective abortion.

There are also new frontiers on the horizon in the science of preselection. Pills that halt men's production of one type of sperm are being
experimented with. Pills or gels that render the woman's environment
inhospitable to one or the other type of sperm are being sought after.

Filters that allow only the smaller male sperm through have been experimented with as well. Even Dr. Shettles, who also practices in his Las Vegas clinic (apparently he likes gambling with the odds), is searching for new methods. He feels that he can achieve a 90 percent success rate by inseminating high in the cervical canal so the more motile, male sperm will reach the egg first. He theorizes that females will be born if the sperms are allowed to age in a sterile petri dish for a few days, as only the stronger, female sperm will survive.

Most people want boys. From early civilization, boys were cherished for their value as hunters and farmers. According to Dr. Roberta Steinbacher, psychologist and chairwoman of the Department of Urban Studies at Cleveland State University, the preference for male children has always been stronger than that for females. She deduces that the effect of a perfected technique and the desire to practice it would be an increased number of males and a decreased number of females in the population. By tilting the gender balance and having more males, we risk increased male homosexuality and polyandry, according to Dr. Steinbacher.

What other effect could perfected techniques of preselection have on society? One cannot help but notice the outcome of sex determination as exemplified in the green turtle and the American alligator, and the possible relation to the extinction of the dinosaur, the first reptile, some sixty-five million years ago. A sudden climate change either up or down could have produced a predominance of one sex. Once there is only one sex of an animal, there can be no more reproduction of the species, and the result is extinction.

Just as we are not green turtles, we are not dinosaurs. We are human beings with the power to choose, rather than allowing nature to take its course in those circumstances that are scientifically changeable. Traditionally, we have believed that controlling and determining life lie only in the hands of the Creator. Lately, however, developments such as life-support systems, test-tube babies, and genetic engineering have challenged the old beliefs. Whereas science was first used to prolong life, it can now be used to alter life, by giving us choices.

FOCUS: DOCUMENTATION

Using Footnotes

As the author of an investigative essay, you must identify the sources of your information. You should refer to the books and periodical articles cited in your paper by using notes. Footnotes—or endnotes, as they are called if they appear on a separate page at the end—tell your audience that you can back up your statements. They also show that you are familiar with the conventions of research technique—in effect, that you know what you're doing.

A footnote number appears twice: once in the text of your paper (usually at the end of a sentence; never at the very beginning) and again at the bottom of the page of text or on the separate page for notes. Here is a typical footnote for a book:

[1]David M. Rorvik, <u>Your Baby's Sex: Now You Can Choose</u> (New York: Dodd, Mead, 1970), p. 48.

You should give this information the first time you cite this book. If you refer to it again, you need only give a short note:

[2]Rorvik, p. 49.

For periodical articles, the following would be typical first and subsequent references:

[3]John Lorber, "Disposable Cortex," <u>Psychology Today</u> (Apr. 1981), p. 126.
[4]Lorber, p. 127.

Other sources that you use may require different styles of documentation. Here are some of the possible citations that you are likely to encounter:

1. A book with more than one author:

[1]Jim Mason and Peter Singer, <u>Animal Factories</u> (New York: Crown, 1980), p. 46.

2. A work without a specified author, often written by some corporate, governmental, or institutional agency:

> [1]Health Effects of Air Pollutants, by the U.S. Environmental Protection Agency (Washington, D.C.: Government Printing Office, 1976), p. 2.

3. A book made up of a variety of essays by a single author:

> [3]Lewis Thomas, "The Iks," The Lives of a Cell: Notes of a Biology Watcher (New York: Viking Penguin, 1974), p. 60.

4. A book made up of a variety of essays by several authors:

> [4]Donald Davidson, "What Metaphors Mean," On Metaphor, ed. Sheldon Sacks (Chicago: University of Chicago Press, 1979), p. 36.

5. An article in a periodical with continuous pagination:

> [5]Lewis Branscomb, "Taming Technology," Science 171 (12 March 1971), 970.

6. An article in a newspaper:

> [6]Jane E. Brody, "Emotions Found to Influence Nearly Every Human Ailment," New York Times (24 May 1983) Sec. C, p. 1.

7. An interview:

> [7]Interview with Dr. George Adams, Assoc. Prof. of Anthropology, Danville College, 20 June 1983.

Using Bibliography

A bibliography is an alphabetized list of works that you have used in preparing your paper. It is placed at the end of your text on a separate page. Your instructor will decide whether you can include sources that you consulted but that are not cited in your text. As you will notice, the form for a bibliographic reference is different from that for a footnote. The bibliographic citation separates elements with periods, rather than with commas, as in the footnote. The second line of a bibliographic entry is indented, unlike the second line of the footnote, which extends to the left margin. The following examples of a footnote and a bibliographic entry will show you the differences.

Footnote: ²Joan Didion, <u>Slouching Towards Bethlehem</u> (New York: Farrar, Straus & Giroux, 1968), p. 87.

Bibliography: Didion, Joan. <u>Slouching Towards Bethlehem</u>. New York: Farrar, Straus & Giroux, 1968.

Some bibliographic entries that you are likely to use follow:

1. A book with more than one author:

     Mason, Jim and Peter Singer. <u>Animal Factories</u>. New York: Crown, 1980.

2. An edited book:

     Sacks, Sheldon, ed. <u>On Metaphor</u>. Chicago: University of Chicago Press, 1979.

3. A work with a corporate author:

     <u>Health Effects of Air Pollutants</u>. U.S. Environmental Protection Agency. Washington, D.C.: Government Printing Office, 1976.

4. An essay published in a collection of essays:

     De Man, Paul. "Intentional Structure of the Romantic Image." <u>Romanticism and Consciousness: Essays in Criticism</u>. Ed. Harold Bloom. New York: W. W. Norton, 1970, pp. 65–77.

5. An article in a periodical with continuous pagination:

> Branscomb, Lewis. "Taming Technology." <u>Science</u> 171
>   (12 March 1971), 963–975.

6. An article in a periodical with separate pagination:

> Begley, S. "How the Brain Works." <u>Newsweek</u> (7 Feb. 1983),
>   pp. 40–47.

7. An article in a newspaper:

> Brody, Jane E. "Emotions Found to Influence Nearly Every
>   Human Ailment." New York Times (24 May 1983), Sec. C,
>   p. 1.

Using the New Method

Another method of citing sources is to give the author's name and the page number in the text and to provide at the end of the paper a list of "Works Cited." To identify the source referred to, the reader can glance quickly from author and page number to the list of works cited. When preparing your paper, you need only to compose your bibliography and insert the author's name and the page number in your written text. This method eliminates the large number of footnotes that make some papers difficult to read because of frequent interruptions in the text. Here is an example of this method of citation:

> According to Frank (160), a mother may not wish to accept the
> rhythms of her infant. A child's development, however, is likely to be
> shaped by a number of forces, all of them interacting in ways that in-
> tensify or reduce the effect of any one of them (Frank 161).

Works Cited

> Frank, Lawrence K. <u>On the Importance of Infancy</u>. New York:
>   Random House, 1966.

As this example illustrates, you can either work the author's name into your own sentence or include it in the parentheses. You might also say:

As Frank states (160), . . .

In Frank's view (160), . . .

Frank reports that (160) . . .

One investigator notes (Frank 160) . . .

In recent years, the trend has been to develop forms of documentation that are clear, coherent, and simple. In the interests of simplicity and efficiency, this second method seems preferable because it virtually eliminates the need for footnotes and places all the names and page references within the text, where they most logically belong. Your list of "Works Cited," arranged alphabetically, will show your readers all the sources that you referred to in your paper. With some practice, you will be able to work the authors' names into your text without undue repetition.

In your readings in scientific articles, you may have encountered a similar method of documentation. In specialized scientific research, it is common to place the author's name and the date of publication in parentheses. Because scientific research changes rapidly, the year of publication would be of great importance in an evaluation of the significance of a specific study. The reader turns from the text to a list of sources following the article to refer to the individual citation. If there is more than one work by an author referred to, the sources are listed by date of publication, starting with the oldest and ending with the most recent.

Before adopting any method of documentation, you will want to make sure that you have discussed with your instructor which form of citation is applicable to your assignment.

SOME PRACTICE WITH DOCUMENTATION

1. Write a footnote for a magazine article entitled "The Compleat Eclipse-Chaser" that appeared in *The Sciences* in the May–June 1983 issue, on pages 24–31. The author is Laurence A. Marschall.

2. Write a footnote for an article entitled "Nerve Cells That Double as Endocrine Cells," written by W. K. Samson and G. P. Kozlowski. It appeared in Volume 31 of *Science*, the June 1981 issue, on pages 445–448.

3. Write a footnote for an essay by Loren C. Eiseley named "Charles Darwin." It appeared on pages 283–293 in a collection of essays entitled *Modern American Prose: A Reader for Writers.* The book was edited by John Clifford and Robert Di Yanni and was published in New York by Random House in 1983.

4. Write subsequent citations for each of the above sources.

5. Write the citations for a list of "Works Cited" using the above sources.

REWRITING

Obtaining Feedback on Your Rough Draft

By now, you are accustomed to getting direct responses to your work. Hopefully, you have grown more comfortable in accepting the comments of others, and they have learned to be more specific about their responses. You may find, however, that your audience's reaction to your research article will be somewhat ambivalent. On the one hand, they may be reluctant to criticize a project that has occupied so much of your time and concentrated effort. On the other hand, you may notice immediately by their reaction whether you have adapted your research materials to their understanding. If they're not quite sure about what level of comprehension you were aiming at, you might have to give your approach to your audience some more thought when you revise your first draft.

--- **AUDIENCE RESPONSE GUIDE** ---

1. **What does the writer want to say in this paper? What is her purpose in writing?**
2. **How does this paper affect the audience for which it was intended?**
3. **How effective has the writer been in conveying her purpose and meaning? Explain.**
4. **How should the paper be revised to better fulfill its purpose and meaning?**

Peer evaluations of the rough draft of "Achieving a Tie Score: One Boy to One Girl" were more difficult to generalize on for this task. Some students felt that they lacked the specific knowledge to evaluate the student's topic and use of sources. They felt that the topic should be adapted in relation to its intended audience.

1. The group concluded that the writer wanted to inform the reader about recent developments in preselecting the sex of unborn children. The implications of this topic are broad and need to be clarified.

2. The group liked the writer's approach to the subject, shared her interest in the topic, and thought it had an appeal to a general audience.

3. The group thought the paper generally clearly organized and effective in its use of sources, but several respondents felt that the language was often confusing and in need of rewriting.

4. They suggested eliminating much of the deadwood and clotted writing and making the structure of paragraphs more clear.

Before reading the revised essay, consider the following discussion of deadwood.

Eliminating Deadwood

In my considered opinion, in the area of accuracy of steering, this driving machine performed in an erratic manner due to the fact that the road was of a wet condition. It is recommended by the inspector that in such a definitely damp and humid weather situation, the vehicle operator act in a manner that exercises extreme caution.

What is wrong with this language? Doesn't it have the sound of authority, of some official writing a report in an official style? If so, isn't it adequate for its intended audience, probably another official? But would the intended reader of such prose, even another inspector, make sense of it? Writers who use such language are really placing a barrier to communication between themselves and their audience. Part of the problem with this kind of writing is that we don't hear the *person* behind the language. Instead there is a mask of pretentiousness disguising a simple statement with lengthy connective expressions ("in the area of," "due to the fact that"); wordy substitutes for common nouns ("weather situation," "vehicle operator"); and the passive voice ("is recommended," "caution is exercised"). The writer wishes to sound important and to appear an expert by avoiding the simple language of clarity:

Because the road was wet, the car was hard to steer. The driver should be careful when it rains.

In trying to explain, we also have a tendency to reach for an abstraction rather than a simple direct statement of fact. This tendency often results in our emphasizing an abstract noun over a verb, just as this writer did in the previous sentence by writing "have a tendency" rather than "tend."

The term *deadwood* is a general label for language that obscures the meaning of a sentence. By cutting out deadwood, we sharpen and clarify our language. We learn to be more direct with our audience, more accurate in our choice of diction, and less tentative in our assertions. The writer who says, "In my opinion, I feel that abortion on demand can be considered counterproductive," is avoiding a direct commitment to a point of view. Instead of saying, "Abortion on demand is wrong," the writer tries to hide behind weak, unconvincing language that qualifies every assertion. A writer does not intend to write deadwood; it is a plain reminder to us all how difficult it is to write clearly and concisely.

Deadwood is often the result of awkward sentence structure as well as poor word choice. In this case, the writer must be more analytical, revising the sentence fully. The following sentences show how to revise statements that hinder communication between writer and audience:

Original: This woman who was boisterous and unruly was thrown out of the restaurant, which was French and therefore elegant, and in which we were eating dinner.

Revised: While we were eating dinner in an elegant French restaurant, a boisterous, unruly woman was thrown out.

This sentence was improved by the use of subordination and the omission of unnecessary modifying clauses.

Original: His car, which was an antique, black Ford, moved in a creeping fashion toward the other cars.

Revised: His antique, black Ford crept toward the others.

The modifying clause is replaced by adjectives attached directly to the noun. *Car* is replaced by the more specific *Ford*.

Original: The pennant-bound club will seize every opportunity to win. They will hound the pitcher with stolen bases. They will punch singles through the infield. And they will always come through with timely hits.

Revised: The pennant-bound ball club will seize every opportunity to win, hounding the pitcher with stolen bases, punching singles through the infield, and always coming through with timely hits.

Too many separate sentences can be combined into one sentence with participial modifiers. The writer must remember to keep these modifiers parallel.

Original: Another theory has been set forth by Sally Langendoen, who has based her theory on the works of Dr. Joseph Stolkowski.

Revised: Another theory, based on the works of Dr. Joseph Stolkowski, has been set forth by Sally Langendoen.

or

Sally Langendoen has set forth a theory based on the works of Dr. Joseph Stolkowski.

In this example, the writer gets rid of repetitive phrasing and also more clearly emphasizes the subject (see also Chap. 1, pp. 13–14, and Chap. 5, pp. 156–165).

What follows is the final draft of the student's research paper "Achieving a Tie Score: One Boy to One Girl." In this final draft, the student has added footnote numbers in the text wherever she felt that it was necessary to document the sources of her information. She also has added an endnote page and a bibliography at the end of her paper.

Compare the rough draft of the student's research paper on pages 235–240 to the revised paper that follows. You might also want to review the peer group evaluation on pages 246–247, as well as your own response, before doing so. In comparing the two versions, you might look for rewritten sentences that have eliminated deadwood. Are there sentences in the revised paper that still need pruning? What other changes has the writer made?

ACHIEVING A TIE SCORE: ONE BOY TO ONE GIRL

Although baby doctors universally believe that an unborn child has an equal chance of being male or female, having the power to choose the sex has preoccupied the minds of prospective parents for ages.[1] Crude forms of preselection were practiced as far back as the Middle Ages, but none of them proved effective.[2] Among the five hundred or more formulas recorded was one that required a woman, in order to produce a son, to drink a mixture of wine and blood and to make love under a full moon while an abbot prayed.[3]

Besides the obvious, satisfying the parents' curiosity to know the sex of their unborn child, there are other values to preselection. A couple can limit family size to the children they desire. Instead of having three boys, a couple who, like my husband and me, really want a girl could limit family size from the beginning by choosing a girl as their first child. Preselection thus has important implications for limiting population growth.[4]

Finding a reliable method of preselection would be a very simple task if we were all green turtles. In conservationists' efforts to save these turtles from extinction, they found that the temperatures in the hatcheries had a direct correlation to the sex of the baby turtle. When incubator temperatures were low—that is, 28°C and below—almost no female turtles were hatched, statistically zero to 10 percent. When temperatures rose above 29.5°C, 95 to 100 percent of the offspring were females.[5] A similar phenomenon was found to be true in other reptiles, including the American alligator, but in reverse: 30°C and below produced females exclusively, and 34°C and above produced all males.[6]

Unfortunately, the methods used to preselect the sex of reptiles have not been found to work for human beings, for temperature level has no relation to the sex of the yet-to-be-conceived child.[7] All theories of sex determination in humans are based on the fact that there are two types of sperm: one carries the X chromosome, which determines females; the other carries the Y chromosome, which determines males.[8]

This fact was first discovered by Dr. Landrum B. Shettles, an associate professor of Obstetrics and Gynecology at Columbia University's College of Physicians and Surgeons. His discovery and identification of male- and female-producing sperm are recognized universally. After viewing live sperm in a phase-contrast microscope, an instrument that throws halos of light over dark objects, he noticed that sperm cells came in two distinct sizes. Examining approximately 500 specimens, he hypothesized that the small, round-headed sperm were the Ys (males) and the larger, oval sperm the X.

Dr. Shettles thought that there must be other differences besides shape. Conducting sperm counts, he found that there were approximately twice as many male as female sperm; yet there are not twice as many men as women. He was convinced that some substance slaughtered the males. Studying the uterus and its secretions, and watching sperm activity in the secretions, Shettles filled capillary tubes with vaginal secretions taken at various times of the menstrual cycle. Then he added sperm at the top and monitored their activity. The female-producing sperm fared better when the solution was more acidic. Because their greater bulk rendered them feistier in the bath, they lived longer. When cervical mucus was taken very close to ovulation, the woman's most fertile, most favorable time for conception, the smaller, faster male-producing sperm fared better. He concluded that the time of intercourse was crucial in determining the child's sex. Two or three days prior to ovulation, when the uterus is slightly acidic, a girl is conceived; and during ovulation, when the environment is alkaline and more favorable, a boy is conceived.[9]

Dr. Shettles determined the time of ovulation by using a temperature chart or by measuring with Tes-Tape paper the pH balance in the uterine mucus. Primarily used to determine sugar levels in diabetics, the paper turns darkest when the woman is just about to ovulate.[10] Dr. Shettles also recommended douching prior to intercourse to reconstruct the acid—alkaline environment of the uterus. A vinegar douche will induce a girl; baking soda, giving the uterus a more alkaline quality, a boy. By combining douching with timing intercourse at or near ovulation, we can expect to get the sex of our choice 80 percent of the time.[11]

Once it became obvious that there are two types of sperm, other scientists sought to separate Y sperm from X sperm so that the chosen specimen could be inseminated into the uterus. In 1974, R. J. Ericsson and his co-workers at the A. G. Schering Company in Berlin separated sperm for the first time. Collecting volunteer sperm and diluting them in Tyrode's solution, the scientists placed them on top of a column, setting them loose in a solution of bovine serum albumin. Those that did not penetrate the solution were separated from those that did. The more motile sperm that made it through the solution were mostly male, and the less motile ones remaining in the solution were mostly female. Once separated, the desired sex sperm sample could be inseminated into the mother-to-be.[12]

Sperm can also be separated by chromosome level. There is a 3 to 4 percent difference in the DNA content of male and female sperm. A technique known as flow cytometric is precise enough to resolve the proportion of X to Y with respect to DNA content. Flow-sorting instruments can separate the DNA content of sperm. A liquid suspension of single cells stained with fluorochrome intersects a beam of excitation light. Optical detectors convert fluorescent flashes into electrical signals, which are then analyzed with a multichannel analyzer. This instrument compares the number of cells in relation to the brightness per cell. When the difference in cell brightness is 3 to 4 percent of the number counted, the male and female sperm can be observed without resolution. This method is preferred by scientists who discount Dr. Shettles's theories based on shape.[13]

Another of Ericsson's methods is the "sperm-separation method," used only to increase the chance of having a son. As mentioned before, when Ericsson separated sperm, the resulting unharmed ones were all male and the ones left in the solution were all female. He then monitored the mother's early-morning temperature for two months to pinpoint ovulation and determined the best day for conception by insemination with male sperm. Any possible harm to the fetus is eliminated, as theoretically only the stronger sperm will be able to survive the procedure, and a healthier child may possibly result. Therefore Ericsson used a combination of three methods: separation, time of ovulation, and insemination.[14]

Another theory has been set forth by Sally Langendoen, a registered nurse, based on the work of Dr. Stolkowski of the University of Pierre, of Marie Curie in Paris, and of Dr. Jacques Lorrain of Sacre-Coeur Hospital in Montreal. Stolkowski and Lorrain determined that eating foods high in sodium and potassium and low in calcium and magnesium results in male births, and that the reverse diet results in female births. Practicing this dietary program with 260 women, they achieved an 81 percent success rate. Ms. Langendoen made two eating regimes for women for the four to six weeks prior to conception attempts. Although husbands can join their wives in this diet for moral support, their cooperation has no effect on the result. When the woman becomes pregnant, there is no need for her to continue dieting. For the birth of a girl, the diet should consist of salt-free foods, lots of milk, and very little meat such as chicken, steak or lamb. Emphasis is placed on foods low in potassium, and on fruits and vegetables such as pears, peaches, apples, beans, and peas. To give birth to a boy, the woman should not consume milk products; should stick to salty meats like bacon, sausage, and ham; and should eat fruits and vegetables such as oranges, grapefruit, bananas, potatoes, artichokes, and mushrooms. Because the boy diet is high in salt, hypertensive mothers-to-be should check with their physicians before trying this diet. Although no one knows how this diet actually works, it must alter either the membrane around the egg or the environment of the uterus to favor male or female sperm.[15]

Of all methods of sex preselection, the most accurate is selective abortion. Through amniocentesis (injection into the uterus to withdraw amniotic fluid), the sex of the fetus can be determined. Therefore, the option of abortion is available to the parent because of the fetus' sex.[16] The idea of abortion flitted through my mind last year after amniocentesis indicated that I was pregnant with my third boy, but my gynecologist advised me that neither society nor the profession was ready to consider selective abortion. Future generations may not consider this process the ethical dilemma that we do today.

In the science of preselection new frontiers are on the horizon. For example, scientists are experimenting with pills that halt men's production of one type of sperm. They are also seeking pills or gels that will render the woman's environment inhospitable to one or the other type of sperm. And they are experimenting as well with filters that allow only smaller males through.[17] Even Dr. Shettles is searching for new methods. By inseminating high in the cervical canal so that the more motile, male sperm will reach the egg first, he feels that he can achieve a 90 percent success rate. When sperm are allowed to age in a sterile petri dish for a few days, females will be born because only the stronger, female sperm will survive.[18]

Most people want boys. From early civilization, boys were cherished for their value as hunters and farmers. According to Dr. Roberta Steinbacher, psychologist and chairwoman of the Department of Urban Studies at Cleveland State University, male children have always been preferred to female children. She deduced that the effect of a perfected technique practiced by many would be a population increase in males and a decrease in females.[19] By tilting the gender balance by having more males, we risk increased male homosexuality and polyandry, said Dr. Steinbacher.[20]

What other effects could further advances in the science of preselection have on society? One cannot help noticing the outcome of sex determination in the green turtle and the American alligator in relation to the extinction, some sixty-five million years ago, of the dinosaur. A

sudden climate change either up or down could have produced a predominance of one sex. Once there is only one sex of an animal, the species can no longer reproduce, and the result is extinction.[21]

We are neither green turtles nor dinosaurs but human beings with
the power to choose, rather than allowing nature to take its course in
circumstances that are scientifically changeable. Traditionally we have
believed that controlling and determining life lie only in the hands of
the Creator. Recent developments such as life-support systems, test-
tube babies, and genetic engineering have challenged old beliefs.
Whereas science was first used to prolong life medically, it can now be
used to alter life by giving us choices.

ENDNOTES

[1]David M. Rorvik, <u>Your Baby's Sex: Now You Can Choose</u> (New
York: Dodd, Mead, 1970), p. 23.

[2]Bonnie Johnson, "Move Over Mother Nature: A New Diet May
Help Moms Select Their Baby's Sex," <u>People Weekly</u> (23 Aug. 1982),
pp. 48–51.

[3]Rorvik, p. 25.

[4]K. Ray, "The Implications of Sex Preselection," <u>Technology
Review</u> (May–April 1980), pp. 76–77.

[5]S. J. Morreale et al., "Temperature Dependent Sex
Determination," <u>Science</u> 214 (1982), 1245.

[6]Mark Ferguson and Ted Joanen, "Alligators: Cue to Dinosaur's
Demise?" <u>Science News</u> (6 Dec. 1975), p. 14.

[7]"The Genetic Basis of Sex Determination," <u>Science News</u> (6 Dec.
1975), p. 52.

[8]Lori Martin, "Your Child's Sex—Can You Choose?" <u>Parents</u> (Oct.
1981), p. 74.

[9]Rorvik, p. 38.

[10]Martin, p. 75.

[11]Martin, p. 76.

[12]"Sex Selection: Technique Not Confirmed," <u>Science News</u> (8
March 1975), p. 38.

[13]A. D. Pinkel et al., "Sex Preselection in Mammals?: Separation of Sperm Bearing Y and O Chromosomes in the Vole microles oregoni," Science 32 (1982), 904–906.

[14]J. Delepine, "Good Housekeeping Gave Us Our Son," Good Housekeeping (Aug. 1982), p. 40.

[15]Johnson, p. 50.

[16]Ray, p. 76.

[17]Ray, p. 76.

[18]Martin, p. 77.

[19]Ray, p. 77.

[20]Ray, p. 77.

[21]Ferguson and Joanen, p. 14.

BIBLIOGRAPHY

Delepine, J. "Good Housekeeping Gave Us Our Son." Good Housekeeping (Aug. 1982), p. 40.

Ferguson, Mark, and Ted Joanen. "Alligators: Cue to Dinosaur's Demise?" Science News (15 May 1982), p. 14.

"The Genetic Basis of Sex Determination." Science News (6 Dec. 1975), p. 52.

Johnson, Bonnie. "Move Over Mother Nature! A New Diet May Help Moms Select Their Baby's Sex." People Weekly (23 Aug. 1982), pp. 48–51.

Martin, Lori. "Your Child's Sex-Can You Choose?" Parents (Oct. 1981), pp. 74–77.

Morreale, S. J., et al. "Temperature Dependent Sex Determination." Science 214 (1982), 1245–1247.

Pinkel, A. D., et al. "Sex Preselection in Mammals? Separation of Sperm Bearing Y and O Chromosomes in the Vole microle oregoni." Science 214 (1982), 904–906.

Ray. K. "The Implications of Sex Preselection." Technology Review (Oct. 1981), pp. 74–77.

Rorvik, David M. Your Baby's Sex: Now You Can Choose. New York: Dodd, Mead, 1970.

"Sex Selection: Technique Not Confirmed." <u>Science News</u> (8 March
    1975), p. 38.

As we explained in the Focus section of this chapter, there is an alternative
method for citing sources, namely to give the author's name and the page
number(s) in the text itself. This alternative method eliminates the need for a
separate footnote page and uses only a list of "Works Cited." As an example
of how this method would be used, we have reproduced the first three pages
of the final draft of the student's paper, substituting this alternative method
for her use of footnotes.

ACHIEVING A TIE SCORE: ONE BOY TO ONE GIRL

Although baby doctors universally believe that an unborn child
has an equal chance of being male or female, as David M. Rorvik
points out, having the power to choose the sex has preoccupied the
minds of prospective parents for ages (23). According to Bonnie
Johnson, crude forms of preselection were practiced as far back as
the Middle Ages, but none of them proved effective (48–51). Among
the five hundred or more formulas recorded was one that required a
woman, in order to produce a son, to drink a mixture of wine and
blood and to make love under a full moon while an abbot prayed
(Rorvik 25).

Besides the obvious, satisfying the parents' curiosity to know the
sex of their unborn child, there are other values to preselection. A
couple can limit family size to the children they desire. Instead of
having three boys, a couple who, like my husband and me, really
want a girl could limit family size from the beginning by choosing a
girl as their first child. Preselection thus has important implications for limiting population growth (Ray 76–77).

Finding a reliable method of preselection would be a very simple
task if we were all green turtles. In conservationists' efforts to save
these turtles from extinction, they found that the temperatures in
the hatcheries had a direct correlation to the sex of the baby turtle.
When incubator temperatures were low—that is, 28°C and below—

almost no female turtles were hatched, statistically zero to 10 percent. When temperatures rose above 29.5°C, 95 to 100 percent of the offspring were females (Morreale 1245). A similar phenomenon was found to be true in other reptiles, including the American alligator, but in reverse: 30°C and below produced females exclusively, and 34°C and above produced all males (Ferguson and Joanen 14).

Unfortunately, the methods used to preselect the sex of reptiles have not been found to work for human beings, for temperature level has no relation to the sex of the yet-to-be-conceived child ("Genetic Basis" 52). All theories of sex determination in humans are based on the fact that there are two types of sperm: one carries the X chromosome, which determines females; the other carries the Y chromosome, which determines males (Martin 74).

This fact was first discovered by Dr. Landrum B. Shettles, an associate professor of Obstetrics and Gynecology at Columbia University's College of Physicians and Surgeons. His discovery and identification of male- and female-producing sperm are recognized universally. After viewing live sperm in a phase-contrast microscope, an instrument that throws halos of light over dark objects, he noticed that sperm cells came in two distinct sizes. Examining 500 specimens, he hypothesized that the small, round-headed sperm were the Ys (males) and the larger, oval sperm the Xs.

Dr. Shettles thought that their must be other differences besides shape. Conducting sperm counts, he found that there were approximately twice as many male as female sperm yet there are not twice as many men as women. He was convinced that some substance slaughtered the males. Studying the uterus and its secretions, and watching sperm activity in the secretions, Shettles filled capillary tubes with vaginal secretions taken at various times of the menstrual cycle. Then he added sperm at the top, and monitored their activity. The female-producing sperm fared better when the solution was more acidic. Because their greater bulk rendered them feistier in the bath, they lived longer. When cervical mucus was taken very close to ovulation, the woman's most fertile, most favorable time for concep-

tion, the smaller, faster male-producing sperm fared better. He concluded that the time of intercourse was crucial in determining the
child's sex. Two or three days prior to ovulation, when the uterus is
slightly acidic, a girl is conceived, and during ovulation, when the
environment is alkaline and more favorable, a boy is conceived
(Rorvik 38).

Dr. Shettles determined the time of ovulation by using a temperature chart or by measuring with Tes-Tape paper the pH balance in
the uterine mucus. Primarily used to determine sugar levels in diabetics, the paper turns darkest when the woman is just about to
ovulate (Martin 75). Dr. Shettles also recommended douching prior
to intercourse to reconstruct the acid–alkaline environment of the
uterus. A vinegar douche will induce a girl; baking soda, giving the
uterus a more alkaline quality, a boy. By combining douching with
timing intercourse at or near ovulation, we can expect to get the sex
of our choice 80 percent of the time (Martin 76)....

WORKS CITED

Delepine, J. "Good Housekeeping Gave Us Our Son." Good
    Housekeeping, Aug. 1982, p. 40.

Ferguson, Mark, and Ted Joanen. "Alligators: Cue to Dinosaur's
    Demise?" Science News, 15 May 1982, p.14.

"The Genetic Basis of Sex Determination," Science News, 6 Dec.
    1975, p. 52.

Johnson, Bonnie. "Move Over Mother Nature! A New Diet May Help
    Moms Select Their Baby's Sex." People Weekly, 23 Aug. 1982, pp.
    48–51.

Martin, Lori. "Your Child's Sex-Can You Choose?" Parents, Oct. 1981,
    pp. 74–77.

Morreale, S. J., et al. "Temperature Dependent Sex Determination."
    Science, 214 (1982): 1245–1247.

Pinkel, D., et al "Sex Preselection in Mammals? Separation of Sperm
    Bearing Y and O Chromosomes in the Vole microle oregoni."
    Science, 214 (1982): 904–906.

Ray, K. "The Implications of Sex Preselection." Technology Review, Oct. 1981, pp. 74–77.

Rorvik, David M. Your Baby's Sex: Now You Can Choose. New York: Dodd, Mead & Co., 1970.

"Sex Selection: Technique Not Confirmed." Science News, 8 Mar. 1975, p. 38.

BECOMING AWARE OF YOURSELF AS A WRITER

1. How efficient were your methods of investigation in writing the research paper? What was the most helpful method you used?

2. Were you able to use your knowledge of other academic subjects to provide you with material for your paper? If so, how were you able to adapt this knowledge for your audience?

3. Was it difficult obtaining information on your topic? What could you have done to find more material?

4. How skillfully were you able to analyze and interpret the usefulness or validity of your sources? Did you encounter any contradictory information in your sources? If so, how did you decide what to accept or reject?

5. How did you convert your source material into your own words? Were there any rough spots that you found particularly difficult to work on? How would you account for them? How did you solve the problems they created?

6. If you are assigned an investigative paper in the future, might you pursue your research any differently? How might you proceed?

7. How does writing for an audience affect the preparation of an investigative paper? What adjustments did you make?

8. Do you see the writing of an investigative paper as mainly an exercise in acquiring factual information, or are there other skills to be learned? What are those skills? How do you think you can use these skills in other writing that you do?

9. What did the author of the student essay do to avoid making her paper an exercise in "sterile fact-gathering"? Would her technique work for you?

PART IV

PERSUASION

INTRODUCTION

In Chapter 8, we turn to a third type of writing, writing that has an aim and purpose different from those of both expressive writing and expository writing. The primary aim in writing to persuade is neither to express the writer nor to explain the subject but to convince the reader of the writer's point of view on a particular issue. In terms of the triangle diagram from Chapter 2, the focus is on the reader rather than on the writer or the subject.

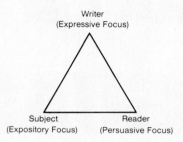

Persuasion, or argumentation, is a common aim in our society. Newspaper editorials aim to persuade, politicians argue their positions in speeches, preachers persuade from the pulpit, advertisers lure readers in the pages of magazines and newspapers. And in our everyday communication with others, we often wish to convince them of our point of view. To learn how to persuade or argue effectively in writing is the purpose of Chapter 8.

8
WRITING PERSUASIVELY

PURPOSE

The tools of persuasion are the abilities to reason well and to use language effectively. But as you develop these abilities, you should take some care in how you use them to influence others. Often, in our society, the tools of persuasion are wielded as weapons, to influence the public through illogical reasoning and seductive language, as in many political speeches and in much advertising. In its extreme form, persuasion can become propaganda, in which a cause is supported regardless of the merits of the arguments used. When studying persuasive techniques, then, it is important to distinguish, as Aristotle himself did, among the different means of argumentation: You can appeal to an audience's logic, emotions, or sense of ethics. (In fact, a distinction is often made between persuasion and argumentation; the former is defined as an appeal to the emotions, and the latter as an appeal to reason.) When appealing to the logic of your readers, you should be careful to be indeed logical and not to mislead them; when appealing to their emotions, you should be careful not to manipulate them; when appealing to their ethical or moral sense, you should be ethical yourself and not lead your readers astray. Perhaps the best argument includes all three appeals, each a counterbalance for the other. In the "Generating Ideas" section of this chapter, we will discuss the forms of logical appeal, including induction and deduction.

Because the emphasis in persuasive writing is on the audience, we will concentrate in the "Audience" section on how you, as a writer, can establish a relationship with your readers so that you can best persuade them to adopt your point of view. From the outset, you must take care to respect your readers even if they differ from you, and especially if they are ignorant of the subject altogether. You should have their attitude uppermost in your mind throughout or seek to foster a positive attitude if none exists. It is also important that you seek to establish your own credibility as an authority on the subject, as well as your sincerity in presenting your point of view. All the facets of writing to an audience that we have discussed thus far should be brought to bear: understanding the audience's frame of reference, role-playing the audience to understand their attitude, determining your voice, and, finally, ascertaining how much depth of information the audience needs about the subject.

The "Audience" section culminates in a discussion of how to appeal to your readers' sense of ethics, and the "Focus" section concentrates on how to phrase your essay in words that will appeal to your audience's emotions.

In the "Writing the Essay" section of this chapter, we present two of the most powerful arguments in American history, the American colonists's "Declaration of Independence" and Martin Luther King's support of his nonviolent tactics in "Letter from a Birmingham Jail." Studying these documents in the light of what you know about their effect on history will dramatize for you the mighty force wielded by an effective argument.

GENERATING IDEAS: INDUCTION, DEDUCTION, AND THE CLASSICAL QUESTIONS

Ideas for argument and persuasion can be generated on a number of levels; for example, one may think through the logic of an argument using inductive or deductive reasoning, then use many of the classical questions as a means to generate ideas to support that reasoning. Induction, deduction, and the classical questions, as they can be used in support of the persuasive aim, are discussed in this section.

Induction

Although inductive reasoning, as a product of the scientific age, arrived on the scene more recently than deduction, which was devised by the Greeks many centuries ago, we will discuss induction first for two reasons: (1) it is simpler than deduction, and (2) you are familiar with the concept of induction from Chapter 7.

In Chapter 7, you used induction as a way of arriving at scientific truth, answering the classical question "What examples are there of it?" Induction as a persuasive tool also answers this question, but the process of arriving at a conclusion is somewhat different from the process used by scientists. The scientific method begins with examples and then forms a conclusion; inductive argumentation uses examples to support a point of view. This distinction can, of course, be pushed too far, for the scientist begins with a hypothesis, and the persuasive writer, hopefully, has looked at the evidence before forming his or her point of view. But there are other differences as well: the scientific writer, for example, works with scientific subjects, whereas the persuasive writer works outside the laboratory with issues, emotions, and opinions.

The major difference is in intent. Scientific writers are more involved in their subject matter than with their audience, whereas persuasive writers marshal their evidence and present it in such a way as to convince their readers. Their emphasis is more on the reader, less on the subject (see the "Audience" section).

There are three types of persuasive induction: sampling, analogy, and causal generalization. Sampling is used to arrive at a conclusion about a group through reference to a certain percentage of that group rather than the entire membership, as discussing or even knowing about every member of a group would be impossible. For example, we might conclude through sampling that Americans want to view escapist movies because so many science-fiction movies have been so successful (for more on sampling, see Chapter 7, p. 213).

Analogy is helpful to an argument because it suggests that things alike in some ways must also be alike in others. You might argue by analogy that hecklers at public meetings are like political tyrants: They take ideas hostage. This statement suggests that hecklers, like tyrants, prevent the free exchange of ideas.

Causal generalization generalizes about many members of a class in order to determine why one member of the class is different. Only one child in a family got measles, and because he was the only one to visit a cousin, the implication is that he contracted the measles while at his cousin's house.

All of these methods must be handled logically, for there are many pitfalls in their use. If you use too few examples or samples, you may not prove your position. Hasty generalizations—for example, we will have a recession every eight years because we had one in 1975 and another in 1983—tend to be unconvincing. Atypical examples also tend to undercut the effectiveness of an argument; thus it may not help much to interview those not on welfare if you wish to argue that the welfare system is working. Moreover it is unfair to ignore examples that contradict your line of reasoning; if some people on welfare feel that the system is not much help to them, there is a way of admitting this contrary evidence (see the section on "Arranging Your Essay," p. 293).

When you argue inductively, it is best to avoid claiming more for your examples than they merit and to avoid making sweeping generalizations as did the cigarette commercial "Everyone who knows smokes Kools." Analogies, too, should be drawn carefully so that there is a sound basis of comparison and not a fleeting or glamorous one: When politicians claim that Latin American refugees will become "feet people" just as the Vietnamese were "boat people" if we do not defend Central America, their analogy is less sound than it might be; what actually causes refugees in either case is war itself, not our unwillingness to become involved.

Finally, in ascribing causal generalizations, watch for the dangers, mentioned in Chapter 5, that can be encountered when using causation: Is X the real cause of Y, or did it just come before it in time? Or is the connection just coincidental? Or is X the only cause of Y? Perhaps the child with the measles contracted the disease in school, rather than from contact with his cousin, or perhaps both the cousin and the classmates had the disease.

The criteria for successful inductive reasoning, then, include the following:

1. Your examples should be of sufficient quantity.
2. They should be randomly selected.
3. They should be accurate and objectively presented.
4. They should be relevant to the conclusion drawn.
5. They should disprove the evidence of the opposition.

SOME PRACTICE WITH INDUCTION

1. Identify the type of induction used in the following passages:

a. "Beasts abstract not," announced John Locke, expressing mankind's prevailing opinion throughout recorded history. Bishop Berkeley had, however, a sardonic rejoinder: "If the fact that brutes abstract not be made the distinguishing property of that sort of animal, I fear a great many of those that pass for men must be reckoned into their number." Abstract thought, at least in its more subtle varieties, is not an invariable accompaniment of everyday life for the average man. Could abstract thought be a matter not of kind but of degree? Could other animals be capable of abstract thought but more rarely or less deeply than humans? . . .

There is by now a vast library of described and filmed conversations, employing Ameslan and other gestural languages, with Washoe, Lucy, Lana and other chimpanzees studied by the Gardiners and others. Not only are there chimpanzees with working vocabularies of 100 to 200 words; they are also able to distinguish among nontrivially different grammatical patterns and syntaxes. What is more, they have been remarkably inventive in the construction of new words and phrases.

On seeing for the first time a duck land quacking in a pond, Washoe gestured "water bird," which is the same phrase used in English and other languages, but which Washoe invented for the occasion. Having never seen a spherical fruit other than an apple, but knowing the signs for the principal colors, Lana, upon spying a technician eating an orange, signed "orange apple." After tasting a watermelon, Lucy described it as "candy drink" or "drink fruit," which is essentially the same word form as the English "water melon." But after she had burned her mouth on her first radish, Lucy forever after described them as "cry hurt food." A small doll placed unexpectedly in Washoe's cup elicited the response "Baby in my drink." When Washoe soiled, particularly clothing or furniture, she was taught the sign "dirty," which she then extrapolated as a general term of abuse. A rhesus monkey that evoked her displeasure was repeatedly signed at: "Dirty monkey, dirty monkey, dirty monkey." Occasionally Washoe would say things like "Dirty Jack, gimme drink." Lana, in a moment of creative annoyance, called her trainer "You green shit." Chimpanzees have invented swear words. Washoe also seems to have a sort of sense of humor; once, when riding on her trainer's shoulders and, perhaps inadvertently, wetting him, she signed: "Funny, funny."

Lucy was eventually able to distinguish clearly the meanings of the phrases "Roger tickle Lucy" and "Lucy tickle Roger," both of which activities she enjoyed with gusto. Likewise, Lana extrapolated from "Tim groom Lana" to "Lana groom Tim." Washoe was observed "reading" a magazine—i.e., slowly turning the pages, peering intently at the pictures and making, to no one in particular, an appropriate sign, such as "cat" when viewing a photograph of a tiger, and "drink" when examining a Vermouth advertisement. Having learned the sign "open" with a door, Washoe extended the concept to a briefcase. She also attempted to converse in Ameslan with the laboratory cat, who turned out to be the only illiterate in the facility. Having acquired this marvelous method of communication, Washoe may have been surprised that the cat was not also competent in Ameslan. . . .

I would expect a significant development and elaboration of language in only a few generations if all the chimps unable to communicate were to die or fail to reproduce. Basic English corresponds to about 1,000 words. Chimpanzees are already accomplished in vocabularies exceeding 10 percent of that number. Although a few years ago it would have seemed the most implausible science fiction, it does not appear to me out of the question that, after a few generations in such a verbal chimpanzee community, there might emerge the memoirs of the natural history and mental life of a chimpanzee, published in English or Japanese (with perhaps an "as told to" after the byline).

If chimpanzees have consciousness, if they are capable of abstractions, do they not have what until now has been described as "human rights"? How smart does a chimpanzee have to be before killing him constitutes murder? What further properties must he show before religious missionaries must consider him worthy of attempts at conversion? . . .

The long-term significance of teaching language to the other primates is difficult to overestimate. There is an arresting passage in Charles Darwin's *Descent of Man:* "The difference in mind between man and the higher animals, great as it is, certainly is one of degree and not of kind. . . . If it could be proved that certain high mental powers, such as the formation of general concepts, self-consciousness, et cetera, were absolutely peculiar to man, which seems extremely doubtful, it is not improbable that these qualities are merely the incidental results of other highly-advanced intellectual faculties; and these again mainly the results of the continued use of a perfect language. . . ."

—**Carl Sagan**, *The Dragons of Eden*

b. When Lincoln at last determined, in July 1862, to move toward emancipation, it was only after all his other policies had failed. The Crittenden Resolution had been rejected, the border states had quashed his plan of compensated emancipation, his generals were still floundering, and he had already lost the support of great numbers of conservatives. The Proclamation became necessary to hold his remaining supporters and to forestall—so he believed—English recognition of the Confederacy. "I would save the Union," he wrote in answer to Horace Greeley's cry for emancipation. " . . . If I could save the Union without freeing any slave, I would do it; and if I could do it by freeing all the slaves, I would do it." In the end, freeing all the slaves seemed necessary.

It was evidently an unhappy frame of mind in which Lincoln resorted to the Emancipation Proclamation. "Things had gone from bad to worse," he told the artist F. B. Carpenter a year later, "until I felt that we had reached the end of our rope on the plan of operations we had been pursuing; that we had about played our last card, and must change our tactics, or lose the game. I now determined upon the adoption of the emancipation policy. . . ." The passage has a wretched tone: things had gone from bad to worse and as a result the slaves were to be declared free!

The Emancipation Proclamation of January 1, 1863, had all the moral grandeur of a bill of lading. It contained no indictment of slavery, but simply based emancipation on "military necessity." It expressly omitted the loyal slave states from its terms. Finally, it did not in fact free any slaves. For it excluded by detailed enumeration from the sphere covered in the Proclamation all the counties in Virginia and parishes in Louisiana that were occupied by Union troops and into which the government actually had the power to bring freedom. It simply declared free all slaves in "the States and parts of States" where the people were in rebellion—that is to say, precisely where its effect could not reach. Beyond its propaganda value the Proclamation added nothing to what Congress had already done in the Confiscation Act.

Seward remarked of the Proclamation: "We show our sympathy with slavery by emancipating the slaves where we cannot reach them and holding them in bondage where we can set them free." The London *Spectator* gibed: "The principle is not that a human being cannot justly own another, but that he cannot own him unless he is loyal to the United States."

But the Proclamation was what it was because the average sentiments of the American Unionist of 1862 were what they were. Had the political strategy of the moment called for a momentous human document of the stature of the Declaration of Independence, Lincoln could have risen to the occasion. Perhaps the largest reasonable indictment of him is simply that in such matters he was a follower and not a leader of public opinion. It may be that there was in Lincoln something of the old Kentucky poor white, whose regard for the slaves was more akin to his feeling for tortured animals than it was to his feeling, say, for the common white man of the North. But it is only the intensity and not the genuineness of his antislavery sentiments that can be doubted. His conservatism arose in part from a sound sense for the pace of historical change. He knew that formal freedom for the Negro, coming suddenly and without preparation, would not be real freedom, and in this respect he understood the slavery question better than most of the Radicals, just as they had understood better than he the revolutionary dynamics of the war.

For all its limitations, the Emancipation Proclamation probably made genuine emancipation inevitable. In all but five of the states freedom was accomplished in fact through the thirteenth amendment. Lincoln's own part in the passing of this amendment was critical. He used all his influence to get the measure the necessary two-thirds vote in the House of Representatives, and it was finally carried by a margin of three votes. Without his influence the amendment might have been long delayed, though it is hardly conceivable that it could have been held off indefinitely. Such claim as he may have to be remembered as an Emancipator perhaps rests more justly on his behind-the-scenes activity for the thirteenth amendment than on the Proclamation itself. It was the Proclamation, however, that had psychological value, and before the amendment was passed, Lincoln had already become the personal symbol of freedom. Believing that he was called only to conserve, he had turned liberator in spite of himself:

"I claim not to have controlled events but confess plainly that events have controlled me."

—**Richard Hofstadter,** "Abraham Lincoln and the Self-made Myth"

c. We should not conclude, either, that the child who has strong ties to his parents is insured against neurosis. We can only say that he will have the best possible measures within his personality to deal with conflict, which may then provide greater resistance to neurotic ills. But a neurosis is not necessarily an indictment of the parent–child relationship; a neurotic child is not necessarily an unloved child, or a rejected child. The child who has never known love and who has no human attachments does not develop a neurosis in the strict clinical meaning of the term. The unattached child is subject to other types of disorders. He might develop bizarre features in his personality, he might be subject to primitive fears and pathological distortions of reality, he might have uncontrollable urges that lead to delinquency or violence, but he would probably not acquire a neurosis because a neurosis involves moral conflicts and conflicts of love which could not exist in a child who had never known significant human attachments. The merit of a neurosis—if there is anything good to be said about it at all—is that it is a civilized disease. The child who suffers a disturbance in his love relationships or anxieties of conscience offers proof of his humanity even in illness. But the sickness of the unattached child is more terrible because it is less human; there is only a primitive ego engaged in a lonely and violent struggle for its own existence.

Indeed, it can be argued that the real threat to humanity does not lie in neurosis but in the diseases of the ego, the diseases of isolation, detachment and emotional sterility. These are the diseases that are produced in the early years by the absence of human ties or the destruction of human ties. In the absence of human ties those mental qualities that we call human will fail to develop or will be grafted upon a personality that cannot nourish them, so that at best they will be imitations of virtues, personality façades. The devastating effects of two world wars, revolution, tyranny and mass murder are seen in cruelest caricature in the thousands of hollow men who have come to live among us. The destruction of families and family ties has produced in frightening numbers an aberrant child and man who lives as a stranger in the human community. He is rootless, unbound, uncommitted, unloved and untouchable. He is sometimes a criminal, whether child or adult, and you have read that he commits acts of violence without motive and without remorse. He offers himself and the vacancy within him to be leased by other personalities—the gang leaders, mob-rulers, fascist leaders and the organizers of lunatic movements and societies. He performs useful services for them; he can perform brutal acts that might cause another criminal at least a twinge of conscience, he can risk his life when more prudent villains would stay home, and he can do these things because he values no man's life, not even his own. All that he asks in return is that he may borrow a personality or an idea to clothe his nakedness and give a reason, however perverse, for his existence in a meaningless world.

We have more reason to fear the hollow man than the poor neurotic who is tormented by his own conscience. As long as man is capable of moral conflicts—even if they lead to neurosis—there is hope for him. But what shall we do with a man who has no attachments? Who can breathe humanity into his emptiness?

—**Selma H. Fraiberg**, *The Magic Years*

2. Observe the use of the types of induction in the following essay. Does the essay meet all of the criteria for effective induction?

I knew a man who went into therapy about three years ago because, as he put it, he couldn't live with himself any longer. I didn't blame him. The guy was a bigot, a tyrant and a creep.

In any case, I ran into him again after he'd finished therapy. He was still a bigot, a tyrant and a creep, *but* . . . he had learned to live with himself.

Now, I suppose this was an accomplishment of sorts. I mean, nobody else could live with him. But it *seems* to me that there are an awful lot of people running around and writing around these days encouraging us to feel good about what we should feel terrible about, and to accept in ourselves what we should change.

The only thing they seem to disapprove of is disapproval. The only judgment they make is against being judgmental, and they assure us that we have nothing to feel guilty about except guilt itself. It seems to me that they are all intent on proving that I'm OK and You're OK, when in fact, I may be perfectly dreadful and you may be unforgivably dreary, and it may be—gasp!—*wrong*.

What brings on my sudden attack of judgmentitis is success, or rather, *Success!*—the latest in a series of exclamation-point books all concerned with How to Make it.

In this one, Michael Korda is writing a recipe book for success. Like the other authors, he leapfrogs right over the "Shoulds" and into the "Hows." He eliminates value judgments and edits out moral questions as if he were Fanny Farmer and the subject was the making of a blueberry pie.

It's not that I have any reason to doubt Mr. Korda's advice on the way to achieve success. It may very well be that successful men wear handkerchiefs stuffed neatly in their breast pockets, and that successful single women should carry suitcases to the office on Fridays whether or not they are going away for the weekend.

He may be realistic when he says that "successful people generally have very low expectations of others." And he may be only slightly cynical when he writes: "One of the best ways to ensure success is to develop expensive tastes or marry someone who has them."

And he may be helpful with his handy hints on how to sit next to someone you are about to overpower.

But he simply finesses the issues of right and wrong—silly words, embarrassing words that have been excised like warts from the shiny surface of the new how-to books. To Korda, guilt is not a prod, but an enemy that he slays on page four. Right off the bat, he tells the would-be successful reader that

- It's OK to be greedy.
- It's OK to look out for Number One.
- It's OK to be Machiavellian (if you can get away with it).
- It's OK to recognize that honesty is not always the best policy (provided you don't go around saying so).
- And it's always OK to be rich.

Well, in fact, it's not OK. It's not OK to be greedy, Machiavellian, dishonest. It's not always OK to be rich. There is a qualitative difference between succeeding by making napalm or by making penicillin. There is a difference between climbing the ladder of success, and macheteing a path to the top.

Only someone with the moral perspective of a mushroom could assure us that this was all OK. It seems to me that most Americans harbor ambivalence toward success, not for neurotic reasons, but out of a realistic perception of what it demands.

Success is expensive in terms of time and energy and altered behavior—the sort of behavior he describes in the grossest of terms: "If you can undermine your boss and replace him, fine, do so, but never express anything but respect and loyalty for him while you're doing it."

This author—whose *Power!* topped the best-seller last year—is intent on helping rid us of that ambivalence which is a signal from our conscience. He is like the other "Win!" "Me First!" writers, who try to make us comfortable when we should be uncomfortable.

They are all Doctor Feelgoods, offering us placebo prescriptions instead of strong medicine. They give us a way to live with ourselves, perhaps, but not a way to live with each other. They teach us a whole lot more about "Failure!" than about success.

— **Ellen Goodman**, "It's Failure, Not Success"

Deduction

Deductive reasoning works quite differently from inductive reasoning: Rather than working from evidence to a conclusion, as does induction, deduction works from an assumption—a generalization that is generally accepted as true— to a specific conclusion. This assumption, called a *premise* in formal logic, leads to a specific conclusion with the help of a "linking statement." Here is an example of deductive thinking:

Assumption: All college students should drink beer.

Linking Statement: John is a college student.

Conclusion: John should drink beer.

Of course, most of us usually do not think according to this process, called a *syllogism* in formal logic. Usually, we think only in the last two steps of the process (formally called an *enthymeme)*. For example, we might argue that because John is a college student, he should drink beer, taking for granted the assumption that all college students should drink beer.

If you decided to argue that we are going to war because we are having an army buildup, your argument similarly would rest on an unspoken assumption, in this case that an army buildup necessarily leads to war.

Assumption: All army buildups lead to war.

Linking Statement: We are having an army buildup.

Conclusion: We are going to war.

You might find it a good idea to construct this syllogism to determine if the assumption on which your argument rests is a sensible (or valid) one. If it is valid that all army buildups lead to war (or that all college students should drink beer, for that matter), then your argument itself makes sense. To say that Peter is cold because he has no coat on is to assume that all people who have no coats on are cold. If the weather is cold, if the people are outdoors, and if they have no heavy sweaters on instead, then your assumption is probably valid. And if your assumption is valid, then your argument is probably valid also.

Deduction is useful when you are trying to persuade your readers of a highly controversial conclusion because, if you can get them to agree with your assumption, you have a good chance of getting them to agree with your conclusion. It is worthwhile, therefore, to learn how to construct an informal syllogism. (Courses in logic instruct one in formal constructions.)

Each of the three statements in a syllogism has two parts, each of these parts appearing in one of the other statements according to the following pattern:

Assumption:　All that has a tendency to become stale needs renewing.
　　　　　　　　　　　　　　　3　　　　　　　　　　　　　　　　2

Linking Statement:　Slang has a tendency to become stale.
　　　　　　　　　　　　　1　　　　　　　　　　　　3

Conclusion:　Slang needs to be renewed.
　　　　　　　　　1　　　　　2

Because your conclusion is usually your shaping idea, begin here to construct your syllogism. By adding a causal conjunction to your conclusion, you can usually arrive at your linking statement: *Slang needs to be renewed* because *it has a tendency to become stale.* You now have all three parts of your syllogism and can construct the third statement accordingly, as the assumption always contains Parts 3 and 2, in that order.

For example, suppose your shaping idea for your argument is "Our involvement in El Salvador is a no-win situation." By adding *because* to this sentence, you can arrive at your linking statement: "Our involvement in El Salvador is a no-win situation because it is a guerrilla war." Diagramming your enthymeme will give you your assumption:

Linking Statement:　El Salvador is a guerrilla war.
　　　　　　　　　　　　1　　　　　　　3

Conclusion:　Our involvement in El Salvador is a no-win situation.
　　　　　　　　1　　　　　　　　　　　　　2

Assumption:　Guerrilla wars are no-win situations.
　　　　　　　　3　　　　　　　2

We should add here that sometimes it is necessary to construct a series or string of syllogisms, in order to clarify just what general assumption lies behind a point that you wish to argue. For example, in a discussion of deductive logic in one class, the students decided to construct an argument in support of handgun control. They found that they had to put together the following series of syllogisms before they could determine the general assumption behind their feeling that handgun possession is immoral:

Syllogism 1:
All persons who kill except in self-defense or in defense of others are immoral.

He killed neither in self-defense nor in defense of others.

He is immoral.

(This syllogism does not establish that he has a handgun, so the students added Syllogism 2 to their argument.)

Syllogism 2:

All in possession of guns are readily equipped to kill in all situations (self-defense, defense of others, and non-defense).

He is in possession of a gun.

He is readily equipped to kill in all situations.

(This syllogism does not establish that the person equipped to kill is likely to kill, so the students added Syllogism 3.)

Syllogism 3:

All men readily equipped to kill are more likely to kill in non-defense situations, as well as in self-defense or in defense of others.

He is readily equipped to kill.

He is more likely to kill in non-defense situations.

(This syllogism does not establish the charge of immorality, so the students added still another syllogism.)

Syllogism 4:

All men more likely to kill in non-defense situations are immoral.

He is more likely to kill in non-defense situations.

He is immoral.

(With Syllogism 4, the students felt that they had clarified the logic behind their argument that handgun possession is immoral.)

Do you think the students' assumptions are valid?

SOME PRACTICE WITH DEDUCTION

Reconstruct the assumptions on which the following arguments (enthymemes) are based. In each case, does the argument seem to rest on a valid assumption?

1. Business is a good major because you can get a job.

2. Toxic waste disposal is a vital issue because undisposed-of poisons can affect our health.

3. The government should continue to subsidize student loans because college tuitions can no longer be afforded by a sizable percentage of the middle class.

4. Playing video games should not be ridiculed because they encourage mind–body coordination.

5. Because high-technology firms promise employment, Americans should train or retrain to enter a high-technology profession.

6. The sexual revolution has been harmful because so many people are contracting herpes.

7. Bilingualism should not be encouraged because studies show that students in bilingual classes do not learn English well.

8. Advertising should not be considered worthless because buying an advertised product makes people feel good.

9. Women should resist the return to ultrafeminine fashions because this trend repudiates the philosophy of the women's movement.

10. Because it appears likely that young marrieds will not be able to afford the downpayment on a house due to high interest rates, they should not hope to have a home of their own.

Deductive Fallacies

As we indicated above, the reason for constructing a syllogism is to determine if your assumption is logical. Below are some of the problems that you might encounter in trying to make this determination.

1. *Faulty analogy:* There are not enough important similarities between the two subjects being compared to really support the conclusions that are being drawn. Although it is often said that the generation of the 1980s is just like that of the 1950s because both are silent, the differences between the two decades are greater than any similarities.

2. *False cause:* The ascribed cause is not really a cause at all or is just one of many factors. Although the women's movement has been blamed for the disintegration of the family, other societal factors are the chief causes.

3. *Begging the question:* The assumption takes for granted what ought to be established by proof. You cannot assume, for example, that a person cannot be believed because he has a reputation as a liar. You must establish proof that he is lying in a particular argument.

4. *Ad hominem:* An argument is formulated on the basis of a person's personal life rather than on the issue itself. To argue that because one is a Catholic one has no business talking about abortion is to stray from one's ideas about abortion to one's religious beliefs.

5. *Ad populum:* An argument is based on appeals to popular biases such as insisting that the nuclear freeze movement must be ignored because it is infiltrated by Communists.

6. *Either/or:* The implication is made that there are only the two options when, in fact, there may be several others. The argument that one is better off "dead than red" is a well-known example of the either/or fallacy.

7. *Red herring:* The audience is diverted from the real issue. Faced with laws insisting on the installation of pollution controls, a company might warn that employees will lose their jobs if the costly controls are installed, thus diverting attention from the legal and environmental issues.

8. *Genetic fallacy:* The class that a person is from, and not the person's own qualifications, becomes the focus of the argument. For example, many people argued that Ronald Reagan could not be a good president because he had been a movie actor.

9. *The bandwagon:* This argument asserts the value of its point of view because "everybody" is doing it. Advertisements often commit this fallacy: "*Atlantic* Subscribers Never Miss" or "All Over the World People Have One Thing in Common: They Start the Evening with Red" (Johnnie Walker Red).

10. *Slanting:* Arguers sometimes use language unfairly to encourage the reader to take their view of the subject. To claim that over 30 percent of a class failed an exam when in fact nearly 70 percent had passed it for the highest percentage of passes ever is an example of slanting, because it emphasizes the small percentage that failed rather than the vast majority that passed.

SOME PRACTICE WITH IDENTIFYING DEDUCTIVE FALLACIES

1. Which assumptions in the exercise on pp. 274–275 can be categorized by one of the logical fallacies?

2. Identify the fallacy in each of the following assumptions:

a. He is an Italian; he must belong to the Mafia.

b. Students, if you continue to protest this regulation, you will be encouraging anarchy in the schools.

c. People who know use Product X.

d. Ted doesn't use deodorant; how could he possibly be a good student-body president?

e. The candidate has been divorced; therefore his qualifications for political office are questionable.

f. If you do not learn computer languages, you will find yourself unemployed.

g. His preposterous suggestion insults all red-blooded Americans.

h. Foreign imports are destroying the U.S. economy.

i. I cannot take this political speech seriously because politicians cannot be trusted.

j. The Republicans are at it again: first Watergate and now "briefinggate."

The Classical Questions in Support of Persuasion

Whether you develop an argument through inductive or deductive thinking, you need proof to support your position. The classical questions are useful in generating ideas that will supply proof for your argument. Because most arguments combine deduction and induction, we direct your attention here to questions that generate proof for both types of argument.

The classical question "What examples are there of it?" can generate a sampling to support an inductive argument. Other inductive questions are "What is it like?" (analogy or analogies) and "What factor not characteristic of others in its class may have caused it?" (causal generalization).

Deductive arguments or portions of arguments can be supported by the material generated by the classical question "What is it?" which may help you argue that your subject, as defined, has certain properties: characteristics, parts, and functions. For example, if you argue that "This gun is a product of human hatred and fear because it is a weapon," then you can base your argument on the assumption that "Weapons are products of human hatred and fear," and that the ownership of guns therefore should be abolished.

Another classical question to ask in support of deduction is "What is it like or unlike?" A variation on this question asks, "How does it compare with the ideal?" If, for example, the ideal is in your assumption that "All good deeds deserve rewards," then you can argue that what you have just done compares favorably with a good deed (and therefore you deserve a reward). Another variation on this question is "How does it compare with my opponent's view?" Explain why she or he disagrees either that you have done a good deed or that good deeds deserve rewards. Still another variation: "How does it compare with the alternatives?" Remind your reader that being rewarded will produce further good behavior, whereas being unacknowledged will lead to indifferent behavior.

A third classical question in the service of deductive proof asks, "How can it be classified?" Corresponding questions are "How can this group be defined?" "What characteristics of the group does my subject show?" and "How does it compare with others in its class?" Because we know that our recent purchase was made by a designer, we classify it as a designer fashion. We also assume that "All designer fashions are well made," and we can therefore argue that this purchase, which has a flaw in it, should be replaced.

SOME PRACTICE WITH THE CLASSICAL QUESTIONS AS MEANS OF GENERATING IDEAS FOR AN ARGUMENT

Which of the classical questions might be useful in generating ideas for the following arguments (deductive and/or inductive)?

1. Natural foods are healthier than processed ones.
2. Dogs are better pets than cats.
3. Cocaine is America's Number One social problem.
4. America should adopt more vigorous measures for feeding the hungry people of the world.

How to Apply the Principles of Induction and Deduction in Generating Ideas for a Persuasive Essay

In order to generate proof for your argument, we suggest that you take the following four steps:

1. Construct a logically sound argument using deduction and/or induction; summarize your main points. Research your issue if necessary to obtain the best proof. If you can find an argument developed by the opposition or one supporting your own point of view, such material should be helpful in constructing your own argument and in acquiring supporting proof.
2. Reevaluate your summary in the light of any conflict between your frame of reference and that of your audience and/or your opponent (your audience may not necessarily be opposed to your point of view, it may be neutral instead). Once you have understood how your audience and/or your opponent would view your argument, you have some idea of what the issues really are.
3. Weigh the merits of the various points of view underlying both sides of the issue, and make a case for the higher priority of the values of your case over those of your opponent. In order to do so, you may have to locate a new assumption that your opponent must agree with. Incorporate your new perspective into your argument by writing a new summary.
4. Use this final summary to write your argument.

For example, a student arguing against coed dormitories might work through the four steps in the following way:

1. **Formulate an Argument:** He formulates his main points using a combination of deduction and induction:

- **Shaping Idea:** Coed dormitories should be abolished because they introduce distractions and tensions into students' lives.
- **Inductive Proof by Example:**

  a. Ned, whose girlfriend lived on his floor, flunked math because he did not want to study.
  b. Jim, who organized nightly dormitory parties, had to leave school for a semester because he was suffering from exhaustion.
  c. Sarah, who developed a nervous condition because her boyfriend moved to another girl's dormitory, withdrew from her classes and her social relations as well.

- **Assumption:** Anything other than their studies that distracts and preoccupies students should be abolished.
- **Conclusion:** Coed dormitories should be abolished.
- **Argument Stated as a Syllogism:**

  Assumption: Anything that distracts and preoccupies students should be abolished.
  Linking Statement: Coed dormitories distract and preoccupy students.
  Conclusion: Coed dormitories should be abolished.

2. **Analyze Audience Frame of Reference:** His readers are new freshmen who either have no opinion on coed dorms or are anxious to try their social wings and are strongly in favor of them. The strongest argument of those supporting these dorms is that they encourage students to gain valuable social experience and thus help them to mature faster. Proof of their argument comes from examples supplied by their older brothers and sisters who have experienced living in coed situations.

  a. Susan, who had always felt awkward and unsure of herself on dates, learned to relax with the opposite sex by coming in contact with them in everyday situations.
  b. John gradually removed the pedestal from beneath women, stopped breaking up with every girl he went out with, and accepted Dorothy even though she didn't meet his ideal.
  c. Carol, who had attended an all-girl high school, enjoyed learning what men thought of her.

Assumption: Anything that encourages maturity should be maintained.

3. **Consider a Higher Priority:** Our writer recognizes that maturity is an important value and now knows that he must maintain that students have more to gain by doing well in their studies than by spending their study time in social pursuits because this is a very competitive world, and a good education is a vital necessity.

4. **Reconstruct Your Argument:** He now reconstructs his argument in the following way:

- **Assumption:** In a competitive world, education must be students' first priority, and anything that interferes with that priority should be abolished.
- **Linking Statement:** Coed dorms interfere with education.
- **Conclusion:** Coed dorms should be abolished.

SOME PRACTICE WITH MAKING A CASE FOR THE HIGHER PRIORITY OF SOME VALUES OVER OTHERS

1. Review the passages by Sagan, Hofstadter, Fraiberg, and Goodman (pp. 266–272). Which, if any, of these authors have recognized the validity of their opposition's viewpoint and have argued for the higher priority of their own? What other attitudes have these authors taken toward their opposition? Can you explain why they have taken these attitudes?

2. Construct the audience frame of reference and the opposition point of view for the following deductive syllogisms; then reconstruct each syllogism so that it rests on an assumption of higher priority:

   a. **Assumption:** High-school teachers should help students to deal maturely with all of the pressures of adolescence.
   Linking Statement: Sex education is necessary if students are to deal maturely with the pressures of adolescence.
   Conclusion: Sex education should be taught by teachers in high school.

   b. **Assumption:** Anything that pollutes the atmosphere should be replaced by nonpolluting substitutes.
   Linking Statement: All gas-powered cars pollute the atmosphere.
   Conclusion: All gas-powered cars should be replaced by nonpolluting vehicles, such as battery- or solar-powered vehicles.

AUDIENCE: PERSUADING YOUR AUDIENCE

As the aim of persuasion differs from the aims of expressive and expository writing, so the role of the audience differs as well. When you engage in expressive writing, although you may wish to make yourself appealing to your audience and therefore may attempt to understand your readers through constructing their frame of reference, role-playing their point of view, and then deciding which of your own voices would be most effective, your purpose is not primarily to persuade your readers; you do not want your readers to adopt your point of view, but simply to accept you enough to enter into your experience.

In expository writing, your aim as a writer is to convey your subject matter, and your concern with your audience leads you to accommodate yourself to any disparity between their background and your own—in education generally and in the subject matter specifically. In order to be aware of any disparities, you must also construct a frame of reference and determine your own voice in writing—as an expert writing to a lay audience, for example.

For the most part, as a writer of persuasion, you can expect that your audience will be familiar with the subject matter already, although they may need some repetition of the basic facts and perhaps some in-depth treatment; what you want is for them to form an opinion about the subject matter, either their first opinion or a replacement opinion. In addition, you may want your readers to act on this newly formed opinion, either in a manner of their own choosing or in a very specific way determined by you. Thus you are demanding more of the audience than you might if you were writing expressive or expository prose, and you must use all the means at your disposal to accomplish your persuasive aim. You must first of all establish a relationship with your audience—you must establish your credibility as a writer, your role, and your voice. Then you must build bridges by establishing that you are aware of the attitude or the frame of reference of the audience and that you esteem your readers despite any differences in their point of view and your own. You must also be aware of how much depth of information your readers need. Although, of course, you must pay a considerable amount of attention to the subject matter itself and to the rational arguments for your point of view, you will also want to consider how to appeal to the emotions of your audience through your use of language and whether you have handled the ethical implications well: those of your own approach as well as those of the situation.

Establishing Credibility

How do you go about building a relationship with your audience? How do you establish bridges between your points of view? Whether your audience is neutral or hostile, a common ground can be established. The first thing that you will want to do is establish your credibility as someone who knows enough about the subject to have a worthwhile opinion about it. Professional writers, of course, have much less difficulty with this part of the task than does the average citizen or the college student. The editorial writers of *The New York Times* or of magazines with national circulation, like *Time* and *Newsweek,* have a built-in credibility by virtue of their position. Likewise, those in the professions arguing about issues in their fields are established authorities.

But how does the average citizen writing a letter to the editor or someone writing to a friend or speaking to his or her classmates establish credibility? One way is to indicate considerable experience with the subject. By narrating your encounters with the issue, you show yourself to be someone who has received firsthand knowledge. Another way is to research your subject thoroughly and to present this research to the reader. By giving background information, on the one hand, and inductive examples from research, as well as experience, on the other, you show yourself to be well versed in your subject matter.

Sometimes the role you choose to play will help you to establish your credibility. You should decide in which of your many roles you will appear most knowledgeable about your subject and select a voice that expresses that role. If you are presenting to your classmates the merits of soccer over lacrosse as a member of both teams, then the voice of a well-rounded athlete gives you added authority. If no knowledgeable voice is available to you, select a voice that indicates that you are involved in your subject. You might, for example, want to argue about state politics, and the voice that would best indicate that you are involved in the subject would be that of concerned citizen. Concerned citizen is, in fact, the most typical voice for the writer of argument to adopt because it allows her or him to identify with her or his audience, who will no doubt want to be considered concerned citizens also.

Adopting the Proper Tone

Once you have chosen your issue and your voice in arguing that issue, you will also want to decide what tone you should adopt. In most cases, your tone should be reasonable as opposed to strident or hostile. But once that is said, there are many combinations possible. As well as reasonable, you can be firm, distant, sarcastic, urgent, moral, full of righteous indignation, weary, chastising, disgusted, humorous, ironic, and so forth. The soccer and lacrosse player, for example, writing to his or her classmates on the merits of soccer, will adopt a tone consistent with his or her own attitude toward the two sports. After all, how much can one dislike lacrosse? His or her tone might, in fact, be humorous. And, too, this writer must take into account the audience's attitude toward lacrosse. Should they enjoy the sport, he or she must adopt a tone that will not offend them.

Thus your subject matter and your voice will help to determine your tone, and so will your audience. When arguing with politicians, for example, editorial writers often feel freer to adopt more extreme tones, such as sarcasm and disgust, than when writing to persuade private citizens. When persuading common citizens to change an opinion on a subject that is dear to their hearts, the writer often chooses a reasonable tone or combines it with humor or a "we're-all-in-this-together" camaraderie.

Analyzing Your Audience

This discussion leads us to the importance of analyzing your audience. You should know your audience's frame of reference in order to proceed. Once you have analyzed that, you know their point of view on the issue. If the audience has not yet formed a point of view, one strategy that you might take is to foster for them a perception of themselves as concerned, reasonable citizens who are willing to act in a reasonable way. If, however, the audience has a point of view, take it into account at all junctures in writing your argument: in deciding on your premises, in adopting your tone, in deciding what action you want the audience to take, and in choosing the language through which you phrase your appeals.

Often your best strategy in arguing is to show esteem for your audience, and to convey this esteem throughout. If you attack your opponents as ignorant or wrong, they probably won't listen to your argument. Instead, adopt the attitude that they are concerned citizens just as you are, and that you "are all in this together." Assume that they want to act in the right manner, just as you do. Be willing to compromise, above all. Very seldom are opposing positions on an issue right and wrong: both sides are right in certain ways and wrong in certain ways. Be willing to recognize this fact as you proceed.

Finally, analyze the depth of your audience's information needs. Do they require background because of lack of acquaintance with the issue? Are they lay readers who can absorb only so much in-depth information? Or are they willing to follow a long, detailed argument? How detailed an argument need you prepare? Analyzing their frame of reference should help you answer this question.

Presenting an Ethical Appeal

In the "Generating Ideas" section, we discussed how to appeal to your audience through the logical means of induction, deduction, and the classical questions. Two other appeals can be made. One is the ethical appeal which depends on the writer's sincerity in approaching the topic; the writer seeks to involve his or her readers in the ethics of the situation as well. How can you establish your sincerity and honesty—your ethics—in approaching your issue? Many professional writers have a reputation that establishes their ethics for them, just as it establishes their credibility. On the other hand, no one quite believes in the honesty or the sincerity of politicians because they usually feel obliged by their party affiliation to argue an issue from the party's point of view. They may sound sincere, sometimes to the point of making people believe in them, but the more dubious audiences often remain just that.

But as an average citizen or a student writer, you have no such baggage either to prove or to disprove your sincerity. You must rely on internal indications, such as your writing carefully, reasonably, and in a straightforward and clear style, making sure to support your points through careful research. Although these internal signs do not prove your honesty, they should appeal to most readers as honest attempts to present a credible argument.

The other appeal is to the emotions, which is made largely through your choice of language. The language of persuasion is discussed in the "Focus" section of this chapter.

SOME PRACTICE WITH PERSUADING YOUR AUDIENCE

Read the following argument and analyze who the writer's audience might be. How aware was the writer of his audience? What appeals has he made to his audience?

We are told that the trouble with Modern Man is that he has been trying to detach himself from nature. He sits on the topmost tiers of polymer, glass, and steel, dangling his pulsing legs, surveying at a distance the writhing life of the planet. In this scenario, Man comes on as a stupendous lethal force, and the earth is pictured as something delicate, like rising bubbles at the surface of a country pond, or flights of fragile birds.

But it is illusion to think that there is anything fragile about the life of the earth; surely this is the toughest membrane imaginable in the universe, opaque to probability, impermeable to death. We are the delicate part, transient and vulnerable as cilia. Nor is it a new thing for man to invent an existence that he imagines to be above the rest of life; this has been his most consistent intellectual exertion down the millennia. As illusion, it has never worked out to his satisfaction in the past, any more than it does today. Man is embedded in nature.

The biologic science of recent years has been making this a more urgent fact of life. The new, hard problem will be to cope with the dawning, intensifying realization of just how interlocked we are. The old, clung-to notions most of us have held about our special lordship are being deeply undermined.

Item. A good case can be made for our nonexistence as entities. We are not made up, as we had always supposed, of successively enriched packets of our own parts. We are shared, rented, occupied. At the interior of our cells, driving them, providing the oxidative energy that sends us out for the improvement of each shining day, are the mitochondria, and in a strict sense they are not ours. They turn out to be little separate creatures, the colonial posterity of migrant prokaryocytes, probably primitive bacteria that swam into ancestral precursors of our eukaryotic cells and stayed there. Ever since, they have maintained themselves and their ways, replicating in their own fashion, privately, with their own DNA and RNA quite different from ours. They are as much symbionts as the rhizobial bacteria in the roots of beans. Without them, we would not move a muscle, drum a finger, think a thought.

Mitochondria are stable and responsible lodgers, and I choose to trust them. But what of the other little animals, similarly established in my cells, sorting and balancing me, clustering me together? My centrioles, basal bodies, and probably a good many other more obscure tiny beings at work inside my cells, each with its own special genome, are as foreign, and as essential, as aphids in anthills. My cells are no longer the pure line entities I was raised with; they are ecosystems more complex than Jamaica Bay.

I like to think that they work in my interest, that each breath they draw for me, but perhaps it is they who walk through the local park in the early morning, sensing my senses, listening to my music, thinking my thoughts.

I am consoled, somewhat, by the thought that the green plants are in the same fix. They could not be plants, or green, without their chloroplasts, which run the photosynthetic enterprise and generate oxygen for the rest of us. As it turns out, chloroplasts are also separate creatures with their own genomes, speaking their own language.

We carry stores of DNA in our nuclei that may have come in, at one time or another, from the fusion of ancestral cells and the linking of ancestral organisms in symbiosis. Our genomes are catalogues of instructions from all kinds of sources in nature, filed for all kinds of contingencies. As for me, I am grateful for differentiation and speciation, but I cannot feel as separate an entity as I did a few years ago, before I was told these things, nor, I should think, can anyone else.

Item. The uniformity of the earth's life, more astonishing than its diversity, is accountable by the high probability that we derived, originally, from some single cell, fertilized in a bolt of lightning as the earth cooled. It is from the progeny of this parent cell that we take our looks; we still share genes around, and the resemblance of the enzymes of grasses to those of whales is a family resemblance.

The viruses, instead of being single-minded agents of disease and death, now begin to look more like mobile genes. Evolution is still an infinitely long and tedious biologic game, with only the winners staying at the table, but the rules are beginning to look more flexible. We live in a dancing matrix of viruses; they dart, rather like bees, from organism to organism, from plant to insect to mammal to me and back again, and into the sea, tugging along pieces of this genome, strings of genes from that, transplanting grafts of DNA, passing around heredity as though at a great party. They may be a mechanism for keeping new, mutant kinds of DNA in the widest circulation among us. If this is true, the odd virus disease, on which we must focus so much of our attention in medicine, may be looked on as an accident, something dropped.

Item. I have been trying to think of the earth as a kind of organism, but it is no go. I cannot think of it this way. It is too big, too complex, with too many working parts lacking visible connections. The other night, driving through a hilly, wooded part of southern New England, I wondered about this. If not like an organism, what is it like, what is it *most* like? Then, satisfactorily for that moment, it came to me: it is *most* like a single cell.

—Lewis Thomas, ''The Lives of a Cell''

1. How did the writer establish his credibility with the audience?

2. What role was the writer playing throughout?

3. What tone would you say he was taking in regard to the issue?

4. What attitude did the writer assume the audience has? To what extent do you think the writer created that attitude for the audience?

5. In what ways has the writer shown esteem for the reader?

6. How much depth of information has the writer supplied?

7. To what extent has the writer appealed to the emotions of the reader? To her or his sense of right and wrong?

8. What role does the writer's use of language play in making his point? What function, for example, does his use of analogy have?

TASK: WRITING A PERSUASIVE ESSAY

Your task for this chapter is to write a persuasive essay. Through your own combination of the methods of induction, deduction, and the classical questions, you should generate support for your point of view on an issue and present a well-reasoned, well-organized argument to your readers.

The issue, the audience, and your purpose in writing are to be selected by you. In order to give your task a context, we would like you to create a life situation or ''case'' in which you take the role of one of the participants in the situation and write an argument to convince one or more other participants of your point of view about an issue that has arisen. In creating your case, you will devise the context, the participants, the issue, your purpose in writing the argument, and the audience for whom it is intended.

Thus, in this task, you are to write not as yourself but as one of the participants in the case that you set up. For example, you might take the role of the manager of a local chemical plant that is considering the installation of costly pollution-control devices. You have been asked by the president of the company to present the company's argument for installing these devices to the other employees. You know that many of your readers may suffer pay reductions as a result of the high costs that the company will incur. How can you best argue your case?

The length of the case and its complexity are up to you. However, you should give your instructor and your peer group enough details about your role and that of your intended audience so that they can construct both frames of reference, and you should also give them enough information about the situation in general and the problem in particular so that they will know as much about your case as you do.

The audience that you select will be either undecided or hostile to your point of view; there is no point in selecting an audience that already agrees with you, as in that case you have no one to convince. Whether hostile or undecided, however, your audience should be interested in your subject and to some extent knowledgeable about it.

In constructing your case, you can proceed in one of two ways: (1) choose an issue that interests you and then build around it a situation containing a specific audience and a purpose for addressing that audience; or (2) choose a situation with which you are familiar, analyze the issues involved, and then select one issue to argue about.

For example, suppose that you want to argue that we should rely more than we do at present on nuclear power for local energy needs. By constructing a case around this issue, you can focus more sharply on whom you are addressing your argument to and why your argument is necessary. Your case might go something like this: You are a homeowner with a family to support in an area where energy costs are high. The local electric company has proposed building a nuclear facility that will lower energy costs to its customers, you and your neighbors. Many of your neighbors, however, are concerned about the dangers of such a facility, and some have formed an antinuclear group. You decide to attend a meeting of this group, to try to convince its members to see your side of the issue. First, you must write out your argument, so that you can present it clearly in what you realize will be a hostile setting. What do you write?

If you choose the second method, start with a situation that you know something about, perhaps one having to do with a job that you hold or with a subject that you are studying; decide what your role is to be; and then select your issue. You might, for example, be studying the period of the American Revolution in a history course, a period in which many important issues were fought over. Adopt a role for yourself from that era, say, the role of a merchant who has decided to back the rebel cause. The Boston Tea Party has just taken place. Write an essay for the local newspaper in which you state why your fellow citizens, many of whom feel that such an act of insurrection is immoral, should support those responsible for the Boston Tea Party.

In focusing on the issue, you might argue from one of the following points of view: You might argue about the merits of the situation, about whether it is "good or bad." Or you might argue about what your subject really means and how it should be interpreted. A third approach is to argue about what consequences will follow from a certain action. Finally, you may want to advocate a certain course of action. Of course, a combination of two or more of these approaches is also possible.

Construct your case before proceeding further. In the following section,

"Writing the Essay," we discuss how to generate ideas for your argumentative essay, how best to address your audience, and how the arrangement patterns that correspond to the classical questions that you have asked can be used to help organize different sections of your essay. Most important, we present patterns of arranging a persuasive essay as a whole. In the "Focus" section, we discuss various considerations in choosing the language of your argument in order to best convince your reader of your point of view.

WRITING THE ESSAY

Generating Ideas Through Induction, Deduction, and the Classical Questions

Now that you have written your case, you know the issue that will form the subject of your essay and the point of view that you will take on that issue. If you have not phrased that point of view as a shaping idea, you will want to do so now. In order to clearly establish the purpose of your argument from the start, word it so that your reader knows whether you are arguing for a course of action ("This should be done"); a value judgment ("This is good/or bad"); an interpretation ("This is what it means and how it should be interpreted"); or a necessary consequence of certain actions or conditions ("This is what will happen").

Once you have your shaping idea, extend it into an enthymeme by linking it to a causal statement through the use of a causal conjunction such as *because* or *as.* Then work out the assumption on which your argument is based by constructing an informal syllogism according to the formula in the "Generating Ideas" section. Examine your assumption(s) for possible fallacious reasoning.

Next, determine the assumption of your opponent. Finally, revise your assumption to take his or hers into account by basing your assumption on a higher priority (see the "Generating Ideas" section).

As we have suggested, most arguments are a combination of induction and deduction. Do be aware, however, that some shaping ideas may not form the conclusion of a syllogism. If you are a scientist arguing that our water sources are plentiful, you may simply be marshaling evidence in a purely inductive argument. At the same time, the possibility that you will be developing a purely deductive argument is remote. Even though your argument may be based on a series of syllogisms in support of your basic conclusion or shaping idea, these conclusions will need inductive support.

You should find the classical questions discussed in the "Generating Ideas" section helpful in generating material for your essay. By making a list of those questions that will generate material on your subject, you can acquire proof for your essay. If you are arguing for a course of action, you might ask what the effects would be and how they would compare with the effects of not acting. If you are arguing the merits (or demerits) of your subject, then you might ask how it compares with the ideal or ask what analogy is effective. When arguing about what a subject means or how it can be interpreted, you might ask what it is, what it will cause, what class it is in, and what examples there are of it. Finally, arguments stating the consequences of a future action ("This is what will happen") can be supported through asking what the effects will be and what will cause those effects, through seeking an analogy, and through making comparisons with alternatives.

It is important that you seek through such questions concrete evidence to present in support of your position: specific examples, statistical information, and factual details. Try to avoid simply praising or condemning a point of view, without offering detailed evidence. And try to make your evidence as concrete as possible. If you give a general reason in support of an argument, back it up with specific details: Thus, if you argue that eighteen-year-olds should be allowed to drink by law because they are expected by society to act in general as responsible adults, back this argument up with references to specific ways in which society does expect eighteen-year-olds to act as responsible adults, and then illustrate your point in even more concrete detail by referring to specific eighteen-year-olds who act as responsible adults in specific ways.

Persuading Your Audience

As you have constructed a case, you virtually have the script for both playing your own role and role-playing that of your audience. Through role playing, you should be able to reconstruct your audience's frame of reference even more fully than you have done in writing the case. Know as thoroughly as you can their point of view on the issue, their education, their values, and the amount of information they have on the subject.

You will also want to analyze the frame of reference and the point of view of the character you are playing, of course, in order to clarify his or her role as well. If this role does not immediately establish your credibility, you might decide to do research on your subject to bolster your authority. Finally, you will want to select a voice that is consistent with your role, the subject, and your knowledge of your audience.

To the extent that the character you are playing is not yourself, keep in mind that you are writing as this character and use his or her voice consistently; as you write, make sure not to lapse into playing yourself at any point in the essay. Rather, develop the argument honestly and sincerely in this voice that you have selected, establishing how the subject engages your values, and remembering as well to relate your argument to the values of the audience.

Arranging Your Essay

The argumentative or persuasive essay has four main divisions: the introduction, the proof, the refutation of the opposing argument, and the conclusion. Following this pattern can help you to organize the material that you generate into an effective and clear presentation.

The introduction to an argumentative essay fulfills the same functions as does any introduction (see Chapter 7, p. 234), although special care must be taken in developing some of its features. It must first of all establish who you are, as the writer—the role you are playing and how the role helps establish your credibility. You cannot introduce yourself, however, without knowing precisely who your audience is and how best to present yourself to them. At the outset, you must set the right tone for your subject and your audience in order to engage them. And then, of course, you must announce your shaping idea: the issue and your point of view on it.

The body of the paper should contain the proof of your argument and your refutation of your opponent's point of view. As we have discussed, you may garner proof through obtaining support for your arguments, whether inductive or deductive, by asking such classical questions as "What examples are there of it?" "What caused it?" "What is it?" "How can it be classified?" and "How does it compare with the ideal, with the opposing argument, with any alternatives, and with others in its class?" The arrangement of this proof thus should correspond to the patterns that we have discussed in previous chapters: cause and effect, comparison and contrast, and process in Chapter 5 and exemplification in Chapter 6 (general to specific) and Chapter 7 (induction).

Two arrangement patterns not presented in earlier chapters are definition and classification. A definition may be as brief as that found in the dictionary, or you may extend it through attributing characteristics, analyzing the parts, stating functions, giving examples, and comparing and contrasting with other subjects. The arrangement pattern for definition may follow any ordering of these features. In the definition below, the nineteenth-century thinker John Stuart Mill argued for the equality of women by defining women's intuitive abilities. He began his argument by defining intuition, but he proceeded largely by comparing and contrasting the thought processes of women with those of men:

The Nature of Women
John Stuart Mill

What is meant by a woman's capacity of intuitive perception? It means, a rapid and correct insight into present fact. It has nothing to do with general principles. Nobody ever perceived a scientific law of nature by intuition, nor arrived at a general rule of duty or prudence by it. These are results of slow and careful collection and comparison of experience; and neither the men nor the women of intuition usually shine in this department, unless, indeed, the experience necessary is such as they can acquire by themselves. For what is called their intuitive sagacity makes them peculiarly apt in gathering such general truths as can be collected from their individual means of observation. When, consequently, they chance to be as well provided as men are with the results of other people's experience, by reading and education (I use the word chance advisedly, for, in respect to the knowledge that tends to fit them for the greater concerns of life, the only educated women are the self-educated) they are better furnished than men in general with the essential requisites of skillful and successful practice. Men who have been much taught, are apt to be deficient in the sense of present fact; they do not see, in the facts which they are called upon to deal with, what is really there, but what they have been taught to expect. This is seldom the case with women of any ability. Their capacity of "intuition" preserves them from it. With equality of experience and of general faculties, a woman usually sees much more than a man of what is immediately before her. Now this sensibility to the present, is the main quality on which the capacity for practice, as distinguished from theory, depends. To discover general principles, belongs to the speculative faculty: to discern and discriminate the particular cases in which they are and are not applicable, constitutes practical talent: and for this, women as they now are have a peculiar aptitude. I admit that there can be no good practice without principles, and that the predominant place which quickness of observation holds among a woman's faculties, makes her particularly apt to build overhasty generalizations upon her own observation; though at the same time no less ready in rectifying those generalizations, as her observation takes a wider range. But the corrective to this defect, is access to the experience of the human race; general knowledge—exactly the thing which education can best supply. A woman's mistakes are specifically those of a clever self-educated man, who often sees what men trained in routine do not see, but falls into errors for want of knowing things which have long been known. Of course he has acquired much of the pre-existing knowledge, or he could not have got on at all; but what he knows of it he has picked up in fragments and at random, as women do.

In arranging the elements of classification, you may define the class, discuss how your subject fits into that class, and/or compare and contrast your subject with other members of the class. Another approach is taken by the authors of the following paragraphs in arguing that athletic competition has no more beneficial effects than intense endeavor in any other field. They first define their class as "problem athletes," then explain how the classification was arrived at, and finally contrast problem athletes with those outside the class.

Sport: If You Want to Build Character, Try Something Else
Bruce C. Ogilvie and Thomas A. Tutko

Types
The problem athletes who made up our original sample displayed such severe emotional reactions to stress that we had serious doubts about the basic value of athletic competition. The problems associated with sport covered a wide spectrum

of behavior, but we were able to isolate major syndromes: the con-man athlete, the hyperanxious athlete, the athlete who resists coaching, the success-phobic athlete, the injury-prone athlete, and the depression-prone athlete.

When we confronted such cases, it became more and more difficult for us to make positive clinical interpretations of the effects of competition. In 1963, we established the Institute for the Study of Athletic Motivation to start research aimed at helping athletes reach their potentials. We wanted to examine normal players as well as problem athletes. To identify sport-specific personality traits, we and Lee Lyon developed the Athletic Motivation Inventory (AMI) which measures 11 traits common to most successful sports figures. We have since administered the AMI to approximately 15,000 athletes. The results of these tests indicate that general sports personalities do exist.

Traits
Athletes who survive the high attrition rate associated with sports competition are characterized by all or most of the following traits:

1) They have great need for achievement and tend to set high but realistic goals for themselves and others.
2) They are highly organized, orderly, respectful of authority, and dominant.
3) They have large capacity for trust, great psychological endurance, self-control, low-resting levels of anxiety, and slightly greater ability to express aggression.

Although the evidence for your argument may be presented through one of the other classical arrangement patterns—as examples of the effects of a cause or as examples of how your subject compares with its alternative—your arrangement pattern may simply list the evidence in response to the question "What examples are there of it?" probably in an order that begins with the least convincing and ends with the most significant. Note the order of examples in this paragraph:

A Case for Rebellion
William O. Douglas

One reading American history and the stirring sentences of our Declaration of Independence would suppose that we would be on the side of the people and against the colonial rulers. *The contrary has been true.* The Dean Achesons who staffed our State Department stood firmly against Indonesian independence for five long years. The Henry Cabot Lodges who manned the United Nations stood resolutely against independence for Morocco or Algeria or Vietnam. By the mid-twentieth century we had become members of a rather plush club whose members wore homburgs, were highly respectable, and stood for the status quo. This was our consistent policy under Truman and Eisenhower. Not until the Kennedy administration did we change. On March 15, 1961, the tide turned when we supported the resolution in the United Nations in favor of Angola and against Portugal.

Until that day we had either voted against independence resolutions or abstained. Until that day we stood with the respectable European colonial regimes and against those who pleaded for independence, at times with raucous voices. Indeed, without our financial support France would not have been able to subdue her subject peoples as long as she did.

Once you have established proof for your shaping idea, your next step is to refute the opposition. Refuting those factors that detract from your argument can gain you further credibility. Not only are you recognizing that another point of view exists, but if that point of view happens to be shared by your audience, then you are also giving them credit for their viewpoint. By stating the objections fairly and then refuting them fairly, you make your own argument more convincing.

Construct your opposing statements by concentrating on what you know about your audience. If your audience is hostile, then you will not want to further arouse their hostility; even a neutral audience will not respond well to a scathing attack. The most useful refutation may well be one that shows the opposition that a higher priority exists, as we discussed in the "Generating Ideas" section.

Sometimes it is also possible to deny the opposing argument by declaring it untrue or invalid under the circumstances. If an opponent has an erroneous grasp of the facts or if his or her facts do not apply in the situation, then you can point this out, remembering to do so tactfully.

The fourth section of an argumentative essay is the conclusion. In this final section, you will want to summarize your proof and restate your major conclusion.

The Declaration of Independence is certainly one of the most famous arguments ever presented in America. An analysis of it will indicate how the writers went about organizing this important document:

The Declaration of Independence, July 4, 1776

The Unanimous Declaration of the Thirteen United States of America
When in the Course of human events, it becomes necessary for one people to dissolve the political bands which have connected them with another, and to assume among the powers of the earth, the separate and equal station to which the Laws of Nature and of Nature's God entitle them, a decent respect to the opinions of mankind requires that they should declare the causes which impel them to the separation.

We hold these truths to be self-evident, that all men are created equal, that they are endowed by their Creator with certain unalienable Rights, that among these are Life, Liberty, and the pursuit of Happiness. That to secure these rights, Governments are instituted among Men, deriving their just powers from the consent of the governed, That whenever any Form of Government becomes destructive of these ends, it is the Right of the People to alter or to abolish it, and to institute new Government, laying its foundation on such principles and organizing its powers in such form, as to them shall seem most likely to effect their Safety and Happiness. Prudence, indeed, will dictate that Governments long established should not be changed for light and transient causes; and accordingly all experience hath shown, that mankind are more disposed to suffer, while evils are sufferable, than to right themselves by abolishing the forms to which they are accustomed. But when a long train of abuses and usurpations, pursuing invariably the same Object evinces a design to reduce them under absolute Despotism, is it their right, it is their duty, to throw off such Government, and to provide new Guards for their future security. Such has been the patient sufferance of these Colonies; and such is now the necessity which constrains them to alter their former Systems of Government. The history of the present King of Great Britain is a history of repeated injuries and usurpations, all having in direct object the establishment of an absolute Tyranny over these States. To prove this, let Facts be submitted to a candid world.

He has refused his Assent to Laws, the most wholesome and necessary for the public good.

He has forbidden his Governors to pass Laws of immediate and pressing importance, unless suspended in their operation till his Assent should be obtained; and when so suspended, he has utterly neglected to attend to them.

He has refused to pass other Laws for the accommodation of large district of people, unless those people would relinquish the right of Representation in the Legislature, a right inestimable to them and formidable to tyrants only.

He has called together legislative bodies at places unusual, uncomfortable, and distant from the depository of their Public Records, for the sole purpose of fatiguing them into compliance with his measures.

He has dissolved Representative Houses repeatedly, for opposing with manly firmness his invasions on the rights of the people.

He has refused for a long time, after such dissolutions, to cause others to be elected; whereby the Legislative Powers, incapable of Annihilation, have returned to the People at large for their exercise; the State remaining in the mean time exposed to all the dangers of invasion from without, and convulsions within.

He has endeavoured to prevent the population of these States; for that purpose obstructing the Laws of Naturalization of Foreigners; refusing to pass others to encourage their migration hither, and raising the conditions of new Appropriations of Lands.

He has obstructed the Administration of Justice, by refusing his Assent to Laws for establishing Judiciary Powers.

He has made Judges dependent on his Will alone, for the tenure of their offices, and the amount and payment of their salaries.

He has erected a multitude of New Offices, and sent hither swarms of Officers to harass our People, and eat out their substance.

He has kept among us, in times of peace, Standing Armies without the Consent of our legislatures.

He has affected to render the Military independent of and superior to the Civil Power.

He has combined with others to subject us to a jurisdiction foreign to our constitution, and unacknowledged by our laws; giving his Assent to their acts of pretended legislation;

For quartering large bodies of armed troops among us:

For protecting them, by a mock Trial, from Punishment for any Murders which they should commit on the Inhabitants of these States:

For cutting off our Trade with all parts of the world:

For imposing Taxes on us without our Consent:

For depriving us in many cases, of the benefits of Trial by Jury:

For transporting us beyond Seas to be tried for pretended offences:

For abolishing the free System of English Laws in a neighbouring Province [Quebec], establishing therein an Arbitrary government, and enlarging its Boundaries so as to render it at once an example and fit instrument for introducing the same absolute rule into these Colonies:

For taking away our Charters, abolishing our most valuable Laws, and altering fundamentally the Forms of our Governments:

For suspending our own Legislatures, and declaring themselves invested with Power to legislate for us in all cases whatsoever.

He has abdicated Government here, by declaring us out of his Protection and waging War against us.

He has plundered our seas, ravaged our Coasts, burnt our towns, and destroyed the Lives of our people.

He is at this time transporting large armies of foreign mercenaries to compleat the works of death, desolation and tyranny, already begun with circumstances of Cruelty & perfidy scarcely paralleled in the most barbarous ages, and totally unworthy the Head of a civilized nation.

He has constrained our fellow Citizens taken Captive on the high Seas to bear Arms against their Country, to become the executioners of their friends and Brethren, or to fall themselves by their Hands.

He has excited domestic insurrections amongst us, and had endeavoured to bring on the inhabitants of our frontiers, the merciless Indian Savages, whose known rule of warfare, is an undistinguished destruction of all ages, sexes and conditions.

In every stage of these Oppressions We have Petitioned for Redress in the most humble terms: Our repeated Petitions have been answered only by repeated injury. A Prince, whose character is thus marked by every act which may define a Tyrant, is unfit to be the ruler of a free People.

Nor have We been wanting in attention to our British brethren. We have warned them from time to time of attempts by their legislature to extend an unwarrantable jurisdiction over us. We have reminded them of the circumstances of our emigration and settlement here. We have appealed to their native justice and magnanimity, and we have conjured them by the ties of our common kindred to disavow these usurpations, which would inevitably interrupt our connections and correspondence. They too have been deaf to the voice of justice and of consanguinity. We must, therefore, acquiesce in the necessity, which denounces our Separation, and hold them, as we hold the rest of mankind, Enemies in War, in Peace Friends.

We, therefore, the Representatives of the united States of America, in General Congress, Assembled, appealing to the Supreme Judge of the world for the rectitude of our intentions, do, in the Name, and by Authority of the good People of these Colonies, solemnly publish and declare, That these United Colonies are, and of Right ought to be Free and Independent States; that they are Absolved from all

Allegiance to the British Crown, and that all political connection between them and the State of Great Britain, is and ought to be totally dissolved; and that as Free and Independent States, they have full Power to levy War, conclude Peace, contract Alliances, establish Commerce, and to do all other Acts and Things which Independent States may of right do. And for the support of this Declaration, with a firm reliance on the Protection of Divine Providence, we mutually pledge to each other our Lives, our Fortunes and our sacred Honor.

1. Discuss the assumptions made in the second paragraph. Are they valid? Under what conditions can such assumptions be considered not valid?

2. On what assumption does the argument for independence rest? Reconstruct the argument as an informal syllogism.

3. Does the Declaration conform to the four-part organization of introduction, proof, refutation, and conclusion? Explain.

4. What are the arguments of the opposition? How does the Declaration refute them and/or appeal to a higher authority?

5. Why have so many examples of America's grievances against the British king been listed? Does this appear to be a sampling or is it presented as an exhaustive list? To what extent do you think it was meant to inform the audience as well as to prove the argument?

6. How did the writers establish their credibility? In what voice did they speak and how did it affect their credibility?

7. Who was the audience for the Declaration? What was their frame of reference and point of view on the issue? What effect do you think the Declaration had on them? What effect does it have on present-day readers?

8. What was the attitude of the writers toward their audience? How did this attitude affect the tone of the piece? How did it affect the writers's ethical appeal?

Writing the Rough Draft

Once you have thought out your argument and assembled your proof for your audience, you are ready to begin writing your essay. Following is the case created by a student and the rough draft of her argument.

<u>Case.</u> I am Rachel McLish, two-time Miss Olympia, and a fervent believer in and practitioner of bodybuilding. You have probably seen me on the Diet Rite commercials with Lee Majors. I have recently been

asked by the editors of <u>Redbook Magazine</u> to write an article for their readers arguing that bodybuilding is good for women. I have agreed to do so because I think their readers can be persuaded of my point of view. If I were to write for some other women's magazines, on the other hand, I might not be able to convince their readers, who are more traditional. Of course, I know that there are still other magazines for women whose readers, like me, are already working out in the gym. <u>Redbook</u> readers are adventurous without being in the avant-garde, and I should be able to win them over.

BODYBUILDING: THE SHAPE OF THE FUTURE

I am a female bodybuilder who has been actively engaged in the sport for many years. When you hear the word <u>bodybuilding,</u> the first thing that comes to your mind is probably a masculine man who is said to be clumsy or muscle-bound. Or a woman who looks manly. Most people's attitudes toward bodybuilding have come a long way, but there are still some who are unaware of its benefits. It is now a respected sport for both men and women. A woman bodybuilder does not lose any of her femininity; she gains sexuality.

What would you rather have—fat or muscle? A shapely, firm body or a spongy, saggy one? I am sure everyone would pick muscle and a shapely, firm body. You don't gain large rippling muscles like the manly woman athletes whom you have seen unless you want them. But you will gain a strong, sleek, sexy body. If you lead a sedentary life, your youthful curves will quickly lose their shape and turn into fat. But if you choose the bodybuilding lifestyle, you will stay young and firm.

Bodybuilders have long had a reputation for being muscle-bound and clumsy. But in reality, bodybuilders build their agility along with their muscles. It is important for a bodybuilder to be agile and flexible in order to help prevent injuries. That is why all professional bodybuilders do stretching exercises as part of their exercise routine.

Another part of their routine is aerobic exercise. This is running, swimming, and cycling. This form of exercise strengthens your heart and lungs.

The most essential part of their routine is weightlifting. This exercise increases your strength and power and gives you a defined, firm body.

Bodybuilders eat only the most nutritious foods. They live on a high-protein diet. The foods that they are allowed, especially when in training for competition, are very restricted.

Bodybuilding is becoming more widely accepted. Because of the American Federation of Woman Bodybuilders, women's bodybuilding especially is a fast-growing sport. I am sure everyone knows Lou Ferrigno and Arnold Schwartzenegger, thanks to their total dedication to the sport.

Bodybuilders are specimens of perfect health. They are fit in all areas, such as strength, agility, flexibility, and muscular and cardiovascular endurance. Let's think of total physical fitness as a chair. One of the chair legs is stretching exercises, the second is aerobic exercises, the third is weight training, and the fourth is nutrition. Each leg needs the other to hold up the chair. If one element is missing, the chair falls. Bodybuilders do not confine themselves to lifting weights. They do all the exercises to keep themselves in the highest physical condition possible.

1. On what assumption did "Rachel McLish" base her argument? What did she hope to accomplish?

2. What proof did she offer to support her argument? What arrangement patterns did she use?

3. What is the view of the opposition? Has she refuted it? What method of refutation did she use, higher priority or denial?

4. How did she take her audience into account? Did she seem to understand *Redbook* readers well? How would she have changed the essay if she were writing to the readers of *Family Circle* or *Ladies' Home Journal?* How would she have changed it if she were writing to *Cosmopolitan* subscribers?

5. What voice and tone did she adopt? Was she sincere in her advocacy of bodybuilding? Explain.

6. How would you revise this draft?

FOCUS: PERSUASIVE LANGUAGE AND THE APPEAL TO THE EMOTIONS

In an effective argument, the writer's words and phrases play an important part because they form the foundation of the emotional appeal. Whereas the logical and ethical appeals are based on content (presenting facts and conclusions based on valid assumptions and establishing one's credibility through research), the emotional appeal evolves largely from how one phrases that content. Of course, in advertising and in propaganda, the words and even the content may be manipulated to appeal to the emotions of the reader, but in honest persuasion, the writer works out a logical argument and then heightens the reader's response through language. In some situations, the writer's audience might not respond to such language, of course; sometimes the members of the scientific community, for example, will be persuaded only by factual content. But in most arguments, the emotional appeal is a significant component.

The tools of persuasive language are many: connotation, figurative language, allusion, repetition, humor, categorical statements, and logical terms. The writer's language must also, of course, be appropriate for the audience and reflect his or her tone.

Connotation

Connotative language is the most commonly used appeal to the emotions. *Connotation* refers to the overlays of meaning that our culture or segments of our culture attach to a word regardless of its denotation, or strictly literal meaning. The denotative meaning of a word is usually the first definition in the dictionary; the connotative meanings follow. Often, as words are so mercurial in our society, the writers of dictionaries cannot keep abreast of the current associations that words have for people. On the other hand, many words that once had fresh connotations have been used so frequently that they have become clichéd and have lost their excitement.

The astute writer is aware of the connotations of words and singles out from a group of possible choices the word that most clearly and freshly states her or his meaning. How many among us, for example, would not prefer to be called *slim* rather than *thin* or *skinny?* Although these words have similar denotations (or literal meanings), their connotations (or associated meanings) are quite different. And if *slim* seems to you to have been overworked, perhaps *slender* seems fresher.

Notice the writer's use of connotation in this paragraph from *Time* magazine that introduces an essay on the acquisition of former President Jimmy Carter's briefing papers by Ronald Reagan's campaign staff before the 1980 debate.

There are moments in American life when events lurch out of context, when the public is hurtled from dim awareness of a seemingly trivial news item into a maelstrom of moral reappraisal. That appears to be happening in the affair that the Washington press corps has predictably dubbed "Debategate."

Words like *lurch, hurtled,* and *maelstrom* create turbulence in us, and when we see them immediately coupled with *American life* and *moral reappraisal,* we may feel fear and insecurity. Although other words and phrases like *moments, seemingly trivial, news item,* and *predictably dubbed* suggest that the cause of the turbulence is trivial, the language of this introduction implies that an apparently unimportant issue may possess real legal or moral significance. In this paragraph, no facts or assumptions are stated directly, but the language has strongly involved the reader's emotions.

The American novelist William Faulkner also made use of connotation in one of the most famous speeches of our time, given when he accepted the Nobel Prize for Literature. Referring to the human fear of being "blown up" in war, he said:

Until he relearns these things, he will write as though he stood among and watched the end of man. I decline to accept the end of man. It is easy enough to say that man is immortal simply because he will endure; that when the last ding-dong of doom has clanged and faded from the last worthless rock hanging tideless in the last red and dying evening, that even then there will still be one more sound: that of his puny inexhaustible voice, still talking. I refuse to accept this. I believe that man will not merely endure: he will prevail. He is immortal, not because he alone among creatures has an inexhaustible voice, but because he has a soul, a spirit capable of compassion and sacrifice and endurance. The poet's, the writer's, duty is to write about these things. It is his privilege to help man endure by lifting his heart, by reminding him of the courage and honor and hope and pride and compassion and pity and sacrifice which have been the glory of his past. The poet's voice need not merely be the record of man; it can be one of the props, the pillars, to help him endure and prevail.

Some of Faulkner's phrases have vividly negative connotations: "ding-dong of doom," "the last worthless rock hanging tideless in the last red and dying evening," "his puny inexhaustible voice." These images are contrasted with words with strong moral, even religious, positive connotations: "man is immortal," "man will not merely endure; he will prevail," "he has a soul, a spirit capable of compassion and sacrifice and endurance," "courage and honor and hope and pride and compassion and pity and sacrifice." Faulkner was not offering a strongly logical argument; rather, through the sheer impact of his words, he hoped to enlist our emotions in affirming that humans will not only endure but prevail.

Figurative Language

Metaphors and similes also aid the writer of persuasion. As we noted in the "Focus" section of Chapter 6, both figures of speech compare one's subject to another that is not really like it in kind but is like it in some other way that the writer has determined. "That car is a monster" is a metaphor in which two unlike things are compared because they both create fear. "The child waddles like (or as) a duck" is a simile because of the injection of the word *like* or *as*. The point of similarity is obvious: both children and ducks waddle. Whereas the comparison in similes is always clearly stated, the comparison may be submerged in metaphor; in "the car growled," the comparison between car and monster is only implied.

These figures of speech abound in the speeches of our presidents and of other leaders. Abraham Lincoln's speeches during the Civil War used and created metaphors that are still famous: he quoted the Bible in asserting that "A house divided against itself cannot stand" and asked that Americans "bind up the nation's wounds." In a speech on the night of Gandhi's death, Indian Prime Minister Jawaharlal Nehru said:

> The light has gone out, I said, and yet I was wrong. For the light that shone in this country was no ordinary light. The light that has illumined this country for these many years will illumine this country for many more years, and a thousand years later that light will still be seen in this country and the world will see it and it will give solace to innumerable hearts. For that light represented the living truth . . . the eternal truths, reminding us of the right path, drawing us from error, taking this ancient country to freedom.

Allusion

Allusion, especially to cultural heroes and myths, is another effective use of language in presenting arguments. Many writers allude to the Bible, which has always been a cornerstone of our own national mythology. We have already quoted a figure of speech from the Bible used by Abraham Lincoln. And Adlai Stevenson, in accepting the nomination as Democratic Party candidate for president in 1952, alluded to Jesus' agony in the Garden of Gethsemane: "I have asked the merciful Father, the Father to us all, to let this cup pass from me. But from such dread responsibility one does not shrink in fear, in self-interest, or in false humility. So, 'If this cup may not pass from me, except I drink it, Thy will be done.' "

Repetition

One of the most frequently used language patterns in persuasion is repetition. Although repetition, if not handled well, can be boring, when handled skillfully, it can achieve quite impressive effects. In one of the most famous speeches of World War II, given after the Battle of Dunkirk, Winston Churchill concluded:

> Even though large tracts of Europe and many old and famous states have fallen or may fall into the grip of the Gestapo and all the odious apparatus of Nazi rule, we shall not flag or fail. We shall go on to the end, we shall fight in France, we shall

fight on the seas and oceans, we shall fight with growing confidence and growing strength in the air, we shall defend our island, whatever the cost may be, we shall fight on the beaches, we shall fight on the landing grounds, we shall fight in the fields and in the streets, we shall fight in the hills; we shall never surrender, and even if, which I do not for a moment believe, this island or a large part of it were subjugated and starving, then our Empire beyond the seas, armed and guarded by the British fleet, would carry on the struggle, until, in God's good time, the New World, with all its power and might, steps forth to the rescue and the liberation of the old.

And Franklin Delano Roosevelt, after the bombing of Pearl Harbor by the Japanese, asked Congress for a declaration of war against Japan. In strikingly effective repetition, he said;

> Yesterday the Japanese government also launched an attack against Malaya.
> Last night Japanese forces attacked Hong Kong.
> Last night Japanese forces attacked Guam.
> Last night Japanese forces attacked the Philippine Islands.
> Last night the Japanese attacked Wake Island.
> And this morning the Japanese attacked Midway Island.

Humor and Satire

Humor can often accomplish for the writer what straight logical argument cannot. Woody Allen, in a speech to the graduating class of 1979, argued that science has failed us:

> Put in its simplest form, the problem is: How is it possible to find meaning in a finite world given my waist and shirt size? This is a very difficult question when we realize that science has failed us. True, it has conquered many diseases, broken the genetic code, and even placed human beings on the moon, and yet when a man of 80 is left in a room with two 18-year-old cocktail waitresses nothing happens. Because the real problems never change. After all, can the human soul be glimpsed through a microscope? Maybe—but you'd definitely need one of those very good ones with two eyepieces. We know that the most advanced computer in the world does not have a brain as sophisticated as that of an ant. True, we could say that of many of our relatives but we only have to put up with them at weddings or special occasions. Science is something we depend on all the time. If I develop a pain in the chest I must take an X-ray. But what if the radiation from the X-ray causes me deeper problems? Before I know it, I'm going in for surgery. Naturally, while they're giving me oxygen an intern decides to light up a cigarette. The next thing you know I'm rocketing over the World Trade Center in bed clothes. Is this science? True, science has taught us how to pasteurize cheese. And true, this can be fun in mixed company—but what of the H-bomb? Have you ever seen what happens when one of those things falls off a desk accidentally? And where is science when one ponders the eternal riddles? How did the cosmos originate? How long

has it been around? Did matter begin with an explosion or by the word of God? And if by the latter, could He not have begun it just two weeks earlier to take advantage of some of the warmer weather? Exactly what do we mean when we say, man is mortal? Obviously it's not a compliment.

In one of the most famous arguments of all time, Jonathan Swift made "a modest proposal" that the Irish eat their children because they were too poor to feed them: "I have been assured by a very knowing American of my acquaintance in London, that a young healthy child well nursed is at a year old a most delicious, nourishing, and wholesome food, whether stewed, roasted, baked, or broiled; and I make no doubt that it will equally serve in a fricassee or a ragout." Because most of his readers were shocked, Swift was very effective in his use of satire, which is the humorous or critical treatment of a subject in order to expose the subject's or the audience's vices or follies. Swift was, of course, not seriously proposing this remedy for the poverty of the Irish, but he wielded the sword of satire in an effort to move the English to alleviate their misery.

Categorical Statements

The writer of argument may speak in categorical statements that emphasize his or her position by assuring the reader that there are no qualifications to the argument and will be no wavering in his or her position. Thus Abraham Lincoln promised, "We shall not fail—if we stand firm, we shall not fail"; Winston Churchill intoned, "we shall defend our island, whatever the cost may be"; and William Faulkner asserted, "I believe that man not only will endure: he will prevail."

Logical Terms

The writer of argument often, of course, uses the terminology of logic in making her or his presentation. In arguing that the poor have every reason for accommodating to poverty, as their situation is "usually hopeless," John Kenneth Galbraith, the economist, stated that the acceptance by the poor of their fate is "a profoundly rational response" and that "The deeply rational character of accommodation lies back, at least in part, of the central instruction of the principal world religions." Through the use of the word *rational*, he hammered away at the prejudices of the rich against the poor, whom the rich blame for accepting their condition.

Tone and Audience

Two other language considerations that the writer of argument must be aware of are how language conveys his or her tone and what language is appropriate to his or her audience. If the tone is serious, then the language must be serious. If the audience is educated, then the language should be educated.

SOME PRACTICE WITH THE LANGUAGE OF PERSUASION

1. Read "Letter from a Birmingham Jail" for Martin Luther King's use of language in attempting to persuade his audience—eight white Alabama ministers who had publicly disavowed his method—to accept his non–violent method of gaining civil rights for American black people.

Letter from a Birmingham Jail
Martin Luther King

I must confess that over the past few few years I have been gravely disappointed with the white moderate. I have almost reached the regrettable conclusion that the Negro's great stumbling block in his stride toward freedom is not the White Citizen's Counciler or the Ku Klux Klanner, but the white moderate, who is more devoted to ''order'' than to justice; who prefers a negative peace which is the absence of tension to a positive peace which is the presence of justice; who constantly says: ''I agree with you in the goal you seek, but I cannot agree with your methods of direct action''; who paternalistically believes he can set the timetable for another man's freedom; who lives by a mythical concept of time and who constantly advises the Negro to wait for a ''more convenient season.'' Shallow understanding from people of good will is more frustrating than absolute misunderstanding from people of ill will. Lukewarm acceptance is much more bewildering than outright rejection.

I had hoped that the white moderate would understand that law and order exist for the purpose of establishing justice and that when they fail in this purpose they become the dangerously structured dams that block the flow of social progress. I had hoped that the white moderate would understand that the present tension in the South is a necessary phase of the transition from an obnoxious negative peace, in which the Negro passively accepted his unjust plight, to a substantive and positive peace, in which all men will respect the dignity and worth of human personality. Actually, we who engage in nonviolent direct action are not the creators of tension. We merely bring to the surface the hidden tension that is already alive. We bring it out in the open, where it can be seen and dealt with. Like a boil that can never be cured so long as it is covered up but must be opened with all its ugliness to the natural medicines of air and light, injustice must be exposed, with all the tension its exposure creates, to the light of human conscience and the air of national opinion before it can be cured.

In your statement you assert that our actions, even though peaceful, must be condemned because they precipitate violence. But is this a logical assertion? Isn't this like condemning a robbed man because his possession of money precipitated the evil act of robbery? Isn't this like condemning Socrates because his unswerving commitment to truth and his philosophical inquiries precipitated the act by the misguided populace in which they made him drink hemlock? Isn't this like condemning Jesus because his unique God-consciousness and never-ceasing devotion to God's will precipitated the evil act of crucifixion? We must come to see that, as the federal courts have consistently affirmed, it is wrong to urge an individual to cease his efforts to gain his basic constitutional rights because the quest may precipitate violence. Society must protect the robbed and punish the robber.

I had also hoped that the white moderate would reject the myth concerning time in relation to the struggle for freedom. I have just received a letter from a white brother in Texas. He writes: "All Christians know that the colored people will receive equal rights eventually, but it is possible that you are in too great a religious hurry. It has taken Christianity almost two thousand years to accomplish what it has. The teachings of Christ take time to come to earth." Such an attitude stems from a tragic misconception of time, from the strangely irrational notion that there is something in the very flow of time that will inevitably cure all ills. Actually, time itself is neutral; it can be used either destructively or constructively. More and more I feel that the people of ill will have used time much more effectively than have the people of good will. We will have to repent in this generation not merely for the hateful words and actions of the bad people but for the appalling silence of the good people. Human progress never rolls in on wheels of inevitability; it comes through the tireless efforts of men willing to be co-workers with God, and without this hard work, time itself becomes an ally of the forces of social stagnation. We must use time creatively, in the knowledge that the time is always ripe to do right. Now is the time to make real the promise of democracy and transform our pending national elegy into a creative psalm of brotherhood. Now is the time to lift our national policy from the quicksand of racial injustice to the solid rock of human dignity.

You speak of our activity in Birmingham as extreme. At first I was rather disappointed that fellow clergymen would see my nonviolent efforts as those of an extremist. I began thinking about the fact that I stand in the middle of two opposing forces in the Negro community. One is a force of complacency, made up in part of Negroes who, as a result of long years of oppression, are so drained of self-respect and a sense of "somebodiness" that they have adjusted to segregation; and in part of a few middle-class Negroes who, because of a degree of academic and economic security and because in some ways they profit by segregation, have become insensitive to the problems of the masses. The other force is one of bitterness and hatred, and it comes perilously close to advocating violence. It is expressed in the various black nationalist groups that are springing up across the nation, the largest and best-known being Elijah Muhammad's Muslim movement. Nourished by the Negro's frustration over the continued existence of racial discrimination, this movement is made up of people who have lost faith in America, who have absolutely repudiated Christianity, and who have concluded that the white man is an incorrigible "devil."

I have tried to stand between these two forces, saying that we need emulate neither the "do-nothingism" of the complacent nor the hatred and despair of the black nationalist. For there is the more excellent way of love and nonviolent protest. I am grateful to God that, through the influence of the Negro church, the way of nonviolence became an integral part of our struggle.

If this philosophy had not emerged, by now many streets of the South would, I am convinced, be flowing with blood. And I am further convinced that if our white brothers dismiss as "rabble-rousers" and "outside agitators" those of us who employ nonviolent direct action, and if they refuse to support our nonviolent efforts, millions of Negroes will, out of frustration and despair, seek solace and security in black-nationalist ideologies—a development that would inevitably lead to a frightening racial nightmare.

Oppressed people cannot remain oppressed forever. The yearning for freedom eventually manifests itself, and that is what has happened to the American Negro. Something within has reminded him of his birthright of freedom, and something without has reminded him that it can be gained. Consciously or unconsciously, he has been caught up by the *Zeitgeist,* and with his black brothers of Africa and his brown and yellow brothers of Asia, South America and the Caribbean, the United States Negro is moving with a sense of great urgency toward the promised land of racial justice. If one recognizes this vital urge that has engulfed the Negro community, one should readily understand why public demonstrations are taking place. The Negro has many pent-up resentments and latent frustrations and he must release them. So let him march; let him make prayer pilgrimages to the city hall; let him go on freedom rides—and try to understand why he must do so. If his repressed emotions are not released in nonviolent ways, they will seek expression through violence; this is not a threat but a fact of history. So I have not said to my people: "Get rid of your discontent." Rather, I have tried to say that this normal and healthy discontent can be channeled into the creative outlet of nonviolent direct action. And now this approach is being termed extremist.

But though I was initially disappointed at being categorized as an extremist, as I continued to think about the matter I gradually gained a measure of satisfaction from the label. Was not Jesus an extremist for love: "Love your enemies, bless them that curse you, do good to them that hate you, and pray for them which despitefully use you, and persecute you." Was not Amos an extremist for justice: "Let justice roll down like the waters and righteousness like an ever-flowing stream." Was not Paul an extremist for the Christian gospel: "I bear in my body the marks of the Lord Jesus." Was not Martin Luther an extremist: "Here I stand; I cannot do otherwise, so help me God." And John Bunyan: "I will stay in jail to the end of my days before I make a butchery of my conscience." And Abraham Lincoln: "This nation cannot survive half slave and half free." And Thomas Jefferson: "We hold these truths to be self-evident, that all men are created equal . . . " So the question is not whether we will be extremists, but what kind of extremists we will be. Will we be extremists for hate or for love? Will we be extremists for the preservation of injustice or for the extension of justice? In that dramatic scene on Calvary's hill three men were crucified. We must never forget that all three were crucified for the same crime—the crime of extremism. Two were extremists for immorality, and thus fell below their environment. The other, Jesus Christ, was an extremist for love, truth and goodness, and thereby rose above his environment. Perhaps the South, the nation and the world are in dire need of creative extremists.

I had hoped that the white moderate would see this need. Perhaps I was too optimistic; perhaps I expected too much. I suppose I should have realized that few members of the oppressor race can understand the deep groans and passionate yearnings of the oppressed race, and still fewer have the vision to see that injustice must be rooted out by strong, persistent and determined action. I am thankful, however, that some of our white brothers in the South have grasped the meaning of this social revolution and committed themselves to it. They are still all too few in quantity, but they are big in quality. Some—such as Ralph McGill, Lillian Smith, Harry Golden, James McBride Dabbs, Ann Braden and Sarah Patton Boyle—have written about our struggle in eloquent and prophetic terms. Others have marched with us down nameless streets of the South. They have languished in filthy, roach-infested jails, suffering the abuse and brutality of policemen who view them as "dirty nigger-lovers." Unlike so many of their moderate brothers and sisters, they have recognized the urgency of the moment and sensed the need for powerful "action" antidotes to combat the disease of segregation.

a. What are the logical components of King's argument? Are they primarily inductive, deductive, or a combination? Did he appeal to a higher priority in refuting his opposition? If so, what higher priority did he establish?

b. What was his attitude toward his audience? How did this attitude affect his tone? What words and phrases indicate what his tone is?

c. King made extensive use of connotative language. What connotative meanings do phrases like the following have, and how do they make an emotional appeal for his argument: "obnoxious negative peace," "unjust plight," "deep groans and passionate yearnings," "dignity and worth of human personality," "prayer pilgrimages," "creative extremists," and "strong, persistent and determined action"?

d. His letter also abounds in figurative language and allusions. What are some of the many metaphors he used? What are some of the allusions? What effects were these intended to have on his readers? Some of his metaphors are clichés like "the time is always ripe." Why would King use clichés in writing to this audience?

e. Repetition is another key element in King's appeal to his reader's emotions. Point out an instance of this repetition and discuss its usefulness.

f. King also presented his argument in categorical statements. Which do you think are most effective in arousing the reader?

g. Where did King insert logical terms, either to denigrate his opponent's use of reason or to support his own logic? How important a role does this type of emotional appeal play? Explain.

h. How did King's audience's frame of reference affect his choice of words? How would his persuasive language have changed if he had been writing to a group of U.S. Senators?

2. Choose one of the following enthymemes and develop it in a paragraph or two. Once you are satisfied with the logic of your argument, revise it by using one or more of the methods of persuasive language. Write to your audience and convey your tone clearly:

Leisure time affects the quality of life more than does work because that is when we have an opportunity to think.

Everyone should participate in games because games can teach us how to compete gracefully.

Stress must be dealt with because it is a constant in modern life.

3. Discuss the use of persuasive language by the framers of the Declaration of Independence (pp. 293–296). Compare and contrast their use of such language with that of Martin Luther King. How can you account for any substantial differences?

REWRITING

Obtaining Feedback on Your Rough Draft

Because persuasive writing depends more on audience response than does any other type of writing, the feedback that you receive on your rough draft will be crucial to the success of your final product. Therefore you must solicit the most thoughtful response. Whether this response comes from your "other, critical self," a peer group, or your instructor, the respondent should play to the best of his or her ability the role that you have established for your audience.

In playing the role of your audience, your respondent should know your audience's frame of reference and their point of view on your subject. He or she should be willing to defend your audience's position in order to elicit from you the most effective argument possible. He or she may indicate to you, for example, that you have not appealed to the most telling higher priority and will need to reevaluate the basis of your argument.

You will want to analyze also how your audience has responded to your language and tone, to your evidence, and to your refutation. At some point, your reader(s) should also switch sides and tell you how to better defend your own position.

Try answering the questions of the "Audience Response Guide" for the student essay on bodybuilding (see pp. 297–298) before you rewrite your essay.

─────── AUDIENCE RESPONSE GUIDE ───────

1. **What does the writer want to say in this paper? What is her or his purpose in writing? What does she or he want the paper to mean?**
2. **How does this paper affect the audience for which it was intended?**
3. **How effective has the writer been in conveying her or his purpose and meaning?**
4. **How should the paper be revised to better fulfill its purpose and meaning?**

The student who wrote the rough draft on "Bodybuilding: The Shape of the Future" obtained the following comments from her peer evaluation group:

1. They knew that she was arguing that because bodybuilding is a necessity to all who are conscious of their appearance and their health, women should pursue the sport.

2. As readers of *Redbook Magazine,* her audience felt that the writer had bridged the gap between the images in the media of the bodybuilding woman as an unattractive athlete, on the one hand, and as a sexual athlete, on the other. They felt her concern about both health and appearance was very convincing.

3. Her readers were impressed by her authoritative, yet friendly presentation. They liked the chair analogy, but they felt the paragraphs in the body of the essay were too short and choppy and suggested she rearrange her material on the different elements of the bodybuilder's routine.

4. They were curious about how bodybuilding relates to the women's movement. They also wanted to be reassured that they would not grow "big" muscles.

How do these comments compare with those that you made? Here is the student's revised draft.

BODYBUILDING: THE SHAPE OF THE FUTURE

I am a female bodybuilder who has been actively engaged in body-building for many years. When you hear the word <u>bodybuilding,</u> the first image that probably comes to mind is a man who is clumsy or muscle-bound and a woman who looks manly. Although some people's attitudes have changed, most are still unaware of the benefits of body-building. Bodybuilding has become more than a sport—it has become a way of life. A woman bodybuilder does not lose any of her femininity; she gains sexuality.

In the past, the woman's place was in the home. She was expected to grow up, get married, have babies, clean, cook, and turn into the all-American frumpy housewife. Well, times have changed; more women have their own careers and goals. Along with career changes have come changes in how women feel about themselves and their bodies. More and more women are discovering bodybuilding as a way of staying fit and youthful.

What would you rather have, fat or muscle? A shapely, firm body or a spongy, saggy one? I am sure everyone would choose muscle and a shapely, firm body. That is the best reason to start bodybuilding. Don't sit back and accept saggy, cellulite bodies as part of nature. And you won't gain large, manly muscles. A woman's level of testosterone, the hormone that causes men to grow large muscles, is generally one tenth that of a man's. Though a woman's muscular strength grows from weightlifting, she does not gain the muscle bulk of the man. Yet she does gain a strong, sleek, sexy body.

Because bodybuilding has long been considered a man's sport, one thinks of bodybuilders as clumsy and muscle-bound, but in reality, bodybuilders build their agility along with their muscles. It is important for a bodybuilder to be agile and flexible in order to prevent injuries.

The program for physical fitness can be compared to a chair. One of the legs on the chair is stretching exercises. Stretching exercises increase flexibility and minimize injuries. These exercises help to keep you agile. The second leg is aerobic exercises. Aerobic exercises are running, swimming, and cycling. These exercises strengthen your cardiovascular system, resulting in keeping a strong heart. The third leg is weight training. These exercises increase your strength and power and give you a defined, firm body. The fourth leg is nutrition. Nutrition is essential in keeping our bodies healthy. You need all four legs to hold up the chair. If one is missing, the chair will fall. And so if one of these components is missing from your routine, then you are not totally fit.

The four legs on the chair of health are part of every bodybuilder's routine; therefore bodybuilders are specimens of perfectly fit human beings. Bodybuilders are fit in all areas, such as strength, agility, flexibility, and muscular and cardiovascular endurance. They are not into just lifting weights. They are totally dedicated to diet and exercise. As men and women develop their physiques, psychological effects also occur, such as self-esteem, confidence, and a new outlook on life.

What changes did the writer make in her rough draft? How can you account for them? What further changes would you suggest that she might make?

Now is the time to revise your own rough draft. With your audience response in mind, perform the necessary functions of revision, adding, cutting, rearranging, distributing, or substituting material in order to develop a better essay.

Once you have revised for content, edit your essay for sentence structure, grammar, and mechanics.

Another essay has been completed.

BECOMING AWARE OF YOURSELF AS A WRITER

1. In presenting your argument, did you convince your audience of your point of view? What methods did you use to convince your audience? How could you have been more convincing? How can you be more convincing in the future?

2. How were you able to use logic in arguing your points? How were you able to achieve sincerity? What effect did your logic and sincerity have on your audience?

3. How were you able to use such elements of language as connotation, metaphor, allusion, and repetition to argue your points effectively?

4. From your work with the techniques of persuasion, can you imagine how such techniques can be misused and abused by those seeking to sell a product or to persuade at any cost? Do you feel more powerful as a writer now that you have begun to develop persuasive skills yourself?

5. What have you learned about responding to the arguments of others by fulfilling this task? How might you argue a particular point differently from how you have argued it in the past?

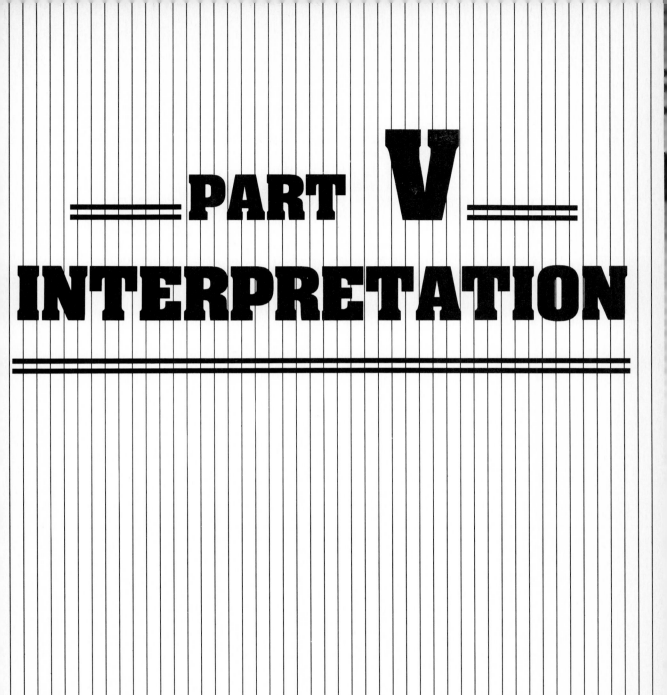

PART V
INTERPRETATION

INTRODUCTION

The act of interpretation is complex. Think, for example, of the problems you face when you want your parents to understand why you like the music of a particular rock star. First, you have to express your own reactions to the music—how you feel about it. Then, you have to explore how and why the music gives you positive feelings. After that, you must explain the music's effect on you in terms your parents can understand. Having done so, you will have put together a convincing explanation of how the rock star's music can be more fully appreciated. You will have put together a piece of critical interpretation.

In Chapter 9, we will ask you to read and then to write a critical interpretation of some poetry. While the paper you write will be primarily explanatory, you will first need to express your feelings about the poetry and then develop a persuasive explanation by exploring the reasons for the effect that the poetry has on you. You will need, in short, to combine many of the skills of expression, exposition, and persuasion that you have learned in the previous chapters.

9

WRITING ABOUT POETRY

PURPOSE

In this chapter, we will ask you to write about poetry. You may write to express your most immediate reactions to and feelings about a poem you have read; you may write to explain or argue something about the poem. But however you choose to approach a piece of poetry, you are looking at and writing about a type of writing that has a purpose somewhat different from that of expressive, expository, or persuasive prose.

More than other types of writing, poetry calls attention to itself as language. Although words are only signs for things and not the things themselves, in literature and especially in poetry the word and the thing become fused in the reader's experience. For example, look at the following poem:

Danse Russe

William Carlos Williams

If when my wife is sleeping
and the baby and Kathleen
are sleeping
and the sun is a flame-white disc
in silken mists

> above shining trees,—
> if I in my north room
> dance naked, grotesquely
> before my mirror
> waving my shirt round my head
> and singing softly to myself:
> "I am lonely, lonely,
> I was born to be lonely,
> I am best so!"
> If I admire my arms, my face,
> my shoulders, flanks, buttocks
> against the yellow drawn shades,—
>
> Who shall say I am not
> the happy genius of my household?

In this poem, the speaker tells us about himself and about his attitude toward the role he plays in his household. He might have written an expressive essay, perhaps developing the narrative component of his poem, telling the story of an incident when, naked, he sang softly to himself in front of a mirror. Or he might have written an essay to explain the meaning of his actions or to argue their validity. Instead, he wrote a poem. If we seek to understand the poem by focusing only on its subject or its speaker or even its possible audience, we ignore what may be its primary reason for being a poem: to convey to us the power and beauty embodied within the patterns and structures of language.

Why did Williams call the sun a "flame-white disc/in silken mists"? Why did he set up the off-rhyme between the words *disc* and *mists?* Why does the phrase "in silken mists" merit a separate line? These are questions whose answers might increase our understanding of the poem's effect on us. They are questions that focus on the imagery, the rhyme, and the rhythm of the poet's language.

What we would like to encourage you to do in this chapter is to look at language with an attentiveness that was not asked of you before. In other writing tasks, you have focused on clearly delineated rhetorical situations. But in reading and writing about literature, you may feel the need to transcend the limitations of the rhetorical triangle of writer, subject, and audience. In responding to a poem, as to a story or a play, you may feel a heightened sensitivity to the essential resources of language itself, such as metaphor or irony and sarcasm. You may sense an extra dimension of expressiveness, a revelation of the possibilities of human creativity that renders any analysis of the literary work tentative and incomplete. No explanation of a Shakespearean sonnet, however ingenious or sensitive to its powerful compression of thought and feeling, seems to substitute completely for a direct experience of the poem itself; an explanation based on a response to the imagery, the rhyme, and the rhythm of its language, though, may illuminate those aspects of the sonnet that distinguish it most significantly from other forms of expression to which the poet might have resorted.

The task for this chapter, then, asks you to write a number of responses to poems, responses that will, we hope, demonstrate an increasing sensitivity to, and awareness of, the complexities and the expressive possibilities of imaginative language. To generate ideas for such a task, you will need to ask questions not only about the subjects or the speakers of the poems but also about the tools of language used by the poets to make the poems.

GENERATING IDEAS: FIGURATIVE LANGUAGE

There are many different questions that you might ask about a particular poem you have read in order to deepen your understanding and appreciation of it. You might ask questions about the speaker of the poem and about his or her voice, situation, and intended audience. You might ask questions about the poem's themes, about the thoughts and feelings it reflects, or about the poem's structure, such as why it begins and ends the way it does. Or you might ask questions about the language used by the poet.

In this section, we want to introduce you to some selected elements of language that you might examine in any poem that you wish to write about. Asking questions about how and why a poet has used one or more of these elements in a poem should help you to generate ideas for writing intelligently about the poem.

Analogy

Much of our thinking centers on making connections between objects and ideas. In order to explain one thing, we frequently bring in an apparently unrelated thing that, on examination, reveals itself to be remarkably linked to the original subject. For example, if we want to indicate that one person is overly dependent on another person, we might say that the first person uses the second "like a crutch." Seeing this connection may give us a greater understanding of the subject. In making this connection, of course, we are making an analogy.

One view of the human mind is that it works as a prolific analogy-making machine, creating analogies or likenesses through its language-generating capacities. Ordinary speech, dreams, advertising, poetry—all are part of this process of analogy production. It is so common a characteristic of everyday speech that we are usually unaware of its presence. When we stand "at the head of the stairs" or speak of the "limbs of a tree," we don't give any thought to the sources of this language. Many of our most common expressions or inherited sayings contain vivid analogies that now seem puzzling, or at least strange enough so that their original analogical connections need to be explained. "Keep your nose to the grindstone" seems simple enough. But what does "Strike while the iron is hot" mean? Perhaps it suggests a berserk housewife taking revenge for her unwanted household labors. Or a group of dissatisfied garment workers staging an unannounced walkout (a "wildcat strike" itself being an example of a common analogical expression). Once we know that the analogy refers to the blacksmith's forge and the need to heat the iron to a sufficient degree before it can be shaped, we understand how this expression refers to timeliness and the need to seize an opportunity (another analogy) when it arises.

The term *figurative* itself suggests some special analogical connection between the potentialities of human speech and the body, the human figure. In Sophocles' *Oedipus the King*, the Sphinx poses the riddle "What walks on four legs in the morning, two legs in the afternoon, and three in the evening?" Oedipus' answer is "Man," because humans crawl on all fours as infants, walk upright on two legs in the prime of life, and then require a cane in old age. In his ability to see through the riddle by recognizing the basic likeness between the times of the day and the stages of human life, Oedipus reveals himself to be a superior interpreter of analogy.

It is perhaps through the Bible that we become most familiar with how analogical language is used to reveal some profound knowledge of human experience that would be restricted in meaning if expressed in literal terms. In the New Testament account of Matthew, Christ combines storytelling with figurative language to create parables that explain in a simple, homely narrative context the mysterious workings of God. Here is the narrative traditionally called the Parable of the Talents (a talent is a substantial amount of gold):

14 For the kingdom of heaven is as a man travelling into a far country, who called his own servants, and delivered unto them his goods.

15 And unto one he gave five talents, to another two, and to another one: to every man according to his several ability; and straightway took his journey.

16 Then he that had received the five talents went and traded with the same, and made them other five talents.

17 And likewise he that had received two, he also gained other two.

18 But he that had received one went and digged in the earth, and hid his lord's money.

19 After a long time the lord of those servants cometh, and reckoneth with them.

20 And so he that had received five talents came and brought other five talents, saying, Lord, thou deliveredst unto me five talents: behold, I have gained beside them five talents more.

21 His lord said unto him, Well done, thou good and faithful servant: thou hast been faithful over a few things, I will make thee ruler over many things: enter thou into the joy of thy lord.

22 He also that had received two talents came and said, Lord, thou deliveredst unto me two talents: behold, I have gained two other talents beside them.

23 His lord said unto him, Well done, good and faithful servant; thou hast been faithful over a few things, I will make thee ruler over many things: enter thou into the joy of thy lord.

24 Then he which had received the one talent came and said, Lord, I knew thee that thou art an hard man, reaping where thou hast not sown, and gathering where thou hast not strewed:

25 And I was afraid, and went and hid thy talent in the earth: lo, there thou hast that is thine.

26 His lord answered and said unto him, Thou wicked and slothful servant, thou knewest that I reap where I sowed not, and gather where I have not strewed:

27 Thou oughtest therefore to have put my money to the exchangers, and then at my coming I should have received mine own with usury.

28 Take therefore the talent from him, and give it unto him which hath ten talents.

29 For unto every one that hath shall be given, and he shall have abundance: but from him that hath not shall be taken away even that which he hath.

30 And cast ye the unprofitable servant into outer darkness: there shall be weeping and gnashing of teeth.

Christ informs his listeners that his story has a concrete meaning: the Kingdom of Heaven can be compared to this sequence of responses of the servants to their lord. The first two servants report success in their use of the talents given to them; the third reports that he has buried his gold, and he is punished for his lack of productivity. The modern reader, aware that the word *talent* denotes a natural aptitude or skill, applies the word figuratively within the context of the narrative. The result is that the story means more than it says; it must be completed by the listener or the reader, who has, in effect, participated in creating the fuller, richer meaning of the story by applying it to himself or herself, or to the possibilities of human experience.

Metaphor and Simile

In poems, the most important use of figurative language may be embodied in metaphor. We have noted in the "Focus" sections of Chapters 6 and 8 that a metaphor is an implied comparison between dissimilar things. In Shakespeare's lines "In me thou seest the twilight of such day/As after sunset fadeth in the west," a metaphor is established comparing the age of the speaker to the end of a day. Perhaps because of the imaginative range of this particular type of trope, or figure of speech, the term *metaphorical* has come to represent figurative language in general. In fact, *metaphor* is almost synonymous with poetic language itself.

Another kind of figure, the simile, is usually linked with metaphor. The simile makes a literal likeness between objects because it joins them with the explicit sign of *as* or *like:*

> This City now doth, like a garment, wear
> The beauty of the morning . . .
> —William Wordsworth

My love is like a red, red rose
That's newly sprung in June,

—Robert Burns

Metonymy

Another term frequently discussed along with metaphor is *metonymy*. In this figure, two terms are linked because of their close association. In the expression "The pen is mightier than the sword" the word *pen,* which refers to the act of writing, and *sword,* which refers to warfare, are both examples of metonymy. One explanation of the human imagination, particularly as it operates in the creation of dreams, is that it works either through metaphor (the substitution of one thing for another) or through metonymy (in which one image generates a series of other images through close association). This version of the human imagination theorizes that the mind is itself structured like a language, obeying the tendency to generate either metaphor or metonymy.

Personification

In personification, an animal, an abstract idea, or an inanimate object is given human characteristics to make the unfamiliar more familiar. In his sonnet "Since There's No Help, Come Let Us Kiss and Part," written in 1619, Michael Drayton used personification to dramatize the hopelessness of his former love relationship, which he actually wishes to revitalize by the end of the poem. Drayton personified love, passion, faith, and innocence to make these abstractions more vivid and dramatic. Indeed, in the poem these personifications almost become characters acting out a dramatic scene.

Since There's No Help

Michael Drayton

Since there's no help, come let us kiss and part.
  Nay, I have done; you get no more of me,
And I am glad, yea, glad with all my heart,
  That thus so cleanly I myself can free;
Shake hands for ever, cancel all our vows,
  And when we meet at any time again,
Be it not seen in either of our brows
  That we one jot of former love retain.
Now at the last gasp of Love's latest breath,
  When, his pulse failing, Passion speechless lies,
  When Faith is kneeling by his bed of death,
  And Innocence is closing up his eyes,
    Now if thou wouldst, when all have given him over,
    From death to life thou mightst him yet recover.

Symbol

The term *symbol* refers to a kind of metaphor, in which no specific comparison is intended. For example, in William Blake's poem "The Sick Rose," published in 1794, the rose carries some of its traditional associations with erotic love and female beauty.

The Sick Rose

William Blake

O Rose thou art sick
The invisible worm
That flies in the night
In the howling storm:

Has found out thy bed
Of crimson joy:
And his dark secret love
Does thy life destroy.

The poem's suggestion of destructive passion in the phrases "invisible worm" and "dark secret love" makes this a disturbing and confusing expression of what is usually a predictable and unthreatening image: a rose. Because of this uncertainty, this deliberate contradiction of the context in which we usually place this object, it takes on the nature of the symbolic. Perhaps Blake was isolating a specific instance of destructive eroticism; or possibly he was creating a poetic world in which both the aggressor and its object are consumed by the very nature of desire. Because we can't really be sure what the poem means—its brevity makes it similar to a riddle or an epigram—we are given the interpretive freedom that the term *symbol* implies. For the modern poet, this freedom has often meant the possibility of removing the constraints of conventional meaning in order to create in language a more suggestive, more imaginative form of expression. And of course, this increased complexity means that the reader must work harder to derive from the poem all that it has to offer.

Imagery

A poet uses the elements of figurative language to create images, pictures that combine with the sounds of the poem (its rhythm, meter, and rhyme) in order to convey the poet's meaning. We respond visually to an image because it pictures something that we can see concretely (*strong as an oak tree*). But an image also may speak to our sense of touch (*soft as a feather*), sound (*loud as a fire alarm*), smell (*foul as garbage*), or taste (*sweet as honey*). In the lines by Burns quoted in the section on metaphor and simile, the rose is a romantic image that pictures how young and beautiful the speaker's beloved is.

Irony

In Blake's poem "The Sick Rose," the image of the rose contradicts the inherited romantic associations that we have with this flower. Here, the apparent incongruity, the distance that separates what we already know about roses from what we perceive of *this* rose, creates a sense of irony. When a phrase or an image is ironic, its literal or assumed meaning is undercut by an implied meaning, one that either the reader or the speaker did not anticipate. Irony often accounts for some of our most important reading or viewing experiences. It gives us insight into the illusions that dramatic or fictional characters create for themselves, for the reader or audience may know what really *is* while the characters see only what *seems*. Oedipus, for example, dedicates himself relentlessly to finding a murderer who turns out to be himself.

SOME PRACTICE WITH FIGURATIVE LANGUAGE

1. In your journal, note your responses to your reading of poems, stories, and plays. Note what interests you, what reminds you of other real or fictional characters whom you have experienced, what questions or doubts you have about certain parts of works or the whole works, and what ironies or complexities you have observed. Use your journal materials as a source of ideas for your work on the task given later in this chapter.

2. Find examples of metaphorical language in the popular media. For what purpose is this language used? How does the writer make sure the reader will understand this language? How original or fresh is this language?

3. Because irony is determined by context, create a verbal context that would make the following statements ironic:

   a. Mr Wadsworth, you certainly are a genius.
   b. Yeah, the little woman is crazy about me.
   c. This is indeed an auspicious occasion.
   d. The grave's a fine and private place,
      But none, I think, do there embrace.
   e. Look on my works, Ye mighty, and despair!

4. Identify and explain the figurative language used in the following lines of poetry; evaluate the effectiveness of each image:

   a. Let not Ambition mock their useful toil,
       Their homely joys and destiny obscure;

> Nor Grandeur hear with a disdainful smile
> > The short and simple annals of the poor.
>
> > > —**Thomas Gray**
>
> b. There is a garden in her face,
> > Where roses and white lilies grow;
> A heavenly paradise is that place,
> > Wherein all pleasant fruits do flow.
>
> > > —**Thomas Campion**
>
> c. I am a part of all that I have met;
> Yet all experience is an arch wherethrough
> Gleams that untraveled world whose margin fades
> Forever and forever when I move.
>
> > > —**Alfred Tennyson**
>
> d. Like as the waves make towards the pebbled shore,
> So do our minutes hasten to their end,
> Each changing place with that which goes before,
> In sequent° toil all forwards do contend.   *succeeding*
> Nativity, once in the main of light,
> Crawls to maturity, wherewith being crowned,
> Crooked eclipses 'gainst his glory fight,
> And Time that gave doth now his gift confound.
> Time doth transfix the flourish set on youth
> And delves the parallels in beauty's brow,
> Feeds on the rarities of nature's truth,
> And nothing stands but for his scythe to mow.
> And yet to times in hope my verse shall stand,
> Praising thy worth, despite his cruel hand.
>
> > > —**William Shakespeare**

5. Compare the use of figurative language in the following two poems by answering the questions after each poem:

Psalm 23

Old Testament

The Lord is my shepherd; I shall not want.

2 He maketh me to lie down in green pastures: he leadeth me beside the still waters.

3 He restoreth my soul: he leadeth me into the paths of righteousness for his name's sake.

4 Yea, though I walk through the valley of the shadow of death, I will fear no evil: for thou art with me; thy rod and thy staff they comfort me.

5 Thou preparest a table for me in the presence of mine enemies: thou annointest my head with oil; my cup runneth over.

6 Surely goodness and mercy shall follow me all the days of my life: and I will dwell in the house of the Lord for ever.

a. How does the speaker see himself in relation to God? Why does he choose the shepherd metaphor?

b. Compare this speaker's tone of voice to Donne's in his poem "Batter My Heart, Three-Personed God":

Batter My Heart

John Donne

Batter my heart, three-personed God; for You
As yet but knock, breathe, shine, and seek to mend;
That I may rise and stand, o'erthrow me, and bend
Your force to break, blow, burn, and make me new.
I, like an usurped town, to another due,
Labor to admit You, but O, to no end;
Reason, Your viceroy in me, me should defend,
But is captíved, and proves weak or untrue.
Yet dearly I love You, and would be lovéd fain
But am betrothed unto Your enemy.
Divorce me, untie or break that knot again;
Take me to You, imprison me, for I,
Except You enthrall me, never shall be free,
Nor ever chaste, except You ravish me.

a. What metaphor is used in lines 1–4?

b. What is the metaphor expressed in lines 5–10?

c. A paradox is a true statement that nevertheless seems to contradict itself. What is the paradox in line 3? Line 14? Are they related?

d. What kind of relationship between mortals and God does Donne express in this poem? How does it compare with the relationship between mortals and God expressed in Psalm 23?

AUDIENCE: THE INFORMED READER

In Chapter 3, you wrote for your teacher in order to experiment with the problem of bridging the gap between yourself and someone whose perspective and ideas on your subject might be quite different from your own. Now we would like you to think about writing for someone who, like your teacher, is informed about a particular field of knowledge. If you are writing a paper for your English teacher about a poem assigned in class, for example, you are writing for an audience that probably knows more about your subject than you do. Indeed, this is usually the case when you write a paper in school. The problem you thus face is not how to bridge the gap between yourself and someone whose interests might be different from yours; in this case, you share your interest in the subject with your reader. Rather, your problem is how to present your own insights into the subject so that your reader, who has already studied the subject, might be interested in and perhaps even enlightened by your views.

On the one hand, you want to try to find something original to say about your subject; your own authentic response may be the one piece of information that you can provide that will be new to your reader. On the other hand, you want to impress your audience with your ability to write about the subject with some knowledge of the issues and to use accurately the vocabulary employed by others in the field; you want to keep your focus not on your response to the subject per se but on what your response contributes to a better understanding of the subject.

As an example of how you might accomplish this, let's consider more specifically how you might write about a poem in order to offer an interpretation that might be read with interest by someone who has more experience in the study of literature than you have.

It is important, of course, to determine just what you think and/or feel about the subject—in this case, a poem. Writing a series of responses to your subject in your journal over a number of days is one possible way to get started. Free writing about your subject is another. But however you go about clarifying your own most immediate ideas, keep in mind that you are not simply going to write expressively about your subject.

It is equally if not more important that you determine what your response helps you to understand about the subject. The more effectively you can explain this, in fact, the more appeal your writing will probably hold for an informed audience. In the case of a poem, you might ask what sort of things the poet has done with language in order to evoke a particular response. Such a question takes you into matters of meaning and technique, but with a limited focus because you are not concerned with explaining everything that the poem might mean or with analyzing all of the techniques that the poet has used. Rather, you are concerned with focusing on how a particular meaning emerges from the poem in a particular way.

Focusing on a particular aspect of a poem is not necessarily easy to do, especially for someone without much practice at it. Reading a poem can be, as you may well know, difficult. The words of a poem written in English may sound familiar, but the way that they work together to create meaning may be puzzling or strange. One poet has likened poetry to dancing. Dancing is similar in many ways to walking, but it is a more conscious activity that requires a knowledge of dance steps, a set of accepted conventions that control your physical movements but free you to express and enjoy the pure pleasure of movement to music. In reading poetry, you learn to enjoy the beauty and expressiveness of language by becoming familiar with the ways in which poets have worked with such conventions of their art as the use of figurative language. In writing about poetry for readers already accustomed to poetry's conventions, one strategy you can take is to focus on the effects of a poet's use of one or more of these conventions.

There also are a number of things that you should probably avoid doing when you write for such an audience. It will serve little purpose, for example, simply to summarize the poem, as your reader can be expected to be familiar with it already. Similarly, a lengthy explanation of historical background or a mechanical counting of a poem's images or poetic devices is not likely to be of much interest to your reader unless it really contributes to an increased understanding of the poem. Although you may need to remind your reader of any one of these things in order to illustrate a point, you do not simply want to list things that your reader knows well enough already.

Another thing that you probably want to avoid is straying too far from the poem itself into a discussion of your personal views of the issues connected with the poem. Thus, if you are writing about a love poem, your personal views on love should be offered, if at all, only to the extent that they help you to explain something about the meaning and technique of the poem. Your personal views are no doubt interesting, but the further you depart from the poem itself, from a discussion of what it says and how it says it, the less you will be contributing to your reader's appreciation of it.

In general, then, when you write on a subject for an audience with experience in that subject, keep the following thoughts in mind:

1. Limit your focus to one or two specific ideas that you have about the subject.
2. Demonstrate your familiarity with the specialized concerns and vocabulary associated with the subject.
3. Explain how your specific ideas both reflect your own understanding or appreciation and will contribute to your reader's understanding or appreciation of a limited aspect of the subject.
4. Avoid writing at length about what your reader already knows, except to the degree that you are using such information to illustrate and explain your own ideas about the subject.
5. Avoid straying from the subject itself, especially by dwelling at length on your personal views of issues associated with the subject.

SOME PRACTICE WITH WRITING FOR AN INFORMED AUDIENCE

1. How might you approach writing about each of the following topics if your audience were to be your peers?

   a. *The National Enquirer*
   b. Fraternity hazing
   c. Sibling rivalry
   d. The Great Depression
   e. The Equal Rights Amendment

Explain how your approach might change if, instead, your audience were to be a teacher with experience in a subject area associated with the topic: a journalism teacher in the case of Topic a, an anthropology teacher in the case of Topic b, a psychology teacher in the case of Topic c, an American history teacher in the case of Topic d, and a political science teacher in the case of Topic e.

2. Read the following poem, which is a traditional Scottish ballad, written anonymously:

Sir Patrick Spens

1
The king sits in Dumferling town,
   Drinking the blude-reid° wine: *blood-red*
"O whar will I get guid sailor,
   To sail this ship of mine?"

2
Up and spak an eldern knicht,
   Sat at the king's richt knee:
"Sir Patrick Spens is the best sailor
   That sails upon the sea."

3
The king has written a braid° letter   *broad*
   And signed it wi' his hand,
And sent it to Sir Patrick Spens,
   Was walking on the sand.

4
The first line that Sir Patrick read,
   A loud lauch° lauched he;   *laugh*
The next line that Sir Patrick read,
   the tear blinded his ee.°   *eye*

5
"Oh wha is this had done this deed,
   This ill deed done to me,
To send me out this time o' the year,
   To sail upon the sea?

6
"Mak haste, mak haste, my mirry men all,
    Our guid ship sails the morn."
"O say na sae,° my master dear,   *so*
    For I fear a deadly storm.

7
"Late, late yestre'en I saw the new moon
    Wi'the auld moon in hir arm,
And I fear, I fear, my dear master,
    That we will come to harm."

8
O our Scots nobles were richt laith°   *loath*
    To weet° their cork-heeled shoon,°   *wet/shoes*
But lang or° a' the play were played   *before*
    Their hats they swam aboon.

9
O lang, lang may their ladies sit,
    Wi' their fans into their hand,
Or ere they see Sir Patrick Spens
    Come sailing to the land.

10
O lang, lang may the ladies stand
    Wi' their gold kems° in their hair,   *combs*
Waiting for their ain dear lords,
    For they'll see them na mair.

11
Half o'er, half o'er to Aberdour
    It's fifty fadom deep,
And there lies guid Sir Patrick Spens
    Wi' the Scots lords at his feet.

a. Which of the following sentences might introduce a discussion of this poem
that would appeal to an informed audience? Which might not? Explain your
reasoning in each case.

1) "Sir Patrick Spens" tells about a sailor who is sent off to sea by a king in
   the middle of winter.

2) In "Sir Patrick Spens," the sailor obeys the king's order to go to sea even
   though he knows he may die.

3) The poem "Sir Patrick Spens" begins with an image of the king drinking
   wine that is described as being "blude-reid."

4) The dangers of sailing on the ocean in winter are dramatized in "Sir Patrick Spens."

b. Each of the following questions might lead to a discussion of "Sir Patrick Spens" that would appeal to an infomed audience. What answers can you develop for these questions? Can you explain why your answers might be of interest to a teacher of literature? Can you think of other questions to ask about the poem that might prove similarly effective in generating ideas that would be of interest to the informed reader?

1) This narrative poem tells its story with a good deal of economy and suggestion rather than complete explanation. What are some of the unexplained details that might puzzle a reader?

2) What kind of portrait of Sir Patrick does the poem give?

3) The storyteller provides images rather than explanation at crucial parts of the story. What images of this kind can you find? How effective are they?

4) To what kind of audience might this poem originally have appealed?

TASK: WRITING ABOUT POETRY

Your task for this chapter is to write an interpretive essay on one or more poems, an essay that will explain your own understanding and appreciation of what the poems mean and how they convey that meaning. Your instructor may suggest that you write on works chosen from the selection of poems in this chapter or on other poems introduced in class. Although you may begin simply by keeping a record in your journal of your initial impressions of and responses to the poems, your goal is to produce a reasoned analysis that will prove of interest to an informed audience.

Your audience most logically will be your English instructor. To hold your instructor's attention, you will want to focus on clarifying how your authentic response to the poems contributes to a better understanding of them. We suggest that you explore how particular conventions of poetry writing, especially conventions of language such as voice and imagery, affect your response to and your understanding of the poems.

In the remaining sections of this chapter, we discuss how asking questions about literary conventions, particularly conventions involving the use of figurative language, can help generate ideas about your subject; how writing for an informed audience can affect the selection and arrangement of your material; how the sounds of words in poetry are a significant aspect of their meaning; and how to revise and edit your rough draft.

WRITING THE ESSAY

Generating Ideas for Writing on a Poem

Writing about a poem is something you do in school, but it's not like the writing you are likely to do in other courses, where you may be asked to explain why the Federal Reserve Board raises or lowers interest rates, or how the genetic material in a cell is arranged. The information that you convey about a poem does not have to come from a textbook or from some other written source of authority. Although many poems make references to the cultural context of another time, requiring the reader to explain words or ideas that have lost their original reference, you don't have to fortify yourself with extensive research on a poet's life or the history of an age. Certainly the more you know about the situation in which a poem was created the more you can bring to your discussion, but of greater importance are the skills you already possess: the ability to empathize with someone else's view of humanity; to respond to a tone of voice that isn't like your own; and to test the personal vision of a poet against your own experiences of life. As reader and as writer, you choose from a unique storehouse of ideas and feelings: your own knowledge of the world based on your having been born in a particular time and place, and having lived through and responded to events that mark the individuality of your existence, yet that also link you to the common experiences of humankind.

Your first step, then, in generating ideas about a poem is simply to register your most immediate responses. We suggest that you begin with journal entries or some other technique, such as free writing, that you find helpful when you want to express your thoughts and feelings as authentically as possible. As you write down your reactions, don't be overly concerned with your ability to infer all the possible shades of meaning in the poem. Also, don't hesitate to compare the poem with others that you have read.

After you establish your initial response, it is a good idea to get to know what other readers, perhaps others in your class, have to say about the poem, and to let them know what you think. Some responses will strike you as more reasonable than others. You might want to incorporate these points of view in your next response to the poem.

This sharing of readings is important because it allows you to develop a continuing process of reading and responding to the poem undertaken by a group of inquiring minds. You can continue on your own by next recording a *process analysis* of your reactions to the poem. As discussed in Chapter 5, process analysis combines elements of narration and exposition to create an explanation that moves through a series of steps. You might, for example, record your response to a series of images in the poem, commenting as you do so on their connection to the speaker's physical or emotional state. This recording process is similar, in a way, to writing a *paraphrase* (see Chapter 7, pp. 225–228), a prose summary of the poem, but here you would be adding your own view of the role that these images play.

In writing about the poem's images, their relationship to the speaker of the poem, and to one another, you are focusing on one particular convention employed by poets. You are looking at the role that the poet's use of figurative language plays in your own understanding and appreciation of the poem, at how the poem is told and how that way of telling affects a reader's ideas about what the poem means. Asking questions about the poem's imagery is one way of generating ideas for writing about the poem. Other questions you might ask that can give you a place to begin in writing about *how* a poem is told include the following:

1. Who is speaking in the poem? What is the situation?
2. What is the tone of voice of the speaker? How is it appropriate to the situation? Does it change during the poem?
3. Is there a specific context (historical, literary, or other) that the reader needs to understand? How important is it?
4. How does the poem end? Is it a surprise, or is the ending anticipated by the speaker's earlier commentary? Does it alter a reader's view of the poem?
5. Are there any other unusual or striking characteristics of language that affect the reader's response or that contribute to the overall experience of the poem? How are they important to the poem as a whole?
6. When you reread the poem—preferably out loud—do you read it differently because of your responses to the previous questions? How would you explain your answer to this question to someone else?

Note that in looking at a poem through these questions, you are not asking at the start what the poem means thematically, what ideas it represents. Too often, when we look first for some recognizable idea or theme, such as love or war or nature, in a poem, we are tempted to discuss the theme without any concern for the imaginative way in which the particular poem expresses its ideas. Such a discussion might be interesting, but it would tell us very little about our experience of *this* poem's unique qualities. Trying to see the poem from the inside, to find out how it works as a poem, will repay you with an increased understanding of and pleasure in the play of language.

SOME PRACTICE WITH GENERATING IDEAS FOR WRITING ON A POEM

Because the task for this chapter asks you to write on one or more poems, the following works and accompanying questions seek to provide you with sufficient material for written analysis and class discussion. Use the questions as guides for identifying some key points of interpretive focus for you to direct toward your own writing, not as devices for determining "right" or "wrong" answers, as on examinations.

The Passionate Shepherd to His Love
Christopher Marlowe

Come live with me and be my love,
And we will all the pleasures prove
That valleys, groves, hills, and fields,
Woods, or steepy mountain yields.

And we will sit upon the rocks,
Seeing the shepherds feed their flocks,
By shallow rivers to whose falls
Melodious birds sing madrigals.

And I will make thee beds of roses
And a thousand fragrant posies,
A cap of flowers, and a kirtle°   *apron*
Embroidered all with leaves of myrtle;

A gown made of the finest wool
Which from our pretty lambs we pull;
Fair lined slippers for the cold,
With buckles of the purest gold;

A belt of straw and ivy buds,
With coral clasps and amber studs:
And if these pleasures may thee move,
Come live with me, and be my love.

The shepherds' swains shall dance and sing
For thy delight each May morning:
If these delights thy mind may move,
Then live with me and be my love.

The Nymph's Reply to the Shepherd
Sir Walter Ralegh

If all the world and love were young,
And truth in every shepherd's tongue,
These pretty pleasures might me move
To live with thee and be thy love.

Time drives the flocks from field to fold
When rivers rage and rocks grow cold,
And Philomel° becometh dumb;   *the nightingale*
The rest complains of cares to come.

The flowers do fade, and wanton fields
To wayward winter reckoning yields;
A honey tongue, a heart of gall,
Is fancy's spring, but sorrow's fall.

Thy gowns, thy shoes, thy beds of roses,
Thy cap, thy kirtle, and thy posies
Soon break, soon wither, soon forgotten—
In folly ripe, in reason rotten.

Thy belt of straw and ivy buds,
Thy coral clasps and amber studs,
All these in me no means can move
To come to thee and be thy love.

But could youth last and love still breed,
Had joys no date nor age no need,
Then these delights my mind might move
To live with thee and be thy love.

1. Ralegh's poem is a response to Marlowe's: Can you note how the nymph's reply diverges in tone and feeling from the invitation of the shepherd?

2. How does the shepherd describe the life he would offer his love?

3. What kind of life is this? Why did Marlowe choose a shepherd to portray the "scene" in this poem? Look up the word *pastoral* and explain its connection to this poem.

4. What can you infer about Marlowe's image of his loved one from the kinds of things he says he will give her? What do these things have in common?

5. What are the major disagreements of the nymph with the shepherd's argument? How would you characterize the nymph?

6. Contrast these views of a shepherd with the view expressed by Psalm 23.

London

William Blake

I wander thro' each charter'd street,
Near where the charter'd Thames does flow,
And mark in every face I meet
Marks of weakness, marks of woe.

In every cry of every man,
In every Infant's cry of fear,

In every voice, in every ban,
The mind-forg'd manacles I hear.

How the Chimney-sweeper's cry
Every blackning Church appalls;
And the hapless Soldier's sigh
Runs in blood down Palace walls.

But most thro' midnight streets I hear
How the youthful Harlot's curse
Blasts the new-born Infant's tear,
And blights with plagues the marriage hearse.

1. Blake repeated a number of words (*chartered, mark*) in the poem. What effect do these repetitions have on a reader?

2. What images characterized London in Blake's imagination? What was he saying about the city and its institutions through his use of such images?

3. How would you describe the speaker's tone of voice in this poem? How would you characterize the speaker?

Composed upon Westminister Bridge, September 3, 1802
William Wordsworth

Earth has not anything to show more fair:
Dull would he be of soul who could pass by
A sight so touching in its majesty;
This City now doth, like a garment, wear
The beauty of the morning; silent, bare,
Ships, towers, domes, theaters, and temples lie
Open unto the fields, and to the sky;
All bright and glittering in the smokeless air.
Never did sun more beautifully steep
In his first splendor, valley, rock, or hill;
Ne'er saw I, never felt, a calm so deep!
The river glideth at his own sweet will:
Dear God! the very houses seem asleep;
And all that mighty heart is lying still!

1. What is the effect of Wordsworth's catalog of city sights? How are they all "silent, bare," and beautiful?

2. By describing the city asleep, Wordsworth was also expressing his view of the city awake. What was that view?

3. What are the different personal feelings that Wordsworth expressed in the poem?

4. Compare Wordsworth's vision of the city with Blake's in the poem "London." How do you account for these contrasting impressions?

On My First Son

Ben Jonson

Farewell, thou child of my right hand, and joy;
My sin was too much hope of thee, loved boy:
Seven years thou wert lent to me, and I thee pay,
Exacted by thy fate, on the just day.
O could I lose all father now! for why
Will man lament the state he should envy,
To have so soon 'scaped world's and flesh's rage,
And, if no other misery, yet age?
Rest in soft peace, and asked, say, "Here doth lie
Ben Jonson his best piece of poetry."
For whose sake henceforth all his vows be such
As what he loves may never like too much.

1. How would you describe the feelings, Jonson expressed on the death of his son, Benjamin, in 1603? Would these feelings have been different if the subject had been an adult?

2. How is the feeling expressed in Line 5 different from the feelings expressed in the rest of the poem, particularly in the last line?

3. In Hebrew, *Benjamin* means "right hand." In line 1, Jonson is thus playing on the words as a means of showing his feeling for his dead son. What effect does this word-play have on the poem?

4. What can you learn about Jonson's attitude toward grief from this poem?

To His Coy Mistress

Andrew Marvell

Had we but world enough, and time,
This coyness, Lady, were no crime.
We would sit down, and think which way
To walk, and pass our long love's day.
Thou by the Indian Ganges' side
Shouldst rubies find; I by the tide

Of Humber° would complain. I would   *River in northern*
Love you ten years before the Flood,   *England*
And you should, if you please, refuse
Till the Conversion of the Jews.
My vegetable love should grow
Vaster than empires and more slow;
An hundred years should go to praise
Thine eyes, and on thy forehead gaze;
Two hundred to adore each breast,
But thirty thousand to the rest;
An age at least to every part,
And the last age should show your heart.
For, lady, you deserve this state,°   *dignity*
Nor would I love at lower rate.
   But at my back I always hear
Time's wingéd chariot hurrying near;
And yonder all before us lie
Deserts of vast eternity.
Thy beauty shall no more be found;
Nor, in thy marble vault, shall sound
My echoing song; then worms shall try
That long-preserved virginity,
And your quaint° honor turn to dust,   *oversubtle*
And into ashes all my lust:
The grave's a fine and private place,
But none, I think, do there embrace.
   Now therefore, while the youthful hue
Sits on thy skin like morning dew,
And while thy willing soul transpires°   *breathes out*
At every pore with instant fires,
Now let us sport us while we may,
And now, like amorous birds of prey,
Rather at once our time devour
Than languish in his slow-chapped° power.   *slow-jawed*
Let us roll all our strength and all
Our sweetness up into one ball,
And tear our pleasures with rough strife
Thorough the iron gates of life:
Thus, though we cannot make our sun
Stand still, yet we will make him run.

1. This poem, intended to persuade the speaker's lady friend to be his lover, is constructed more like a legal argument than a love poem. Each stanza begins with a word that sets the argument for that section:

    "Had we . . ." (really "if we had . . .")

    "But . . ."

    "Now therefore . . ."

What is the main idea in each section of the poem?

2. What tone of voice is characteristic of each section?

3. How does the speaker provide concrete images for abstractions like time and space?

4. How persuasive is the speaker? Is there anything missing from his argument? If so, how would he explain its absence?

5. For what kind of woman is this language intended?

6. What examples of irony are there? How are they used?

Channel Firing

Thomas Hardy

That night your great guns, unawares,
Shook all our coffins as we lay,
And broke the chancel window-squares,
We thought it was the Judgment-day

And sat upright. While drearisome
Arose the howl of wakened hounds:
The mouse let fall the altar-crumb,
The worms drew back into the mounds,

The glebe cow drooled. Till God called, "No;
It's gunnery practice out at sea
Just as before you went below;
The world is as it used to be:

"All nations striving strong to make
Red war yet redder. Mad as hatters
They do no more for Christés sake
Than you who are helpless in such matters.

"That this is not the judgment-hour
For some of them's a blessed thing,
For if it were they'd have to scour
Hell's floor for so much threatening. . . .

"Ha, ha. It will be warmer when
I blow the trumpet (if indeed
I ever do; for you are men,
And rest eternal sorely need)."

So down we lay again. "I wonder,
Will the world ever saner be,"
Said one, "than when He sent us under
In our indifferent century!"

And many a skeleton shook his head.
"Instead of preaching forty year,"
My neighbor Parson Thirdly said,
"I wish I had stuck to pipes and beer."

Again the guns disturbed the hour,
Roaring their readiness to avenge,
As far inland as Stourton Tower,
And Camelot, and starlit Stonehenge.

1. In what tone of voice does God speak?

2. What other voices are there in the poem?

3. How did Hardy make this a convincing view of humankind?

4. What is the significance of the place names in the last stanza?

Trying to Talk with a Man

Adrienne Rich

Perhaps my life is nothing but an image of this kind; perhaps I am doomed to retrace my steps under the illusion that I am exploring, doomed to try and learn what I should simply recognize, learning a mere fraction of what I have forgotten.   —ANDRÉ BRETON, *Nadja*

Out in this desert we are testing bombs,

that's why we came here.

Sometimes I feel an underground river
forcing its way between deformed cliffs
an acute angle of understanding
moving itself like a locus of the sun
into this condemned scenery.

What we've had to give up to get here—
whole LP collections, films we starred in
playing in the neighborhoods, bakery windows
full of dry, chocolate-filled Jewish cookies,
the language of love-letters, of suicide notes,
afternoons on the riverbank
pretending to be children

Coming out to this desert
we meant to change the face of
driving among dull green succulents
walking at noon in the ghost town
surrounded by a silence

that sounds like the silence of the place

except that it came with us
and is familiar
and everything we were saying until now
was an effort to blot it out—
Coming out here we are up against it

Out here I feel more helpless
with you than without you
You mention the danger
and list the equipment
we talk of people caring for each other
in emergencies—laceration, thirst—
but you look at me like an emergency

Your dry heat feels like power
your eyes are stars of a different magnitude
they reflect lights that spell out: EXIT
when you get up and pace the floor

talking of the danger
as if it were not ourselves
as if we were testing anything else.

1. What does *it* refer to in the line "Coming out here we are up against it"? What does *it* say about the speaker and the man she is talking to?

2. How does the quotation by the twentieth-century surrealist French poet André Breton relate to the speaker's state of mind?

3. Compare this poem with Marvell's "To His Coy Mistress." What would the speaker in one poem say about the other? How well would they understand one another?

The Oven Bird

Robert Frost

There is a singer everyone has heard,
Loud, a mid-summer and a mid-wood bird,
Who makes the solid tree trunks sound again.
He says that leaves are old and that for flowers
Mid-summer is to spring as one to ten.
He says the early petal-fall is past
When pear and cherry bloom went down in showers
On sunny days a moment overcast;
And comes that other fall we name the fall.
He says the highway dust is over all.
The bird would cease and be as other birds

But that he knows in singing not to sing.
The question that he frames in all but words
Is what to make of a diminished thing.

1. How does the poet's placement of the word *loud* affect the sense of the poem as well as the sound?

2. How is the oven bird unlike other birds?

3. What is the "other fall" the speaker refers to?

4. The last four lines are more abstract than the previous lines, which speak of concrete things like flowers, leaves, and highway dust. Coming at the end of the poem, what kind of reading attention should we give them? For example, what is meant by "a diminished thing"? Why is it that the bird "knows in singing not to sing"?

5. What other kind of singer could the speaker have in mind? Why would this singer continue singing?

The Vacuum

Howard Nemerov

The house is so quiet now
The vacuum cleaner sulks in the corner closet
Its bag limp as a stopped lung, its mouth
Grinning into the floor, maybe at my
Slovenly life, my dog-dead youth.

I've lived this way long enough,
But when my old woman died her soul
Went into that vacuum cleaner, and I can't bear
To see the bag swell like a belly, eating the dust
And the woolen mice, and begin to howl

Because there is old filth everywhere
She used to crawl, in the corner and under the stair.
I know now how life is cheap as dirt,
And still the hungry, angry heart
Hangs on and howls, biting at air.

1. What is the meaning of the title?

2. How has the death of the speaker's wife affected him?

3. How does the cliché "cheap as dirt" receive a new meaning in the poem?

4. What effect did his wife have on the speaker when she was alive?

5. What is the speaker's attitude toward the vacuum cleaner?

6. How does alliteration, the repetition of initial consonant sounds, function in the last two lines?

7. Compare this poem with Jonson's "On My First Son." Are there any similarities of tone or figurative language?

Writing on Poetry for an Informed Audience

In the previous section, we suggested that one possible step you might take to generate ideas about a poem is to write a process analysis in which you record your response to a particular aspect of the poem, to a particular convention or set of conventions used by the poet. To make the results of such a process analysis of interest to someone with experience in literary study, you should take the further step of explaining how the conventions that you focus on are used in the poem to convey a particular meaning. In following this procedure, you are limiting your focus to a specialized concern of students of poetry in order to explain your own and to contribute to others' understanding of how the poem's art affects a reader's appreciation of it.

To address the audience of this chapter's task, seek to find this sort of limited focus for examining the poems you choose to write on. As we suggested in the Audience section of this chapter, avoid writing at length either on what your reader already can be expected to know about the poem or on your personal views of issues associated with the poem.

What follows here is a poem by William Shakespeare, "That Time of Year Thou Mayst in Me Behold," along with a commentary that illustrates how you might develop a limited focus on the poem that demonstrates your familiarity with one specialized concern of poetry, the use of metaphor. Read the poem, then the commentary. Although your instructor may wish you to read the poem in a different way, this doesn't mean that the commentary is wrong, nor does it mean that there is any other completely right reading of this poem. Part of the benefit of reading poetry is learning to accept the fact that diversity and multiplicity of interpretation are not signs of faulty education. They are what make us human, and a good poem allows for a full spectrum of human responses.

That Time of Year
Thou Mayst in Me Behold
William Shakespeare

That time of year thou mayst in me behold
When yellow leaves, or none, or few, do hang
Upon those boughs which shake against the cold,

> Bare ruined choirs, where late the sweet birds sang.
> In me thou seest the twilight of such day
> As after sunset fadeth in the west;
> Which by and by black night doth take away,
> Death's second self, that seals up all in rest.
> In me thou seest the glowing of such fire,
> That on the ashes of his youth doth lie,
> As the death-bed whereon it must expire,
> Consumed with that which it was nourished by.
> > This thou perceiv'st, which makes thy love more strong,
> > To love that well which thou must leave ere long.

Your first reaction to this poem might actually stand in the way of a full understanding and appreciation of what is happening in it. For some, the name *Shakespeare* is an intimidating one, full of unpleasant associations with high-school reading assignments or torturous exams. For others, the formal but obsolete terms of address *thou* and *thy* and the archaic verb forms *mayst, fadeth,* and *seest* indicate a kind of expression hopelessly out of touch with anything remotely resembling the modern world. Of course, the ideal reader of poetry keeps an open mind and tries to meet the poem on its own ground, suspending judgment until after the poem has been experienced and understood.

One first step that you might take is to read the poem out loud. This is not an unusual request of a student reading poems as part of a college course in writing, but if you are sitting alone in a room, it seems incongruous to speak to no one but yourself. Nevertheless, reading a poem out loud gives you the opportunity to re-create the voice in the poem, making you aware that poems—no matter how formal or artificial to the eye—contain a human voice expressing some unique outlook on life. Reading out loud also restores to poems some vestige of their origins in oral storytelling, song, or prayer and makes the reciter more attuned to the *how* of the poem, namely, the musical and verbal resources that the poet has incorporated within it.

Your initial reading aloud of this poem will reveal one person speaking to another, most likely a younger person than the speaker. Three long sentences, each four lines long, are followed by a unit of two lines that concludes the poem. The speaker emphasizes how a certain state of being can be found "in me." Surely, in the first part of the poem, he is not pointing to some kind of internal map or X-ray picture of his interior, but directing his listener to some likeness that exists between the speaker and "that time of year," namely, the season of autumn. This comparison between a person's life and a season of the year is a natural and commonplace one; it joins the speaker to the listener, who is not as old as the speaker but may be someday. The next part of this image of autumn metaphorically depicts the empty bare branches of the trees as an old church in ruins, a reminder of the music that once sounded through it. This poignant image of recollection and loss concludes the first part of the poem and prepares us for the next.

The second part of the poem states another metaphorical connection, this time between the speaker and twilight. Just as autumn fades into winter, with its suggestion of coldness and desolation, twilight will subside into night, and with night, sleep, "death's second self," or sleep's imitative link to death, a reminder of what is soon to come. This overt reference to death, although indirectly tied to the speaker, intensifies the listener's awareness of the speaker as an aging man.

In the last metaphor of the poem, the speaker connects himself again (the repeated "in me's" gaining in force and emphasizing the identification of the speaker with nature's qualities of change and decay) with an image of finality, the glowing coals of a fire. This is the most physically intense of the three images, for it conveys suggestions of material extinction, of the loss of youth and its accompanying sexual passion. The fire is seen here in its last stages, embers lying on a bed of ashes that itself was once the wood that fed, or "nourished," the fire. Ironically, what once gave it life will now be responsible for its end.

Although all three images are different, yet connected to the speaker's own fate, they could not be arranged in any other sequence. The poem begins with a rather uncertain passage of time: autumn, yes, but just when in that season? The line that describes autumn expresses a certain vagueness, as if one's perception of one's own or another's aging is gradual, lacking in physical immediacy. Twilight is of shorter duration, and one responds more personally to the sensuous glow in the sky that nevertheless is a prelude to night and darkness. The image of glowing embers, however, is the most physically intense of the three. This stage of a fire feels the hottest, and yet it is soon gone. The images move in time from a season to a brief moment, just as they become more vital in their connection to human emotion.

The concluding lines suggest that the speaker's impassioned comparison will strengthen the listener's appreciation of his friend and even increase the worth of the speaker, who, beginning the poem with a pathetic reference to barrenness and lost youth, ends almost triumphantly with a reminder of his still burning vital powers. The poem is made of three simple, natural metaphors. In combination they achieve a beautiful acceptance of life's briefness within the compressed space of the sonnet form.

You might make use of this commentary in order to develop a shaping idea in terms of which you could arrange your thoughts about the effect and significance of Shakespeare's use of metaphor in the sonnet. What might your shaping idea be? Can you explain why it might be of interest to an informed audience? Once you have given some thought to your answers to these questions, go on to the next section, "Arranging the Essay," to see how students like yourself moved from developing an initial response to a poem to arranging a rough draft that might appeal to a teacher of literature.

ARRANGING THE ESSAY

First Responses: Journal Entries

In one class, students wrote entries in their journals about their reading. Here are some of their comments on the poems given earlier in the chapter:

1. I think Nemerov in "The Vacuum" felt guilty over the way he treated his wife when she was alive. He won't allow the vacuum in his life to be filled. He must have taken her for granted while she was alive and now is just lazy and angry over the loss of his wife's services. I'm not sure how he really felt about her when she was alive. Perhaps he only saw her as a housekeeper and not a lover or companion.

2. In "The Passionate Shepherd to His Love," the poet doesn't say anything about a meaningful relationship. He wants to have a sexual relationship with her but with no commitment to the future. Marvell also just wants to seduce his girl, even though he doesn't promise her any gifts as the shepherd does. Both consider women their play toys and not much more than that.

3. Blake's poem "London" gives a strong sense of how London felt to this particular observer: cluttered and oppressive. The word play here emphasizes and connects the strong emotions that he associated with his life there. When he repeats the words <u>every</u> and <u>cry,</u> for example, it gives the reader a sense of total despair. These people are victimized and have no power over their own lives. Blake must have been really angry at what he saw around him and used the observer as a stand-in for his feelings.

4. Donne loves God and is willing to do anything for him, even get himself beaten up or captured by some enemy. He can't seem to control his emotions and wants God to take over. He must be pretty weak if he has to call on God for every little thing. In Psalm 23, at least, the poet knows that God will take care of him and doesn't have to make a big deal out of his suffering. I like the psalm better

because the writer is more acceptant and sure of himself. Donne
seems to make a lot of noise about nothing—or very little anyway.

What would you say of these students' responses to the poems they chose? How well did they respond to the problems posed by each poem? For example, Writer 2 criticized the poets for their attitude toward women. Because both poems were written centuries ago, is this a valid criticism to make? Which writer showed the most understanding of the language of poetry?

In class discussion students recognized that they were often too hasty in arriving at generalizations about their poems. They frequently ignored the concrete imagery in order to come to some conclusion about the idea or theme of the poem. They found it difficult to grasp the connections made by the uses of figurative language. And they tended to judge the poems, or the speakers in the poems, by standards and values that would have meant little to the people in that time. In their next response, the class attempted to expand their explanations through example and analysis. Most students decided to develop their interpretations by comparison and contrast. They felt that this method offered the best opportunity for uncovering the significant characteristics of each poem.

Comparison and Contrast

In preparing a comparison and contrast of two poems, the first consideration is your choice of poems to be interpreted. Two poems like Marlowe's and Ralegh's shepherd poems are fairly obvious possibilities because one poem is a direct response to the other and imitates, even repeats, the language of the first poem. Still, you need to derive from each poem a significant idea or guiding principle that unites the imagery in the poem into a coherent whole. This thematic statement is present in the tone of the shepherd's voice as he woos his desired nymph; in the list of material objects that he offers her; and in the form of the argument that he arranges to "move" her to his point of view. Ralegh's poem seizes on these attributes to reverse them, to argue in a way that will point out the absurdity of Marlowe's shepherd's idealized life.

Your comparison, then, would focus on these major points of comparison. As you learned in Chapter 5, you might develop your discussion of both poems by either the part-by-part or the whole-by-whole method. In your introduction, you should inform your reader of the basis for your comparison, some main point of similarity or difference that you will emphasize. Of course, there is not much point in choosing two poems so obviously different that there is really no common ground between them. On the other hand, there is not much for the reader to learn from a comparison that takes two poems on, say, marriage and says only that both poems show a man and a woman loving, courting, marrying, and dying. The impatient reader will say, "Fine, but how were their relationships different, how did each poem look at love and marriage from a unique point of view?''

Similarity and difference, then, are like opposite ends of a magnet: they attract. If two poems seem obviously different, you might try to show your reader that there are surprising similarities that reveal interesting qualities in both poems. If both poems, however, seem fairly similar, your analysis might point out significant differences, differences that affect how these poems should be read. Whether you choose to write about differences or similarities, the points you emphasize should be relevant to your reader's experience of the poem. They should focus on the poem as a whole and should add to the reader's understanding and perception. A paper, for example, on ''Wordsworth's and Blake's London: Two Nineteenth-Century Views of the Modern City'' might talk about matters of importance to both poems and might analyze specific uses of figurative language.

Many lyric poems like the ones included in this chapter are short enough so that you can say almost everything you understand about them, but because their language is so thickened with connotation and implication, you should be careful to notice how figurative language or musical devices are used. Your shaping idea might make some comparative statement, preferably in one sentence, about the use of figurative language in the two poems. Instead of saying, ''Blake viewed London as a modern hell, a city of suffering and despair; Wordsworth saw London as a distantly observed work of art,'' you can combine your ideas within a complex sentence through the use of subordination: ''Whereas Blake viewed London as a modern hell, a city of suffering and despair, Wordsworth's London was a distantly observed work of art.'' Your comparative statement might also reflect your judgment on the two poems, as when we compare we often do so to say that we like one thing better than another: ''Although both Marlowe and Marvell tried to create persuasive arguments for seduction, Marvell's poem contains a richer and more profound use of figurative language.''

Writing the Rough Draft

Writer 2 above wrote an introduction for a first draft:

In Marlowe's "The Passionate Shepherd to His Love" and Marvell's "To His Coy Mistress," both male characters are in the process of wooing a female. Although the settings are quite opposite, the message is the same. Both consider women their play toys and not much more than that.

This introductory paragraph makes a comparative statement, but as it concludes that the poems convey the same message, there seems little of interest for the informed reader, who already knows that both poems contain speakers attempting to persuade women to be their lovers. This writer also remained determined to show that both poems place women in demeaning roles. Again, the writer has ignored the context of the poems in order to present the two poets as modern male chauvinists dressed in Elizabethan costume.

Writer 3 wrote this introductory paragraph for a first draft:

The poet uses poetry to evoke emotions in the reader by carefully choosing words that represent and express genuine human feelings. Poetry is the poet's way of responding to those issues that are permanent and eternal in human life, issues like the loss of innocence, the love of man and woman, humans' place in nature, and the destruction brought by time and death. However, some poets write about less permanent topics that they feel very strongly about, such as their city, their country, or the society they live in. A good example can be seen in William Blake's "London" and William Wordsworth's "Composed upon Westminster Bridge, September 3, 1802."

1. What is this writer's shaping idea? Is it in the form of a comparative statement?
2. Is this an appropriate introduction for these two poems?
3. Why did the writer begin with a generalization about poetry? How effective is it?

Here is the first writer's rough draft:

HOWARD NEMEROV'S "THE VACUUM" AND ADRIENNE RICH'S "TRYING TO TALK WITH A MAN": A COMPARISON

Both "The Vacuum" by Howard Nemerov and "Trying to Talk with a Man" by Adrienne Rich are poems that deal with the relationships between man and woman. The relationships in these poems are similar in some respects, but at the same time quite different. Whereas the man is the speaker in "The Vacuum," bereaved over the loss of his wife, it is the woman who is speaking in "Trying to Talk with a Man," discontented with the direction the relationship has taken.

Nemerov stated in his poem that the man believes when his wife passed away her soul entered into a vacuum cleaner. In attempting to decipher why his wife picked a vacuum cleaner as her place of residence in the afterlife, one becomes very interested in the image of a vacuum. A vacuum, by definition, is a portion of space (left) unoccupied or unfilled with the usual or natural contents. His wife's demise has definitely left such a vacuum in his life.

A vacuum in the more tangible sense is a tool of housework, that work traditionally performed by a woman. The man seems to remember his wife in her role as a housekeeper rather than in that of a lover or companion. In retrospect, he sees her cleaning under the stairs and in the corners rather than remembering her enjoying life at some more pleasant activity. It is with much regret that he now dwells on the way he took his wife for granted while she was alive. By making the vacuum human (giving it a mouth and lungs), he is preserving his wife's image in the house, but at the same time, he is allowing the memory of her servitude to haunt him. The fact that he cannot bring himself to use the vacuum demonstrates the guilt he feels over the disregard he showed for his wife in the past. At the same time, he is lazy, and therefore, angry over the loss of his wife's services.

Although he realizes that death has terminated his relationship with his wife, he will not permit the vacuum in his life to be filled. The use of the phrases "old filth" and "cheap as dirt" reinforces the feeling of disgust toward himself that remains for the poor treatment of his wife while she was still alive. The vacuum is the instrument used to remove the dirt; now his guilt has rendered the vacuum useless. This is the reason he seems to see the vacuum smiling into the floor, holding back the laughter at this lazy man who is lost without the services of his wife.

In Adrienne Rich's poem "Trying to Talk with a Man," the wife is lamenting the loss of the relationship itself. Unlike the man in "The Vacuum," who has only unpleasant memories, the woman in Rich's poem can remember pleasant times spent in the pursuit of more lighthearted activities. From love letters to suicide notes, it was a time filled with intensity in the relationship. Although it may have had its ups and downs, the relationship was solid and meaningful. The woman feels that there is still a chance to recover what they once shared, even though it is a very slim chance. The "underground river" between the two of them (described as "deformed cliffs") is the slim chance ("acute angle of understanding") that remains.

Now the relationship has deteriorated to a point where only superficial feelings and communications exist. She goes to the desert with her man, a lonely and barren place. It is the type of place one would go to test a bomb. It is here in the desert, far from the distractions of everyday life, where she hopes they will be able to communicate and, in so doing, to salvage the relationship. What she quickly comes to realize, however, is that they have brought with them the same silence and loneliness that the desert provides. When a bomb is to be tested in the desert, there is intensity and explosiveness in the air. After the test is finished, there is only silence. So, too, is their relationship: where once there was intensity and explosiveness between them, now there is silence. It takes a desert setting to convince her that the relationship is doomed, just like the doom that is associated with the testing of bombs. There is sound in the desert, such as the sound of the wind blowing through the cactus, but it is meaningless because there is no one there to hear it. When she tries to talk to him, it is like wind in the desert; no one is listening. Nothing of value grows in the desert; so too, nothing of value is growing between them.

In both of these poems, the speaker is regretful of things that have been lost by time, and both understand that the love relationship is over. The end of love is just as final for Rich as it is for Nemerov.

1. What is the writer's shaping idea? Is anything missing from the introductory paragraph?
2. Has the writer produced sufficient evidence from the poems to establish the ideas about both speakers?
3. Is the conclusion effective? Could it have strengthened the paper by being expanded?

4. Are any of the interpretive statements inadequate? Are any perceptive and interesting?
5. How well has the writer understood the poems' figurative language?

Now begin to write your first draft.

FOCUS: THE SOUND OF POETRY

The sun shone bright and clear. . . . The branches of the hollies pendent with their white burden, but still showing their bright red berries, and their glossy green leaves. The bare branches of the oaks thickened by the snow.

—**Dorothy Wordsworth,** *Journal,* Feb. 17, 1798

And they shall beat their swords into ploughshares, and their spears into pruning hooks.

—Isaiah 2:4

A little more than kin and less than kind.

—*Hamlet,* I, 2, l. 65

The writers of these quotations had little in common, but in one respect, they approached language in the same way. All were conscious of how the sounds of words are deeply intermingled with their meanings. To a large extent, the meanings of their statements are created by the fusing of words into units of verbal music. Each writer chose words that have similar initial consonant sounds—a simple device of repetition called *alliteration.* But each writer used alliteration to serve his or her purpose, so that a commonplace element of language sound becomes a way to create imaginative meanings as well. Dorothy Wordsworth's prose description of a winter scene is made more lyrical and expressive by such combinations as "sun shone," "still showing," "bright red berries," and "glossy green." The translator of the King James Bible emphasized the contrast between war and peace by opposing swords and spears to ploughs and pruning hooks. And Shakespeare revealed Hamlet's bitterness toward his uncle, King Claudius, by playing on the various meanings of *kin* and *kind,* words that would usually go together comfortably but are here made ironically to repel each other, just as Hamlet is intuitively repelled by his uncle, his father's murderer.

In the poet's choice of words, the interplay of sound and meaning is an even more vital part of the poem's expression. Blake's "London" refers to the "chart'red street" and the "chart'red Thames." The word *chartered* usually meant that some piece of property was legally given out for commercial purposes, but the repetition of the word gives it a more important connection with the repeated use of *marks* and the suggestion that the people of London carry the physical marks of suffering on their faces, just as the city of London is marked out or mapped out for those who own it. In addition, both words carry the association of oppression and suffering, even though the dictionary meaning of the words would not fully convey this association. We refer to this tendency of a word to accumulate emotional associations and attitudes as its *connotation;* the dictionary meanings, as its *denotation* (see Chapter 8, pp. 299–300). When Burns said his beloved was like a rose, he counted on the reader's associating the rose with the qualities of youthful female beauty and vitality. In Frost's "The Oven Bird," the word *fall* carries its usual denotation as a season of the year, but the connotation of the word conveys a darker suggestion of the Original Fall in Paradise. One meaning does not supplant the other; they coexist to give the poem a greater range of expression.

In their choice of words, poets do not stray far from the world of concrete things. "No ideas but in things," said one American poet, William Carlos Williams. He meant that only in our direct perception of the physical world could we become receptive to the power of poetic language. "The greatest poverty is not to live in a physical world," said another American poet, Wallace Stevens. Just as we suggested you "show," not "tell," in trying to express an experience (see Chapter 1, pp. 13–16 and Chapter 2, pp. 49–50), the poet evokes the sensuous world in concrete images rather than in abstract terms. When John Keats wanted to write a poem that would capture the essence of autumn, he chose images that would convey its abundance and swelling ripeness:

> To bend with apples the mossed cottage-trees,
> And fill all fruit with ripeness to the core;
>   To swell the gourd, and plump the hazel shells
> With a sweet kernel . . .

Mostly simple monosyllabic words. Some readers think poems must be bulging with obscure polysyllabic words and perfumed adjectives. If you look again at the words in the poems in this chapter, you will see that the vast majority of them are taken from the permanent store of our everyday vocabulary; like Donne's "knock, breathe, shine, and seek to mend," or the Twenty-third Psalm's "though I walk through the valley of the shadow of death." There are levels of diction in poetry, ranging from the high or formal to the low or colloquial, but most poems fall somewhere in between. The genuinely skilled poet can take the ordinary word and put it in a striking context. Then it is no longer ordinary. Here is a short poem by Robert Frost that says simply and beautifully what many human beings have observed about life:

Nothing Gold Can Stay

Nature's first green is gold,
Her hardest hue to hold.
Her early leaf's a flower;
But only so an hour.
Then leaf subsides to leaf,
So Eden sank to grief,
So dawn goes down to day.
Nothing gold can stay.

It would be difficult to change a word in this poem and not alter the unity of meaning and music that Frost created. As leaf subsides, as Eden sank, as dawn goes down to day (an unusual way to look at the change from dawn to day), we re-create this falling rhythm in our reading of the poem. The poem is not so much "about" our perception of change and mortality as it is an embodiment or imitation of it. In your reading of poems, try to be conscious of this unity of word and sound.

REWRITING

Obtaining Feedback on Your Rough Draft

If other members of your class are analyzing the same poem that you are, you may feel that your analysis lacks some of the insights that you heard in others' drafts. It is not unusual to find that in a group writing on specific poems, different insights emerge. Don't feel that you have read inadequately; consider instead how open-ended literature can be. If the poem is a great one, many convincing readings will emerge. Of course, you might modify your reading in light of the analyses you heard, but it's up to you to determine whether others' readings are justified by the evidence that they draw from the poem.

At this point you will want to submit your rough draft to your "other self," your teacher, or your peers in order to get feedback on it. Also, try answering the questions of the "Audience Response Guide" about the student essay in this chapter before you begin work on rewriting your essay on poetry.

─────── **AUDIENCE RESPONSE GUIDE** ───────

1. **What does the writer want to say in this paper?**
2. **How does this paper affect the audience for which it was intended?**
3. **How effective has the writer been in conveying his or her purpose and meaning?**
4. **How should the paper be revised to better fulfill its purpose and meaning?**

Peer evaluations of the first student writer's rough draft revealed how important a shaping idea is. Many papers had fine individual perceptions to express but lacked an overall thematic or formal principle to give them coherence and unity. True, it is often difficult to get a handle on a literary work, particularly a poem, but without a specific direction for your interpretation, your reader will be woefully confused and your perceptions wasted.

1. Peer readers found that the purpose needed clarification. Saying that one speaker is a man and the other a woman did not seem very important. They felt a clearer, more sharply pointed introduction was necessary.

2. The writer provided his audience with some valuable commentary on the poems. He made both poems yield some new insights for his audience.

3. Some readers felt that he overemphasized the element of the speaker's guilt in "The Vacuum." Some questioned whether this was really important in the poem; others said that there was little direct evidence for it. Perhaps the writer read some of his own emotions into the poem.

4. The comparison between the two poems needed to be made more explicit. The conclusion contained a valuable comparative statement, but it needed to be expanded. Some ambiguous sentences needed revision.

Here is how the student rewrote his essay in response to the comments he received from his peers.

HOWARD NEMEROV'S "THE VACUUM" AND ADRIENNE RICH'S "TRYING TO TALK WITH A MAN": A COMPARISON

In poems that deal with the relationships between men and women, there is often expressed the feeling of loss that somehow inevitably follows love. Both "The Vacuum" by Howard Nemerov and "Trying to Talk with a Man" by Adrienne Rich explore this emotion of discontent, but in quite different ways. Whereas the speaker in "The Vacuum" is a man bereaved over the loss of his wife, the woman who is speaking in "Trying to Talk with a Man" is concerned with the direction that her relationship with a man has taken. For the bereaved husband, there is only the bitterness of loneliness; for the woman, however, there is the chance that she will be able to communicate her feelings to another. Both poems use an effective metaphor to express the speakers' emotions.

The man in Nemerov's poem states that when his wife died, her soul entered into a vacuum cleaner. For the reader, this is an interesting image to explain. By definition, a vacuum is a portion of space unoccupied or unfilled with the usual or natural contents. His wife's death has definitely left such a vacuum in his life. In the more tangible sense, however, a vacuum is a tool of housework, the work traditionally performed by a woman. The man seems to remember his wife in her role as housekeeper rather than as lover or companion. In retrospect, he sees her cleaning under the stairs and in the corners rather than remembering her enjoying life at some more pleasant activity, for it is her ability to give order and purpose to life through her dedication to housework that is represented by the vacuum. By making the vacuum human (giving it a mouth and lungs), he is preserving his wife's image in the house, but at the same time, he is allowing the memory of her dedication and energy to haunt him. That he cannot bring himself to use the vacuum perhaps also demonstrates the guilt that he feels for the way he took her servitude for granted.

Although he realizes that death has terminated his relationship with his wife, he will not permit the vacuum in his life to be filled. The use of the phrases "old filth" and "cheap as dirt" reinforces the feeling of disgust toward himself that remains now that his wife's animating spirit is gone. The vacuum is the instrument used to remove the dirt; now his sense of desolation has rendered the vacuum useless. The vacuum seems to be smiling into the floor, holding back laughter at this man who is lost without the guiding hand of his wife.

In Adrienne Rich's poem, the woman laments the loss of her relationship with the man but feels that there is still a chance to recover what they once shared, even though a very slim chance. The "underground river" between them, forcing its way between "deformed cliffs," is the slim chance, or "acute angle of understanding," that remains. Once they had an intense relationship with much that was solid and meaningful. Now the relationship has deteriorated to a point where only superficial feelings and communications exist. She goes to the desert with her man. It is a lonely and barren place, the type of place where one would go to test a bomb. Here in the desert, far from the distractions of everyday life, she hopes that they will be able to communicate and, in so doing, salvage their relationship. What she quickly comes to realize, however, is that they have brought with them the same silence and loneliness that the desert provides.

When a bomb is to be tested in the desert, there is intensity and explosiveness in the air. But after the test is finished, there is only silence. So, too, is their relationship. Where once there was intensity and explosiveness between them, now there is silence. It takes a desert setting to convince her that the relationship is doomed, just as in the doom associated with the testing of bombs. There is sound in the desert, such as the sound of the wind blowing through cactus, but it is meaningless because no one is there to hear it. When she tries to talk to him, it is like wind in the desert—no one is listening. Just as nothing of value grows in the desert, so, too, nothing of value is growing between them.

In both poems the speakers regret what they have lost in the course of their lives. In two powerful metaphors, the vacuum and the desert, they mourn this loss and reflect on what they had once enjoyed. But both understand that loss is usually permanent. The saddened husband is left with his "hungry, angry heart ... biting at air." The woman recognizes that out in the desert, she feels "more helpless with you than without you": whether it is the finality of physical death, as in Nemerov's poem, or of emotional death, as in Rich's, the speakers have arrived at a moment of revelation in their lives that will always remain with them. There is a kind of inconclusiveness about both speakers, but the reader knows that they will never be as they once were.

Quoting Lines of Poetry

Although most poems are short and the text may be readily available, you might want to quote one or more lines of your poem for emphasis or to point out a poetic device or meaning. You can quote words, phrases, and one or two lines of a poem by making the quotation grammatically a part of your sentence:

The speaker in Blake's "London" is disturbed most by "How the youthful Harlot's curse/Blasts the new born Infant's tear" and corrupts the whole institutionalized structure for containing human sexual desire: marriage, or as the poet calls it, "the marriage hearse."

Notice the diagonal slash mark used to separate one line from the next. If you quote at greater length, you must set the quotation apart from your text by ending the last line of your text with a colon, dropping down a double-spaced line on your page, indenting the lines of the quotation ten spaces from the left-hand margin, and single spacing between these lines. Should you wish to quote several lines but to omit one or two that come between, use a row of spaced dots to show that one or more lines have been omitted. If you wish to leave out one or more words in a quotation, use three spaced dots (ellipsis):

> Batter my heart, three-personed God; for You
> As yet but knock, breathe, shine, and seek to mend;
> That I may rise and stand ... bend
> Your force to break, blow, burn, and make me new.
>
> . . . .
>
> Take me to You, imprison me, for I,
> Except You enthrall me, never shall be free,
> Nor even chaste, except You ravish me.

For more information on the mechanics of ellipsis and quotation, see the appropriate sections in the Handbook, pp. 400–403.

Now, revise and edit your essay before submitting it to your instructor.

BECOMING AWARE OF YOURSELF AS A WRITER

1. Now that you have studied others' use of figurative language, are you more aware of your use of such language in your own writing?

2. In what situations would you use your study of figurative language in other areas of learning, such as history, sociology, or economics?

3. What have you learned about yourself as a reader of poems that can help you become a better writer?

4. Have your opinions about poetry changed since you began to write about your responses to poems?

5. What would be the most important piece of advice that you would give to a reader who is faced with an unfamiliar poem?

6. Would you omit the study of poetry from the modern college curriculum? What argument would you offer for its omission? Against?

7. How difficult was your task for this chapter compared to the tasks of the previous chapters? Were there any specific problems that you encountered in this task? What do you think caused these problems?

HANDBOOK

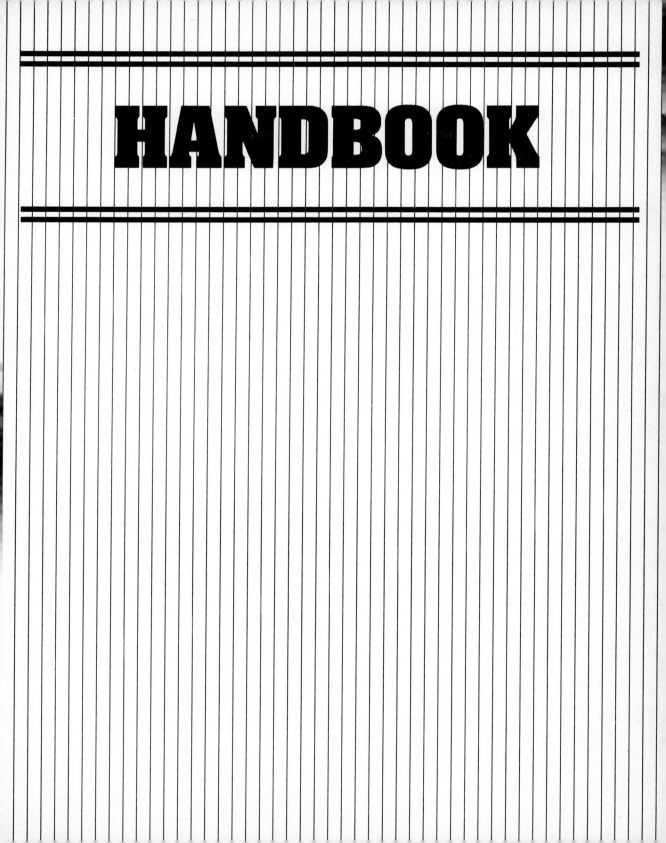

Grammar

Parts of Speech

The Noun
The Pronoun
The Verb
The Adjective
The Adverb

The Conjunction
The Conjunctive Adverb
The Preposition
The Article

Parts of Sentences

The Subject
The Predicate

The Complement

Base Sentences

Phrases and Clauses

The Phrase
The Clause

Combined or Expanded Sentences

Awkward Sentences

Faulty Coordination or Subordination
Incomplete Sentences

Mixed Sentences
Inconsistent Point of View

Common Grammatical Errors

Faulty Agreement
Faulty Reference
Case Errors
Misplaced and Dangling Modifiers

Faulty Parallelism
Run-on Sentences and Comma
Splices
Sentence Fragments

Punctuation

The Period
The Question Mark
The Exclamation Point
The Comma
The Semicolon
The Colon

The Dash
Parentheses and Brackets
The Ellipsis
Quotation Marks
The Apostrophe

Mechanics

Capitalization
Italics
Abbreviations

Numbers
Hyphenation
Spelling

Grammar

PARTS OF SPEECH

The Noun

A noun designates a person, a place, an object, a quality, or an idea. It names something.

A common noun refers to a member of a general class of things, such as an *artist,* a *town,* a *car, beauty, goodness.*

A proper noun names a specific person, place or thing, such as *Pablo Picasso* or *St. Louis, Missouri.* It may name a particular kind of common noun, such as a *Model-T Ford.* Proper nouns are capitalized.

Most nouns are either singular or plural. The plural is formed with *s* (one *car,* two *cars)* or *es* (one *sandwich,* two *sandwiches).* A few nouns form the plural by a change in their spelling (one *child,* many *children;* one *man,* many *men).* Refer to a good dictionary if you are uncertain about the plural form of any noun.

Adding an apostrophe and an *s* to most nouns indicates possession or ownership (the *woman's* car).

The Pronoun

A pronoun substitutes for a noun or a noun phrase. The noun that a pronoun replaces is called the *antecedent* of the pronoun.

Pronouns help a writer to sound less repetitious, as in the sentence

Joe drove his new car home,

where the pronoun *his* has replaced the proper noun *Joe's.*

Pronouns fall into one of the following categories:

Personal Pronouns. Personal pronouns take different forms, depending on whether they are used as subjects (subjective form), as objects or indirect objects (objective form), or to indicate ownership (possessive form):

361

	Subjective		Objective		Possessive	
	Singular	Plural	Singular	Plural	Singular	Plural
1st person	I	we	me	us	my, mine	our, ours
2nd person	you	you	you	you	your(s)	your(s)
3rd person	he, she, it	they	him, her, it	them	his, her(s), its	their(s)

Reflexive Pronouns:

myself	himself
ourselves	herself
yourself	itself
yourselves	themselves

Indefinite Pronouns:

all	few
another	many
any	most
anybody	nobody
anyone	no one
anything	none
both	one
each	some
everybody	somebody
everyone	someone
everything	something

Demonstrative Pronouns:

this	these
that	those

Relative Pronouns   Relative pronouns introduce noun or adjective clauses:

who (subjective)	which
whom (objective)	that
whose (possessive)	

Interrogative Pronouns   Interrogative pronouns ask questions:

who/whom	which
whose	what

The Verb

A verb expresses an action *(to drive)* or a state of being *(to live)*. The root or plain form of any verb is the infinitive, the form listed in the dictionary and usually combined with *to*. This plain form is altered in a variety of ways, depending on how the verb is being used.

All verbs add *s* or *es* to the plain form in order to indicate third-person singular present (she *drives*, he *lives);* the only exceptions are *to be* (she *is*) and *to have* (he *has)*.

What are called *regular verbs* add *d* or *ed* to the plain form in order to indicate the past tense (he *lived).* What are called *irregular verbs* indicate the past tense by more radical alterations of form (she *drove,* he *swam).*

Most verbs form the past participle, which indicates a completed action, by adding *d, ed, n,* or *en* to the plain form *(lived, driven),* although again there are irregularly formed past participles of verbs such as *to do (done)* or *to keep (kept).* The present participle, which indicates a continuing action, is formed by the addition of *ing* to the plain form of a verb *(living, driving, doing, keeping).*

Refer to a dictionary if you are uncertain about the past tense or the past participle of a verb. Any good dictionary lists the past tense if it is irregular, the past participle, and the present participle of a verb.

A verb can be combined with an auxiliary or helping verb to indicate different relationships between the action or state of being that the verb describes and the passage of time (tense), or the actor (voice), or the writer's view of the action (mood). The modal auxiliaries are *can, could, do, does, did, may, might, must, shall, should, will,* and *would.*

Tense.   Verb tense indicates the relationship between an action or state of being and the passage of time. The present tense indicates that something is taking place now (I *live,* you *live,* he or she *lives,* we *live,* you *live,* they *live).* The past tense indicates that something was completed in the past (he *lived,* she *drove).* The future tense indicates that something will take place in the future (she *will drive).*

Each of these three tenses may be formed by use of the past or the present participle. The combination of a past participle with a form of the auxiliary verb *to have* produces what are called the *perfect tenses,* which focus on a completed action: present perfect (I *have driven,* she *has driven);* past perfect (she *had driven);* and future perfect (she *will have driven).* The combination of a present participle with a form of the auxiliary verb *to be* produces what are called the *progressive tenses,* which focus on an ongoing or continuing action: present progressive (I *am living,* you *are living,* he *is living,* we, you, they *are living);* past progressive (I *was driving,* you *were driving,* she *was driving,* we, you, they *were driving);* and future progressive (she *will be driving).*

More complex combinations of verb forms are possible, for example, the present perfect progressive (she *has been driving),* which focuses on an ongoing action in the past.

Voice.   A verb may be either active or passive, depending on whether the subject of the verb is performing the action (she *drives* the car) or is being acted on (the car *was driven* by her; she *was driven* crazy by her car). The passive voice is formed with a past participle and the auxiliary verb *to be.*

Mood.   A verb may be formed to reflect any one of three different moods or attitudes: the indicative mood states a fact or an opinion (she *drives* carefully), or it asks a question *(does* she *drive* carefully?); the imperative mood gives commands or directions *(drive* carefully); the subjunctive mood expresses doubt or uncertainty (I'm not sure that she *should drive* at all), or it states a condition (if she *were to drive* carefully, she'd make me feel better), or it expresses a suggestion or a wish (I'd like it if she *would drive* carefully), or it states a requirement (it is important that she *be* a careful driver). Note that the subjunctive employs *be* (rather than *am, is,* or *are*) in the present tense and *were* (rather than *was*) in the past tense.

The Adjective

An adjective modifies a noun by describing a particular attribute of it (a *blue* car), by qualifying it (a *good* car), or by specifying it (the *second* car; *my* car). In qualifying a noun, an adjective may limit *(that* car) or broaden *(any* car; *most* cars) the meaning of the noun.

An attributive adjective comes immediately before or after the noun it modifies (it is a *dangerous* car). A predicate adjective is separated from its noun by a linking verb (the car is *dangerous).*

An adjective often can be identified by its suffix: *-able, -ous, -full, -less, -ic, -er, -est.* The last two suffixes indicate the comparative and superlative forms of many adjectives *(happy, happier, happiest).* Other adjectives form the comparative and superlative by combining with *more* and *most (dangerous, more dangerous, most dangerous).*

The Adverb

An adverb modifies a verb (she drives *slowly),* an adjective (the road is *dangerously* steep), another adverb (she drives *more* slowly), or a complete clause or sentence *(evidently,* she is a careful driver).

Many adverbs are formed by adding *ly* to an adjective:

shy, shyly	beautiful, beautifully
nice, nicely	hopeless, hopelessly
terrible, terribly	comical, comically
dangerous, dangerously	

Adverbs often specify when something happened (the storm ended *today;* I got lost *again);* where it happened (it was colder *inside* than *outside;* I tried to call you *there);* the manner in which it happened (she left *quickly;* she spoke *hoarsely);* or the extent or degree to which it happened (she *almost* lost her wallet; he *never* thought about it).

Most adverbs form comparatives and superlatives by combining with *more* and *most,* although a few add *er* and *est (soon, sooner, soonest).*

The Conjunction

A conjunction links one part of a sentence to another part. It joins words, phrases, and clauses to one another, showing the relationships between them; for example, the coordinating conjunction *and* shows equality between two parts of a sentence, whereas the subordinating conjunction *because* indicates a cause-and-effect relationship.

Coordinating conjunctions link words or phrases or clauses of equal grammatical rank. They may link one word to another (dogs *and* cats), one phrase to another (in the house *or* in the car), or one clause to another (I like candy, *but* I am on a diet). The coordinating conjunctions are *and, but, or, nor, for, so,* and *yet.*

Correlative conjunctions work in pairs, such as *both . . . and, not only . . . but also, either . . . or, neither . . . nor (either* knock on the door *or* ring the bell).

Subordinating conjunctions link dependent clauses, which cannot stand by themselves as sentences, to independent clauses, which can stand by themselves as sentences (she took the blue car *because* it is faster). Subordinating conjunctions include *after, although, as, because, before, if, in order that, once, since, so, than, unless, until, when, whenever, where, wherever,* and *while.*

The Conjunctive Adverb

Conjunctive adverbs, or sentence connectors, link independent clauses. Like conjunctions, they focus attention on the nature of the relationship between the clauses, although often they do so more emphatically. In the sentence

They could not get their car started; consequently, they walked home,

the conjunctive adverb *consequently* emphasizes the cause-and-effect relationship between the two clauses.

Whereas coordinating conjunctions are usually preceded by a comma, conjunctive adverbs are usually preceded by a semicolon. Also, whereas both coordinating and subordinating conjunctions always stand between the two parts of the sentence that they join, a conjunctive adverb may be moved around within the second clause:

They could not get their car started; they, consequently, walked home.

Conjunctive adverbs include the following:

accordingly	as a result	conversely	for instance
also	besides	earlier	further
afterward	certainly	finally	hence
anyway	consequently	for example	however

in addition	meanwhile	on the other hand	thereafter
indeed	moreover	otherwise	therefore
instead	nevertheless	similarly	thus
in the same way	next	still	undoubtedly
likewise	nonetheless	subsequently	
later	now	then	

The Preposition

A preposition links a noun, a pronoun, or a group of words functioning as a noun to some other word in a sentence. It indicates the relationship in time, space, or logic between the linked words (the car is *in* the garage).

Prepositions include the following:

about	behind	except	onto	toward
above	below	for	out	under
across	beneath	from	outside	underneath
after	beside	in	over	unlike
against	between	inside	past	until
along	beyond	into	regarding	up
among	by	like	round	upon
around	concerning	near	since	with
as	despite	of	through	within
at	down	off	throughout	without
before	during	on	to	

The noun linked to another word by a preposition is called the *object* of the preposition. The combination of the preposition, its object, and any words modifying the object is called a *prepositional phrase.* In the prepositional phrase *in the garage,* the preposition is *in,* the object is *garage,* and the modifier is *the.*

Prepositional phrases usually function as adjectives or adverbs in sentences. The phrase *in the garage* is adverbial, describing where the car is located.

The Article

The articles are *a, an,* and *the.* They modify nouns. *A* and *an* are indefinite; *a car* could mean any car. *The* is definite; *the car* indicates a specific car.

The article *a* precedes nouns that start with a consonant sound *(a rocket).* The article *an* precedes nouns that start with a vowel sound *(an astronaut).*

PARTS OF SENTENCES

The Subject

A subject is a noun (or a word or a group of words serving as a noun) that tells who or what is doing the action or experiencing the state of being expressed by the verb in a clause. In the main clause

The boy's mother had to drive home slowly,

mother is the simple subject, the noun without any modifiers; *the boy's mother* is the complete subject, the noun with its modifiers.

A pronoun, of course, may act as a subject, but other parts of speech may do so also. For example, in the sentence

Driving home took a long time,

the gerund phrase *driving home* serves as a noun and is the subject.

The Predicate

A predicate is usually said to include all parts of a clause other than the subject and its modifiers. A simple predicate is the verb and its auxiliaries, such as the verb *to drive* and its auxiliary *had* in the sentence

The boy's mother had to drive home slowly.

The complete predicate includes any modifiers of the verb *(slowly)* and any complements *(home)*.

The Complement

A complement is a word or a word group that completes or modifies the subject, the verb, or the object of a clause.

Subject complements are called *predicate adjectives* or *predicate nominatives*. A predicate adjective follows a linking verb (often a form of *to be* or a verb like *to become, to appear,* or *to seem)* and modifies the subject, as does the adjective *cautious* in the sentence

She is cautious.

A predicate nominative is a noun (or a noun substitute) that follows a linking verb and defines the subject more specifically, as does the noun *driver* in the sentence

She is the driver of the car.

Verb complements are called *direct* and *indirect objects*. A direct object is a noun (or a noun substitute) that names who or what is affected by the action of the verb. In the sentence

She gave the keys to him.

the direct object is *keys,* and the indirect object is *him.* An indirect object is a noun (or its substitute) that names to or for whom or what the action is done.

Object complements are adjectives and nouns (or their substitutes) that modify direct objects. In the sentence

She gave the car keys to him.

car is an object complement.

BASE SENTENCES

The most basic sentence structure is a simple subject and predicate:

She drives.

This structure is often expanded by the addition of complements to the predicate:

She drives the car cautiously.

Such base sentences may be combined with others to form longer, more complicated sentence structures. These longer sentences may be composed of clusters of words (usually phrases) that act as free modifiers, and/or coordinate clauses, and/or subordinate clauses. See the "Focus" section of Chapter 5 (pp. 156–163).

PHRASES AND CLAUSES
The Phrase

A phrase is a group of words that acts as a single part of a speech. Unlike a clause, it has no subject and predicate.

The following are the most common types of phrases:

The Noun Phrase.   A noun phrase is a noun *(car)* and its modifiers. The most common modifiers are articles *(the* car), adjectives (the *blue* car), and prepositional phrases (the blue car *in the garage)*. A noun phrase functions as a single noun in a sentence. In the sentence

The blue car in the garage is mine.

the noun phrase functions as the subject.

The Verb Phrase.   A verb phrase is a verb *(drive)* and its auxiliaries *(should* drive). It may be expanded by the addition of one or more adverbs (should drive *slowly),* prepositional phrases (should drive slowly *on this road),* or complements (should drive the *car* slowly on this road).

The Prepositional Phrase.   A prepositional phrase is a preposition combined with its object and any modifiers. It usually functions as an adjective or an adverb in a clause. In the sentence

The girl at the beach likes to swim.

the prepositional phrase *at the beach* functions as an adjective; in the sentence

She likes to swim at the beach.

the same phrase functions as an adverb.

The Infinitive Phrase.   An infinitive phrase consists of an infinitive form of a verb along with its subject, and/or object, and/or modifiers. In the sentence

We expected John to tell his mother right away.

John is the subject of the infinitive *to tell, mother* is the object, and *right away* is an adverbial modifier; within the sentence, this infinitive phrase functions as the direct object of the verb *expected* and so is being used as a noun. An infinitive phrase may also be used as an adjective:

John is the person to tell his mother.

or as an adverb:

John left to tell his mother.

The Participial Phrase.   A participial phrase consists of a past or present participle along with its object and/or any modifiers. Participial phrases function as adjectives. In the sentence

Soaked to the skin, they came in out of the storm.

the participial phrase *soaked* (past participle) *to the skin* modifies the pronoun *they.* In the sentence

Soaking wet, they came in out of the storm.

the participial phrase *soaking* (present participle) *wet* functions similarly.

The Gerund Phrase.   A gerund phrase consists of an *-ing* verb when it serves as a noun, along with its subject, and/or object, and/or any modifiers. Gerund phrases function as nouns. In the sentence

His driving the car recklessly made her nervous.

the gerund phrase consists of the gerund *driving* along with its subject *(his),* its object *(car),* and an adverbial modifier *(recklessly);* the entire phrase serves as the subject of the sentence.

The Absolute Phrase.   An absolute phrase consists of a noun or pronoun and a participle, along with any modifiers. It modifies a whole base sentence rather than a single word within the base sentence. In the sentence

The car skidding on the rain slick road, the driver held his breath.

the phrase preceding *the driver* is absolute; it has its own subject *(car)* and modifies the whole base sentence. Compare it to the participial phrase that follows and modifies only *the car* in the following sentence:

The driver held his breath as he felt the car skidding on the rain-slick road.

The Clause

A clause is a group of words that contains a subject and a predicate.
A main or independent clause can stand alone as a sentence:

He drove to the bank.

Two or more main clauses may be linked to form a single sentence with a coordinating conjunction, or a semicolon, or a conjunctive adverb:

He drove to the bank, and he deposited the money.

or

He drove to the bank; and he deposited the money.

or

He drove to the bank; then he deposited the money.

A subordinate or dependent clause cannot stand alone as a sentence because it is introduced by either a relative pronoun, such as *that* or *which*, or a subordinating conjunction, such as *because* or *if* or *when*. Subordinate clauses function as nouns, adjectives, or adverbs in a sentence. Noun clauses and adjective clauses usually begin with a relative pronoun. Adverbial clauses always begin with a subordinating conjunction. In the sentence

That you drive carefully is a comfort to me.

the noun clause *(that you drive carefully)* acts as the subject. In the sentence

The new front tire, which he just bought yesterday, went flat today.

the adjective clause *(which he just bought yesterday)* modifies the noun *tire.* In the sentence

When he hit the brakes, the car swerved to the left.

the adverbial clause *(when he hit the brakes)* modifies the verb *swerved.*

COMBINED OR EXPANDED SENTENCES

Base sentences may be combined or expanded to form compound, complex, or compound-complex sentences. A base sentence, or simple sentence, consists of a single main clause:

The red sportscar in the garage is mine.

A compound sentence consists of two or more main clauses linked by a coordinating conjunction, a semicolon, or a conjunctive adverb:

The red sportscar in the garage is mine; however, I might sell it.

A complex sentence consists of one main clause and one or more subordinate clauses:

Although I will miss driving the car, I will sell it if I can get a good price.

A compound-complex sentence consists of two or more main clauses and one or more subordinate clauses:

The red sportscar in the garage is mine, but I might sell if it I can get a good price.

A simple sentence, then, may be expanded into one with a more complicated structure by the addition of phrases, by the coordination of one or more main clauses, or by a combination of main clauses with subordinate and relative clauses. See the "Focus" sections of Chapters 5 (pp. 156–163) and 6 (194–199) for additional discussion of sentence length and style.

AWKWARD SENTENCES

Sentences become awkward or confused for many reasons: a writer may employ faulty coordination or subordination, may omit necessary sentence elements, may mix elements that are incompatible, or may make inconsistent shifts in point of view.

Faulty Coordination or Subordination

When the logical connection between two coordinated clauses, phrases, or words is unclear, the writing suffers from faulty coordination: in the sentence

She likes to drive, but her teeth hurt.

the coordinating conjunction *(but)* fails to make clear why the writer has chosen to link the subject's feelings about driving to the subject's problems with her teeth.

When the logical connection between a subordinate clause and a main clause is unclear, the writing suffers from faulty subordination: in the sentence

Because my brakes failed, I hit the tree instead of the pedestrian.

the subordinating conjunction *(because)* fails to explain why the driver hit the tree rather than hitting the pedestrian. Often faulty subordination occurs when a writer subordinates what seems to be the main idea of the sentence: the sentence

> When I hit the tree, I had never had an accident before.

might be better revised so that the emphasis falls on the main point:

> Although I had never had an accident before, I hit the tree.

Incomplete Sentences

Incomplete sentences are missing necessary words or phrases.

In a compound construction, a word that functions as but differs grammatically from a preceding word should not be omitted. For example, in the sentence

> The car was given an oil change, and its flat tire (was) fixed.

the second *was* might be omitted; but if the subject of the second clause were plural, its verb could not be so shortened:

> The car was given an oil change, and its wheels (were) aligned.

An incomplete sentence also results when a comparison is made incompletely or illogically. In the sentence

> My car is faster.

a reader is not told what the car is faster than. In the sentence

> She likes the car better than her brother.

a reader is uncertain if the subject likes the car better than she likes her brother or better than her brother likes the car.

If two things are being compared that are not really comparable, the sentence will be logically incomplete. In the sentence

> The engine in his car was more powerful than most of the other cars in the race.

an engine is being compared to other cars rather than to the engines of other cars.

Incomplete sentences also result when a writer omits a needed article or preposition. For example, the sentence

The boy has both a talent and love of fixing engines.

is incomplete because the preposition *for* is needed after the word *talent* and the article *a* is needed before the word *love*.

Mixed Sentences

In a mixed sentence, two parts are presented as compatible either in grammar or in meaning when they actually are incompatible. For example, in the sentence

After driving all night made him feel exhausted.

a prepositional phrase *(after driving all night)* is being treated ungrammatically as a subject and is linked to a predicate *(made him feel exhausted)*.
In the sentence

Driving all night is when he feels exhausted.

an adverbial clause *(when he feels exhausted)* is being equated, illogically, with a noun substitute *(driving all night)*. When a predicate does not apply logically to a subject in this way, it is called *faulty predication.* A linking verb, like *is,* should connect a noun with another noun that is logically comparable to it, as in the revised sentence

Driving all night is an activity that makes him feel exhausted.

Do not link a subject and a predicate together that are not logically comparable, as in the sentence

The use of seat belts was invented to save lives.

The *seat belts* themselves, not their *use,* were invented to save lives.

Inconsistent Point of View

A sentence or a paragraph can become awkward if there are logical inconsistencies in the verb tense or mood or voice. In the sentence

He drove the car home and parks it in the garage.

the writer has shifted confusingly from past to present tense. In the sentence

I was mad when I failed the driving test because I practiced for so many weeks before taking it.

the point of view with regard to verb tense is awkward because the verb *practiced*, which indicates an action that was completed before the test was taken, should be placed in the past perfect tense *(had practiced)*. In the sentence

If you are caught speeding, you would get a ticket.

the shift from indicative to subjunctive mood is a confusing inconsistency; *would* should be changed to *will*. In the sentence

Ann waxed the car after it had been washed.

the shift from active voice *(Ann waxed the car)* to passive voice *(it had been washed)* creates an ambiguity about who actually washed the car; if Ann washed it, the subordinate clause might be better revised to read *after she had washed it.*

A sentence also may become awkward if there are inconsistencies in person or number with reference to pronouns. In the sentence

If one drives too slowly on the highway, you can cause an accident.

the shift from the third person *(one)* to the second person *(you)* is confusing. Similarly, if in this sentence the writer had substituted *they* for *you,* the shift from singular *(one)* to plural *(they)* would have been awkward.

COMMON GRAMMATICAL ERRORS

Faulty Agreement

A verb should agree in person and number with its subject. A pronoun should agree in person, number, and gender with its antecedent.

Subject/Verb Agreement.   In the sentence

Her car runs well.

the third-person-singular subject *(car)* and the third-person-singular verb *(runs)* are in agreement. If the subject were to become plural *(cars)*, the verb would have to be altered to a plural form *(run)*. If the subject were plural in form but singular in meaning, however, it would take a singular verb:

The news is good.

When a phrase comes between a subject and its verb, do not make the verb agree with a noun in the phrase rather than with the subject:

The car with new tires and new brakes costs (SINGULAR) more than the other cars.

Phrases beginning with *in addition to* or *as well as* do not change the subject's number:

Her car, as well as the other two, was (SINGULAR) broken into.

A compound subject joined by *and* usually takes a plural verb. One exception occurs when the parts of the subject refer to a single entity:

Ice cream and cake is (SINGULAR) my favorite dessert.

Another exception occurs when a compound subject is preceded by *each* or *every:*

Every car and truck on the lot was (SINGULAR) sold.

The indefinite pronouns tend to be singular:

Each of them is (not *are)* right.
Everyone is (not *are)* doing it.

All, any, none, and *some* may be either singular or plural:

Some of his time is (SINGULAR) spent at home.
When they get home at night, some of them watch (PLURAL) television.

Two singular subjects joined by *or* or *nor* take a singular verb:

Either Ann or Al is going to pick up the pizza.

Two plural subjects joined by *or* or *nor* take a plural verb:

Either the girls or the boys are going.

If one of the subjects is singular and one is plural, however, the verb agrees with the subject that is closer to it:

Ann or the boys are going.
The girls or Al is going.

When a sentence begins with *there,* the subject tends to follow the verb. Special attention should be paid to agreement:

There was one hole in the muffler; there were two holes in the tire.

When *there* precedes a compound subject, the verb is singular if the first part of the subject is singular:

There is a hole in the muffler and two flat tires.

When a subject complement follows a linking verb, make sure that the verb agrees with the subject, not with its complement:

Cars and trucks are my hobby.
My hobby is cars and trucks.

A collective noun, which names a group of individuals, takes a singular or a plural verb, depending on whether the group is acting as a unit or as separate individuals:

The team is traveling to the game by bus.
The team are traveling to the game in their own cars.

A singular verb follows a title, a word that is being defined, and a word denoting some form of measurement (weight, an amount of money, a period of time):

Forty thousand miles is a lot to put on a car in a year.

When a relative pronoun is the subject of a clause, the verb should agree in number with the antecedent of the relative pronoun. In the sentence

She is one of those drivers who never get a ticket.

the antecedent of *who* is *drivers,* and hence the verb *get* is plural.

Pronoun/Antecedent Agreement.   In the sentence

Ann washed her car.

the third-person-singular feminine pronoun *(her)* agrees with its third-person-singular feminine antecedent *(Ann).* If the antecedent were changed in person, number, and/or gender, the pronoun would have to be changed accordingly:

Joe washed his car.

Joe and Ann washed their cars.

(Note that in the last example the word *cars* is pluralized because Joe and Ann washed different cars; if they washed a single car that they owned together, the object *car* would be singular.)

A compound antecedent joined by *and* usually takes a plural pronoun. One exception occurs when the parts of the antecedent refer to a single entity:

The soldier and patriot was given a ticker tape parade by his home-town neighbors.

Another exception occurs when the compound antecedent is preceded by *each* or *every:*

Each car and truck was parked in its proper place.

The indefinite pronouns, when they serve as antecedents, usually require a singular pronoun:

Everybody will have a chance to take his or her turn.

When the gender of the antecedent is not specifically masculine or feminine but both, two singular pronouns *(his or her)* are used. It is acceptable to substitute a plural pronoun *(their)* in such cases. Simply to write either *his* or *her* in reference to an indefinite antecedent is now considered sexist.

Note that sometimes it is awkward to follow an indefinite antecedent with a singular pronoun, as in the sentence

When everybody arrived, I asked him or her to sit down.

Substituting *them* for *him or her* in this sentence does not really clarify matters. The sentence might be better revised to read

When all of them arrived, I asked them to sit down.

or

As each of them arrived, I asked him or her to sit down.

Two singular antecedents joined by *or* or *nor* take a singular pronoun:

Neither Ann nor Sally washed her car.

Two plural antecedents joined by *or* or *nor* take a plural pronoun:

Neither the girls nor the boys washed their cars.

If one of the antecedents is singular and the other is plural, the plural antecedent should come second and the pronoun should agree with it:

Neither Ann nor the girls washed their cars.

Note that in this last example, if the word *cars* were made singular *(car)*, it would indicate that Ann and the girls own one car together.

A collective noun, when used as an antecedent, takes a singular or a plural pronoun, depending on whether it refers to a group that is acting as a unit or as separate individuals:

The family is coming in its car.
The family are coming in their cars.

Faulty Reference

A pronoun should refer clearly to its antecedent. If there is any ambiguity or confusion about who or what the antecedent of a pronoun is, the pronoun reference is faulty.

If there is more than one possible antecedent, the sentence should be revised. The sentence

Sam told Don that he had used his car.

might be revised to read

Sam said to Don, "I used your car."

The sentence

He hit the ball on the roof, and it fell down.

might be revised to read

After he hit it on the roof, the ball fell down.

Ambiguity may result if the pronoun is placed too far away from its antecedent in a long sentence. In the sentence

The lake is large and pretty with a cabin on the shore and plenty of fish in it.

does the pronoun *it* refer to the cabin or to the lake?

Ambiguity often results when a pronoun such as *this, that, which,* or *it* refers to an entire clause rather than a specifically defined antecedent. In the sentence

We drove all morning and then stopped for a picnic lunch, which made me sleepy.

the relative pronoun, which, could refer to the drive and/or the lunch. The reference would be clearer if it were less broad:

We drove all morning, which made me sleepy, and then we stopped for a picnic lunch.

Another way to clarify the reference would be to define the antecedent more specifically:

We drove all morning and then stopped for a picnic lunch; the drive combined with the lunch made me sleepy.

A similar kind of error involves the use of a pronoun whose antecedent is implied rather than specifically expressed. In the sentence

In George Orwell's novel *1984,* he describes a world where love is a crime.

no specific antecedent for the pronoun *he* is named; if the reference is intended to be to Orwell, the sentence should be revised to make this intention clear:

In his novel *1984,* George Orwell describes a world where love is a crime.

Often this sort of ambiguity results when a writer employs the pronoun *it* or *they* or *you* without a definite antecedent: in the sentence

In college, they expect you to type your papers.

no possible antecedent for *they* is mentioned. Note also that when the pronoun *it* is used in more than one way in a sentence, the results are often confusing:

Because it is hot by the lake, it looks inviting.

Finally, the pronoun *which* should not be used to refer to people. Use *who* to refer to people, *which* to refer to animals or objects or places. *That* may refer both to people and to animals, objects, or places.

Case Errors

The most common case errors involve the use of a subjective form of a pronoun when an objective form is required or the use of an objective form of a pronoun when a subjective form is required.

Generally, the subjective forms should be used if the pronoun is part of the subject of a clause:

The truck driver and I (SUBJECTIVE) stopped at the light.

The light turned green before we (SUBJECTIVE) drove on.

The subjective case is also used for a subject complement after any form of the verb *to be:*

It is I (SUBJECTIVE).

It was they (SUBJECTIVE) who went home last.

The objective forms should be used if the pronoun is a direct object in a clause:

Joe invited her (OBJECTIVE) and me (OBJECTIVE).

an indirect object in a clause:

Joe lent him (OBJECTIVE) the car.

or the object of a preposition:

Joe is in love with her (OBJECTIVE).

Note that the objective forms should be used not only when a pronoun is the object of an infinitive:

Joe wanted to give her (OBJECTIVE) the car.

but also when the pronoun is the subject of an infinitive:

Joe wanted him (OBJECTIVE) to return the car.

There are a number of situations in which many writers find the choice of case confusing:

When the first-person-plural pronoun is used with a noun, its case depends on how the noun is being used. If the noun is a subject, the writer should use *we* along with it:

We students love summer vacation.

If the noun is an object, the writer should use *us* along with it, as in the following sentence, in which the noun *students* is the object of the preposition *of:*

All of us students love summer vacation.

When a pronoun is used as an appositive, appearing next to a noun that it helps to identify or explain, its case depends on how the noun is being used. If the noun is a subject, the appositive pronoun should be in the subjective case:

Three boys, Joe, Sam, and I (SUBJECTIVE), went camping.

If the noun is an object, the appositive pronoun should be in the objective case:

Joe went camping with two other boys, Sam and me (OBJECTIVE).

Who is always used to refer to a subject; *whom* is always used to refer to an object. If you are writing a question, use a personal pronoun to formulate the answer first; the case of the personal pronoun in your answer will indicate whether you should start the question with *who* or *whom:* the answer

She is the judge.

should be rephrased into the question

Who is the judge?

The answer

She sentenced him to a fifty-dollar fine.

should be rephrased into the question

Whom did she sentence to a fifty-dollar fine?

When *who* or *whom* is used in a subordinate clause, the case depends on how the pronoun is being used in the clause. The case depends upon the use of the pronoun in the clause no matter how the clause itself is being used in the sentence. In the sentence

A judge is a person who is honest.

who is the subject of the clause *who is honest;* the clause itself modifies the direct object, *person.* In the sentence

A judge is a person whom most people trust.

whom is the object of the modifying clause *whom most people trust.* If you rewrite the clause as a separate sentence, substituting a personal pronoun for *who* or *whom,* the proper choice of case is often clarified:

She *(who)* is honest. Most people trust her *(whom).*

Finally, the possessive form of a pronoun should be used before a gerund, an *ing* verb that is being used as a noun:

I approved of his (POSSESSIVE) going out with my sister.

Misplaced and Dangling Modifiers

Misplaced Modifiers. A modifier is misplaced if its position in a sentence causes ambiguity about just what part of the sentence it is modifying. For example, in the sentence

I gave the shirt to my brother with the red pinstripes.

the prepositional phrase *with the red pinstripes* is misplaced: Does it modify *brother* or *shirt?* The sentence should be revised to read

I gave the shirt with the red pinstripes to my brother.

Similarly, a subordinate clause can be misplaced. In the sentence

He parked the car in the garage after he had washed it.

did the subject wash the car or the garage? Again, one can revise the sentence simply by moving the misplaced modifier to another position:

After he had washed it, he parked the car in the garage.

Usually, a modifier should be placed as closely as possible to the word or words that it is meant to modify. This is particularly important when a writer is using what are called *limiting modifiers,* single-word adverbs such as *almost, exactly, hardly, just, nearly, only,* and *simply.* Misplacing one of these modifiers can change the meaning of a sentence radically. Thus you might write

The old Ford is the only car that I will drive.

if you are unwilling to drive any other car, but

The old Ford is the car that only I will drive.

if no one else but you is willing to drive the old Ford.

   Sometimes a writer positions a modifier so that a reader cannot determine if it modifies the words that come right before it or the words that come right after it. Such modifiers are called *squinting modifiers.* For example, in the sentence

Joe had told her in May they would go to the beach.

did Joe tell her *in May* that they would go to the beach at some future time, or did Joe tell her that they would go to the beach *in May?* A squinting modifier should be repositioned away from the part of the sentence that it is not meant to modify:

In May, Joe had told her they would go to the beach.

or

Joe had told her they would go to the beach in May.

Dangling Modifiers.   A dangling modifier is a phrase or clause that does not sensibly describe any specific word in its sentence. For example, in the sentence

Arriving after midnight, the house seemed deserted.

the only word that the opening phrase could modify is *house,* but clearly it is not the house that arrived after midnight; the actual word that the phrase modifies is missing, and the sentence must be revised to include it:

Because we arrived after midnight, the house seemed deserted.

   A writer most often produces dangling modifiers by starting or ending a sentence with a phrase that lacks a subject itself, such as the participial phrase that starts the sentence

Soaked to the skin, the walk home in the rain was no fun.

or the infinitive phrase that ends the sentence

An umbrella should be taken to walk in the rain.

Also an elliptical clause, a subordinate clause in which the subject is unstated but understood, often becomes a dangling modifier. In the sentence

When I was only a small boy, I often went fishing.

the opening clause might be made elliptical by the omission of *I was;* if this elliptical clause is then used to introduce a main clause in which the subject is no longer *I,* a dangling construction results:

When only a small boy, my father often took me fishing.

To correct a dangling modifier, add the missing word or words to which it refers. You can do this by changing the subject of the main clause:

When only a small boy, I was often taken fishing by my father.

You can also do it by rewriting the dangling modifier as a complete subordinate clause:

When I was only a small boy, my father often took me fishing.

Faulty Parallelism

Faulty parallelism occurs when elements in a sentence or a paragraph that express comparable ideas and that perform similar grammatical functions are expressed in different grammatical form. In the sentence

Walking on the beach relaxes him more than a swim.

the parallelism is faulty because one comparable idea, *walking on the beach,* is expressed as a gerund phrase, whereas the other, *a swim,* is expressed as an unmodified noun. The sentence might be revised to read

Walking on the beach relaxes him more than swimming in the ocean.

or

A walk on the beach relaxes him more than a swim in the ocean.

Elements linked by coordinating or correlative conjunctions should be expressed in parallel form. To correct the faulty parallelism of the sentence

He is an excellent musician, a talented dancer, and puts on an exciting performance.

you might rephrase the last of the coordinated elements:

He is an excellent musician, a talented dancer, and an exciting performer.

As an alternative, you might subordinate the last element:

> He is an excellent musician and a talented dancer who puts on an exciting performance.

Note that faulty parallelism often occurs with correlative conjunctions because the writer omits a preposition or an infinitive marker *(to)* after the second conjunction: in the sentence

> He was overtired not from working too hard but sleeping too little.

a second *from* should be added after *but;* in the sentence

> She told him either to wait for her or leave.

a second *to* should be added after *or,* or perhaps a parallel prepositional phrase should be added after *leave,* such as *without her.*

Run-on Sentences and Comma Splices

A run-on sentence (also called a *fused sentence)* occurs when a writer fails to separate two or more main clauses with any punctuation; for example,

> He likes music he likes to dance.

A comma splice occurs when a writer links two or more main clauses with commas; for example,

> He likes music, he likes to dance.

A run-on sentence or a comma splice can be corrected simply if each main clause is punctuated as a separate sentence:

> He likes music. He likes to dance.

A second option is to link the main clauses with semicolons:

> He likes music; he likes to dance.

A third option is to link the main clauses with coordinating conjunctions:

> He likes music, and he likes to dance.

A fourth option is to link the clauses with subordinating conjunctions or relative pronouns, leaving only one main clause:

He likes music because he likes to dance.

Run-ons and comma splices often result when a writer links two or more main clauses with conjunctive adverbs. Conjunctive adverbs, like *also, however,* and *then,* should always follow either a semicolon or a period when they are being used to link main clauses.

He likes to dance, therefore he likes music.

is a comma splice; it should be repunctuated to read

He likes to dance; therefore he likes music.

or

He likes to dance. Therefore he likes music.

Note, however, that comma splices are used effectively by writers to emphasize the link or the contrast between ideas, particularly if the main clauses expressing the ideas are short and are phrased in a parallel fashion. The following sentences might make their point more effectively as one long comma splice:

I love the circus. I love the clowns. I love the acrobats. I love the side show. I love the whole spectacle.

Similarly, two or more contrasting ideas expressed in parallel phrasing may be punctuated as a comma splice to emphasize the contrast:

She did not hate him, she pitied him.

Sentence Fragments

A fragment is a part of a sentence that is punctuated with an initial capital letter and a final period as if it were a complete sentence. A sentence fragment may lack a subject, as does the verb phrase

Drove home at night.

It may lack a verb, as does the noun phrase

The boy on the bicycle.

It may lack both a subject and a verb, as does the prepositional phrase

On the beach.

It may include both a subject and a verb but begin with a subordinating conjunction, as does the subordinate clause

Because I love strawberries.

or with a relative pronoun, as does the relative clause

Which is my favorite.

If a fragment lacks a subject and/or a verb, you can correct it by adding the missing part or parts:

He drove home at night.
The boy on the bicycle left.
She is walking on the beach.

You can also correct it by linking it to a complete sentence:

He stayed for dinner, then drove home at night.

If a fragment is a dependent clause, you can correct it by rewriting the clause as an independent or main clause:

I love strawberries.

You can also correct it by linking it to a complete sentence:

I like vanilla but prefer chocolate, which is my favorite.

A fragment often results when a writer adds on information after completing a sentence. The added information might be the answer to a question:

What kind of day was it? A great day.

The information might be a modifying word or phrase:

My uncle is a conservative man. Old-fashioned.

He is a farmer. Living off the land.

Or the information might be a clause that further explains or qualifies:

She pitied him. Even though he was cruel to her.

Like comma splices, fragments can be used effectively by a writer for emphasis. Instructions are often written as fragments:

Bake in preheated oven (425°). One hour. Remove. Let cool before slicing.

Sometimes a definition is easier to remember if it is written in fragments:

Alcoholism. A disease. Both physiological and psychological.

A description may sometimes be made more vivid if some of the images that compose it are fragments:

The schoolroom was quiet. Empty desks. Rows of them. The board cleaned of chalk. The afternoon light fading outside the closed windows.

In general, because a fragment isolates a piece of information, it focuses a reader's attention on that information. If a writer can make use of fragments for this purpose without confusing the reader, there is no reason not to employ them on occasion.

Punctuation

The conventions of punctuation that follow are more complete than those offered in the "Focus" section on sentence combining in Chapter 5 (pp. 156–165). The basic information about how punctuation marks can help a reader to follow the separations or links that you wish to make between sentences and parts of sentences is the same.

THE PERIOD

A period is one way to end a sentence. It may be used to end any declarative sentence, any statement:

She is at the office.

It may be used to end a mild command:

Think about it.
Let me know.

It may be used to end an indirect question, a report of what someone has asked:

She wondered why they had to leave so early.

Periods are also used with many abbreviations: cities (N.Y.C., L.A.); states (Pa., Ill., Ariz.); names (Franklin D. Roosevelt); titles (Mr., Ms., Dr., Rev.); degrees (B.A., Ph.D., D.D.S.); months (Sept.); addresses (St., Ave., Rte.); Latin abbreviations (ibid., etc., et al.). Note that when an abbreviation is the last element in a sentence, a single period is used both to end the abbreviation and to end the sentence:

He lives in Washington, D.C.

Periods are not used with the capital letter abbreviations of technical terms (FM, IQ); organizations (NFL, AFL-CIO); corporations (CBS, IBM); or government agencies (FBI, TVA). Nor are periods used with acronyms, pronounceable words formed from the initial letters in a multiword title (NATO, VISTA).

Additional information on abbreviations is offered below in the section on abbreviations.

THE QUESTION MARK

A question mark is used to end a direct question:

What do you want to be when you grow up?

Note that if you write a series of questions, each is followed by a question mark:

He asked, "What profession do you think you will enter? Medicine? Law? Business?"

Note also that a question mark is never combined with another question mark or with a period or comma or exclamation point. The question

Who asked, "What do you want to be when you grow up?"

does not take a second question mark after the final quotation mark. The statement

He asked her, "What profession do you plan to enter?"

does not take a period after the final quotation mark.

A question mark may also be used within parentheses to indicate uncertainty within a statement:

My grandfather was ninety-two (?) when he remarried.

Someone—my brother Al (?)—borrowed my favorite shirt.

THE EXCLAMATION POINT

An exclamation point is used after a sentence or a phrase or a word that expresses a strong emotion:

Leave me alone!

What a wonderful day!

Yes! I must go home right now!

Its use should be reserved to indicate unusually strong emphasis.

Note that an exclamation point should not be used in parentheses to express amazement or irony or sarcasm, as in the sentence

My brother borrowed (!) my favorite shirt.

The context should indicate that a word, in this case *borrowed*, is being used ironically.

THE COMMA

A comma is used, above all else, to prevent misreading, by signaling that the reader should pause slightly before reading on. For example, although a comma is not absolutely required following a short introductory phrase, sometimes inserting one can clarify a sentence: in the sentence

After tomorrow morning choir practice will begin.

the meaning is different depending on whether a comma is inserted following *tomorrow* or following *morning.* Alternatively, it is sometimes necessary to omit a comma at a point in a sentence where one would ordinarily be inserted: in the line

The woods are lovely, dark and deep.

the poet Robert Frost left out the comma that ordinarily would be inserted after *dark;* had he inserted the comma, the three adjectives would have seemed equivalent descriptions of the woods; by omitting the comma, Frost suggested that the phrase *dark and deep* modifies *lovely,* that the woods are lovely because they are dark and deep. Commas, then, should be used with common sense as tools that can help a reader see how words, phrases, and clauses in a sentence are meant to be linked together or set apart from one another.

Generally, a comma is used to set off an introductory word, phrase, or clause from the rest of the sentence:

Undoubtedly, the villain will be caught. To catch him, the authorities will set a trap. Once the trap is set, we can sit back and relax.

Certainly, the comma may be omitted after a single introductory word or a short introductory phrase or clause if no confusion will arise as a result. Note that a comma is not needed after an introductory conjunction:

Yet the villain may escape.

A comma is inserted before a coordinating conjunction that links two main clauses in a sentence:

The authorities are armed with the most modern investigative tools, but the villain may prove too clever for them.

If the main clauses are short, however, and no confusion will arise, the comma may be omitted:

The authorities have set a trap but the villain may escape.

See the following section of the semicolon for information about when a semicolon should replace a comma that links two main clauses.

Note that a comma should not be inserted between two words or phrases that are joined by a coordinating conjunction. In the sentence

The authorities, and the criminal are clever.

the comma after *authorities* should be omitted.

Commas are used to separate two or more adjectives that precede a noun that they modify equally:

The criminal is a clever, ingenious thief.

If the adjective nearer the noun is more closely related to the noun in meaning, however, no comma should separate it from the preceding adjectives:

The authorities have clever legal minds.

If you can rearrange the adjectives or insert the conjunction *and* between them without changing the meaning, the comma should be used: thus you might write the phrase *an ingenious, clever thief* or *a clever and ingenious thief,* but you would not write *legal, clever minds* or *clever and legal minds.*

Commas are used to join three or more words, phrases, or clauses in a series:

> The thief is tall, dark, and handsome. He is suspected of stealing a diamond tiara in New York, a ruby brooch in Paris, and a pearl necklace in Singapore. His manners are charming, his victims are never suspicious of him, and his real name is a mystery.

The final comma in the series, the comma that comes before the conjunction, is regularly omitted by some writers and is regularly inserted by others. It is probably best to use the final comma consistently, except when you wish to emphasize the link between the final two items in a series, to identify the final two items as a single element:

> The thief is handsome, tall and dark.

See the following section on the semicolon for information about when semicolons should replace commas that separate items in a series.

Commas are used to set off a nonrestrictive modifier, a phrase or clause that offers additional (in a sense, parenthetical) information about an element in a sentence. Because the information offered by a nonrestrictive modifier is not essential to the meaning of the sentence, the modifier can be omitted without causing any confusion in the reader's mind. In the sentence

> The left front tire, which had forty thousand miles on it, blew out.

the relative clause *which had forty thousand miles on it* is nonrestrictive; the basic meaning of the sentence is that the left front tire blew out; it is not essential to know that the tire had forty thousand miles on it.

On the other hand, in the sentence

> The tire that had forty thousand miles on it blew out.

the relative clause *that blew out* is restrictive; if it is omitted, the reader has no way of knowing which tire blew out. A restrictive phrase or clause is not set off with commas.

Note that although both nonrestrictive and restrictive clauses may begin with *which,* only restrictive clauses begin with *that.*

An appositive, a noun or noun phrase that renames or further identifies the noun immediately before it, also may be nonrestrictive or restrictive. In the sentence

> My brother John is a Marine.

John is an appositive that further identifies the writer's brother. Because it is not set off by commas, it is restrictive, essential to the meaning of the sentence; presumably, the writer has other brothers, so he must distinguish his brother John from his brother Michael or his brother Arthur. if the sentence is rewritten

>   My only brother, John, is a Marine.

the appositive is nonrestrictive; the writer has only one brother, and his brother's name happens to be John.

Commas may be used to set off an absolute phrase:

>   The day drawing to a close, we headed home.

A phrase of contrast:

>   Speed, not strength, is a boxer's most important asset.

A conjunctive adverb:

>   He got home, however, before the rain started.

An additional explanation or example preceded by such expressions as *for example, namely,* and *such as:*

>   His favorite sports are team sports, such as baseball and soccer.

A noun of address:

>   John, you must get up now.

Also, a comma follows the salutation in a personal letter.

Conventional usage requires that commas separate the items in a date, an address, or the name of a place. Within a sentence, each date, address, or place is also followed by a comma, unless it appears at the end of the sentence:

>   On December 7, 1942, the weather was mild in New York.
>   His old address is 705 Walton Avenue, Mamaroneck, New York.

One final note: never use a comma to separate a subject from its verb or a verb from its object, unless there are words between them that must be set off by commas. Thus you might write

>   My brother, John, is a Marine.

setting off *John* as a nonrestrictive appositive; but you should not write

My brother John, is a Marine.

Similarly, you might write

She ate, not a dietetic snack, but a hot fudge sundae.

setting off the phrase of contrast; but you should not write

She ate, a hot fudge sundae.

For the use of commas with quotation marks, see the section below on quotation marks.

THE SEMICOLON

A semicolon may be used, instead of a period, to separate two main clauses:

She loves to roller-skate; he loves to ice-skate.

A semicolon is used to emphasize that two or more main clauses are closely related in meaning:

Someone had left a window open; it was freezing in the house.

A semicolon is used between two main clauses when the second clause contains a conjunctive adverb:

In the morning he jogs; however, yesterday morning he slept late.

Note that the semicolon in this instance may be replaced by a period, in which case the first letter of the second clause is capitalized. Note also that the semicolon may be used even if the conjunctive adverb does not immediately follow the initial clause:

In the morning he jogs; yesterday morning, however, he slept late.

In this case, a comma is inserted both before and after the adverb.
When two main clauses are linked by a coordinating conjunction, it is helpful to use a semicolon, rather than a comma, before the conjunction if the clauses are long and/or contain internal punctuation:

Driving down the icy mountain road, he downshifted, pumped the brakes, and honked the horn as he rounded each curve; and he breathed a sigh of relief when, rounding the last curve, he saw the road level out before him.

Similarly, it is helpful to separate the items in a series with semicolons when those items are long and/or contain internal punctuation:

It was a scary drive because the road was icy, steep, and narrow; the night was dark, and one of the headlights was out; and the car, with its worn tires, kept skidding each time he drove around a sharp curve.

Note that a semicolon should not be used between a phrase and a clause. In the sentence

To get up early; he sets the alarm.

the semicolon should be omitted; it may be replaced by a comma.

Similarly, a semicolon should not be used between a main clause and a subordinate clause. In the sentence

He always sleeps late; if the alarm fails to ring.

the semicolon should be omitted.

Also, a semicolon should not be used to introduce a list. In the sentence

You need the following ingredients; eggs, butter, milk, flour, and chocolate chips.

the semicolon should be replaced by a colon.

THE COLON

A colon is used to introduce a list or series:

There are many different writing tools: the pencil, the pen, the typewriter, and now the word processor.

Note, however, that a colon should not be used to introduce a list if the colon interrupts the completion of a main clause by coming between a verb and its object or a preposition and its object. Thus, the colon is omitted before the lists in the following sentences:

Some different writing tools are the pencil, the pen, and the typewriter.

A pencil is made of lead, rubber, and wood.

A colon is used to introduce an explanation or summary of the statement that it follows:

She writes only with a pencil or a pen: She hates to type.

Note that the sentence following the colon may begin with either a capital or a lowercase letter.

A colon may be used instead of a comma to introduce a quotation. See the section below on quotation marks.

A colon is also used to separate a subtitle from a title *(In Bluebeards's Castle: Some Notes Towards the Redefinition of Culture)*; to separate the hour from the minute in a time reference (2:15 P.M.); to separate chapter from verse in a biblical citation (Genesis 19:24–28); and after the salutation in a formal letter (Dear Mr. President:). For the use of colons in footnote and bibliographic entries, see the ''Focus'' section of Chapter 7 (pp. 000–000).

THE DASH

A dash (two hyphens when you are typing) indicates a sudden interruption in tone or thought:

She looked sincere—although looks can be deceiving—when she testified in court.

To replace the two dashes in the preceding example with parentheses would suggest that the interrupting clause is less relevant; to replace the two dashes with commas would make the interruption less emphatic.

A dash may be used to lend greater emphasis to an appositive:

My mother—a wonderful woman—is coming to visit.

It may be used to set off a word, a phrase, or a clause that summarizes a preceding list:

Men, women, children—people of all ages love the circus.

It may be used to emphasize an important idea at the end of a sentence:

There was nothing wrong with their marriage—but she wanted more from life.

Note also that a dash may replace a colon before a list, although it is considered less formal than a colon.

PARENTHESES AND BRACKETS

Parentheses

Parentheses are used to enclose words, phrases, and clauses that are not essential to the meaning of a sentence or paragraph but that clarify or comment on a point made in the sentence or paragraph. Parenthetical expressions may offer—

Factual information:

On the day that Pearl Harbor was attacked (December 7, 1942), my father was studying in his dormatory room.

Examples:

He likes any kind of pasta (spaghetti, linguine, or ravioli), as long as it is smothered in tomato sauce.

Explanations:

The suicide squeeze (in which the batter bunts and the runner on third races for home) is one of baseball's most exciting plays.

Qualifications:

He said he was so upset (although "angry" may be a better description) that he could not eat or sleep.

When a complete sentence is enclosed in parentheses, it needs no capital letter at the start or period at the end if the parentheses fall within another sentence:

The day that he left home (it was a sad day for all of us), rain fell all morning.

Note that although a comma may follow the closing parenthesis within a sentence, no comma comes before the opening parenthesis.

When a complete sentence is enclosed in parentheses that fall between two sentences, the sentence in the parentheses does begin with a capital letter and end with a period:

The day that he left home, rain fell all morning. (It was a sad day for all of us.) In the afternoon, however, the sky cleared.

Parentheses also are used to enclose cross-references: (see Freud's *Totem and Taboo*, p. 27); and to enclose letters or numbers that label items in a list:

There were a number of reasons that he preferred taking the train to driving: (1) he could sleep on the train; (2) the train got him there faster; and (3) he did not have to worry about parking his car when he arrived.

Brackets

Brackets are used to enclose your own explanations, comments, and corrections within a quotation from another writer. They may be used to add information:

E. B. White believes that *"Walden* [published in 1854] is an oddity in American letters."

They may be used to enclose a substitute word or phrase for a part of a quotation that, without the substitution, would be unclear, as in the following sentence, where the bracketed name has replaced the pronoun *his*:

E. B. White writes that *"Walden* is [Henry David Thoreau's] acknowledgement of the gift of life."

Note that the Latin word *sic* may be placed in brackets after an error in a quotation to indicate that the error was made by the author of the quotation. Also, brackets replace parentheses that are inserted within parentheses.

THE ELLIPSIS

An ellipsis is three periods separated from one another by single spaces. It indicates that material has been omitted from a quotation. If a comma, a semicolon, or a colon precedes the ellipsis, it is dropped. If a complete sentence precedes the ellipsis, the period ending the sentence is retained and is followed by the periods of the ellipsis.

Look at the following quotation from an essay by E. B. White on Thoreau's *Walden:*

Thoreau said he required of every writer, first and last, a simple and sincere account of his own life. Having delivered himself of this chesty dictum, he proceeded to ignore it. In his books and even in his enormous journal, he withheld or disguised most of the facts from which an understanding of his life could be drawn.

To omit the phrase "first and last" from the first sentence along with the entire second sentence, two ellipsis marks are necessary:

Thoreau said he required of every writer . . . a simple and sincere account of his own life. . . . In his books and even in his enormous journal, he withheld or disguised most of the facts from which an understanding of his life could be drawn.

Some writers use ellipsis marks to indicate that they have omitted material at the end of a quoted message:

"In his books and even in his enormous journal, he withheld or disguised most of the facts. . . . "

Others feel that the ellipsis is unnecessary in this case.

Note that an ellipsis may be used to indicate a pause or an incompleted statement in dialogue or quoted speech:

"Oh, no . . . " she said; then her words were drowned in tears.

Note also that a line of ellipsis marks across the full width of an indented quotation is used to indicate that one or more paragraphs of prose or lines of poetry have been omitted.

QUOTATION MARKS

Quotation marks are used to enclose words, phrases, or sentences that are quoted directly from speech or writing:

The mayor said he was "confident" that he would win reelection. According to the local paper, however, his popularity is "the lowest that it has been since his term began." In yesterday's editorial, the paper threw its support to his opponent. "While the incumbent has done a respectable job," the editorial said, "his opponent is better qualified in every respect."

Note that an indirect quotation, which reports what someone has said or written, but not in the exact words, should not be enclosed in quotation marks.

Single quotation marks are used to enclose a quotation within a quotation:

Yesterday's editorial went on to say, "The challenger's promise that she will hire more teachers, 'even if it means raising taxes,' is another reason that she has earned this paper's support."

Note that if you are quoting more than a single line of poetry, you should mark the line divisions with slashes:

Frost wrote, "The woods are lovely, dark and deep, / But I have promises to keep."

If you are quoting more that three lines of poetry or more than four lines of prose, you should not use quotation marks; instead, use identation to indicate where the quotation begins and ends. End the sentence introducing the quotation with a colon, double-space both above and below the quotation, indent the quotation itself ten spaces from the left-hand margin (and an additional five spaces to start a new paragraph), and single-space the lines of the quotation. Note the following example, in which quotations from Thoreau and Frost are each preceded by an introductory sentence:

Thoreau's optimism is apparent in the following passage from *Walden:*

> I think that we may safely trust a good deal more than we do. We may waive just so much care of ourselves as we honestly bestow elsewhere. Nature is as well adapted to our weakness as to our strength. The incessant anxiety and strain of some is a wellnigh incurable form of disease.

Frost seemed more careworn when he wrote:

> The woods are lovely, dark and deep,
> But I have promises to keep,
> And miles to go before I sleep,
> And miles to go before I sleep.

Quotation marks are used to indicate the title of a part or a chapter of a book ("Economy" is the first chapter of *Walden*); the title of an essay ("The Angry Winter," by Loren Eiseley); the title of a short story ("Rip Van Winkle," by Washington Irving); the title of a short poem ("To His Coy Mistress," by Andrew Marvell); the title of a magazine article ("What Do Babies Know?" in *Time*); the title of a song ("Yesterday," by the Beatles); or the title of an episode of a television or radio series ("The Miracle of Life," on *Nova*). Note that quotation marks are not used around the title on the title page of a paper that you have written.

Quotation marks are used by some writers to indicate that they are raising a question about the way a word is being used:

What he called his "new" car turned out to be a ten-year-old wreck.

Note, however, that when they are defining a word, most writers set it off by italicizing it. See the section on italics below.

When a single word or phrase is placed within quotation marks, no punctuation is needed to introduce it. When one or more sentences are placed within quotation marks, either an introductory comma or an introductory colon is needed. Some writers use a comma before a single sentence, a colon before two or more sentences:

He said, "Let's go home now." She replied: "First I've got to stop at the bank. Then we'll go home."

Other writers use a comma to introduce quoted speech and a colon to introduce quoted writing.

Use a comma at the end of a quoted sentence that is followed by a tag:

"I think that we may safely trust a good deal more than we do," Thoreau tells us.

If the quoted sentence is a question or an exclamation, however, it should end with a question mark or an exclamation point:

"Do you agree with Thoreau?" he asked.

In either case, the tag begins with a lowercase, not a capital, letter.

If a tag interrupts a quoted sentence, it is set off by two commas:

"I think," Thoreau wrote, "that we may safely trust a good deal more than we do."

If a tag is placed between two quoted sentences, the first quoted sentence is followed by a comma, the tag is followed by a semicolon or a period, and the second quoted sentence begins with a capital letter and ends with a period:

"Nature is as well adapted to our weakness as to our strength," Thoreau wrote; "The incessant anxiety and strain of some is a well-nigh incurable form of disease."

Note that at the end of a quotation, a period or a comma is always placed inside the closing quotation mark, and a semicolon or colon is always placed outside the closing quotation mark. A dash, an exclamation point, or a question mark is placed inside the closing quotation mark only if it is part of the quotation:

"Do you understand?" she asked.

If the dash, exclamation point, or question mark applies to the whole sentence, however, it is placed outside the closing quotation mark:

Does anyone understand what Thoreau meant when he wrote that "we may safely trust a good deal more than we do"?

THE APOSTROPHE

An apostrophe followed by *s* is used to form the possessive case of singular and plural nouns that do not end in *s*: the *boy's* dog, the *man's* property, *women's* rights, *children's* toys.

Singular common nouns ending in *s* also take an apostrophe followed by *s* to form the possessive: the *boss's* daughter, the *business's* manager. Singular proper nouns ending in *s* may form the possessive with an apostrophe followed by *s* or with an apostrophe alone: *Doris's* house or *Doris'* house, Mr. *Jones's* apartment or Mr. *Jones'* apartment. There are a few singular nouns ending in an *s* or a *z* sound that form the possessive with an apostrophe alone: for *conscience'* sake, *Moses'* law. Often such forms are rephrased to omit the apostrophe altogether: *for the sake of conscience, the law of Moses.*

An apostrophe alone is used to form the possessive case of plural nouns that end in *s*: *babies'* cribs, the two *boys'* tree house, the *Joneses'* apartment, the *Smiths'* home.

An apostrophe followed by *s* is added to the last word of a compound noun to indicate possession: my *sister-in-law's* car, *somebody else's* truck.

Only the last of two or more nouns takes the apostrophe (and the *s*, if needed) to indicate joint possession: the phrase *the boy and girl's dog* indicates that the boy and the girl own one dog together; if this phrase is revised to read the *boy's and girl's dogs,* it indicates that the boy and the girl each own one or more dogs individually.

An apostrophe followed by *s* is used to form the possessive of indefinite pronouns: *everybody's* favorite ice cream, *someone's* dirty laundry. Note, however, that the possessive personal pronouns do not require an apostrophe to indicate ownership:

This house; that is *hers.*

I like *their* house, but *its* backyard is so small.

An apostrophe is also used to indicate that letters, words, or numbers have been omitted in contractions: *can't* (cannot), *doesn't* (does not), *don't* (do not), *he's* (he is), *I'll* (I will), *isn't* (is not), *it's* (it is), *I've* (I have), *ma'am* (madam), *o'clock* (of the clock), *she's* (she is), *they're* (they are), *you're* (you are), *we're* (we are), *weren't* (were not), *who's* (who is), *won't* (will not), *'84* (1984). Note that the contraction *would've* means *would have;* do not write *would of* instead of *would've*. Better yet, do not use this contraction; write *would have.*

Note also that the personal pronouns *its, their, your,* and *whose* should not be confused with the contractions *it's, they're, you're,* and *who's.* See the section below on spelling for examples of the proper use of each of these pronouns and contractions.

An apostrophe followed by *s* is used to form the plural of numbers that are written as figures, letters, and words that are referred to as words: three *10's,* the 1950's, the '60's, five *b*'s, two more *but*'s.* Some writers omit the apostrophe with numbers and/or letters. The apostrophe is unnecessary when you spell out the plural of a date: the sixties.

---

*Note that individual numbers, letters, and words referred to in this way are italicized, but that dates are not. See the section below on italics. Also, the apostrophe followed by *s* is not italized.

Mechanics

CAPITALIZATION

To capitalize a word, make the first letter of the word a capital letter.
Capitalize the first word of a sentence:

She hates to type.

Capitalizing the first word of a sentence that follows a colon is optional:

She writes only with a pencil or a pen: She (*or* she) hates to type.

Capitalizing the first word of a direct quotation is necessary if the original begins with a capital letter:

I said to my sister's teacher, "She hates to type."

Capitalize proper nouns, such as the names of specific persons, places, events, institutions, and organizations:

Aunt Sally   the Renaissance
George Washington   World War I
Fifth Avenue   the New York Public Library
Los Angeles   Mamaroneck High School
the Rocky Mountains   Michigan State University
Lake Michigan   the Internal Revenue Service
the Pacific Ocean   the Boy Scouts of America
France   the Boston Red Sox
Africa   the United Nations
Jupiter

Note that common nouns like *avenue, mountain, lake, ocean, high school,* and *university* are capitalized when they are part of the name of a place or an instutition.

The article preceding a proper noun and any preposition that is part of a proper noun are not capitalized.

Capitalize proper adjectives formed from proper nouns:

a *Shakespearean* play
an *American* car
the *Republican* party

Capitalize trade names:

Scotch tape
Kleenex tissues
a *Xerox* copier

Capitalize the names of the points of the compass when they refer to specific geographical regions:

the *Midwest*
the *North Pole*
Western civilization

Do not capitalize the points of the compass when they simply indicate direction:

a *southerly* wind

Capitalize the days of the week, the months of the year, and holidays.
Capitalize the names of religions, their followers, and their sacred books:

Protestantism	Muslims
Judaism	the Bible
Christians	the Koran

Also capitalize all words used to designate the deity, including pronouns:

He	the *Lord*
His	*Allah*
God	*Buddha*

Capitalize abbreviations of academic degrees (B.A., Ph.D., M.D.); titles (Mr., Jr., Dr.); and all letters of acronyms (NATO, NASA, VISTA).

Capitalize a title that comes before a proper name or that substitutes for a proper name:

President Reagan is seeking reelection. The President announced his plans to run for a second term.

Do not capitalize a title that does not specifically refer to a proper name:

The president in our system of government is limited to two terms in office.

Similarly, do not capitalize a word designating a relationship *(father, aunt)*, unless it forms part of or sustitutes for a proper name:

My brother went to pick up Uncle George at the station.

Capitalize all words in the title of a book or a chapter of a book; of a magazine or newspaper or an article in either; an essay; a short story; a poem; a musical composition; a painting; a play; a film; or a television or radio show. Note, however, that no article, conjunction, or proposition of less than 5 letters is capitalized unless it is the first word of the title:

For Whom the Bell Tolls
Romeo and Juliet
Gone with the Wind

Always capitalize the first person singular pronoun, *I*.

ITALICS

Italic type slants upward to the right. It is used to set off words and phrases. In a typed or handwritten paper, you italicize a word or phrase by underlining it.
Italics are used to give emphasis to a word:

I don't want to know what *she* thinks; I want to know what *you* think.

Italics are also used to set off a word that is being treated as a word:

What does the word *love* really mean?
Why must you preface everything you say with *I think?*

Italics are used to identify a foreign word or phrase not yet accepted as a standard English expression: the phrase *carpe diem* is italicized, whereas the phrase per diem is not. Consult a dictionary to check whether a foreign expression is italicized.
Italics are used to indicate the title of a book *(Walden)*; a long poem (the *Odyssey)*; a play *(Romeo and Juliet)*; a magazine *(Time)*; a newspaper (the Philadelphia *Inquirer*); a pamphlet *(Common Sense)*; a published speech (the *Gettysburg Address)*; a long musical work *(Rubber Soul)*; a work of visual art (the *Mona Lisa)*; a movie *(Star Wars)*; and a television or radio show *(60 Minutes)*. Note, however,

that the Bible and the books within it are neither italicized nor placed in quotation marks, although they are capitalized:

Genesis is the first book of the Bible.

Italics are also used to indicate the names of trains (the *Orient Express);* ships (the *Queen Elizabeth II);* airplanes (the *Spirit of St. Louis);* and spacecraft *(Apollo 8).*

ABBREVIATIONS

The more formal you wish to make your writing, the less you should abbreviate words and phrases. Although special abbreviations may be used regularly in the technical writings of business, law, scholarship, and science, common abbreviations should be used only moderately in most formal writing. If you are uncertain about whether or not a term should be abbreviated, spell it out fully.
Titles that accompany a proper name may be abbreviated:

Ms. Jones   Mary Stuart, D.D.S.
Dr. Smith   John Doe, Jr.
Rev. Wilson

Note that some writers feel that the titles of religious, government, and military leaders should be spelled out in full:

the Reverend Martin Luther King
Senator John Glenn
General George Patton

Titles should not be abbreviated when they appear without a proper name:

I called the doctor for an appointment.

Titles of academic degrees are an exception:

I received my B.A. this June.

Well-known abbreviations of organizations, corporations, people, and some countries are acceptable. When they are comprised of the first letters of three or more words, they are usually written without periods:

FBI   FDR
YMCA   JFK
ITT   USA
NBC   USSR

Abbreviations that specify a date or a time of day are acceptable:

621 B.C.   10:30 A.M.
A.D. 1983   1:17 P.M.

Note also that the abbreviations for number (*no.*) and dollars (*$*) may be used with specific numbers: *no.* 9, $5.50. None of these abbreviations should be used without a specific numerical reference: in the sentence

I feel asleep in the P.M.

P.M. should be changed to *afternoon*.
Note that if an abbreviation comes at the end of a declarative sentence, the period that marks the end of the abbreviation also marks the end of the sentence:

We left at 3:30 P.M.

If an abbreviation comes at the end of question, the question mark follows the period that marks the end of the abbreviation:

Did you leave before 3:00 P.M.?

In formal writing, the following should not be abbreviated:
Units of measurement, such as *inches* (*in.*) or *pounds* (*lbs.*). Long phrases such as *miles per hour* (*mph*) are an exception.
Geographical names, such as *Fifth Avenue* (*Ave.*) or *California* (*Calif.*). USA and *USSR* are exceptions, as are *Mount* (*Mt. Washington*) and *Saint* (*St. Louis*).
Names of days, months, and holidays, such as *Wednesday* (*Wed.*), *September* (*Sept.*), or *Christmas* (*Xmas*).
Names of people, such as *Charles* (*Chas.*) or *Robert* (*Robt.*).
Academic subjects, such as *economics* (*econ.*) or *English* (*Eng.*).
Divisions in books, such as *page* (*p.*), *chapter* (*chap.*) or *volume* (*vol.*). These abbreviations are acceptable, however, in footnote and bibliographic entries, and in cross-references, in a formal research paper.
Note finally that common Latin abbreviations that may be used in parenthetical references in informal writing, such as *e.g.*, (*for example*), *etc.* (*and so forth*), and *i.e.* (*that is*), should be replaced by their equivalent English phrases in formal writing:

In some of the songs in *Blood on the Tracks*, for example, "Idiot Wind," Dylan returns to the biting social criticism of his early career.

NUMBERS

Like abbreviations, numbers written as figures are used only moderately in formal writing, as compared to their regular use in technical and informal writing.

Generally, in formal writing, numbers are spelled out if they can be expressed in one or two words:

He lived to be one hundred years old.

If a number is hyphenated, it is considered one word:

The car has eighty-two thousand miles on it.

If spelling out a number takes more than two words, the number should be written in figures:

The book has 372 pages.

Note, however, that if several numbers appear in a sentence or a paragraph, they should be spelled out or written in figures consistently:

In the crowd of 275 people attending the rehearsal of the circus, there were only 25 grown men and 37 grown women; all the rest, a total of 213, were children.

Use figures to write the following: a date (*September 2, 1947*); a time of day (*8:45 A.M.*); an address (*705 Walton Avenue*); a telephone number (*631-6303*); an exact sum of money (*$12.42*); a decimal (*a 4.0 grade average*); a statistic (*37 percent*); a score (*7 to 3*); a volume, chapter, and/or page number in a book (*Volume 3, Chapter 10, page 105*); and an act, scene, and/or line number in a play (*Act II, Scene 3, lines 12–14*).

Note, however, that if the name of a street when the street is numbered can be spelled out in one or two words, it should be (*42 Fifth Avenue*), unless a word such as *East, West, North,* or *South* precedes the street name (*42 East 57th Street*). Also, a figure in round numbers may be written out (*ten cents, two o'clock, a hundred miles*).

Finally, always spell out numbers that begin a sentence:

Thirteen is my lucky number.

If the number requires more than two words to be spelled out, rearrange the sentence: the sentence

275 people attended the rehearsal.

should be revised to read

The rehearsal was attended by 275 people.

HYPHENATION

A hyphen is used to divide a word between the end of one line and the beginning of the next line. The hyphen should be placed only at the end of the first line, never at the start of the second. The last word on a page should not be divided with a hyphen.

When dividing a word with a hyphen, break the word only between syllables (*divi-sion, hyphen-ation*). Consult a dictionary to check the syllable breaks in a word. Words that have a prefix or a suffix should be divided between the prefix and the root (*dis-approve*) or between the root and the suffix (*happi-ness*). A compound word should be divided between the two words that form the compound (*air-plane*).

Never divide a word of only one syllable; for example, the word *dropped* cannot be divided between the two *p*'s.

Some writers prefer not to divide a word so that a single letter is left at the end of a line (*a-men*) or so that fewer than three letters appear at the start of a line (*com-ic*). Also, some writers prefer not to divide a word if the division creates a pronunciation problem (*con-science*).

A hyphen is also used to form some compound nouns (*a vice-president*) and some compound adjectives when they appear before a noun (*a hard-boiled egg*). Note that many compound nouns are simply written as one word (*playhouse*) or as two words (*hair stylist*). Many compound adjectives are written as one word (*childlike*) or as two words when they appear after a noun in a sentence (*he is well known*). Consult a dictionary to check whether a compound noun or adjective should be written as a single word, as a hyphenated word, or as two words.

A hyphen is used to join a prefix to a proper noun (*un-American*). It is not used to join a prefix to a common noun, adjective, or a verb (*superpatriot, profile, rejoin*), unless it is needed to avoid a misreading; for example, it is used to distinguish the word *re-creation* (something that has been created over again) from the word *recreation* (relaxation).

A hyphen is used to divide compound numbers written as words between *twenty-one* and *ninety-nine*. Some writers use the hyphen to divide fractions written as words (*three-fourths*).

Finally, hyphens are used in a series such as the following: *a two-and-one-half-, a three-, or a four-minute egg.*

SPELLING

The most important thing to keep in mind with regard to spelling is that you should consult a dictionary whenever you have any doubt about whether you have spelled a word correctly. If, in addition, you keep a notebook in which you list the words that you misspell frequently, along with their proper spelling, you will have a valuable tool that you can use whenever you are proofreading a paper. Always proofread your papers for spelling.

Beyond these preparations, there are a few basic rules that you can follow to avoid common spelling errors:

Put *i* before *e*, except after *c* or when pronounced like *a*, as in *neighbor* or *weigh*. Thus, write *believe* or *grief*, but *ceiling* or *receive*. Other exceptions to the rule of putting *i* before *e* include *either, leisure, foreign, seize,* and *weird*.

Generally, a final *e* is dropped before a suffix that begins with a vowel:

love, lovable, loving
imagine, imagination, imaginary
grieve, grieving, grievous

Some exceptions are *changeable, courageous, mileage, shoeing*.

Generally, a final *e* is retained before a suffix that begins with a consonant: *lovely, arrangement, fineness*. Some exceptions are *truly* and *judgment*.

Generally, a final *y* is changed to *i* before a suffix is added to a word:

beauty, beauties, beautiful
copy, copies, copied

One exception occurs when the suffix is *ing*: *copying*. Another exception occurs when the final *y* comes after a vowel:

obeyed, days, journeys

Generally, in a one-syllable word that ends in a consonant preceded by a single vowel, the final consonant is doubled before a suffix that begins with a vowel:

drop, dropped
slap, slapping
win, winner

However, when the final consonant of a one-syllable word is preceded by two vowels or by a vowel and another consonant, the final consonant is not doubled before a suffix that begins with a vowel:

cool, cooler   park, parking
real, realize   strong, strongest

Generally, in a word of two or more syllables that ends in a consonant, the final consonant is doubled before a suffix that begins with a vowel, if the accent falls on the last syllable of the word and if a single vowel precedes the final consonant:

begin, beginning
occur, occurred
regret, regrettable

The final consonant is not doubled if the accent does not fall on the last syllable:

enter, entered

Nor is it doubled if the final consonant is preceded by two vowels or by a vowel and another consonant:

despair, despairing
return, returning

Note: Avoid the common mistake of joining words that should be written separately, such as *a lot* and *all right*, or separating words that should be joined, such as *together* and *throughout*.

Finally, many times spelling errors arise because a writer confuses two words that sound alike but that differ both in spelling and in meaning. Such words are called *homonyms*. The following is a list of some commonly confused homonyms:

Accept/except.   *Accept* is a verb meaning "receive" or "agree to":

He accepted her terms.

Except is used most often as a preposition meaning "but for" or "other than":

I like every kind of music except rock and roll.

As a verb, *except* means "leave out" or "exclude":

Excepting his accountant, no one knows how rich he is.

Advice/advise.   *Advice* is a noun meaning "recommendation" or "guidance":

She gave her son good advice.

Advise is a verb meaning "give advice to":

She advised him to study hard.

Affect/effect.   *Affect* is used most often as a verb meaning to "change" or "influence":

The jury's decision was affected by her testimony.

It also can mean "pretend to feel":

He affected amusement, even though he was really quite angry.

Effect is used most often as a noun meaning "result" or "consequence":

The side effects of the medicine are unknown.

As a verb, *effect* means to "bring about" or "perform":

The senator's efforts effected a change in the tax laws.

All ready/already.   *All ready* means "completely prepared":

She was all ready to leave.

Already means "by this time" or "by that time":

The game was already half over when we got there.

All together/altogether.   *All together* means "in a group":

The family was all together at my aunt's house last Thanksgiving.

Altogether means "completely" or "entirely":

He changed his mind partially but not altogether.

An/and.   *An* is an article:

I ate an apple.

And is a coordinating conjunction:

I love apples and oranges.

Buy/by.   *Buy* is a verb meaning "purchase":

We need to buy a new car.

By is most often used as a preposition meaning "near to," "through," or "with":

The house by the station was destroyed by fire.

By is also used as an adverb:

The time went by.

Conscience/conscious.   *Conscience* is a noun meaning "a sense of right and wrong":

She thought about cheating, but her conscience kept her from doing it.

Conscious is an adjective meaning "aware" or "awake":

He was conscious for a few minutes after the accident, but then he passed out.

Every day/everyday.   *Every day* means "daily":

She jogs two miles every day.

Everyday means "common," "ordinary," or "regular":

"Oh," she said, "this old thing is just an everyday dress."

Formally/formerly.   *Formally* means "in a formal or ceremonious way":

He was dressed formally, in a white tuxedo, at his wedding.

Formerly means "previously," or "at an earlier time":

She was formerly a student, but now she works on Wall Street.

Hear/here.   *Hear* is a verb meaning to "perceive," to "listen," or to "learn" by the ear or by being told:

I hear you are leaving town.

Here is an adverb meaning "in or to or at this place or point":

I am not leaving; I am staying right here.

Its/it's.   *Its* is a possessive pronoun:

He likes the car but not its price.

It's is a contraction meaning "it is":

Unfortunately, it's too expensive.

Know/no.   *Know* is a verb meaning to "understand," "perceive," or "be aware of":

Do you know what I mean?

No is used as an adverb to express denial, dissent, or refusal:

No, I do not understand.

No is also used commonly as an adjective meaning "not any" or "not at all":

I have no idea what you mean.

Later/latter.   *Later* refers to time:

I have to finish a paper right now so I'll call you later.

Latter refers to the second of two things previously mentioned:

When David fought Goliath, the former used his brain, the latter used only his brawn.

May be/maybe.   *May be* is a verb phrase:

My brother, who is overseas, may be coming home.

Maybe is an adverb meaning "perhaps":

Maybe he will sell it, if he gets a good enough offer.

Peace/piece.   *Peace* is a noun meaning "freedom from war or strife," "harmony," or "calm":

Why can't we live in peace with one another?

Piece, used as a noun, means "a limited quantity or part of something" (*a piece of land*), or "a specimen of workmanship" (*a piece of music*), or "an individual article in a set or a collection or a class" (*a piece of furniture*). *Piece* is also used as a verb meaning to "mend" or "join together":

A detective pieces clues together to solve a mystery.

Principal/principle.   *Principal,* used as a noun, means "chief administrator":

The school principal ran the assembly.

It also means a "capital sum of money":

He had to pay the interest on the principal of his car loan.

Principal, used as an adjective, means "main" or "most important":

The principal reason that I fear cats is the memory I have of being scratched as a child.

Principle is a noun meaning "rule" or "basic truth" or "law":

He followed the principle of doing unto others as he would have them do unto him.

Right/write.   *Right,* used as an adjective, means "proper," "correct," "genuine," or "legitimate":

Apologizing was the right thing to do.

Right, used as a noun, means a "just claim" or a "privilege" (*freedom of speech is a basic right*). Used as an adverb, it means "directly" or "exactly" (*do it right now*) or the opposite of "left." Used as a verb, it means to "set up" or to "set in order":

It took a crane to right the fallen statue.

Write is a verb meaning "trace words on paper" or "communicate" or "compose":

My sister is writing a novel.

Sight/site.   *Sight,* used as a verb, means to "observe" or to "perceive with one's eyes":

The sailor on the mast was the first to sight land.

Sight, used as a noun, means "vision" or "spectacle":

After the food fight, the dining room was a sight to behold.

Site is used most often as a noun meaning "location":

This hill is the site we have chosen to build the house on.

Site is also used as a verb meaning to "locate." Note: Do not confuse *sight* or *site* with *cite,* a verb that means to "refer to" or to "mention":

The lawer cited the case of *Jones* v. *Jones* in his argument before the judge.

Some/sum.   *Some* is used as an adjective, an adverb, or a pronoun to indicate a certain unspecified number, amount, or degree of something:

We are having dinner with some friends.

Sum, used as a noun, means a "total" or a "quantity":

One million dollars is a large sum of money.

Sum is also used as a verb meaning to "combine into a total" or to "form an overall estimate or view of":

The lawyer summed up her case for the jury.

Than/then.   *Than* is a conjunction used in making comparisons:

I like the blue shirt better than the yellow.

Then is an adverb used in referring to the passage of time:

He put the cake in the oven; then he waited an hour before checking to see if it was done.

Their/there/they're.   *Their* is a third-person-plural possessive pronoun:

Their car is in the driveway.

There indicates a place:

The kids will like the park, so let's go there.

There is also used in the expressions "there is" and "there are." *They're* is a contraction meaning "they are":

I always root for the home home team, even when they're having a bad year.

Threw/through.   *Threw* is a past-tense form of the verb "to throw":

He threw the ball to her.

Through is used as a preposition, an adverb, and an adjective meaning "in one end and out the other," "between or among," "during the whole period of," "having finished," "by means of," or "by reason of":

She finished the marathon through sheer willpower.

Note: Do not employ the popular shortened form *thru* for *through*; similarly, avoid the shortened form *nite* for *night* or *tho* for *though*.

To/too/two.   *To* is a preposition that indicates place, direction, or position:

We have flown to the moon.

To also forms the infinitive with all verbs:

I'd like to get to know you.

Too is an adverb meaning "also" or "excessively":

She is too tired to go out tonight.

Two is a number:

Two plus two equals four.

Were/we're/where.   *Were* is a past-tense form of the verb to "be":

They were not home.

Were is also used to form the subjunctive mood:

If they were home, we would visit them.

We're is a contraction meaning "we are":

We're planning to go on our vacation next month.

Where is used as an adverb or as a conjunction to indicate a place or a position:

Where are the keys? They are where you left them.

Who's/whose.   *Who's* is a contraction meaning "who is":

Who's coming to the party?

Whose is a possessive form of the pronoun who:

Whose party is it?

Your/your're.   *Your* is a possessive form of the pronoun you:

I saw your sister today.

You're is a contraction meaning "you are":

She said that you're leaving for college this week.

INDEX

A-to-Z arrangement, 51–53
Abbreviations, 390–391, 407, 409–410
Abrams, M. H., 234
Absolute phrase, 370, 394
Abstractness, style adjusted for, 196
Acronyms, capitalizing, 407
Active voice, 363
Ad hominem argument, as deductive fallacy, 275
Ad populum argument, as deductive fallacy, 276
Addition, for revising, 64–66, 169
Address, commas used with, 395
Adjective, 364, 393–394, 412
Adjective clause, 371
Adjective cluster, 159
Adjusting style. *See* Style
Adverb, 364, 365–366, 395
Adverb cluster, 159
Adverbial clauses, 371
Agreement, 375–379
Airplanes, italics used with names of, 409
Allen, Woody, 17, 302–303
Alliteration, 350
Allusion, as persuasive language, 301
Analogy. *See* Figurative language
Analysis, exposition for, 117
Analyzing audience, for persuasion, 283
Antecedent, of the pronoun, 361
Apostrophe, 361, 404–405
Appositive, 394–395
Argumentation, 263. *See also* Persuasion
Aristotle, 138, 263
Arrangement. *See also* Comparison and contrast; Shaping idea
A to Z, 51–53

cause and effect, 150
classification, 290, 291–292
definition, 290–291
description for, 117–118
duration, 51–53
examples, 292–293
flashback, 54–55
generalization and specification for, 187–190
process analysis, 115–116, 151–152
of persuasive essay, 290–296
rearranging, 97–98
styles of (*see* Exposition; Narration)
Article, 366
Assumption, in deduction, 272–273
Attributive adjective, 364
Auden, W. H., 4
Audience
    common reader as, 142–144, 148–149
    depth of information needed by, 107–111
    frame of reference of, 43–45, 49, 107, 279
    informed, 324
    lay, 216–218
    persuading, 281, 289
        analyzing audience for, 283
        credibility established for, 281–282
        ethical appeal presented for, 283–284
        frame of reference of audience for, 279
        with persuasive language, 303
        proper tone for, 282–283
    point of view of, 39–41, 46, 48, 49–50, 107

for research paper, 229–230
role-playing the, 165–166
shared sense of form and value for addressing, 180–181, 186–187
style shaped by, 194–195
writing for publications as, 144, 148–149
Austen, Jane, 17
Authentic voice, 11–16, 21
Auxiliary verb, 363

Balanced phrasing, for eloquent style, 197
Bandwagon, as deductive fallacy, 276
Base clause, 162
Base sentences, 157, 368, 371, 372
Begging the question, as deductive fallacy, 275
Bellow, Saul, 119–121
Biblical citation, colon used with, 398
Bibliography, 223–225, 242–244, 255–256
Blake, William, 321, 322, 333–334
Body, of persuasive essay, 290
Brackets, 402
Brill, A. A., 108–109
Brody, Jane, 231
Burns, Robert, 320

Campion, Thomas, 323
Capitalization, 406–408
Case
    errors in, 381–383
    writing a, 137–170
Casing the subject, writing a case as, 137–170
Categorical statements, as persuasive language, 303

Causal generalization, as persuasive
    induction, 265, 266
Causal relationships, classical
    questions considering, 140
Cause and effect, 150
Chronological order, for writing
    about an incident, 51–53
Churchill, Winston, 301–302, 303
Clark, Ramsey, 91–92
Classical questions, 138–141,
    146–147
  for generating ideas, 277,
    288–289
  for persuasion, 277
  for writing about what you know,
    174
Classification, for persuasive paper,
    290, 291–292
Clause, 370–371
  base, 162
  punctuation with, 162, 396–397
  subordinate, 158
Cluster of words, 158–159, 368
Coffin, Robert P. Tristram, 127
Colon, 162, 397–398, 402–403
Comma, 162, 392–396, 402–403
Comma splice, 386–387
Common noun, 361
Common reader
  role-playing the, 165–166
  writing for, 142–144, 148–149
Commonplace book, 4. *See also*
    Journal
Comparative adjective, 364
Comparative adverb, 364
Comparison and contrast, 150–151
  commas used to set off phrase of,
    395
  exposition for, 116–117
  whole-by-whole method as,
    150–151
  for writing about poems, 345–346
Compass, capitalizing points of, 407
Complement, of sentence, 367–368
Complete predicate, 367
Complex sentence, 372
Compound adjectives, 412
Compound-complex sentence, 372
Compound noun, 412
Compound number, 412
Compound sentence, 372
Concluding sentence, of paragraph,
    89–90
Conclusion
  in deduction, 272–273
  in persuasive essay, 293
Concreteness, style adjusted for, 195
Conjunction, 56, 162, 365, 393

Conjunctive adverb, 365–366, 395
Connotative language, 299–300,
    351
Consolidating, 207–208
Contractions, 404
Contrast. *See* Comparison and
    contrast
Conventions, for addressing an
    audience, 180–181
Coordinate clauses, 368
Coordinating conjunctions, 365, 393
Coordination
  for paragraph development,
    125–126, 127–128
  of sentences, 372
Correlative conjunction, 365
Credibility, establishing to persuade
    audience, 281–282
Cross-references, parentheses
    enclosing, 399
Cutting, for writing rough draft, 86

Daily journal. *See* Journal
Dangling modifier, 384–385
Dash, 162, 398, 403
Dates
  abbreviations for, 410
  commas used with, 395
Days of week, capitalizing, 407
Deadwood, eliminating, 247–249
Declaration of Independence,
    293–296
Deduction
  for generating ideas, 288–289
  for a persuasive essay, 278–280
Deductive fallacies, 275–276
Definition, as arrangement for
    persuasive paper, 290–291
Deity, capitalizing, 407
Demonstrative adjective, 57
Demonstrative pronoun, 362
Denotation, 351
Dependent clause, 371
Depth of information, for audience,
    107–111, 113–115
Description, for writing about a
    place, 117–118
Details, in essay about an incident,
    53–56
Dialogue, for writing about a place,
    118
Didion, Joan, 90
Dillard, Annie, 153–154
Direct object, 368
Distributing, for revising, 169
Documentation, 185
  bibliography for, 242–244,
    255–256

footnotes for, 227–233, 241–242,
    243, 249–255
plagiarism and, 185, 227
"Works Cited" list, 244–245,
    256–259
Donne, John, 324, 351
Douglas, William O., 292–293
Drayton, Michael, 320
Duration, of essay on incident, 51–53

Early, Tracey, 163
Editing, 66
  consolidating for, 207–208
  distributing for, 169
  paragraphs, 135
  sentence combining for, 169–170
  substitutions for, 134
  transitions for, 134–135, 169
Effects, 140, 150. *See also* Cause and
    effect
Eiseley, Loren, 51–53
Either/or, as deductive fallacy, 276
Elbow, Peter, 69, 71
Eliminating deadwood, 247–249
Ellipsis, for quotations, 226–227,
    234, 400–401
Elliptical clause, 384–385
Endnotes, 241. *See also* Footnotes
Enthymeme, 272, 288
Episode. *See* Phase, writing about a
Ethical appeal, presenting to
    persuade audience, 283–284
Evaluation, 140, 165. *See also*
    Feedback
Examples
  as arrangement for persuasive
    essay, 292–293
  parentheses for, 399
Exclamation, quotation marks with,
    403
Exclamation point, 392, 403
Explanation
  as exposition form, 83
  persuasion as, 263–311
  punctuation with, 395, 398, 399
  research paper as, 210–259
  writing about poetry as, 315–356
  writing about what you know as,
    173–208
Exploration
  writing about a place as, 103–135
  writing a case as, 137–170
Explorer's questions, 104–106,
    112–113, 140–141
Exposition, 104, 116
  process analysis containing, 151
  in the service of narration, 82,
    83–85

for writing about a place, 116–117
in writing on a significant episode, 85–86

False cause, as deductive fallacy, 275
Faulkner, William, 160, 300, 303
Faulty analogy, as deductive fallacy, 275
Feedback
    on persuasive argument, 308–311
    on research paper, 246–247
    on writing a case, 165–168
    on writing about an incident, 62–64
    on writing about a phase, 95–97
    on writing about a place, 130–133
    on writing about poetry, 352–355
    on writing about yourself, 28–31
    on writing about what you know, 201–207
Fenton, Patrick, 115–116
Figurative language
    analogy
        classical questions considering, 140
        faulty, 275
        as persuasive induction, 265, 266
        in poetry, 317–319
    for eloquent style, 198
    imagery, 321, 331
    irony, 198, 322
    metaphor
        for eloquent style, 198
        for persuasion, 300–301
        in poetry, 319, 341–343
    metonymy, 320
    personification, 320
    for persuasion, 300–301
    simile
        for eloquent style, 198
        for persuasion, 300–301
        in poetry, 319–320
    symbol, 321
Final product, 31–32
Flashback technique, for writing about an incident, 54–55
Footnotes, 227, 233, 241–242, 243, 249–255
Foreign words, italics used with, 408
Fragments, of a sentence, 387–389
Fraiberg, Selma H., 269–270
Frame of reference
    of audience, 43–45, 49, 107, 279
    writer's, 39–41
Franklin, Ben, 179
Free modifiers, 158–159, 162–163, 368

Free writing, 69–72, 138
    for generating ideas, 77–79, 330
    for journal, 8
Freud, Sigmund, 109
Frost, Robert, 339–340, 351–352, 402
Fused sentence, 386–387
Future progressive tense, 363
Future tense, 363

Gathering information, for research paper, 174–176
Gathering sources, for research paper, 223–225
Generalization
    for arrangement, 187–190
    causal, 265, 266
    for generating ideas, 185–186
    hasty, 213, 265
    for significance of information, 177
    sweeping, 265
Generating ideas, 104–106, 112–113
    classical questions for, 138–141, 146–147, 174, 277, 288–289
    deduction for, 288–289
    explorer's questions for, 104–106, 112–113, 138, 140–141
    free writing for, 71–72, 77–79, 138, 330
    generalization for, 177–179, 185–186
    induction for, 213–214, 220–221, 288–289
    journal for, 138, 330, 344–345
    journalist's questions for, 34–38, 48, 138
    reading or media experiences for, 176, 182–185
    for writing about poetry, 317–322, 330–331
Generating a subject, reading or media experiences for, 182–185
Genetic fallacy, as deductive fallacy, 276
Goodman, Ellen, 270–272
Gornick, Vivian, 59
Grammatical errors, 375–389
Gray, Thomas, 322–323
Gerund phrase, 370

Hardy, Thomas, 337–338
Harrington, David V., 108
Hasty generalization, 213, 265
Helping verb, 363
Hofstadter, Richard, 268–269
Holidays, capitalizing, 407

Homonyms, spelling of, 414–421
How, as journalist's question, 34–38
Humor, as persuasive language, 302–303
Hyphenation, 411, 412

Ideas, dash used with, 398. *See also* Generating ideas; Shaping ideas
Imagery, 321, 331
Imperative mood, 364
Impression, giving in writing about a place, 119–122
Incident, writing about, 33–66
Incomplete sentence, 373–374
Indefinite pronoun, 362
Independent clause, 370–371
Indirect question, 390
Induction, 210, 212
    for generating ideas, 213–214, 220–221, 288–289
    for persuasive essay, 264–266, 278–280
Inference, reader's frame of reference from, 45
Infinitive phrase, 369–370
Information
    depth of for audience, 107–111, 113–115
    gathering, 174–176
    presentation of, 173–208
Informed audience, writing poetry for, 324–326, 341–343
Informing. *See* Explanation
Initial response, for generating ideas for writing on poetry, 330, 344–345
Interpretation, as exposition skill, 83
Interrogative pronoun, 362
Interview
    footnote for, 242
    for induction, 221
    of reader, 44–45
Introduction
    of persuasive essay, 290
    of research paper, 234
Investigative essay. *See* Research paper
Irony, 198, 322
Irregular verb, 363
Italics, 408–409

Jacobs, Jane, 126
Jefferson, Thomas, 17, 293–296
Jonson, Ben, 335
Joseph, Chief, 129
Journal, 4–18
    essay based on, 18–32

Journal (*cont.*)
    for generating ideas for writing on
        poetry, 138, 330, 344–345
Journalist's questions, 34–38, 48,
        125, 138

Keats, John, 351
Key words, as transitions, 56, 57
King, Martin Luther, 304–306
Kreps, Juanita, 93

Language. *See also* Figurative
        language; Persuasive language
    alliteration, 350
    connotation, 299–300, 351
    denotation, 351
    sound of poetry achieved with,
        350–352
Latin abbreviations, 410
Lay audience, 216–218
Leonard, George, 118
Library, gathering sources for
        research paper from, 223–225
Lifton, Robert Jay, 125
Limiting modifiers, 383–384
Lincoln, Abraham, 303
Linking statement, in deduction,
        272–273
Lists, punctuation with, 162, 397,
        398, 399–400
Logic. *See* Deduction; Induction;
        Persuasion
Logical terms, as persuasive
        language, 303
Loose sentence, for eloquent style,
        197–198

Macrorie, Ken, 13
Main clause, 370–371
Mannes, Marya, 90, 128
Marlowe, Christopher, 332
Marvell, Andrew, 335–336
Mauriac, François, 89–90
Mead, Margaret, 178
Media experience, for generating
        ideas and subject, 182–185
Melville, Herman, 89
Metaphor. *See* Figurative language
Mill, John Stuart, 290–291
Misplaced modifier, 383–384
Mixed sentence, 374
Modifiers
    free, 158–159, 162–163, 368
    misplaced and dangling, 303–385
Months of the year, capitalizing, 407
Mood, of verb, 363–364
Moorhouse, Geoffrey, 160–161
Morris, Wright, 195

Names
    of a place, 395
    titles with, 407, 408–409
Narration, 81
    process analysis containing, 151
    for writing about an incident,
        50–56
    for writing about a place, 115–116
    for writing on a significant
        episode, 81–82
Narrative paragraph, 98
Nehru, Jawaharlal, 301
Nemerov, Howard, 340
New York Times Index, The, 223
Newman, Edwin, 117
Newspaper article, documenting,
        242, 244
Nominal sentence, 197
Nonrestrictive modifier, commas
        used to set off, 394
Note taking, for research paper,
        225–228
Notebook. *See* Journal
Noun, 361
    of address, 395
    compound, 412
Noun clause, 371
Noun cluster, 158
Noun phrase, 369
Numbers, 404–405, 410, 411–412

Object complement, 368
Object of the preposition, 366
Objective pronoun, 361–362,
        381–382
Observation, for induction, 213–214,
        220–221
Observing a situation, writing a case
        as, 137–170
Ogilvie, Bruce C., 117, 291–292
Olson, Eric, 125
Outlining, for research paper,
        228–229
Overriding impression, in writing
        about a place, 119–122

Pagination, of final product, 31
Paragraph. *See also* Free writing
    cause and effect for, 150
    coordination for, 125–126, 127–128
    editing, 135
    explorer's questions for, 104–106,
        112–113, 140–141
    faulty parallelism in, 385–386
    journalist's questions for, 34–38,
        48, 125, 138
    part-by-part comparison and
        contrast method for, 150–151

process analysis for, 152
    rearranging, 97–98
    structure, 88–91
    styles of development (*see*
        Description; Exposition;
        Narration)
    subordination for, 126–128
    topic sentence, 98, 125, 127, 128
    transitions, 98
    whole-by-whole comparison and
        contrast method for, 151
Parallelism, faulty, 385–386
Paraphrase, for research paper, 227
Parentheses, 391, 399–400
Part-by-part method, of comparison
        and contrast, 150–151
Participial phrase, 370
Participles, of verbs, 363
Parts of speech, 361–366
Passive voice, 363
Past participle, of verbs, 363
Past perfect tense, 363
Past progressive tense, 363
Past tense, 363
Perfect tenses, 363
Period, 390–391, 403, 410
Periodic sentence, for eloquent style,
        197–198
Periodical articles, documenting,
        241–242, 244
Personal observation, for induction,
        213–214, 220–221
Personal pronoun, 361–362
Personification, as figurative
        language, 320
Persuasion, 263–311
Persuasive induction, 264–266
Persuasive language, 299
    allusion, 301
    appropriateness of, to audience,
        303
    categorical statements, 303
    connotation, 299–300
    figurative language, 300–301
    humor and satire, 300–301
    logical terms, 303
    repetition, 301–302
    tone as consideration of, 282–283,
        303
Petrunkevitch, Alexander, 129
Phase, writing about a, 68–99
Phrase, 366, 369–370, 395
Place, writing about a, 103–135
Plagiarism, 185, 227
Plural noun, 361
Poetry
    quoting, 401–402
    writing about, 315–356

Point of view, of audience, 39–41, 46, 48, 49–50, 107
Polanyi, Michael, 214
Possession, indicating, 361
Possessive case, apostrophe for, 404
Possessive pronoun, 361–362
Predicate, 367
Predicate adjective, 364, 367–368
Predicate nominative, 367–368
Prefixes, hyphen with, 412
Prejudice, writing case about, 137–170
Premise, in deduction, 272–273
Preposition, 366
Prepositional phrase, 366, 369
Present participle, of verb, 363
Present perfect progressive tense, 363
Present perfect tense, 363
Present progressive tense, 363
Present tense, 363
Process analysis, 115–116, 151–152
Progressive tenses, 363
Pronouns, 361–362, 367
  agreement with antecedent, 377–379
  case errors, 381–383
  faulty reference and, 379–380
  possessive, 404
Proofreading, 31–32
Proper adjectives, capitalizing, 407
Proper name, titles with, 409
Proper noun, 361, 406, 408
Proper tone, adopting to persuade audience, 282–283, 303
Punctuation, 162, 390–405
Purpose in writing, style shaped by, 194

Qualifications, parentheses for, 399
Question, exploring a
  writing about a place as, 103–135
  writing a case as, 137–170
Question mark, 391, 403
Questions. *See also* Classical questions
  explorer's, 104–106, 112–113, 140–141
  journalist's, 34–38, 48, 125, 138
  quotation marks with, 403
Quotation
  brackets with, 400
  capitalizing, 406
  colon used to introduce, 398
  for dialogue, 118
  ellipsis for, 226–227, 234, 400–401
  in note taking, 226–227

of poetry, 355–356
  quotation within, 401
  in research paper, 232–234
  sic with, 400
  specifying source of, 185 (*see also* Documentation)
Quotation marks, 118, 185, 391, 401–403

Ralegh, Walter, Sir, 332–333
Reader. *See also* Audience
  common, 142–144, 148–149, 165–166
  informed, 324–326, 341–343
  lay, 216–218
Reader's Guide to Periodical Literature, The, 223
Reading, for generating ideas, 176, 182–185
Rearranging, in revising, 97–98
Reasoning. *See* Deduction; Induction
Recording, for generating ideas for writing on poetry, 330–331
Red herring, as deductive fallacy, 276
Reference, faulty, 379–380. *See also* Documentation
Reference works, for preliminary bibliography, 223–225
Reflexive pronoun, 362
Refutation, in persuasive essay, 293
Regular verbs, 363
Relative pronouns, 362
Repetition, 126, 301–302
Representative sampling, 213
Research paper, 210–259
Revising, 64, 65. *See also* Feedback
  adding, 65–66
  consolidating, 207–208
  cutting, 86
  deadwood elimination, 247–249
  distribution for, 169
  distributing, 169
  rearranging, 97–98
  substituting, 133–134
Rewriting, 28–31 *See also* Feedback
Rich, Adrienne, 338–339
Roethke, Theodore, 89
Role-playing
  of audience, 165–166, 281, 289
  point of view from, 46, 48
Roosevelt, Franklin Delano, 302
Rough draft, 23–25, 165
  cutting and pasting for, 86
  for essay on an incident, 56
  of research paper, 235–240
  rewriting (*see also* Feedback; Revising)

Rousseau, Jean-Jacques, 16

Sagan, Carl, 58, 266–268
Salutation, punctuation used with, 395, 398
Sampling, for persuasive induction, 265
Sancton, Thomas, 92–93
Satire, as persuasive language, 302–303
Self-expression
  voice as means of, 73–74
  writing about an incident as, 33–36
  writing about a phase as, 68–69
  writing about yourself as, 3–32
Semicolon, 162, 393, 396–397, 403
Sentences
  abbreviations at end of, 410
  awkward, 372–375
  base, 157, 368, 371, 372
  combining, 156–157, 371–372
    base sentences for, 157
    for editing, 169–170
    free modifiers for, 158–159
    subordinate clauses for, 158
  comma splices, 386–387
  complex, 372
  compound, 372
  compound-complex, 372
  deadwood in, 247–249
  declarative, 390
  faulty parallelism in, 385–386
  fragments, 387–389
  incomplete, 373–374
  inconsistent point of view in, 374–375
  length and rhythm of, 160–161
  loose and periodic, 197–198
  mixed, 374
  nominal, 197
  numbers in, 411–412
  parentheses enclosing, 399
  parts of, 367–368
  punctuation of, 162
  run-on, 386–387
  verbal, 196
Series, punctuation used with, 394, 397, 412
Shakespeare, William, 323, 341–343, 350
Shaping idea, 19, 21–22, 26
  for arrangement, 187
  for persuasion, 279
  for writing a case, 149–150
  for writing about a phase, 80–81
Shaping subject, 25–27

Shared sense of form and value, for
    addressing an audience,
    180–181, 186–187
Ships, italics used with names of,
    409
Sic, 400
Simile. *See* Figurative language
Simple predicate, 367
Simple sentence. *See* Base sentence
Simple subject, 367
Single quotation marks, 401
Slanting, as deductive fallacy, 276
Sources, for research paper, 223–225.
    See also Documentation
Specification, for arrangement,
    187–190
Speech, parts of, 361–366
Spelling, 413–421
Squinting modifiers, 384
Stevens, Wallace, 351
Stevenson, Adlai, 301
Straight summary, as exposition
    form, 83
Street names, 411
Strunk, William, Jr., 198
Style
  adjusting
    for abstractness, 196
    for concreteness, 195
    nominal sentence for, 197
    verbal sentence for, 196
  components, 194–195
  eloquent
    balanced phrasing for, 197
    figurative language for, 198
    irony for, 198
    loose and periodic sentences for,
      197–198
Subject
  determining what to say about, 22
  generating, 182–185
  of sentence, 367
  shaping the, 25–27
Subject complement, 367
Subject/verb agreement, 375–377
Subjective pronoun, 361–362,
    381–382

Subjunctive mood, 364
Subordinate clause, 158, 368, 371
Subordinating conjunction, 365
Subordination
  for paragraph development,
    126–128
  of sentences, 372–373
Substituting, for editing, 133–134
Subtitle, colons used with, 398
Summary
  colon to introduce, 398
  in exposition, 83
  in research paper, 227
Superlative adjective, 364
Superlative adverb, 364
Sweeping generalizations, 265
Swift, Jonathan, 303
Syllogism, 272–273
Symbol, as figurative language, 321

Tabloids, readership of, 143
Taking notes, for research paper,
    225–228
Talese, Gay, 34–36
Tennyson, Alfred, 323
Tense, of verbs, 363
Thomas, Lewis, 284–285
Thoreau, Henry David, 102, 200,
    402
Thurber, James, 93–94
Time references, 398, 410
Titles
  of books, 408–409
  of essay, 31
  of people, 407–408, 409
  quotation marks with, 402
Tone, persuasive language
    considering, 282–283, 303
Topic, for writing about research,
    221–222
Topic sentence, of paragraph, 78,
    88–90, 125, 126, 127, 128
Toynbee, Arnold, 178
Trade names, capitalizing, 407
Trains, italics used with names of,
    409
Transitional phrase, 56–58

Transitions, 56–58
  for editing, 66, 134–135, 169
  free modifier as, 162–163
  in paragraphs, 98
Trippett, Frank, 129
Tutko, Thomas A., 117, 291–292
Twain, Mark, 161
Typing, of final product, 31

Underlining, italics indicated by, 408
Understatement, for eloquent style,
    198
Unity, distributing for, 169
Updike, John, 94

Verb, 362–364, 375–377
Verb cluster, 159
Verb complement, 368
Verb phrase, 369
Verbal sentence, for style, 196
Voice
  as a means of self-expression,
    73–74
  of verb, 363
  for your reader, 73–76, 79–80

What, as journalist's question, 34–38
When, as journalist's question, 34–38
Where, as journalist's question,
    34–38
White, E. B., 127, 177, 183,
    188–189, 194, 195, 198, 200,
    400
Who, as journalist's question, 34–38
Whole-by-whole method, of
    comparison and contrast,
    150–151
Why, as journalist's question, 34–38
Wicker, Tom, 57
Williams, William Carlos, 315–316,
    351
Wordsworth, Dorothy, 350
Wordsworth, William, 319, 334
"Works Cited," list of, 244–245,
    256–259

Yourself, writing about, 3–32